The Archaeology of Animals

SIMON J. M. DAVIS

The Archaeology of Animals

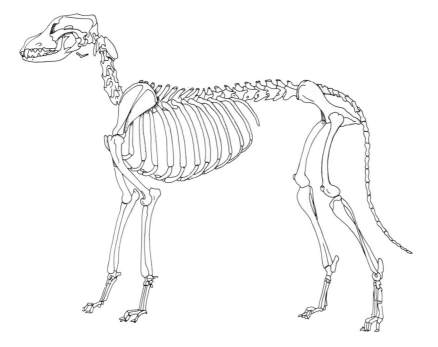

Yale University Press   New Haven and London

Published 1987 in Great Britain by Batsford Ltd.
Published in the United States 1987 by Yale University Press

Printed in Great Britain

Library of Congress catalog card number: 87–50381
International standard book number: 0–300–04065–2

10 9 8 7 6 5 4 3 2 1

Contents

'. . . on this neutral territory between Palaeontology and Archaeology a wide field is opened for investigation, which must eventually lead to a great extension of our knowledge of the history of primeval Man.'

Joseph Prestwich,
read before the Royal Society, London,
26 May 1859   (Prestwich, 1861)

A Note to the Reader

Many of the archaeological sites discussed in this book date to the last fifty or so millennia. Since the 1950s the analysis of radiocarbon (^{14}c) content has been used to date organic remains extending as far back in time as 45,000 years. However, it is now known that radiocarbon dates do not necessarily equal real or calendar dates. The convention, followed herein, is to use bc for radiocarbon dates, and BC for their calibrated equivalent in calendar years.

See also Clark, R.M. (1975) A calibration curve for radiocarbon dates. *Antiquity* 49, 251–66.

Acknowledgements

While writing this book I have been fortunate in having had the help of many friends and colleagues. I am particularly grateful to Leslie Aiello, Philip Armitage, Alan Boyde, Barry Brown, Anneke Clason, Diana Davies, Margaret Deith, Caroline Grigson, Andrew Jones, John Kahn, Peter King, Richard Klein, Anthony Legge, Richard Meadow, Terry O'Connor, Rosemary and Sebastian Payne, Michael Ryder and Anthony Warshaw who all read parts of the manuscript, corrected errors, and offered me valuable advice. William Waterfield and John Kahn between them kindly undertook the task of critically reading and improving the whole manuscript.

Numerous people have been generous in providing me with their photographs and drawings; they are credited in the legends to the figures. I thank my mother Evelyn who drew many of the small animal-sketches, my sister Sara Midda, and Odile le Brun who gave me advice on how to do the graphs and charts, Mr Haycox and his staff at University College press who set the type for the labels in the figures, and Raymond Lee who helped me to draw the maps.

While the writing of this book has kept me occupied since 1984, it is to some extent the product of fifteen exciting years 'doing bones' in Israel, Persia, Cyprus, and England. During this time I have received much support and hospitality from innumerable friends. Special thanks go to Sebastian Payne, who has, during my stays in Ankara, Kranidi and Cambridge, and in our constant exchange of views, taught me much about zoo-archaeology; and to John Kahn who has helped me to overcome writer's cramp, to dismantle stacked nouns, and to tackle my otherwise turgid circumlocution.

I am also grateful to Sam Berry, Duncan O'Dell and Pat Edwards for their kindness and help at University College, to Sara and Lucy and colleagues in the 'Fly House' for their moral support, and to my parents who have always encouraged my interest in natural history and who made all this possible.

List of illustrations

Glossary

Allele   any of the different forms of a gene that occupy the same place on the chromosome

Alveolus   the tooth socket in a mammal's jaw

Ameloblasts   ectodermal epithelial cells that secrete enamel in the formation of a tooth

Apatite   a mineral which consists mainly of calcium phosphate, with either fluorine or chlorine, or both. It crystallizes in a hexagonal form

Articular   that which is situated at a joint

Assemblage   a group of fossils/artefacts occurring together in the same stratigraphic level

Aurochs *or* **Urus**   this was the 'wild ox' ancestor of our domestic cattle

Bezoar   a stone found in the stomach or intestine of some animals, mostly ruminants. Bezoar stones consist of layers of organic matter deposited round some foreign substance, used in traditional medicine. The wild goat ('Bezoar goat') of the Near East is the best-known source of these stones

Carnassial   those teeth adapted for cutting by a scissor-like action. In carnivores (dogs and cats, for example), the carnassial teeth are the fourth premolar in the upper jaw and the first molar in the lower jaw

Cementum   a bone-like material deposited around a tooth, often the root only

Cestode   a class of parasitic Platyhelminthes commonly called tapeworms

Chondroclasts   large cells whose function is the destruction of cartilage. Such destruction is termed 'chondroclasis'

Cline   a character gradient; continuous variation in the expression of a character through a series of contiguous populations, often associated with a change in the environment

Collagen   a protein, usually in fibrous form, that is the major constituent of cartilage and bone

Commensal   an organism living with another and sharing its food. Both species usually benefit from this association

Cursorial   those animals which are adapted for running, such as cats and antelopes

Cyst   the enclosing membrane (protective covering) round the resting stage of an organism, e.g. the encysted larvae of parasitic worms

Cytoplasm   the substance of a cell exclusive of the nucleus

Dasyuridae   a family of carnivorous marsupial mammals

Dentine   the bone-like layer beneath the enamel and surrounding the pulp cavity in a tooth. Ivory consists of dentine

Dermal ossification   bone formation which occurs within the embryonic 'dermal' or surface layer of an embryo

Diagnostic character   a character that unambiguously differentiates one taxon from others, e.g. the shape of the metacarpal condyles differentiates between sheep and goat

Diaphysis   the shaft of a long bone

Dimorphism   a condition in which a population or species has two genetically determined morphological types, e.g. sexual size dimorphism, in which the sexes are of different sizes

Diphyodont having two sets of teeth. This condition exists in the mammals which replace their teeth once only: the deciduous or 'milk' teeth are replaced by the permanent teeth

Distal that which lies further away from the body, e.g. the hand is distal to the shoulder

Ectoderm the outer of the three embryonic, or germ, layers of an animal

Electrophoresis a technique for separating mixtures of organic molecules, based on their different rates of travel in an electric field. Electrophoresis is commonly used by geneticists to separate the proteins produced by the various alleles of a particular gene in an individual

Endochondral beginning or forming within the cartilage

Enzymes proteins, produced by living organisms, which act upon specific biochemical reactions in living organisms. 'Enzymes' are approximately analogous to 'catalysts' in chemistry

Epiphysis any part or process of a bone (usually at its end) which is formed from a separate centre of ossification and later fuses with the bone

Epitaxy oriented intergrowth between two solid phases. The surface of one crystal provides, through its lattice structure, preferred positions for the deposition of the second crystal

Epithelium the tissue that covers, or lines, an organ or organism

Exoskeleton a hard supporting structure formed around the outside of the body, as in insects

Exostosis an outgrowth of bone tissue (from a bone), usually the result of trauma or disease

Guanaco a South American camelid ruminant artiodactyl

Histogram a chart which depicts quantites in the form of bars whose lengths are proportional to the quantities they represent

Histology the study of the detailed structure of animal (or plant) tissues, and their microscopic morphology

Hypsodont teeth with high crowns—usually adapted for chewing abrasive food such as grass (e.g. the cheek teeth of sheep, goats and antelopes)

Infundibulum in reference to mammal teeth, this is a 'funnel' or 'pouch' of enamel which penetrates

down part of the central portion of the tooth from its occlusal surface

Karyotype the chromosome complement of a cell, individual, or group of animals (or plants)

Keratin the organic substance (a scleroprotein) which forms horn, claws, nails, and hooves of mammals. Hair and feathers also contain much keratin

Lamella in bone—a small plate of bone, for example surrounding a Haversian canal

Macropods a family of marsupial mammals that includes the kangaroos and wallabies

Madder a herb, *Rubia peregrina*, from which the dyestuff madder (alizarin) is derived

Malacology the study of molluscs, i.e. snails, clams, squid, etc. (Conchology is the study of the hard parts, shells, only of molluscs)

Mastodon large extinct mammal resembling the elephant, characterized by having pairs of nipple-shaped tubercles on the crowns of the teeth

Mesenchyme a diffuse tissue formed chiefly from the middle germ layer (mesoderm). In vertebrates, the connective tissues, bone and cartilage, are formed from mesenchyme

Mesoderm the middle of the three embryonic or germ layers found in developing 'higher' animals

Metaphysis the growing end of the diaphysis of a developing long bone, situated next to the epiphysis

Moa a large extinct New Zealand bird related to the kiwi

Nematodes a group of worm-like animals which are distinguished by their cylindrical body covered with a cuticle

Odontoblasts mesodermal cells that secrete dentine in the formation of a tooth

Osteoblast a bone-forming cell

Osteoclast a cell which destroys bony tissue

Osteocyte a bone cell developed from an osteoblast

Osteon a unit of bone which consists of a Haversian canal and its surrounding lamellae of bone

Otolith *or* **'Ear stone'** calcareous particles in the inner ear of many vertebrate animals, concerned with balance and movement

Pademelon a popular name given to small wallabies of the genera *Setonyx* and *Thylogale*. They are the least kangaroo–like macropods

Papilla   a small conical protuberance or nipple

Pedicle   a short stem or process

Periostial membrane, periosteum   the tough fibrous membrane which covers the surface of the bones except on their joint surfaces. The periostial membrane is tightly adherent to the bone surface, and it is from this membrane that new bone is laid down on the surface of young developing bone

Prodomesticates   those wild animal species which were subsequently domesticated

Rancholabrean   a 'faunal period' at the end of the Pleistocene named after the tar-pit deposits at Rancho la Brea in Los Angeles

Sacrum   that region of the vertebral column (backbone) to which the pelvic girdle is attached. In mammals the sacrum usually consists of several vertebrae which fuse

Saithe   coalfish = *Pollachius virens*

Secodont   teeth which are adapted for cutting

Silica   a hard mineral substance (silicon dioxide) which is contained in the cell walls of certain plants, e.g. grasses. Sand, flint and glass are largely silicon dioxide

Synovial membrane   the inner layer of the articular capsule in a joint which secretes the lubricating fluid

Taphonomy   the study of the environmental phenomena and processes that affect organic remains after death, including the process of fossilization, e.g. what happens to the various bones of a skeleton after an animal's death, how they are scattered, and which are preserved as fossils

Tasmanian devil   a predatory marsupial, *Sarcophilus ursinus*

Teleosts   the true bony fishes

Ungulate   hoofed animals. This term is now used in a popular sense to include two orders of mammals: (1) Perissodactyls, or odd-toed ungulates (e.g. horses, tapirs, rhinoceroses), and (2) Artiodactyls, or even-toed ungulates (e.g. antelopes, goats, cattle)

Vicugna   a South American camelid ruminant artiodactyl

INTRODUCTION

Bones and antiquaries, a nineteenth-century prelude

This book is about zoo-archaeology (also known as archaeozoology): the study of fossilised faunal (i.e. animal) remains from archaeological sites. These remains are derived mainly, though by no means exclusively, from the hard parts such as bone, tooth and shell of animals eaten in antiquity. Zoo-archaeology is thus basically the study of the garbage of ancient peoples' meals. Remains of animals which were used for other purposes like transport and decoration, or which happened to co-exist with early humans, are also sometimes found. And on rare occasions even hair and wool are preserved.

Our human and earlier hominid ancestors have been traced back in time several million years—a span which encompasses the geological Quaternary period, or Pleistocene and Holocene epochs. For much of this period our ancestors' remains are associated with those of animals, so zoo-archaeology may be regarded as Quaternary palaeontology.

Zoo-archaeology, along with other specialist sciences such as physical anthropology, archaeobotany, geology and chemistry, all serve to build up for the archaeologist a more complete picture of our ancestors' way of life and the environment they inhabited. But zoo-archaeology is the study of animal remains (here termed 'archaeofaunal remains'), which not only reflect human behaviour patterns, but which can also reveal much about the animals themselves. Given the detailed chronology now available to archaeology, these archaeofaunal remains provide a unique opportunity to study the evolution of animal species through a short but finely divided period—the envy of any palaeontologist studying fossils from earlier periods and interested in micro-evolution (small-scale changes occurring over short spans of time). So, zoo-archaeology bridges two disciplines—palaeozoology and anthropology/archaeology.

THE PURPOSE OF THIS BOOK

This book is intended primarily for students of archaeology and anyone with an interest in both natural history and the history of our own species. My aim in writing it has been to describe how zoo-archaeologists go about studying faunal remains from archaeological sites, and to explore the nature of these remains, and some of the information they may provide. This occupies the first part of the book. The second part outlines the long relationship between people and animals. This starts with our early ancestors in Africa and ends in post-medieval Britain. This part concentrates on a few specific problems from a restricted number of geographical localities—usually those where there has been considerable archaeological excavation. I have not attempted to write an exhaustive survey of zoo-archaeology. The inquiring reader is encouraged to delve into the fast-growing body of literature on the subject, some of which is included in the list of references at the end.

But first let me briefly describe how the subject developed in its early days, that is in the nineteenth and early twentieth centuries.

FAUNAL REMAINS ASSOCIATED WITH ANCIENT MAN

Zoo-archaeology represents another dimension of the study of our ancestors' way of life. Two important contributions which archaeofaunal remains have made are, first, in establishing the antiquity of man, and, second, in unravelling the food-producing revolution—the change from hunting to herding livestock, formerly termed the 'Neolithic revolution'.

As late as 1859 Joseph Prestwich complained (Prestwich, 1861) that 'The conclusion, in fact, that man did not exist until after the latest of our geological changes and until after the dying out of the great extinct mammals, had become almost a point of established belief.'

Until the mid-nineteenth century it was customary to take the biblical narrative of the creation literally. According to James Usher, Archbishop of Armagh (1581–1656), the world was created in 4004 BC (9.00 am on 23 October according to a later scholar). So when in 1797 John Frere, High Sheriff of Suffolk, Member of Parliament for Norwich, and country squire, found at Hoxne in Suffolk flint artefacts '. . . weapons of war, fabricated and used by a people who had not the use of metals' associated with 'some extraordinary bones, particularly a jaw-bone of enormous size, of some unknown animal, with the teeth remaining in it', tempting him 'to refer them to a very remote period indeed; even beyond that of the present world' (Frere, 1800), he was duly ignored. Similar associations of human remains with extinct animal bones were reported in Germany (Daniel, 1975:25).

These finds in Germany and England were treated with scepticism, and were explained away by one means or another. An 'elephant' (presumably mammoth) found with a 'British weapon' in Gray's Inn Lane, London, at the end of the seventeenth century was considered to have been imported by the Roman emperor, Claudius (Daniel, 1975:26). The remains of Neanderthal man, found in 1857 near Dusseldorf in Germany, were thought of as having belonged variously to some poor idiotic hermit, or to an ailing Cossack deserter (Reader, 1981)!

Despite its lack of recognition at the time, Frere's communication in the journal *Archaeologia* in 1800 must be one of the earliest published contributions to zoo-archaeology.

In the 1830s a customs official from Abbeville in northern France, Jacques Boucher de Perthes (Daniel, 1975), studied the 'diluvial' remains of man and extinct animals found in nearby quarries. In Sicily the palaeontologist Hugh Falconer found hippopotamus and elephant bones with small flint implements resembling obsidian knives from Mexico. Like Frere's report, these two were given a cold reception. By 1859, however, the geologists Sir Joseph Prestwich and Sir John Evans, after visiting Perthes in Abbeville, became convinced of the authenticity of Perthes' as well as Frere's and other reported finds. They communicated their opinions to the Royal Society in that year (this was the same year that Charles Darwin, *Origin of species* was published). Prestwich (1861:309) wrote: 'It might be supposed that in assigning to Man an appearance at such a period, it would of necessity imply his existence during long ages beyond all exact calculations; for we have been apt to place even the latest of our geological changes at a remote, and, to us, unknown distance.'

During the second half of the nineteenth century, thanks to geologists and other scientists such as Charles Lyell, Lord Kelvin, Thomas Huxley and Charles Darwin, the great age of the earth and the antiquity of our ancestors came to be appreciated. In England further evidence came in the mid-nineteenth century with William Pengelly's re-excavation of caves in south Devon which yielded remains of man contemporary with bones of such extinct animals as lion, hyaena, bear, mammoth, rhinoceros and reindeer (Daniel, 1975:58).

The first major contribution therefore of zoo-archaeological remains was in providing proof of the antiquity of man. Once this was established the next task was to rationalize prehistoric remains into some kind of chronology. Much pioneering work in establishing a sequence of archaeological periods was done in Denmark by antiquaries like Christian Jurgensen Thomsen and J. J. A. Worsaae. The magistrate and palaeontologist, Edouard Lartet (1801–71) explored cave sites in France. He recognized changes in the species composition of different cave strata, and distinguished four periods according to their associated animals: (1) cave bear period, (2) woolly mammoth and rhinoceros period, (3) reindeer period and (4) aurochs or bison period. His was an early attempt to classify archaeological remains on the basis of non-archaeological data (Daniel, 1975:101).

By 1870 a chronological framework in archaeology was accepted. Excavations now began to be conducted rigorously by men like the antiquarian Worsaae and the soldier turned archaeologist General Augustus Pitt-Rivers. Both stressed the importance of careful excavation and preservation of even ordinary or 'trifling' objects. Faunal remains were now studied for their contributions to our understanding of early human behaviour and economy.

Early zoo-archaeology proper, in the sense of specialist studies of archaeofaunal remains, is often associated with two Swiss workers: L. Rütimeyer and J. Ulrich Duerst. In 1862 Rütimeyer described the mammal bones from Neolithic lakeside dwellings in Switzerland. He was perhaps the first to distinguish between bones of domestic animals such as sheep, pigs and cattle, and bones of their wild ancestors. His observation of cut-marks on fox bones led him to infer that this animal was consumed by humans. Further work on the origin of domestication was done by Duerst, who spent nearly three years from 1904–07 studying half a ton of animal bones from excavations carried out by Pumpelly and Schmidt at Anau in Russian Turkestan. He claimed (Duerst, 1908) to be able to show, via a reduction of size and a change in texture of the bone itself, the transition of wild cattle, and sheep to their domestic descendents. The osteological investigation of the origin of domestic animals was now under way.

After chronology and domestication, the next contribution which archaeofaunal remains made was in reconstructing the environment of the past. An early example is Dorothea Bate's now famous *Dama-Gazella* graph. In the 1930s, on advice from her mentor, Frederik Zeuner (whose later book on domesticated animals, published in 1963, is still a standard text), Bate plotted the frequencies in different strata of the Mount Carmel caves (excavated by Dorothy Garrod) of two animals each characteristic of a different habitat. She was able to deduce climatic changes during the Upper Pleistocene of the Levant. Her study was an early example of the use of quantitative data in zoo-archaeology (her results are discussed in Chapter 3).

As archaeology grew, so did the interest in the geographic origin of food production. Eduard Hahn at the end of the nineteenth century suggested that many animals were first domesticated in the Near East. Gordon Childe termed this first attempt to control our source of food the 'Neolithic Revolution'. The plant geneticist Nikolai Ivanovich Vavilov, who later tragically perished in the Stalinist purges, sought to determine what he termed centres or hearths of domestication. Interest in the early origin of food production took Robert Braidwood, of the Oriental Institute in Chicago, to the Near East in the late 1940s and 1950s. He was accompanied by a zoologist—Charles Reed. It was Reed in the late 1950s who questioned (Reed, 1961) some of the assumptions being made at that time concerning the domestic status of many of the animals found on excavations. Reed set the stage for a more rigorous approach by subsequent investigators to the origin of domestication (see Chapter 6).

The origin and subsequent evolution of livestock breeds have for a long time been a major subject of study in Germany. Since the 1950s, one renowned pioneer of the use of zoo-archaeology to this end has been Joachim Boessneck, together with his students (the 'Munich school'). Besides studying in great detail faunal remains from European and Near Eastern archaeological sites, he has made important contributions to our understanding of the osteology of domestic livestock and to basic methods now used by zoo-archaeologists.

The 1970s saw a huge increase in the number of people investigating archaeofaunal remains. An international conference of zoo-archaeologists was held in 1971 in Budapest. Out of this grew the International Council for Archaeozoology (ICAZ)—founded in 1976 in Nice. Subsequent meetings were held in Groningen in 1974 and Stettin in 1978. And at the fourth conference held in London in 1982 over 200 people participated from over 30 different countries. Anneke Clason of the Biological-Archaeological Institute of the University of Groningen (Poststraat 6, 9712 ER Groningen, The Netherlands) is currently the secretary of ICAZ. She publishes an annual newsletter containing information on conferences, new publications, an address-list and a list of current research projects and other items that might be of general interest to zoo-archaeologists. An annual bibliography is published by Hans-Hermann Muller of the Central Institute for Ancient History and Archaeology of the Academy of Sciences of the DDR. Much of what these zoo-archaeologists have been studying forms the basis of this book.

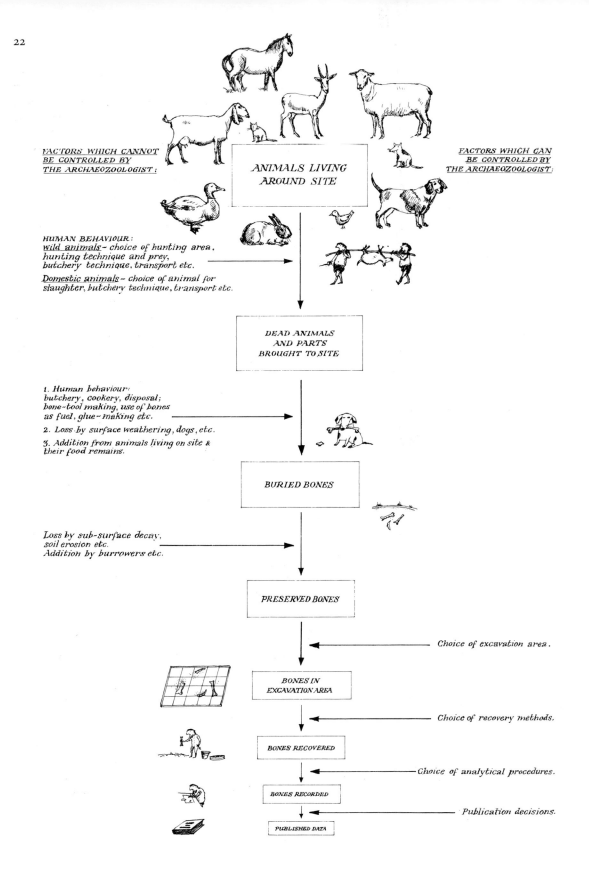

ANIMALS LIVING
AROUND SITE

*FACTORS WHICH CANNOT
BE CONTROLLED BY
THE ARCHAEOZOOLOGIST:*

*FACTORS WHICH CAN
BE CONTROLLED BY
THE ARCHAEOZOOLOGIST:*

HUMAN BEHAVIOUR:
wild animals – *choice of hunting area,*
hunting technique and prey,
butchery technique, transport etc.

Domestic animals – *choice of animal for*
slaughter, butchery technique, transport etc.

DEAD ANIMALS
AND PARTS
BROUGHT TO SITE

1. Human behaviour:
butchery, cookery, disposal;
bone-tool making, use of bones
as fuel, glue-making etc.

2. Loss by surface weathering, dogs, etc.

3. Addition from animals living on site &
their food remains.

BURIED BONES

Loss by sub-surface decay,
soil erosion etc.
Addition by burrowers etc.

PRESERVED BONES

Choice of excavation area.

BONES IN
EXCAVATION AREA

Choice of recovery methods.

BONES RECOVERED

Choice of analytical procedures.

BONES RECORDED

Publication decisions.

PUBLISHED DATA

CHAPTER ONE

Methods and problems in zoo-archaeology

Zoo-archaeology as a discipline in its own right has only become established during the last 20–30 years. Most zoo-archaeologists originally trained either as zoologists or as archaeologists. They have worked in different parts of the world—often quite independently of one another. This has led to the development of different methods—particularly the ways of counting and measuring bones. Perhaps the most serious shortcoming is that investigators vary in their ability to identify bones correctly.

In its early days, a zoologist called upon to analyse archaeofaunal remains was merely expected to provide a list of identified species. Today we know that much more than mere 'laundry lists' of species can be obtained. Quantitative data like the age distribution and sex ratios of each species present may tell us how they were exploited in antiquity: for example, were they hunted or husbanded, and, if the latter, were they kept primarily for meat or wool and milk? Our job then is to extract as much zoological and anthropological information as possible from what is just a pile of bones.

This chapter discusses some of the methods used by zoo-archaeologists, and describes various pitfalls which must be avoided before drawing conclusions from archaeofaunal data. The next chapter details the structure and development of bone and teeth.

1.1 Some of the factors which may have affected archaeofaunal data. On the left are factors over which the archaeologist has no control, and on the right are those which can be controlled. *Drawing by Sara Midda. After Meadow, 1980 and Payne, 1985*

THE ORIGIN OF AN ARCHAEOFAUNAL ASSEMBLAGE

A long chain of events occurs between the original collection and slaughter of animals in antiquity, their incorporation within an archaeological site, their ending up on the faunal analyst's workbench, and their final publication. One sometimes wonders whether there is any similarity between a published bone report and the animals exploited by ancient humans. In an ideal situation the data and conclusions contained in the final faunal report would reveal something about the original population of animals exploited by man. Sadly, this is rare. But let us assume that some information may be gleaned from the faunal debris associated with archaeological excavations. Basically there are two sets of factors which may modify archaeofaunal data (fig. 1.1).

A first set of possible modifications is beyond our control. This set relates to the behaviour of early man and various animals, and peculiarities of the site such as soil acidity and humidity. A second set of modifications, however, can be controlled by the archaeologist and faunal analyst, and has to do with the way we go about excavating, recovering and finally studying the faunal remains.

An understanding of these two sets of modifying factors which intervene between prehistoric fauna and published faunal report should alert us to some of the dangers when drawing environmental and cultural conclusions in zoo-archaeology.

THE PRIMARY ACCUMULATION OF AN ARCHAEOFAUNAL ASSEMBLAGE

Humans

It is usually assumed that humans alone were responsible for accumulating archaeofaunal remains. This is a logical assumption for medium-large animals (rabbit- to cow-sized), particularly when their bones display cut and butchery marks which only flint or metal blades could produce (fig. 1.2). Fig. 1.3 illustrates how lamb, beef, and pork is butchered today in Britain.

The majority of bones we excavate derive from animals that were intentionally killed for their slaughter products (i.e. primary products such as meat, hides, sinews, bones etc). A fundamental problem in zoo-archaeology, to which we all too infrequently address ourselves, is what do these bones really represent in terms of the living animals and man's exploitation of them. Consider an extreme present-day example: the Maasai cattle herders in East Africa. The Maasai are primarily dependent upon the cow for its milk (and sometimes blood too). Examination of the debris from a temporary encampment may not reveal any trace of cattle—the mainstay of their economy—for they may only be rarely slaughtered. Also, animals exploited, say, for traction or riding, may not necessarily have been consumed and may only be represented by an occasional bone introduced by scavenging dogs. The problem of correlating between excavated bones and the economic importance of the animals in antiquity is far from being resolved. In particular other animals often play a part.

Hyaenas

A carnivore known to play a bone-scavenging role is the hyaena. While this animal has not formed an association with humans, the possibility that carcasses jettisoned from a settlement have been scavenged by hyaenas, or even that an assemblage of fossil bones

1.2 Carcass cutting in antiquity: these bones show typical cut marks. Shown here are butchered bones of red deer, horse, pig and cow astragali and distal humeri from archaeological sites (see Driesch and Boessneck, 1975). *Photograph courtesy Angela von den Driesch and Joachim Boessneck*

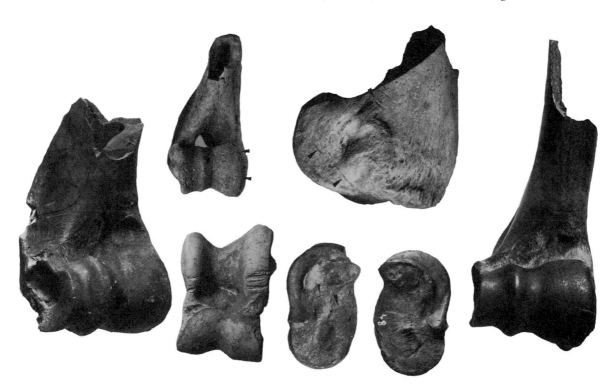

LAMB

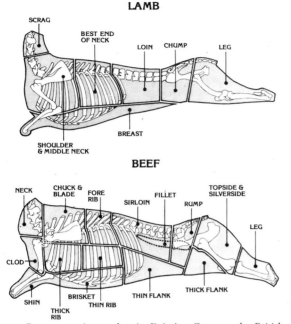

BEEF

PORK

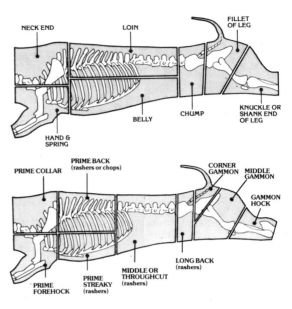

1.3 Carcass cutting today in Britain. *Courtesy the British Meat promotion executive*

was once a hyaena den has to be considered. Hyaenas are more efficient at crushing and digesting bone than dogs. They leave only the tooth-row sections of upper and lower jaws and the very robust long-bone ends from the largest mammals. A typical hyaena-den bone assemblage will therefore consist primarily of just these elements. I recently studied a collection of bones from an Aceramic Neolithic cave site in the northern Negev which contained an abundance of mandibles and horn cores, just as did a nearby recent hyaena den. I concluded that the Neolithic assemblage had at the very least been extensively scavenged by hyaenas in antiquity.

Richard Klein (1975) suggests that human food remains can be separated from carnivore refuse by the amount of carnivore remains themselves within such refuse—a carnivore:ungulate ratio. This is because carnivores typically feed upon other carnivores more frequently than does man, so a high ratio may indicate carnivore involvement, and a low ratio, human. The bone-collecting activities of hyaena as well as leopards and porcupines in Africa are discussed in great detail in Charles Brain (1981), *The Hunters or the Hunted*. He concludes that many of the very early accumulations of animal bones associated with man's ancestor *Australopithecus* in South Africa as well as the bones of Australopithecines themselves

may well have been formed by large carnivores. *Australopithecus* was hunted rather than hunter (see Chapter 5).

Owls

Most owls feed nocturnally on small mammals and birds which they swallow whole. However, the owl obligingly does not allow the bones to pass into the stomach with its acidic digestive juices. Instead it regurgitates most of the animal bones (and hair) as a pellet, usually while it is roosting. Favourite roosting places are trees, and ledges overhanging cliffs or caves. In the latter case layer upon layer of small mammal (and bird) bones accumulate—the result of countless hundreds of rejected owl pellets. The owl was probably the main agent responsible for introducing rodent, small insectivore and bird bones in cave sites. Some larger owls will also catch the young of slightly larger animals, and in Africa the Cape Eagle owl will take hares, hyrax and even fawns of antelopes (Brain, 1981:122). The absence of suitable roosting places above ancient settlements probably accounts for the paucity of small mammal remains in most archaeological sites which are not inside caves or under overhanging cliffs. Exceptions are instances where burrowing rodents have managed to penetrate the archaeological layers. Such cases can often be recognised by the following clues: (1) the overlying strata may show disturbance; (2) such rodents may consist of complete skeletons; and (3) they are sometimes suspiciously fresh in appearance.

Owls usually foray up to about 2–3km from their roost. Therefore a small-mammal assemblage in an archaeological cave deposit derives from prey introduced by owls from the immediate vicinity. A sequence of such assemblages should give an indication of the local faunal succession and hence, by inference, vegetational and climatic changes. Caution is required, though. Owls, like most predators, tend to specialise, and concentrate on one or a few particular prey species. The range of species preyed upon and returned to the roost will not necessarily reflect the naturally occurring spectrum of species. Analysis of small-mammal remains from cave sites (usually from the early Stone Ages) is a specialization in itself. (For identifying remains in British owl pellets, see Yalden, 1977.)

MODIFYING FACTORS

Humans

Most archaeological bones represent the garbage of ancient people's meals; consequently skeletons have become widely scattered as a result of butchering. Prehistoric people also tended to subject bones to rather drastic treatment, notably roasting them and fragmenting them to extract the marrow. They also split and shaped some bones into tools. The only ones which may escape such treatment are the small phalanges, carpals and tarsals. Teeth generally fare better.

Fragmentation may be the result of (1) butchery and pounding of bones in order to liberate the marrow, (2) unintentional trampling, and (3) unintentional breakage resulting from excavation. The last is recognised by its fresh appearance and the different staining (usually lighter) of the fractured surface. Trampling in antiquity results in fairly simple fractures—in the mid-shaft region for example. Deliberate percussion for marrow extraction leaves very little of the diaphysis intact and of course produces a debris of numerous bone chips and splinters. The edges of the broken ends are jagged and frequently a scar identifies the original point of impact. It is difficult, usually impossible, to reassemble long bones—particularly in large assemblages where bones have suffered extensive fragmentation. However 'kill sites' such as those of the North

American plains and East Africa sometimes contain the remains of one or a few large mammals. In these cases an attempt to reconstruct the skeleton, having mapped the exact position of each bone fragment, can reveal how the carcass was dismembered. One important question is: did early Palaeolithic humans scavenge big game or hunt big game? This topic, and the possible roles of other animals such as dogs and hyaenas, will be discussed later.

Most assemblages comprise fragmented mandibles (sometimes only isolated teeth), skull fragments, bits of ribs and vertebrae. Most of the recognizable parts of long bones consist of the articular ends only. None of the later Stone Age sites in the Near East I have seen contains any complete long bones.

Sometimes bones show signs of fire. Burning shrinks bone, particularly when done for a long time or at high temperatures. I have seen calcined bones (they are blue–white in colour) which have shrunk to about half their natural size. Burnt bones should not be measured.

Dogs

Payne and Munson (1985) have investigated the destructive effect dogs may have on different bones. They fed whole goat limbs and several species of small animals to two large dogs, observed what they did and collected the resulting debris. The dogs were able to break and extensively chew most of the long bones. Most fragments smaller than about 2.5cm diameter were swallowed and subsequently either vomited or passed out with the faeces (fig. 1.4). In

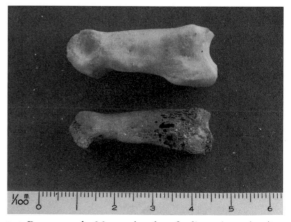

1.4 Payne and Munson's dog-feeding investigation. *Above:* fresh goat first phalanx; *below:* goat first phalanx after passage through a dog's digestive tract and recovery from its faeces. *Photograph courtesy Sebastian Payne*

either case these smaller fragments become heavily attacked by stomach juices resulting in either their complete disappearance or varying degrees of etching. In one experiment, one of the dogs was fed the heads and feet of 37 squirrels, but when the surviving bone was examined only 14 individuals could be accounted for.

Etched surfaces of digested bone are often shiny, and any broken edges wafer-thin and sharp. Once seen, this kind of treatment is easily recognisable in archaeological bone, and distinction from simple soil erosion is made by comparing large and small fragments. Dogs will not swallow fragments whose diameter exceeds *c*2.5cm; soil corrosion will affect small and large fragments alike. In the Israeli archaeofaunal sequence (fig. 6.21, Davis, 1985) the first evidence of digested small bones—particularly phalanges and tarsals of the gazelle—comes from the Natufian culture period (between 10,300 and 8500 bc). It corroborates other evidence (Chapter 6) for early dog domestication at that time.

Geological factors

These zoological and cultural modifying factors lead one to wonder whether there is any relation between what we find preserved on a site and what early people ate. Consider an extreme example: the excavation of Fort Ligonier, which was a British army relay station between Carlisle and Pittsburgh during the French and Indian war. Historical records tell us that it was garrisoned from 3 September 1758 to the spring of 1766 (2364 days) by as many as 4000 men. The daily meat ration was 1lb per soldier. However, the bone recovered and analysed by John Guilday (1970) suggests a total meat consumption of no more than 4000lb for the entire period—enough to sustain the full garrison for only one day, or only two men for the length of time of the human occupancy. As Guilday states, this kind of calculation is clearly ridiculous. Besides much of the meat consumed was salted pork, most probably off the bone. No doubt too, bone and other garbage was cast out some distance from the station. At most, the bone assemblage provides just an estimate of the relative importance of the various meat animals.

The disappearance of bones prior to or during the formation of an archaeological (or geological) deposit has stimulated much inquiry. This is a branch of palaeontology termed taphonomy, which was defined by the palaeontologist Efremov in 1940 as 'the

study of a process in the upshot of which the organisms pass out of the different parts of the biosphere and, being fossilized, become part of the lithosphere'. Much of this work (in archaeology) was prompted by Raymond Dart who studied the animal remains from the early hominid site of Makapansgat in South Africa. He found that some parts of the skeleton were grossly underrepresented. Dart postulated that these missing bones were those used by *Australopithecus* as clubs (such as humeri) and left outside the cave, while the commonly represented mandibles had been selectively brought back to the cave for use as saws and scrapers to form part of what he called an osteodontokeratic industry.

Charles Brain (1967) suspected another, and simpler, cause for the unequal representation of skeletal elements at Makapansgat—their destruction prior to fossilization. He tested his suspicion by collecting the bones from garbage jettisoned around modern Hottentot goatherders' villages on the Namib plain. These goat bones had already suffered breakage for marrow extraction, chewing, gnawing by dogs and scavenging by crows, but they had not been used to manufacture tools.

He plotted the frequencies with which different parts of the skeleton were represented. The plots he obtained (fig. 1.5) were very similar to those of the animal bones from Makapansgat, and it became clear that those parts which survive best are the ones most resistant to the rigours of chewing and weathering. For example the solid early-fusing distal end of the humerus survives well, while its spongy late-fusing proximal end is hardly represented at all. Thus the differences of hardness between various parts of the skeleton is an important factor determining their frequencies in death assemblages.

At one Palaeolithic site (at Mount Carmel) I witnessed total bone destruction: all that was left was a layer of fine yellow powder. Bone preservation tends to be good in alkaline and calcareous soils, and bad in acid and sandy ones. Gordon and Buikstra (1979) showed a direct correlation between the acidity of the soil (its pH) and bone preservation in human burial sites. In slightly acidic soils (pH 6.5) adult skeletal remains may be difficult to study and infant bones are reduced to powder.

So far I have discussed factors which modify the composition of an archaeofaunal sample before and during its fossilization: (a) initial culling of animals and whether by humans, hyaenas or owls, (b)

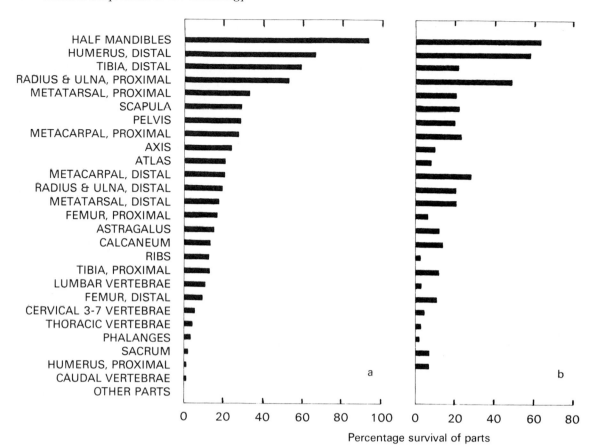

HALF MANDIBLES
HUMERUS, DISTAL
TIBIA, DISTAL
RADIUS & ULNA, PROXIMAL
METATARSAL, PROXIMAL
SCAPULA
PELVIS
METACARPAL, PROXIMAL
AXIS
ATLAS
METACARPAL, DISTAL
RADIUS & ULNA, DISTAL
METATARSAL, DISTAL
FEMUR, PROXIMAL
ASTRAGALUS
CALCANEUM
RIBS
TIBIA, PROXIMAL
LUMBAR VERTEBRAE
FEMUR, DISTAL
CERVICAL 3-7 VERTEBRAE
THORACIC VERTEBRAE
PHALANGES
SACRUM
HUMERUS, PROXIMAL
CAUDAL VERTEBRAE
OTHER PARTS

Percentage survival of parts

1.5 Brain's study of differential preservation of bones. (a) The percentage survival of different parts of the goat skeleton in the vicinity of modern Hottentot villages, based on a minimum of 64 individual goats. (b) The percentage survival of bovid skeletal parts from the Lower Pleistocene site Makapansgat, South Africa, arranged in the same order as (a). *From Brain, 1967.*

subsequent treatment of carcasses/bones by man (butchery, cooking, tool production, trampling) or dogs and (c) the effects of factors like soil acidity upon the incorporation of remaining bones into the fossil record. These factors are all beyond the control of the zoo-archaeologist.

Assuming some faunal remains are preserved in a site, I shall now discuss factors which we can control, i.e. those which result from archaeological and post-excavation procedure.

IN THE FIELD : THE ARCHAEOLOGIST AND RECOVERY TECHNIQUES

The faunal analyst should ideally be present 'on site'. This allows a feel for its location and immediate environs to be gained, and also permits emergency treatment to be carried out, such as consolidation of bones disintegrating on exposure.

An archaeologist has to work in close cooperation with the faunal-analyst. In the past, and sadly often even today, many archaeologists have concentrated their attention on written records, coins, pots and architecture. Bones with their clues about the ancient economy have been thrown away, or at best relegated to an appendix at the back of the excavation report. Among archaeologists specializing in earlier periods such as the Stone Ages, with little or no pottery, and certainly no written remains, the record has been better since prehistoric sites yield little besides stones and bones.

Besides appreciating the value of faunal remains, a competent archaeologist should be aware of the importance of factors like methods of sampling and of the need to acquire a comparative osteological collection. Let us address the first problem: how were the faunal remains collected?

The days of 'laundry-list' faunal reports are now over, with zoo-archaeology adopting a quantitative approach. However, as in any branch of science dealing with numerical and metrical data, very careful attention must be paid to the processes which generate such data. In our case this includes not only the effects of various weathering agents on faunal remains prior to their excavation (i.e. before and during fossilization) but also the methods used in the recovery of archaeofaunal remains on site.

For a long time in archaeology, and regrettably on many digs even today, finds retrieved during an excavation are simply those that were noticed by the excavators. A scrupulous zoologist enquiring about the apparent lack of phalanges and other small bones in the collection would be assured that great care had been taken by the excavators, and that every single splinter of bone was meticulously collected. Despite such care, it is now realized that a bias operates favouring the recovery of easily recognisable elements such as long-bones and mandibles. This calls for the employment of more objective recovery techniques—a requirement long recognised by certain archaeologists, particularly those digging Mesolithic assemblages with their tiny chipped stone tools or microliths. Many of these archaeologists took to sieving the excavated soil in order to retrieve these microliths, and in so doing recovered most of the small bones too.

Sebastian Payne, a zoo-archaeologist who works mainly in Turkey and Greece, is largely responsible for drawing our attention to the problem of biased recovery. He noted (Payne, 1975) the lack of smaller bones in many published faunal reports. For example at a site in Greece, whose fauna comprised mainly sheep, goats and cattle, the proportion of sheep/goat to cattle mandibles was 3:1, but for third phalanges the ratio was reversed: cattle third phalanges were ten times more frequent than those of sheep/goat. Sheep/goat phalanges are small and therefore difficult to pick out from the dirt and debris of an excavation. There is a similar body-part discrepancy in my own data from Tel Yarmout, a Bronze Age site in Israel, where sieving has not so far been carried out (table 1.1). Which of the skeletal elements represents the true frequency of animals at both of these sites?

	Sheep/Goat	Cattle
M$_3$s/posterior mandibles	92	3
Distal humeri	89	8
Distal radii	36	2
Distal tibiae	73	8
Astragali	47	9
Third phalanges	7	12

Table 1.1 Bone counts from one of the levels at Tel Yarmout, Israel. Sieving was not carried out.

Payne then undertook a series of sieving experiments (fig. 1.6) while participating in the excavation of Sitagroi, a mound site in Greece. He processed the dumped earth excavated fairly rapidly by pick. Bones retrieved by the excavators were kept separate from those that they missed but which he was able to recover in the sieve. The results are astounding (table 1.2). His example shows how numerous bones, particularly smaller parts of the skeleton and isolated teeth, are lost when sieving is not carried out. Needless to say sieving or lack of sieving has an important effect upon the recovery of the unfused epiphyses from young animals, so that estimates of

	Cattle		Pig		Sheep/Goat	
	recovered in trench	missed in trench recovered in sieve	recovered in trench	missed in trench recovered in sieve	recovered in trench	missed in trench recovered in sieve
Single teeth	6	10	1	41	1	128
Mandible and skull fragments with teeth	2	2	5	10	1	6
Long bones and metapodials	12	7	5	21	13	73
Phalanges, carpals and tarsals	9	13	1	35	0	111

Table 1.2 Payne's (1972) sieving experiments at Sitagroi, Greece. Note how recovery in the trench is more efficient for larger animals and larger bones.

1.6 Wet sieving in action. *Photograph courtesy Sebastian Payne*

1.7 Wet sieving often produces large quantities of invaluable small teeth and bones—sorting these can be tedious but rewarding. *Photograph courtesy Sebastian Payne*

the proportion of juveniles in a sample may be severely biased in the absence of sieving. (An epiphysis is the separate centre of ossification at the end of a long bone which fuses when a mammal matures—see next chapter.) Without sieving there is little chance at all of recovering the bones of the smaller mammals such as rodents, shrews and small carnivores. Payne further recommends wet sieving in preference to dry sieving. Water not only washes the bones rendering them more visible, but also liberates bone fragments from clods of soil. The use of wet as opposed to dry sieving is especially important when fine-mesh screens are used to extract microfaunal remains such as rodent bones and teeth (fig. 1.7). Partial recovery therefore is a problem easily remedied by wet sieving. A quick glance at a table giving body-part frequencies may provide an immediate impression of how well the sample was recovered. Moreover, findings such as these illustrate how important it is to publish data in full and of course to describe the methods of recovery.

Archaeological context

When analysing the finds it is most important to record the archaeological context (square, level, etc.) of each identifiable bone, so that different levels and different areas of the site can be separately analysed and compared with one another. The nature of each context should also be considered—be it living floor, dump, butchering area, altar or any other type of special area. Variability within a site can reveal what kinds of activity were being carried out and where. Differences between levels may indicate economic or climatic trends which occurred in the course of the site's occupation. Where spatial and intra-site variation exists data for the layer or site as a whole are only meaningful when a large area has been sampled. One interesting example I encountered which illustrates the importance of organizing data according to place of origin (locus), comes from the Iron Age site of Tel Qiri near Hazorea in Israel. Here most of the bones at five particular places on the site (reckoned by the archaeologist to have been cultic) were sheep/goat right fore-limbs, many from young individuals (table 1.3). So, presumably, the priests at ancient Hazorea offered kid and lamb right forequarters.

An important problem when dealing with archaeofaunal remains is the reliability of the context (such as the stratum) from which they are supposed to have

Locus number		1065 L	1065 R	1044 L	1044 R	1074 L	1074 R	1146 L	1146 R	1064 L	1064 R
SHEEP/GOAT											
Scapula	F	2	33	—	4	—	7	—	4	—	4
Scapula	U	—	16	—	3	—	4	—	3	—	—
Humerus (distal)	F	2	34	—	8	—	8	—	5	—	7
Humerus (distal)	U	2	3	—	1	—	1	—	1	—	—
Radius (distal)	F	—	7	—	2	—	2	—	1	—	2
Radius (distal)	U	—	11	—	4	2	4	—	—	—	1
Metacarpal (distal)	F	—		—		—		—		—	
Metacarpal (distal)	U	—		—		—		—		—	
Femur (distal)	F	—	1	—	—	—	—	—	—	—	—
Femur (distal)	U	1	—	—	—	—	—	—	—	—	—
Tibia (distal)	F	1	—	—	1	—	—	1	—	—	—
Tibia (distal)	U	—	1	—	—	—	—	—	—	—	—
Calcaneum	F	1	1	—	—	—	—	—	—	—	—
Calcaneum	U	—	1	—	—	1	—	—	1	—	—
Astragalus		—	—	—	1	1	—	—	—	—	—
Metatarsal (distal)	F	—		—		—		—		—	
Metatarsal (distal)	U	2		—		—		—		—	
Third phalanx		—	—	—	1	1	—	—	1	—	—
CATTLE											
Radius (distal)	F	—	—	—	—	—	1	—	—	—	—
Calcaneum		—	—	—	—	—	1	—	—	—	—
Third phalanx		1	—	—	—	—	—	—	—	—	—

Table 1.3 Bone counts from five loci at Tel Qiri, an Iron Age (twelfth–eighth centuries BC) site near Hazorea, Israel. L and R refer to left and right, F and U refer to fused and unfused epiphyses.

There is clear evidence for a preference for right sheep/goat forelimbs. See Exodus 29:2 and Leviticus 7:32 for references to selection of a particular side of a sacrificial animal. This practice was apparently once widespread in the near East.

come. Animal bones are not like coins or pots. They have not changed much in the last 100,000 years, so they cannot be assigned to any particular culture or period. The analyst must exercise extreme caution when dealing with mixed loci.

Many bones, particularly those which have lain in calcareous soil for numerous millennia, accumulate a deposit of calcrete (calcium carbonate) around them making identification difficult, and measurement impossible. Sometimes this deposit may be prised off with a dental tool; however, thicker deposits may require more drastic treatment such as use of a mechanical vibratory pick. An alternative method, but one which weakens fossilised bone, is immersion in a dilute solution of acetic acid. This preferentially reacts with calcrete, leaving bone intact. This method is suitable for rapid treatment of large samples, may take several hours, and must be followed by several hours' thorough washing in fresh water to remove all trace of acid. Afterwards, cleaned bone has to be thoroughly dried, and reinforced with a consolidant. One substance I have used (perhaps not the best, however) is a plastic—polyvinyl acetate. The bones are immersed in an acetone solution of this plastic for one or two hours, and then removed from the solution and allowed to dry in a well-ventilated room.

AT THE WORKBENCH: IDENTIFICATION AND THE IMPORTANCE OF A COMPARATIVE COLLECTION

Following cleaning and mending, faunal remains have to be identified. Since most zoo-archaeologists will compare the fossils with modern forms, the first step in fossil bone identification is to establish a comparative collection of reliably identified, aged and sexed skeletons of modern animals. Animal speciation and gross morphological changes (except among certain domestic animals) are usually thought to take tens or even hundreds of thousands of years to occur. This means that, apart from possible small changes in size, wild animal remains found on archaeological sites will closely resemble their present-day descendants. Collections of modern animals may therefore be used as a basis for comparison and identification, although we have to remember that animals are constantly evolving and undergoing morphological changes, even if only slowly. As we deal with fossil assemblages which are progressively older, it becomes increasingly difficult to fit the fossil animals into the framework of zoological criteria already established for identifying modern animal species.

In regions which have long had a museum tradition, such as Europe and North America, there may be sufficient comparative material in local natural history museums. Museum collections seldom possess more than one or two specimens from each locality, and many have in the past restricted their collecting to skulls and skins. Besides the skull, a zoo-archaeologist needs disarticulated limb bones. Since we are dealing with samples, and since all living things vary, the collection of large numbers of each animal species is important. A zoo-archaeologist joining an expedition to remoter parts of the world will have to start from scratch. This means going out to collect the local fauna: a slow, laborious and often smelly business, which requires hunting, trapping and retrieving dead animals from roads. Some enterprise is necessary, and the aid of local inhabitants is often a great help. A good place to obtain local domestic livestock is the abattoir, but from my own experience limb excision and decapitation must be supervised to prevent confusion between limbs and heads of different animals.

Defleshing large mammals (sheep, goat, pig and so on) can be quite unpleasant. There are a number of methods for doing this: one method involves removing as much muscular tissue as possible, simmering at just below boiling point for an hour and then maceration (i.e. allowing to rot in water). The latter may take several weeks. The use of biological washing powder, or an enzyme such as trypsin, may speed up this process.

The establishment of good comparative collections is most important. Very little is known about variation within the species such as differences between sexes (sexual dimorphism) and age-related change (ontogenetic variation), even for most of our domestic animals.

In the absence of a comparative collection, there are several good books or 'bone-atlases' which provide detailed drawings of many of the commoner animal bones one is likely to find on an archaeological site. Three examples for European animals are Ian Cornwall (1964), *Bones for the archaeologist*, Lavocat (1966) *Faunes et flores pré-historiques de l'Europe occidentale* and Elisabeth Schmid (1972), *Atlas of animal bones for prehistorians*. And one example for East Africa is Rikki Walker (1985), *A guide to post-cranial bones of East African animals*.

Identification of bones and teeth of mammals to their families (and even genus) is usually fairly straightforward. Distinguishing between two or more closely related species, however, may be difficult. And distinction at this level is, as we shall see later, often extremely important. Let me give a few useful examples which I have encountered in my own work.

In Europe and the Near East, the bane of most zoo-archaeologists' lives is the distinction between sheep

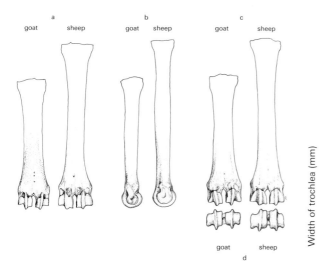

a   b   c

goat   sheep   goat   sheep   goat   sheep

goat   sheep

d

1.8 The distinction between sheep and goat metacarpals. (a) Posterior, (b) lateral, (c) anterior, and (d) plantar views of sheep and goat metacarpals to show the small differences between them. *Drawing by Judith Ogden*

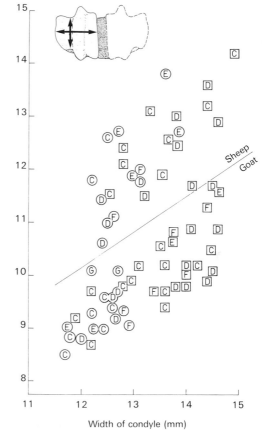

Width of trochlea (mm)

Sheep
Goat

Width of condyle (mm)

and goat bones and teeth. Such a distinction is often important in reconstructing the ancient economy and in earlier periods, in the reconstruction of the geographical distribution of these two animals. Joachim Boessneck (Boessneck *et al.*, 1964; Boessneck, 1969) has compiled and illustrated criteria for making the sheep-goat distinction for many parts of the skeleton. I have found the distal metacarpal relatively easy to identify (fig. 1.8), and Payne (1969) devised a series of measurements which, when plotted (fig. 1.9), also make this distinction. He (Payne, 1985) has also noted ways of separating juvenile sheep and goat teeth (fig. 1.10). Other bones are not so easy for separating the sheep from the goats. I personally feel confident about identifying metacarpals, metatarsals, astragali and first phalanges, but many others have to remain in a 'sheep/goat' category.

To study the origin of domestic equids (horse and donkey) it is essential, in the Near East at any rate, to distinguish between ass, onager, horse, and the little-known and now extinct *Equus hydruntinus* (the 'Otranto ass'). Besides southern Italy, where it was first discovered, the Otranto ass was once widespread in southern Europe and the Levant (Davis, 1980). It may have been related to the zebras. Figs. 1.11 and 1.12 show how these equid molars and metacarpals may be distinguished.

1.9 Metacarpals of modern sheep and goats from Kermanshah, Persia. Two measurements suggested by Payne (1969) taken on the condyles for distinguishing between these two species. Plots of sheep fall above the line, and goats below. Besides separating sheep from goat, most of the older male goats can be distinguished from the females. Males are represented by squares, females by circles. The letters C, D, E, F, and G refer to the dental age (Payne, 1973) of the individual: C = 6–12 months, D = 1–2 years, E = 2–3 years, F = 3–4 years, G = 4–6 years. Several young male goats (in dental stage C and whose epiphyses are unfused) fall among the females, so sex ratios of juvenile animals cannot safely be deduced.

Equids and sheep/goat are just two groups of animals whose bones are often difficult to tell apart. Some other problematical groups often encountered in zoo-archaeology are: cattle and bison; cattle and water buffalo; the South American camelids (llama, alpaca, guanaco); dromedary and bactrian camels; the house mouse and its wild relatives; and the hedgehogs.

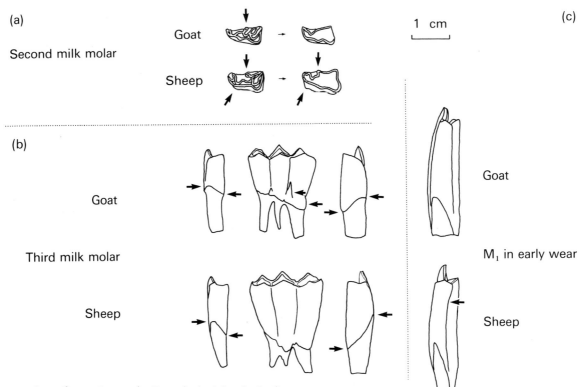

(a)

Goat

Second milk molar

Sheep

1 cm

(c)

(b)

Goat

Third milk molar

Sheep

Goat

M₁ in early wear

Sheep

1.10 Juvenile caprine teeth: Payne's (1985) criteria for distinguishing between sheep and goat. (a) Second deciduous molar, very young on the left and older on the right. (b) Third deciduous molar in mesial, external, and distal views. (c) First molar in mesial view. The arrows point to features which help make the distinction. *From Payne, 1985*

buccal

anterior (mesial)

a   b   c

protocone

3cm

lingual fold

buccal fold

a'   b'   c'

anterior (mesial)

buccal

1.11 Dental criteria for distinguishing between three equid groups. (a) Horse, (b) zebra/*Equus hydruntinus*, and (c) ass/onager. *Above:* occlusal views of upper molar (M¹ or M²) teeth, and *below:* lower molars (M₁ or M₂). The enamel folds only are shown. In the upper molars notice the shape of the protocone: elongated in the horse, triangular and short in zebras/*E. hydruntinus*, and oval in ass/onager. In the lower molars notice: first, the lingual fold. This is generally 'U' shaped in horses, and 'V' shaped in the other two groups. Second, the buccal or external fold makes a partial penetration of the adjacent folds (metaflexid and entoflexid) in horse molars (but not premolars); it completely penetrates between the flexids in zebra and *Equus hydruntinus* molars (but not premolars) and there is no penetration in ass/onager molars and premolars. The scale is 3cm long.

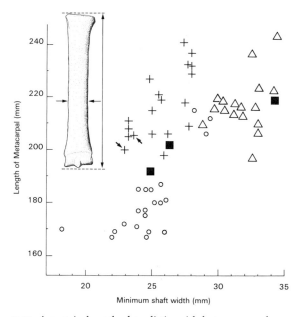

1.12 A metrical method to distinguish between ass, horse and onager metacarpals. Plot of length against minimum shaft width. Ass = circles, horse = triangles, and onager = crosses (the two arrowed plots belong to the Syrian onager). Note that there is some overlap between all three equids; therefore it would not always be possible to identify species using this method alone. The three squares are plots of three metacarpals from Arad, an Early Bronze Age site in the Negev, Israel. These probably belonged to two asses/onagers and a horse.

IDENTIFIABILITY AND COUNTING

Archaeologists often ask me what fragments of bone are identifiable, and what have to be relegated to the pile of unidentifiable splinters. Many are suprised that identifiability bears little relation to size. For example, a single isolated rodent molar barely visible to the naked eye may be identified to species, while a 12cm shaft splinter can only be referred to as 'large mammal'. Different parts of the skeleton vary in their distinctiveness. Ribs, shaft splinters, vertebrae and skull fragments are exceptionally difficult to identify. A general rule is that most bone fragments—especially from limb and foot—which include an articular surface can be identifiable at least to family and often to genus and species. Most teeth, even isolated ones, and articular ends of long bones (especially, in the case of ungulates, distal metapodials) are reasonably distinct and therefore easier to

identify, although age- and sex-dependent variation can complicate matters.

Ideally every scrap of bone should be identified. However, the task of processing thousands of bones can be overwhelming and calls for compromise. Most workers decide to identify, register, and measure a restricted number of skeletal parts (table 1.4 gives a list of the ungulate bones I register). These are usually ones which are (1) better preserved, (2) easier to identify and (3) more useful in providing age, sex and mensural information. The inclusion of bones from different parts of the skeleton will indicate whether any particular part of the body was preferentially selected. It is also important to count left and right limb-bones separately.

HEAD
  Mandible—posterior part/isolated third molar tooth (L/R).

SHOULDER GIRDLE and FORELIMB
  Scapula—glenoid articulation (L/R).
  Humerus—distal epiphysis (L/R).
  Radius—distal epiphysis (L/R).
  Metacarpal—distal epiphysis.

PELVIC GIRDLE and HIND LIMB
  Ischium—acetabular part (L/R).
  Femur—distal epiphysis (L/R).
  Tibia—distal epiphysis (L/R).
  Astragalus (L/R).
  Calcaneum (L/R).
  Metatarsal—distal epiphysis.

PHALANGES
  First phalanx—complete (l/r).
  First phalanx—proximal epiphysis (l/r).
  First phalanx—distal articulation (l/r).
  Third phalanx (l/r).

Table 1.4 Diagnostic zones of the ungulate skeleton which I identify, register and include in my counts for calculating species frequencies. Limb-bones from the left or right side of the animal (L/R) are listed separately. Phalanges from the left and right side of the limb (l/r) are also listed separately. No attempt is made to distinguish between metapodials from left and right limbs.

Having dug, cleaned, sorted to area/level and identified the faunal remains, we next have to assess the relative importance of each species. This may be calculated by adding the 'Number of Identifiable fragments of bones of each Species' (NISP) and expressing it as a percentage of the total number of bone-fragments in that level/area/site. There are three potential sources of bias here.

I have already mentioned the first possible source of bias: it derives from unequal recovery. In table 1.1, the bone counts from Tel Yarmout, the total NISP count indicates that cattle comprised 11 per cent of the fauna, but the mandibles alone suggest a mere 3 per cent. Since sieving was not undertaken at Yarmout, and given the results of Payne's sieving experiments, the low figure is probably nearer the truth. Before calculating the percentages of different species it is important to check for any discrepancies in the body-part frequencies. In cases where there are obvious biases (absences of smaller species' phalanges for example) better estimates of species frequencies are probably to be made from the easily visible (in excavation) elements such as mandibles.

The second source of bias is less serious and can easily be rectified. Not all mammals have the same number of diagnostic bones. One example might be a comparison between horse, cow and pig. The horse has, in the course of its evolution, reduced the lateral metapodials to small splint bones and lost all lateral digits. A horse limb, therefore, possesses one metapodial and one set of phalanges, while a cow limb (like sheep, goat and antelope) has one 'cannon bone' (derived from two longitudinally fused metapodials) and two sets of phalanges, and a pig limb has four separate (i.e. not longitudinally fused) metapodials and four sets of phalanges. Thus a little arithmetic manipulation has to be performed in order to standardize bone counts across the species spectrum. For example, cattle phalangeal counts could be halved, pig lateral metapodials and phalanges not included in the counts at all, pig central metapodials counted as halves, and equid phalange counts doubled.

The third source of bias, also easy to rectify, may derive from the differential fragmentation of bones. What was once a single bone may be included in a count as several fragments. In an estimate of frequencies, animals whose bones were subjected to greater fragmentation would then seem to be more common. This can sometimes happen to very large animal skeletons. John Watson's (1979) 'diagnostic zones' concept overcomes this bias. Each 'zone' is small and unlikely to be fragmented, but still large enough to be identified to species. It should not be possible to count the same bone more than once with any one zone. The same zone, however, should be present in all species under consideration, and counts for each zone must be recorded separately. Watson lists 88 'diagnostic zones' which are derived from parts of the skull, limb and feet bones. My own list (table 1.4) which is shorter, still includes zones and bones scattered throughout the skeleton.

LIVESTOCK VERSUS DEADSTOCK

Archaeologists often ask how many animals are represented in a given site, in order to estimate how many people the site could have sustained, and for how long. An individual mammal skeleton equals well over 200 complete bones and many more pieces if it is fragmented. If the numbers of each bone element per species, left or right (i.e. the 'diagnostic zones'), are scored separately, then it is possible to ascertain the 'Minimum Number of Individuals' (MNI). For example there are two humeri—one left and one right—so 18 left and 23 right sheep humeri must have come from at least 23 sheep.

Minimum counts of different species are not necessarily a guide to their economic importance. Different animals provide different quantities of meat: 200 hare and 10 cow bones do not mean that the hare was the mainstay of the economy. One way of estimating the economic importance (for example protein value) of each species is simply to multiply the numbers of individuals of each species by their average carcass weight. Since there is a direct relation between mammal skeleton weight and meat weight some zoo-archaeologists prefer to weigh all the bones found. Weights per species should therefore show the dietary contribution made by each animal. Of course if one species, for instance the cow, was exploited for its secondary products such as milk and power, the matter becomes rather more complicated. Similarly bones for the most part only represent what was killed. They do not necessarily reflect the proportions of husbanded animals—the 'life assemblage'. Consider a village with more live cows than pigs. Sows can produce many offspring per year: the cow can only have one or two. Therefore large numbers of pig bones in a village 'death assemblage' may simply reflect different reproductive rates.

ON TAKING MEASUREMENTS

Just as there are many attitudes concerning the identification of bones, many views exist upon the approach to adopt in measuring them. Some only measure one type of bone, frequently the teeth; others may take several measurements of every bone. It is of the greatest importance when measuring bones to explain exactly how those measurements were taken. This is best done by publishing sketches of the bone or tooth in question with unambiguous lines joining the points across which the calipers were lain. (In fig. 1.13 some of the measurements I take on certain bones are given.) Failing this, one of the reference works which give sketches of standard osteological measurements may be cited. Two early works of this nature are Hue, *Musée Osteologique* (1907) and Duerst, *Vergleichende Untersuchungsmethoden am Skelett bei Saugern* (1928). Neither are easy to find. Recently Angela von den Driesch (1976)

1.13 Some of the measurements I take on certain ungulate bones commonly found in Near Eastern archaeological sites. (a) Bovid/cervid distal metapodial; (b) bovid/cervid astragalus; (c) bovid/cervid distal humerus; (d) pig distal humerus. Measurements on these bones are relatively easy to define.

published a *Guide to the Measurement of Animal Bones from Archaeological Sites*. Using a standardized system has the advantage of allowing various workers to compare measurements with one another. Given time, a body of standardized mensural data will accumulate in the literature which will become a valuable source of data to study size changes both through time and across the globe. But why take measurements at all?

Most mammal species can be characterized on the basis of their size. Sometimes size is the main criterion for distinguishing between closely related species, as for example, in gazelles; in the absence of any appreciable morphological differences, the zoo-archaeologist will have little else to go on. Hence the first reason for measuring bones is simply to aid their identification. Furthermore publication of measurements helps other workers confronted with similar material.

Besides such interspecific size differences, there is much within-species variation of size, which is extremely relevant to zoo-archaeology; in particular sexual dimorphism and age related variation. 'British Archaeological Reports' (BAR) have recently published a useful volume of papers on these two subjects, edited by Wilson, Grigson and Payne (1982).

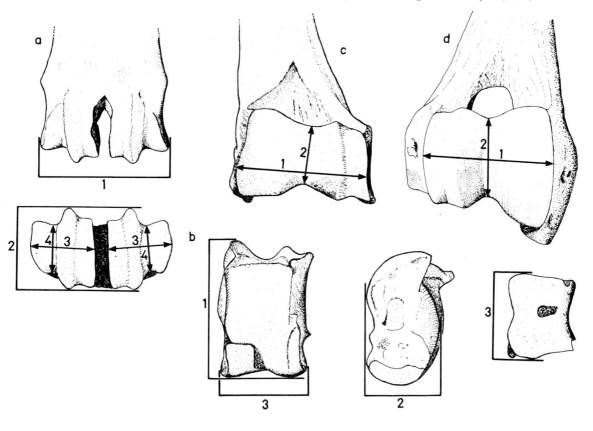

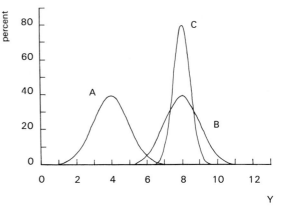

1.14 Age-dependent variation. A sheep mandible which exhibits severe interdental attrition—especially between first and second molars. *Specimen from West Hill, Uley, Gloucestershire. Photograph courtesy Bruce Levitan*

1.15 Basic biometry: the mean (average) and variance of a sample of measurements (such as length of a particular bone). Sample (a) has a mean of 4, while sample (b) has a mean of 8; both have the same variance. Sample (c) also has a mean of 8, but less variance. *From* Biometry, *1969, by Sokal and Rohlf, fig 6.3, W.H. Freeman & Co*

Teeth—particularly of herbivores—display a considerable degree of age-related variation. For example the length of the whole tooth row in an adult sheep mandible may decrease by as much as 15 per cent in the course of the living animal's life; this being due to the tapering of each tooth towards its base and interdental attrition (fig. 1.14). It is not therefore a good idea to characterize a herbivore on the basis of its tooth row length. However, if an easily measured variable alters significantly with respect to age in a known way, then the age at death of an animal can be estimated. So among the herbivores we have just such a variable: the height of their high crowned molar teeth. They are worn down gradually. Given a large enough sample of teeth the age-related culling strategy can be deduced. Such data can help determine the wild or domestic status of a species represented, and if the latter, can indicate for what purpose the animal was reared, whether for meat or for secondary products.

Living things possess inherent variability. An understanding of this is particularly important when we try to compare specimens and samples. The need to have objective (scientific) means of comparison was the factor which stimulated the birth of biometry, a branch of the science of statistics which deals with measurements of things biological.

Measurements taken of a sample of specimens tend to fall into a characteristic pattern of variation about either side of an average or mean. Graphic portrayal of the frequency of a biological measurement will usually produce a characteristic bell-shaped or Gaus-

sian curve which is symmetrical around the mean value. The shape of the curve describes the amount of variation. The wider the curve, the greater the variance of our variable (fig. 1.15).

Of course we usually have only a small sample at our disposal. Measuring provides a good estimate of the actual average size of the whole population from which our sample came. The probability that our estimate is a good one is dealt with in that section of statistics known as hypothesis testing (for details of which the reader should consult a textbook of biometry). The works of Simpson, Roe and Lewontin (1960), and Sokal and Rohlf (1969) are recommended.

Another source of variation which is not always fully appreciated is age-dependent variation. In mammals, once epiphysial fusion has occurred, longitudinal growth of long bones ceases. Growth in width of, say, the epiphyses will usually (but not always) have ceased too. However, if we measure across an area of tendon attachment, old individuals may appear to be wider due to the growth of extra bone around the point of tendon attachment (exostosis). Therefore it is important when taking measurements to control for age-dependent variation.

AGE AT DEATH

Having dealt with size differences between individuals, let us now discuss what is probably, for zoo-archaeology, the most important source of within-species variation: the age of an animal at death. Age data can reveal much about the economy: hunting capability, the origin of domestication and the mode of exploiting livestock. There are two kinds of ageing methods: (a) juvenile-adult distinction (epiphysial fusion; deciduous-permanent dentition) and (b) continuous distinction (dental age-classes). Much work has now been done on modern sheep and goat mandibles, with a view to being able to age their ancient ancestors.

Both methods of ageing archaeological bone suffer from possible preservational discrepancies. Bones and teeth of young animals, being incompletely ossified, are more likely to have been destroyed post mortem. Hence it is usually only possible to give a minimum estimate of the number of juveniles compared to adults, and the juvenile dental age classes have to be treated with caution. Let us now examine in some detail the various methods used for estimating age.

Epiphysial fusion
(The embryological development of bone is described in the next chapter.) Different epiphyses fuse at different ages: some around birth, most by the end of the juvenile period. For example in lambs the coracoid fuses to the scapula 3–4 months after birth. A count of scapulae with missing (unfused) coracoids will therefore tell us how many new-born lambs were culled. The first phalanx epiphysis fuses between 6–10 months, and the distal tibia around 12–15 months. Fusion counts of each of these three bones should in theory at least reveal in which of these four age groups (o—3–4 months, o—6–10 months, o—12–15 months, older than 12–15 months) the sheep had been preferentially slaughtered. If, for example, most coracoids and first phalanges are fused, but a large percentage of tibiae are unfused, it is logical to assume that this percentage of sheep was culled towards the end of the first year of life (between 6–10 and 12–15 months). However, the problem of unequal preservation of (a) unfused versus fused epiphyses and (b) different parts of the skeleton complicates the picture.

The phenomenon of epiphysial fusion has been well studied in man, dog and laboratory rodents.

Studies on epiphysial fusion in various breeds of the domestic dog (Smith and Alcock, 1960, for example) show that there is surprisingly little variation between breeds, between sexes, and even between individuals. Whether this is true of domestic and wild ungulates remains to be seen. Tove Hatting (1983), in her studies of fusion in Gotlandic sheep, finds that castration probably delays fusion. Nonetheless, counting unfused and fused epiphyses separately does provide a very approximate picture of the age-related culling pattern. Since measurements taken of the distal metacarpal in many ungulates (see above) can separate some or even all the specimens into their respective sexes as well as age groups culled—young or adult—it is sometimes possible to relate age to sex. The sex ratio of the juveniles may be compared to the sex ratio among adults. In many husbandry systems the optimum slaughter age is towards the end of the juvenile period when rapid growth has ceased and the meat gain no longer increases relative to fodder input. Most males are culled while young, whereas the females are kept longer for reproduction and perhaps milk and wool. Only a small proportion of males are maintained for stud purposes. Kurdish pastoralists told me that the adult sex ratios among their sheep and goat flocks are of the order of one male for every 10–30 females. The ability to recognize such sex-age related culling will help us trace the origin of animal husbandry.

Unfortunately knowledge of epiphysial fusion in many domestic animals (especially ungulates) and most wild animals is still in a somewhat rudimentary state: fusion ages are imprecise, and we know little about their variation, as well as differences between breeds and differences related to the nutrition level. Many of the earlier works dealing with the subject are unreliable. Data based upon X-ray analyses may also be unreliable. What appears unfused on an X-ray plate may in reality be newly fused and vice versa. Some recent sources of fusion data (mostly based on very small samples) are: Garcia–Gonzalez (1981), Smith (1967 in Noddle 1974) for sheep, Bullock and Rackham (1982) and Noddle (1974) for goats, Bull and Payne (1982) for pigs and wild boar, and Davis (1980) for gazelle. In table 1.5 I present a summary of some of these data.

Dental age classes
Tooth wear is one of the oldest techniques for age determination, and is particularly applicable to large

Bone/Epiphysis	red fox (weeks)	grey-hound (weeks)	Goth sheep (months)	Clun forest sheep (months)	Aragon sheep (months)	feral and domestic goats (months)	Israeli gazelles (months)
Scapula-Coracoid	9–11	–	–	4	3– 4	9–11	3– 6
proximal Humerus	29	–	24–30	27	30–42	23–48	–
distal Humerus	15–18	25–29	2– 4	4– 6	2– 4	11–12	c. 2
proximal Radius	20	–	2– 4	4	1.5– 3	4– 9	c. 2
distal Radius	28	45–47	15–30	20	18–36	33–48	12–18
distal Metacarpal	19–21	by 31	15–22	15	12–18	23–30	10–16
proximal Femur	28	c. 45	15–23	17–19	18–36	23–36	10–16
distal Femur	25–26	by 47	15–23	18–20	24–36	23–48	10–18
proximal Tibia	28	43–59	15–30	20–25	24–36	23–?36	12–18
distal Tibia	23–24	41–43	13–15	14	12–15	19–?24	8–10
Calcaneum-Tuber calcis	–	–	15–17	–	12–18	23–48	10–16
distal Metatarsal	20–22	by 37	15–23	15	12–18	23–30	10–16
proximal first Phalanx	16–19	by 27	6– 9	8–10	6– 8	11–24	5– 8
(fore-feet	16–18						
hind-feet	17–19)						

Table 1.5 The approximate ages of epiphysial fusion. The data for greyhounds and Clun forest sheep are based on radiological analysis, and so are probably not reliable for archaeological purposes. These data come from: Harris, 1978 (red fox); Smith and Allcock, 1960 (greyhound); Hatting, 1983 (Goth sheep); Smith in Noddle, 1974 (Clun forest sheep); Garcia-Gonzalez, 1981 (Aragon sheep); Noddle, 1974 (feral and domestic goats); and Davis, 1980 (Israeli gazelles).

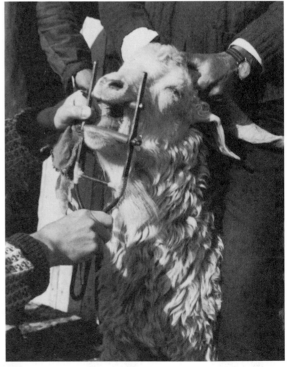

1.16 and **1.17** Payne and Deniz in central Turkey, examining tooth eruption and wear in modern Angora goats. By using an 'adjustable speculum' they were eventually able to examine the mandibular cheek teeth of up to 20 animals per hour. *Photographs by Gail Bull, courtesy Sebastian Payne*

herbivores (e.g., before making a purchase, one 'looks a horse in the mouth'). The last 15 years have seen the publication of several important papers which deal with the ageing of herbivore mandibles. Some establish criteria for assigning a given mandible to a particular age class on the basis of dental eruption and the pattern on the occlusal (biting) surface. The main contributors to this kind of methodology have been Eşref Deniz and Sebastian Payne (1982), working on Anatolian sheep and goats (figs. 1.16 and 1.17). Other studies deal with the rates at which the tooth-crowns are worn down, such as those undertaken by C. A. Spinage (1972; 1973) and Richard Klein (Klein and Cruz–Uribe, 1984). They have devised mensural methods linking dental crown height with age in several animals which were important sources of meat to Palaeolithic people. We shall briefly discuss the underlying principles of both these methods.

The Deniz–Payne method is easy to apply to archaeofaunal sheep and goat mandibles, even fragmented ones. The sequnce of eruption, replacement and dental wear patterns form the basis of their method: deciduous (milk) molars are replaced by adult pre-molars, while adult molars erupt sequentially: the first molar (M_1) before the second molar

(M_2) and lastly the third (M_3). Following eruption, each tooth comes into bite and gets worn down. For example the molar teeth have four enamel covered cusps—an anterior pair and a posterior pair. A 'valley' (infundibulum) separates each pair of cusps. As the cusps come into wear, the superficial capping of enamel is worn away, exposing the underlying core of the tooth. The biting surface of a lightly worn sheep or goat tooth will have a characteristic pattern consisting of four crescents like letter 'C's as depicted in fig. 1.18. Further wear results in the isolation of the infundibular enamel in the centre from the outer enamel so that the 'valleys' become 'lakes'. This is a relatively long-lasting stage, lasting between 16 months and 40 months on average in the Angora goat first lower molar (fig. 1.19) as the infundibulum penetrates (like a finger in a glove) most of the way down the crown. In a very worn tooth the inner

1.18 The Deniz-Payne method of ageing sheep/goat mandibles. This figure depicts a typical wear sequence for the lower first and second molars, and the shorthand symbols used to represent each wear stage. Enamel is shown white, dentine black. Notice the interdental attrition; tooth length decreases as enamel on anterior and posterior surfaces is worn away by the adjacent tooth. *From a drawing by G. Hill, in Payne, 1973*

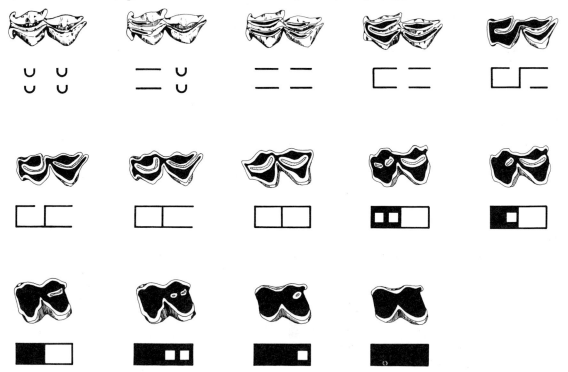

M₁ — Females

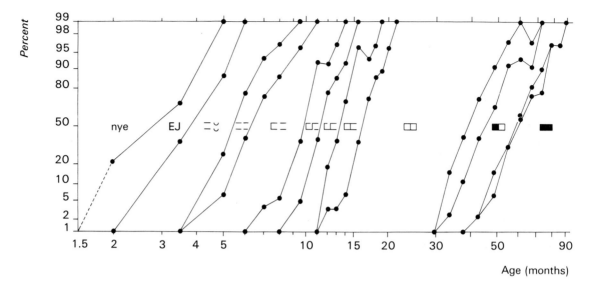

Age (months)

1.19 The Deniz–Payne method of ageing sheep/goat mandibles. A graph to show the different M₁ wear stages (as in **1.18**) in female angora goats. Deniz and Payne plotted the percentage of goats in their flocks which had attained a certain wear stage against age in months, from birth to old age. 'nye' = not yet erupted, the tooth has not yet cut through the gum. 'EJ' includes teeth that are erupting and those with some wear visible on the enamel only, but no dentine is yet exposed. The 50 per cent intercept provides a measure of the average age at which a change from one wear stage to the next occurs. Notice that there is considerable variation in the times taken for goats to pass from one wear stage to the next. This variation increases (in absolute terms) with age. *From Deniz and Payne, 1982*

'lake' of enamel will completely disappear. Complete loss of the infundibulum leaves the core of the tooth filled with dentine only. Finally in very worn teeth little is left of the tooth except small isolated pegs— the roots. As with eruption, the age of infundibular isolation and disappearance in the molars is sequential: M₁ before M₂ and lastly M₃.

Deniz and Payne have described nine age classes into which a sheep/goat mandible may be placed, on the basis of the stage of dental eruption and the degree to which enamel infoldings are still visible on its occlusal surface.

The ages when teeth erupt are presumed to be largely genetically controlled and should therefore be relatively consistent for different individuals. Deniz and Payne show that for younger individuals in their flocks this is indeed the case. Deviations of only one or two months occur. Hence it should be possible to assign a fairly accurate age to juvenile sheep/goat mandibles.

The rate of tooth wear, measured by the age when a tooth 'passes' from one wear stage to the next, is significantly affected by such factors as the coarseness of forage and the amount of sand in the soil (which inevitably gets incorporated in the food). Hence the relation between tooth wear-stage and actual age may vary considerably between populations for the older individuals. For example passage from stage G to H may occur as early as 7 or as late as 10 years.

This apparent handicap may, however, be an advantage. With stable tooth eruption ages, but wear rates which vary with food quality, we have a potential means for investigating sheep and goat grazing and feeding conditions in antiquity. For example, in two of their three flocks of Anatolian goats, Deniz and Payne observed greater wear on the third milk molar relative to the eruption and early wear of M2. They suggest that this indicates poorer grazing conditions among these two flocks.

Another method of age estimation for herbivorous animals makes use of a dental dimension which varies strongly with age: the decreasing height of the tooth crown. It can be applied to animals with high-crowned teeth whose roots are closed (i.e. where tooth growth ceases early, fixing maximum crown height and where no enamel is accreted to the crown base ruling out the open-rooted rodent incisors). This

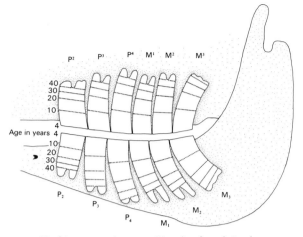

method is ideally suited to the equids and bovids—mammals which dominate many of the archaeofaunal samples in the Old World (figs. 1.20 and 1.21). It has been developed by C. A. Spinage, and Klein (1979) has applied it to the collections of zebra, gazelle, eland, buffalo, giraffe and rhinoceros in many South African Stone Age sites (Chapter 5).

In this method the crown height of a given tooth is measured from the occlusal surface to the crown-root junction down one side of the tooth: this for the buccal (external) side of mandibular teeth (fig. 1.22) and the lingual (internal) side of maxillary teeth. Attrition tends to follow a negative exponential course, with rapid wear in the young and slow wear

1.20 Herbivore tooth wear. Sketch of teeth in the upper and lower jaws of an adult horse to show their rate of wear. Dotted lines depict the crown heights when 10, 20, 30, and 40 years old. *From Willoughby, 1974*

1.21 Plot of upper first molar crown height against age for the plains zebra *Equus burchelli boehmi*. The vertical lines show range, and the outline sketches depict the appearance of M¹ at various ages. *From Spinage, 1972*

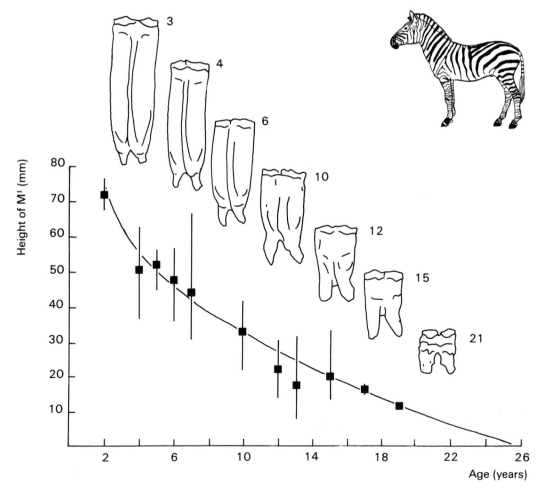

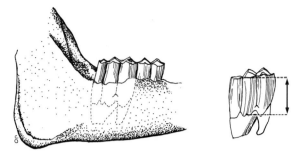

1.22 Crown height measurement. External view of the posterior part of a gazelle mandible showing how the height of the M₃ crown may be measured. *Drawing by Judith Ogden*

in the old. When an ungulate's teeth are worn right down feeding becomes impossible and it dies. With large samples of teeth, a plot of their crown heights will therefore indicate the age composition of the animals killed—the 'death assemblage'.

SEXUAL VARIATION

Most mammals display sexual size dimorphism, males usually being larger than females. An exception is the hare, in which the doe is larger than the buck. For some animals, such as goats and cows, dimorphism is great enough to allow us to estimate the sex ratio within a sample of bones. However, the presence of castrated animals complicates matters considerably. Castration probably delays epiphysial fusion allowing long bones to continue longitudinal growth, and these may become long and slender.

Sex ratios can provide some clues about the economy of an early culture. Which parts of the skeleton can be sexed and which cannot is therefore an important question to which we must devote some attention. The skulls of complete horned or antlered artiodactyls (these are the cloven-hoofed ungulates) can usually be sexed. Males have larger horn cores than females, and in the latter the horn cores may be absent. In most deer species the males have antlers and the females do not. The reindeer is an exception: both sexes carry antlers. Unfortunately, it is rare to find whole skulls on archaeological sites. With the pig mandible, the boar may be differentiated from the sow by its possession of tusk-like canines. Similarly the presence of a canine (the dog tooth) is more frequent among stallions than mares. In general, however, mammalian mandibles and

teeth display little or no sexual size dimorphism, so a comparison of tooth-row lengths or size of individual teeth is unlikely to yield information on the sex ratio in a sample. Male equids, rodents and carnivores have penis bones, some male birds have metatarsal spurs, and the male's pubis is more robust than that of the female in many ungulates. But penis bones and spurs are seldom found in archaeological material and pelvises are usually crushed. So which bones are useful to the zoo-archaeologist for sexing?

Some work on the sexing of modern specimens is now available which facilitates interpretation of the fossils. Metapodials are undoubtedly the most useful of all the ungulate bones for sexing purposes. Firstly they frequently survive and are easy to measure, secondly they tend to be relatively easy to identify to the species level and, thirdly, the epiphysial fusion

1.23 Size difference between sexes of modern gazelles (*Gazella gazella*) from northern Israel. The two measurements on each of the two metacarpal condyles are taken in the manner shown in **1.9**. For each individual, the plots of each condyle are joined by a thin line. Males are represented by squares, females by circles. Metacarpals with fused distal epiphyses are shown black, and unfused (i.e. juvenile) white. Note that sexes overlap by approximately 30 per cent. This means that while the sex of a single distal metacarpal cannot necessarily be determined, a sex bias in a large sample should be visible.

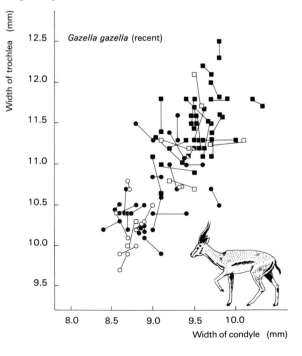

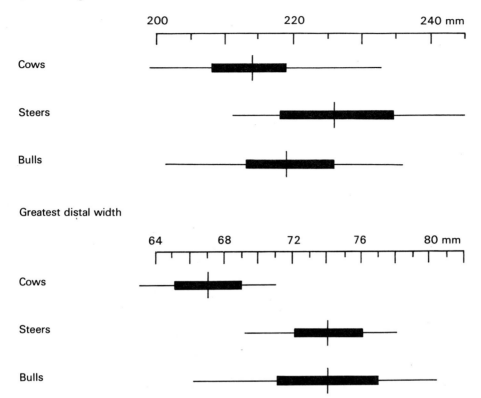

1.24 Size difference between sexes and castrates of modern cattle. Metacarpal measurements of the Schwarzbuntes breed given in Fock (1966). There is considerable overlap between the three groups in their lengths, and a marked difference in their widths, although the steers and bulls cannot be separated. Vertical line represents the mean, horizontal bar the standard deviation of the mean, and horizontal line the range. *From Grigson, 1982*

towards the end of the juvenile period enables easy discrimination between young and adult specimens. However, castrates again complicate matters, as they are difficult to distinguish from both males and females. Fock's (1966) work on the German 'Schwarzbunte' breed of cattle (fig. 1.24) shows that there is a degree of sexual dimorphism in the distal breadth of the metacarpal (but little in length). In other words males have more robust metacarpals than females. However, there is some overlap of sexes (i.e. some robust females are indistinguishable from slender males), which means that a single metapodial cannot be sexed with absolute certainty, although given a large enough sample an estimate of the probable sex-ratio can be made.

I have collected over 60 modern skeletons of the North Israeli gazelle. Here too measurements taken on the distal end of the metacarpal show that some degree of separation of the sexes is possible (fig. 1.23). The degree of overlap between the sexes appears to be similar in sheep metacarpals as can be seen in fig. 1.9 which shows plots for 14 modern domestic Persian sheep. This poor separation contrasts with the 21 modern domestic goats where there appears to be good separation of sexes (fig. 1.9). (These were sheep and goats which I purchased in a Persian abattoir, and where decapitation and limb excision was under my supervision.) Note also that some of the juvenile male gazelle, sheep and goat measurements fall within the female area on the graphs. These smaller specimens presumably represented very young juveniles which had not completed ossification of their condyles by the time of slaughter.

Failure to take sexual size dimorphism into account has sometimes led investigators into identifying two instead of one species.

SYNTHESIS

Towards the end of the preliminary analysis the zoo-archaeologist will have identified and recorded all the animals represented, their frequencies, and various within-species data such as size, sex and age, butchery marks and pathology. All these data should have been related to their stratigraphic provenance. The most important stage now is overall synthesis, and comparing the results with data from other sites. Hypotheses concerning environmental change, evolution of the animal species and human cultural development can be formulated.

A very rough guide to how much information can be gleaned from different sizes of sample would be as follows: 10 identified bones will tell us which species were exploited; 100 identified bones can tell us roughly in what proportion man exploited them; 1000 identified bones will just be enough to provide us with intra-specific information such as the proportion of different age groups and sexes culled. In a sample of 10,000 identified bones there should be enough mandibles to plot a continuous age distribution of the herbivores. Of course a sample as large as 10,000 bones can be divided into smaller samples, for example one for each different stratum within the site. These might still be large enough to provide a breakdown into age groups and sexes, and it would then be possible to discover whether changes had occurred during the occupation of the site.

Because so much of zoo-archaeological inference is based upon inter-site comparison, zoo-archaeologists must publish their results in as much detail as possible. A bone report should include body-part numbers for each species per level, individual bone measurements, drawings and photographs, detailed description of methods—including screen-mesh size and how sub-samples were taken for fine sieving. Unfortunately few journals will publish these kinds of data in full, and only accept results and discussions of findings, and at most statistical summaries of measurements (mean and standard deviation, for example). In such cases, the full data should still be made available to other workers by archiving them in accessible libraries. An alternative is to gather all the data in a microfiche appended at the back of the report. During the last 10 years there have been attempts to organize some kind of central computerized storage of bone data (measurements especially), but this aspect of zoo-archaeology is still at an early stage, and we must await its maturity in the coming decades.

Three other books which the student of zoo-archaeology will find useful are:

Chaplin (1971), *The study of animal bones from archaeological sites*
Hesse, and Wapnish (1985), *Animal bone archaeology.*
Ryder (1968), *Animal bones in archaeology*

CHAPTER TWO

What are bones and teeth?

The bulk of the faunal debris found on an archaeological site consists of mammal bone and teeth. Bird, reptile and fish bones and mollusc shells are found too, but generally in smaller quantities. Of what substances are bones and teeth composed and how do they form? This chapter will briefly describe how bones and teeth develop in the growing animal, and what they look like under the microscope. Without a thorough understanding of hard tissue biology, it is difficult to make sense of archaeofaunal data. Bones and teeth are not bits of pottery or stone tools.

Dry bone in a museum can be deceptive in that it appears inanimate and immutable. But in the living animal this is far from the truth. Bone is a connective tissue, and like muscle, nerves and blood, it is a living substance. Although seemingly hard, it is plastic and is supplied with blood vessels. Throughout an animal's life bone undergoes continuous renewal and reconstruction. It responds to external stimuli: increased use may result in excessive growth (hypertrophy). An example of this is osseous outgrowths (exostoses) resulting from strain, as found in overworked beasts of burden. Disuse results in atrophy. For example astronauts and cosmonauts are reported to suffer up to 15 per cent reduction of bone density (in weight bearing bones) while on journeys in outer space, and even greater losses are common in long-term bedridden patients (Goode and Rambaut, 1985).

Bones provide the main struts which support the body, and areas for muscle attachment. Bones protect the vital organs of the head and chest, and enclose the bone-marrow where red blood cells are formed.

Bone serves as a store of readily mobilizable calcium salts—important in the regulation of their concentration in body fluids such as the blood. There is a continuous turnover of the constituents of bone. Laboratory experiments show that by administering radioactively labelled calcium phosphate to adult rats, about 30 per cent of the phosphorous deposited in the skeleton was removed in a mere three weeks (Le Gros Clark, 1971:74). Much re-channelling of calcium salts takes place in pregnant females to aid in the development of the foetal skeleton and deer do likewise while their antlers are growing. Dairy cows producing optimum quantities of milk may suffer calcium depletion in their bones, which become rarefied. This problem can become acute under conditions of malnutrition.

GENERAL STRUCTURE OF BONE (fig. 2.1)

Bones are either cylindrical (long bones of the limbs), flat (skull, girdles, ribs) or irregular (vertebrae) in shape. When sectioned longitudinally, a long bone of an adult mammal consists of a cylinder of dense (compact or cortical) bone, with spongy (trabecular or cancellous) bone at either end, and an internal marrow cavity. Surrounding the outside of the shaft is a membrane—the periosteum— which continues around the synovial, or joint cavity (where two bones articulate). Thus the articular end of a long bone is not covered by periosteum, but by a thin layer of cartilage providing a frictionless surface for articulation. The whole joint is bathed by synovial fluid, contained within the synovial cavity.

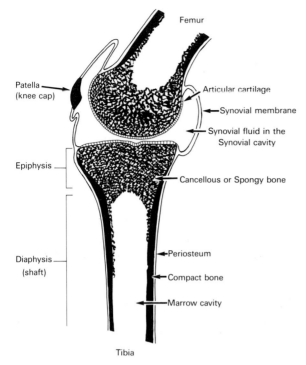

2.1 The knee: a synovial joint. Diagrammatic longitudinal section through the lower (distal) part of the femur and upper (proximal) part of the tibia of a fully grown mammal to show the main structures.

CHEMISTRY AND BIOMINERALIZATION

At the chemical level, bone is a combination of inorganic and organic matter. The inorganic 'bone mineral' is a crystalline calcium phosphate salt which resembles the mineral apatite. The organic component consists of collagen and other organic substances. Collagen, with its huge molecules (macromolecules), forms long fibres. (During ossification calcium salts infiltrate these fibres to form a densely packed matrix.)

The mineral content of fresh bone is approximately 65 per cent (table 2.1) and provides the bone with its rigidity and compressive strength. The organic component (35 per cent) provides elasticity and added strength. With its two major constituents, bone may be likened to fibreglass in which two components, glass and resin, have quite different properties from the composite. While the elasticity of bone is intermediate between that of collagen and

	Organic	Inorganic
Bone	35%	65%
Dentine	20%	80%
Enamel	0.5%	99.5%

Table 2.1 The chemical composition of mammalian hard tissues; fat-free dry weight. From Bloom and Fawcett, 1975.

apatite, its tensile strength is greater than either collagen or apatite individually.

How, at the molecular level, does bone formation occur? One suggestion is that body fluids are supersaturated with bone minerals, and that crystallization of the latter takes place over a protein template of collagen fibres by a process known as 'epitaxy' or crystal overgrowth (Simkiss, 1975). This process could be the basic mechanism whereby calcareous structures are formed throughout the animal kingdom. For example, egg-shell formation is initiated by small masses of protein nuclei from which crystals grow out in all directions forming so called 'spherulites' (Simkiss, 1975). But asking how tissues are able to calcify really poses the question why tissues do not calcify, since collagen is a widespread protein in the body and one of the main constituents of connective tissue. Fleisch and Neumann (1961) have hypothesized the general presence of an inhibitor substance which prevents calcification from occurring. They suggest that besides the presence of collagen, around which calcium phosphate might crystallize, an enzyme (in this case a phosphatase) must be locally available for the destruction of the inhibitor(s) in the blood.

THE EMBRYOLOGICAL CLASSIFICATION OF BONES

In the vertebrate skeleton bones may be classified according to their embryological origin as being either dermal or cartilage. Dermal or membrane bones may have originated in the beginning of vertebrate evolution as flat bony plates similar to fish scales. In mammals, dermal bones comprise part of the skull roof, protecting the brain. Cartilage or endochondral bones comprise most of the mammal skeleton: inner bones of the skull, ribs and vertebrae, girdle bones (except the clavicle), and limb bones such as long bones, hand and foot bones and finger-bones (phalanges). Endochondral bones, especially of the limbs, are perhaps the most important for us in archaeology since they are the ones most frequently found preserved as fossils. What does bone tissue consist of at the microscopic level?

BONE HISTOLOGY AND OSSIFICATION (fig. 2.2)

Bone is composed of cells enclosed within a solid matrix. There are three main kinds of bone cell: osteoblasts, osteocytes, and osteoclasts. The osteoblast lies on the bone surface. Osteoblasts secrete bone matrix, and in so doing they become surrounded and entrapped by matrix and cease synthesizing and are then termed osteocytes. The osteoclast also lies on the bone surface. Osteoclasts are large multinucleate cells which destroy bone by acid demineralization of apatite and then enzymatic digestion. This localized destruction leaves small pits.

INTRAMEMBRANOUS OSSIFICATION — BONE FORMATION WITHIN MEMBRANES

Development of dermal bones is a relatively simple process whereby bone forms directly in connective tissue. Ossification starts within a central condensation of collagen fibres and osteoblasts and then expands outwards. As growth proceeds, the bone thickens, becomes more dense, and takes the form of a 'plate'. This plate extends until, in the case of skull bones, it touches the margins of an adjacent bone plate. The junction between them is termed a suture. Many sutures only completely close up later in the animal's development; some, even in late adulthood, and provide one way of determining age at death of a skull.

2.2 Scheme to show the arrangement of cells and matrix in surface bone, osteon bone, and dentine. *From Alexander McNeil,* The Chordates, *Cambridge University Press, 1981 second edition fig 3–17*

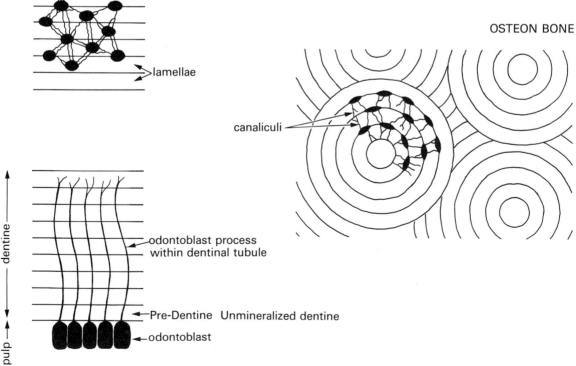

SURFACE BONE

osteocyte

lamellae

OSTEON BONE

canaliculi

dentine

pulp

odontoblast process within dentinal tubule

Pre-Dentine Unmineralized dentine

odontoblast

DENTINE

ENDOCHONDRAL OSSIFICATION — BONE FORMATION WITHIN CARTILAGE

A cartilage bone is partly formed from a cartilage model or template already present in the foetus. Each cartilage model is a diminutive version of the future bone. Endochondral ossification occurs in a process whereby cartilage is first eroded away, and bone secreted into the resulting spaces left behind by the cartilage cells.

Growth

Besides cartilage replacement, bone is also laid down by osteoblasts on the bone surface around the outside of the developing bone and around the inside.

Unlike most other tissues of the body bone cannot grow by any simple process of expansion; osteocytes cannot divide and grow like cartilage cells. Therefore the process of longitudinal growth in a bone has to take place within a zone of cartilage. In most reptiles and birds this growth zone is situated at the articular end of the bone, but in mammals, perhaps to facilitate accurately fitting joint surfaces, bone ends, as well as some points of muscle attachment, become well formed and ossify early in life. These are the epiphyses. The zone of proliferating cartilage is a thin disc between the end or epiphysis and the shaft or diaphysis. This cartilagenous disc is known as the epiphysial plate. A bone may have epiphyses, and therefore epiphysial plates, at both ends or at one end only. However, some bones like the carpals and most tarsals are single units as far as their ossification is concerned: they have no epiphyses. Let us follow through the development of a limb bone from foetus to adult.

Fig. 2.3 shows the stages in the development of a limb bone. In the foetus, before any sign of ossification, a cartilage model of the prototype bone is formed (stage A). Cartilage cells in its central region next undergo enlargement at the expense of the intervening cartilage matrix. The latter becomes mineralized. At the same time, a collar or cylinder of bone is deposited by osteoblasts in the periosteal membrane around the outside of the central region of the model (stages B and C). Mineralized cartilage is broken down by special cells, chondroclasts, leaving spaces which allow the ingrowth of blood vessels. Among the many cells transported into the bone

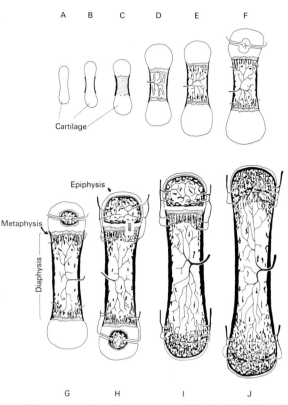

2.3 Diagram to show how a mammalian 'cartilage bone' develops from foetus to adult. Bone is black, calcified cartilage is stippled. *From Bloom and Fawcett, 1975.* (A small part of the section in stage 'H' is shown enlarged in **2.4**.)

centre by these invading blood vessels are cells which will become bone-forming cells, or osteoblasts. Some calcified cartilage remains in the form of struts separating what were columns of cartilage cells and this cartilage serves as a temporary scaffold upon which bone matrix is deposited. We have now reached stage D. This central region of bone formation is referred to as the 'primary centre of ossification', a term which distinguishes it from the 'secondary centres' which develop later, in the epiphyses.

Continued growth

Following the initial development of the primary centre of ossification, the adjacent cartilage cells at either end of this centre undergo rapid cell division resulting in the formation of columns of cells. Each column is separated by bars of cartilage matrix. The processes already described above for the primary centre then occur, but in an orderly fashion such that different zones may be recognized (stage E, for

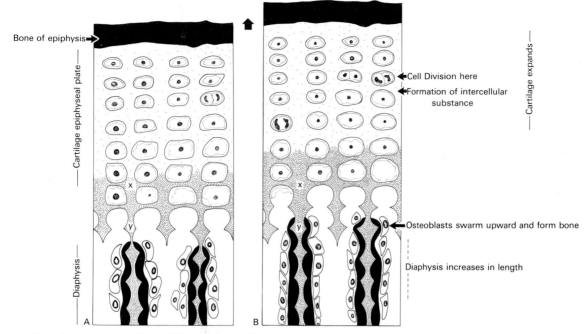

Bone of epiphysis

Cartilage epiphyseal plate

Diaphysis

A

B

Cartilage expands

Cell Division here

Formation of intercellular substance

Osteoblasts swarm upward and form bone

Diaphysis increases in length

2.4 An enlarged section of part of the epiphysial plate and diaphysis to show the changes which occur during a short period of growth. Cartilage is lightly stippled, calcified cartilage is heavily stippled, and bone is black. Stage 'A' on the left precedes stage 'B' on the right. The sites labelled x and y are fixed points and remain at the same level in both diagrams. Note how cartilage cells divide, secrete new intercellular substance and 'push up' the epiphysis, while the levels of calcified cartilage and bone advance simultaneously. *From A.W. Ham, 1952, Journal of Bone Joint Surgery 34–A, 701*

example). At some distance from the primary centre is a zone in which the cartilage cells divide (fig. 2.4): this is the zone which produces longitudinal growth. Next, as we move toward the centre of the diaphysis, is a zone of maturation where the cells enlarge. This is followed by a zone of hypertrophy characterized by (a) very large cells and (b) deposition of calcium salts in the intervening bars (scaffolding) of cartilage matrix. At the shaft (diaphyseal) end of the columns of cells, the open ends of the resulting lacunae are invaded by osteoblasts brought in by the blood vessels, and bone matrix is secreted over the calcified cartilage bars and subsequently mineralized. The net result of all these processes is that the diaphyseal bone elongates to 'keep pace' with the rapidly dividing and enlarging cells at either end. The transitional zone where advancing bone replaces the cartilage is known as the metaphysis. We are now at stages E/F.

In the next stage secondary centres of ossification appear at either both or one end of the bone, and the processes of (1) cartilage cell hypertrophy, (2) invasion of blood vessels, and (3) ossification proceed until most of the epiphyseal cartilage is replaced by bone (stage H/I). All that remains is a thin disc of cartilage separating epiphysis from diaphysis—the epiphyseal plate. This is the active zone of growth which contains the columns of differentiating and proliferating cartilage cells responsible for longitudinal bone-growth. A fine balance exists between the growing away (from diaphysis) of the proliferating cartilage cells on the one hand and replacement by bone matrix on the other.

When cartilage cell proliferation ceases the epiphyseal plate disappears (stage J) and the epiphysis is said to have 'fused' or 'closed'. Longitudinal growth comes to an end. In our own leg bones for example, this occurs in our late teens when we reach adult height.

Each epiphysis in the mammalian skeleton has its own predetermined age of closure which may be from before birth to the very end of the juvenile or growing period. The timing of our own skeleton's development is now well known, and women attain skeletal maturity one or several years before men. Reliable data for many of our domesticated livestock are unfortunately lacking. Hence for archaeofaunal material it is difficult to make more than vague estimates of age-related culling practices based upon counts of unfused and fused epiphyses found.

Increase of girth and remodelling in long bones
(figs. 2.5 and 2.6)

During longitudinal growth substantial remodelling occurs in two regions: the diaphysis and the metaphysis (both of which are enveloped by a membrane—the periosteum). Remodelling ensures that the developing bone retains its overall shape.

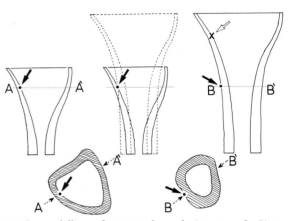

2.6 Remodelling of compact bone during growth. Since bone deposition and resorption can only occur at a surface, every point within compact bone must have been exposed on a surface at one time. By referring back to **2.5** it is possible to understand that a point 'A' on the inside of the bone at level A–A' soon becomes point 'B' on the outside of that bone at level B–B' as growth in length occurs, and metaphysis becomes diaphysis by decreasing girth. 'x' is the relative position in the older bone of the original point 'A'. *From Enlow, 1963; Principles of bone remodelling, Charles Thomas*

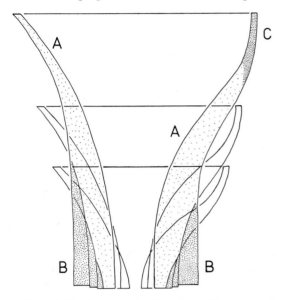

2.5 Remodelling in a growing long-bone. Bone can only be secreted at surfaces—either on the inner surface (shown lightly stippled) or by the periosteum (heavily stippled). Internally formed bone develops as the metaphysis (A) is progressively reduced in girth while bone-length increases. Increase in girth of the diaphysis (shaft) is by periosteal bone deposition (B). At c localized increase in width occurs by periosteal bone deposition. *From Enlow, 1963; Principles of bone remodelling, Charles Thomas*

(a) *Diaphysis.* Around the diaphysis osteoblasts on the surface of the bone deposit successive layers of compact bone. The shaft thus increases in girth keeping pace with the longitudinal growth in the epiphysial region. At the same time the marrow cavity enlarges by osteoclastic resorption of the inner surface of the shaft. There is a delicate balance between the rate of external apposition and the rate of internal resorption to ensure that the former slightly exceeds the latter. Thus the bone widens and its shaft wall thickens.

(b) *Metaphysis.* At the end of the diaphysis and adjacent to the epiphysial plate is the region known as the metaphysis. Since the metaphysis is broader than the contiguous diaphysis, a substantial amount of metaphysial 're-shaping', particularly a reduction of diameter, is necessary as metaphysis becomes diaphysis. Here the reverse of the growth and remodelling processes already described above for the middle of the diaphysis occurs. Remodelling at the metaphysis is brought about by periosteal resorption (by local osteoclasts) and deposition of bone onto the inside surface (by osteoblasts). Without remodelling, bone growth by equal apposition over all surfaces would result in ungainly and heavy bones. This happens in a rare disease, *diaphysial aclasis*, in which the osteoclasts do not function properly (Le Gros Clark, 1971:94).

A simple and elegant technique for demonstrating the way bone growth occurs was used by J.C. Brash (1934) and others. It utilizes the madder plant whose edible roots contain a red dye related to alizarin which stains newly-formed bone. Growing pigs may be fed a diet of madder, followed for example, by a three-week madderless period before slaughter. This is known as the 'indirect madder method'. New bone of the madderless period shows up white against a background of the red (maddered) bone tissue (fig. 2.7).

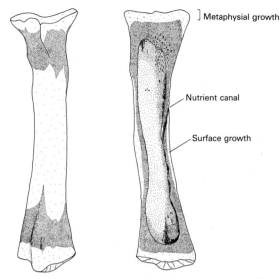

]Metaphysial growth

Nutrient canal

Surface growth

2.7 The indirect madder method for demonstrating long-bone development. A growing pig, in this case 282 days old when slaughtered, was fed on a diet of madder which stains growing bone red. Thirty days prior to slaughter, madder was removed from the diet. Bone formed during this madderless period appears white in section. The diaphysis and its growing ends, the metaphyses, are shown here. The unfused epiphyses have been removed. Dyed bone is shown heavily stippled. *From Brash, 1934*

Epiphysial fusion marks the end of longitudinal growth. A long bone with fused epiphyses will have attained maximum length, although occasionally further remodelling may alter certain parts of the shaft.

Internal reorganization of bone

Bone is formed by the apposition of layers or lamellae, each one several microns thick. Connections between bone cells are maintained via long cell processes contained within minute pores known as canaliculi. The wall of a bone's shaft may consist of many lamellae, at least in the early stages of development and while remodelling takes place. Animals develop another kind of bone as they get older, known as Haversian bone. It contains numerous canals (Haversian canals).

Each Haversian canal is surrounded by characteristic concentric cylinders of bone. And each canal with its concentric cylinders is known as a secondary osteon or Haversian system. Secondary osteons are formed as part of a remodelling process in which osteoclasts digest long tunnels through the matrix. Each tunnel so formed is then filled by the formation of concentric cylinders of bone secreted by osteoblasts in association with the blood vessels.

Replacement of bone tissue continues throughout life, and under the microscope several succeeding generations of Haversian systems may be observed in specimens of adult bone (fig. 2.8). The time it takes for a Haversian system to form in adult man is said to be about four–five weeks. It is this continuous internal change which provides the plasticity enabling bone to modify its shape and re-adapt to new mechanical stresses.

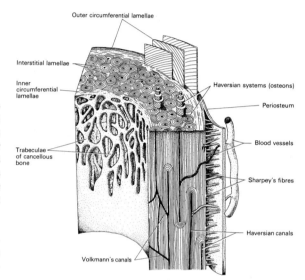

Outer circumferential lamellae

Interstitial lamellae

Inner circumferential lamellae

Haversian systems (osteons)

Periosteum

Blood vessels

Trabeculae of cancellous bone

Sharpey's fibres

Haversian canals

Volkmann's canals

2.8 A section of the shaft of a long-bone showing the arrangement of lamellae in the osteons or Haversian systems, the interstitial lamellae and the outer and inner circumferential lamellae, and blood vessels. *From Bloom and Fawcett, 1975*

THE MAMMAL SKELETON

A mammal's skeleton may be divided into the following functionally distinct regions: skull, vertebral column, rib cage, limb girdles, and limbs (figs. 2.9 and 2.10).

The skull is a composite structure containing both endochondral and dermal bones. It protects the brain, eyes, and ears, supports the mouth with its teeth and tongue, and provides attachment for the jaw muscles.

A series of vertebrae constitutes the vertebral column or backbone. Each vertebra is a solid disc, the centrum, with a dorsal neural arch, through which passes the spinal cord. A combination of interlocking joints and ligaments provides the backbone with both

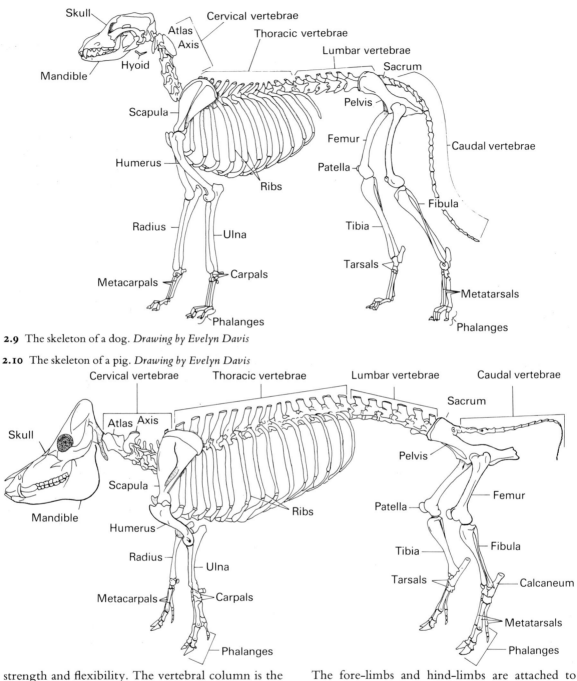

2.9 The skeleton of a dog. *Drawing by Evelyn Davis*

2.10 The skeleton of a pig. *Drawing by Evelyn Davis*

strength and flexibility. The vertebral column is the body's main supporting strut: to it are attached the limbs, by means of their girdles, and the ribs.

Each rib is attached at its dorsal end to a thoracic vertebra. Collectively, the ribs form a cage, which encloses and protects the heart and lungs: organs of the thoracic cavity. The rib cage with its musculature and diaphragm functions like a bellows, pumping air in and out of the lungs.

The fore-limbs and hind-limbs are attached to pectoral and pelvic girdles respectively. These girdles provide attachment for the limb muscles, and also connect limb to body. In the large cursorial mammals, such as horses, antelopes, cattle and deer, as well as the carnivores, the pectoral (shoulder) girdle consists of the plate-like scapula only. It has lost its rigid attachment to the rest of the skeleton, and 'floats' within muscles outside the rib cage. The shoulder of these fast running animals is therefore very flexible. This both increases gait and reduces the amount of head-jarring suffered when fore-feet hit the ground. In locomotion the hind-limbs provide most of the thrust which is transmitted directly to the vertebral column by way of the pelvis. So the pelvic girdle has to be firmly attached to a series of fused vertebrae—the sacrum.

The bones of both fore- and hind-limbs conform to a similar basic pattern (fig. 2.11). Moving away from the body, we observe a single proximal bone— the one attached to the limb girdle. Then we observe two parallel bones. In most large cursorial mammals these two distal bones have fused together, limiting any unnecessary rotatory movement.

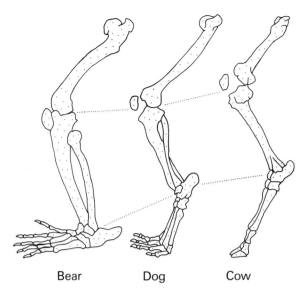

Bear   Dog   Cow

2.12 The three basic kinds of limb and locomotory arrangements in mammals. From left to right: plantigrade—the whole foot is in contact with the ground (e.g. human and bear feet). Digitigrade—only the toes are in contact with the ground. The metapodials, usually somewhat elongated, are now functionally part of the limb, and hence make it longer which increases the stride (e.g. carnivores). Unguligrade—only the last digit, usually surrounded by a hoof, touches the ground. These animals, such as horses, cattle, antelopes, walk on 'tip-toes' and their first and second phalanges are functionally part of the limb, which gives them an even longer stride. In many fast-running ungulates, redundant lateral digits and lateral metapodia have become reduced or even lost altogether.

2.13 Skeleton of the human hand compared with that of three ungulates with varying degrees of metapodial fusion/loss and digit loss. Note that the horse has lost all but the central toe; second and fourth metapodials have been reduced to slender splints. The cow (like antelopes, sheep, goat etc.) has retained only the third and fourth digits. Metapodials III and IV have fused longitudinally. The pig has reduced but not lost digits II and V, and the two central metapodials are not fused. Metapodial III is shown in black, and metapodial IV stippled. *From Clevedon Brown and Yalden 1973*

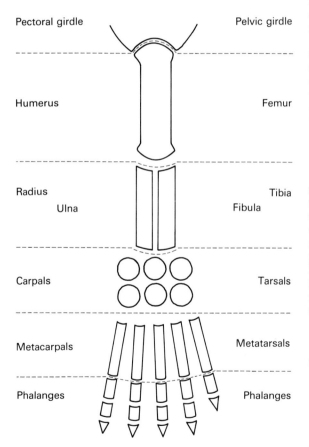

Pectoral girdle		Pelvic girdle
Humerus		Femur
Radius Ulna		Tibia Fibula
Carpals		Tarsals
Metacarpals		Metatarsals
Phalanges		Phalanges

2.11 The vertebrate limb. Scheme showing the general arrangement of bones in the fore-limb (labelled on the left) and hind-limb (labelled on the right). In the course of vertebrate evolution, numbers and relative sizes of different limb elements have altered.

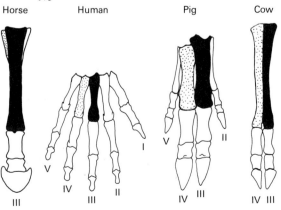

Horse   Human   Pig   Cow

Further down the limb we come to the wrist or ankle, formed by a series of small bones—the carpals and tarsals respectively. To them are attached the metacarpals and metatarsals (known collectively as metapodials). At the end of each metapodial are attached the phalanges or finger bones. In the course of evolution, stride in many mammals has been increased by a lengthening of the metapodials. This is most marked in the ungulates (deer, cattle, antelopes, horses etc), which have further increased stride by raising all but the terminal phalanx off the ground. They effectively walk on 'tip-toes'. Reduction or loss of the lateral metapodials and digits in many of these fast-running animals has made their feet lighter, and hence reduced the effort required to overcome inertia during locomotion. The artiodactyls (even-toed un-gulates such as deer, cattle and antelopes) walk on the two central toes (they are cloven-hoofed), and perissodactyls (odd-toed ungulates), such as horses, on one central toe only (figs. 2.12 and 2.13).

TEETH

Unlike fish and reptiles which continually replace their teeth, most mammals only replace theirs once. They have two sets of teeth (i.e. they are diphyodont); the deciduous (milk or primary) and the adult (permanent or secondary) dentition (fig.

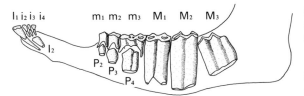

2.14 Young goat mandible showing the deciduous teeth (lower-case letters) and their permanent or adult replacement teeth (upper-case letters). In the course of their evolution, bovids have lost the first premolar tooth. *From Payne, 1982*

2.14). The evolutionary development of a single replacement of teeth is linked to the accurate alignment and occlusion of upper against lower teeth. This means that mammals are able to chew their food extensively before swallowing it. Reptiles gobble large chunks of food which seldom remain very long in the mouth. Mammals can also chew and breathe simultaneously since they have evolved a secondary

palate whereby the air passage by-passes the mouth. Thorough mastication is particularly important to herbivores who must puncture the cell walls of their plant food. Despite herbivores' relatively efficient chewing apparatus and digestive tract, they spend most of their time eating. A cow may spend most of its day grazing and chewing the cud.

There are four basic kinds of tooth in the mammal, each located in a particular part of the jaw (for directional terms see fig. 2.15). These regional differences are a characteristic of mammals. The four types are: (1) incisors at the front of the mouth, (2) canines, (3) pre-molars, and (4) molars at the back of the jaws. Both incisors and canines have deciduous precursors. The pre-molars are preceded by the deciduous molars (sometimes called deciduous pre-molars). The molars are not preceded by deciduous teeth.

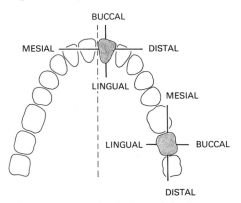

2.15 Diagrammatic occlusal view of the human jaw to explain the directional terms (buccal = labial = external, and lingual = internal).

A full complement of all four tooth types would include (this only applies to the Eutherian or 'higher' mammals) three incisors, one canine, four pre-molars and three molars in each jaw half, making a total of 44 teeth. A shorthand notation for an animal's dental complement is the 'dental formula': the numbers of teeth in both upper and lower half jaws are written like a fraction. Our own formula for the permanent dentition is:

$$\frac{2123}{2123}$$

We, along with Old World monkeys and apes, have lost both first and second pre-molars. For dogs the dental formula is:

$$\frac{3142}{3143}$$

Dogs have lost the upper third molar. For sheep, goats, cattle, and deer the dental formula is:

$$\frac{0033}{3133}$$

They have no incisors or canines in the upper jaws.

In the course of mammalian evolution tooth numbers have been reduced in response to altered feeding habits.

General structure of mammalian teeth

A mammalian tooth consists of two parts: (a) the crown, or that part of the tooth which is at some time exposed above the gum, and (b) the root, which remains below the gum line (fig. 2.16). The region where the two meet is sometimes referred to as the neck. The area of the crown which makes contact with its opposite tooth (upper against lower jaw) is known as the occlusal or chewing surface.

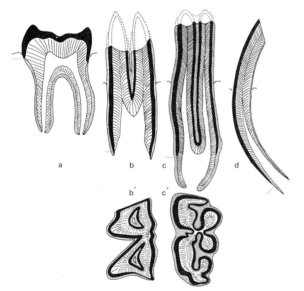

2.16 Some mammal mandibular teeth in longitudinal section (shown above), and in occlusal or biting surface view (shown below). Enamel is shown black, dentine hatched, and cementum stippled. The continuous line shows the top of the gum, and the dotted line separates crown above from root below. (a) The human molar has low rounded cusps; high crowned hypsodont teeth are: (b) sheep molar, (c) ass molar, and (d) rodent incisor.

Most or all of the crown is covered by a hard white crystalline substance, the enamel. (This is absent from all but the tip of an elephant's tusk, and from the internal surface of rodent and rabbit incisors.) Under the enamel and extending into the root is a bone-like substance called dentine (or ivory). This surrounds the pulp chamber which contains blood vessels, nerves etc. The roots, and sometimes part or all of the crown, are covered by a thin layer of cementum. The tooth sits in a cavity in the jaw-bone known as the alveolus.

The shape of the crown with its cusps (biting points or ridges) provides the basis upon which a tooth is described.

Insectivorous mammals such as shrews and hedgehogs have retained a crown structure similar to that of the first mammals of some 190 million years ago. They possess sharp pointed cusps for piercing the tough exoskeleton of their insect prey. In the carnivores the anterior part of the first lower molar and fourth upper pre-molar have become modified to perform a very efficient scissor-like or break-shear action. These are the 'secodont' carnassial teeth used for cutting meat.

The Miocene epoch of some 20 million years ago saw a great expansion of grasslands. Unlike fleshy tree foliage, grass contains silica which can rapidly abrade teeth. Several groups of mammals, particularly ungulates (especially bovids and equids), evolved in these grasslands. Many ungulates have overcome the problem of rapid tooth wear by (a) developing high crowned (or hypsodont) teeth, and (b) infolding the outer enamel layer (the latter gave rise to the complex patterning to be seen on the occlusal surface of their teeth when these are worn) and (c) covering the crown with a layer of bone-like substance—cementum—which helps prevent chipping of the enamel in bovids and equids. Because enamel is harder than dentine, which is in turn harder than cementum, the chewing surface of these hypsodont teeth remains rough as each of these substances is abraded differentially. The enamel folds jut out from the occlusal surface as small sharp ridges—rather like a crude version of a carpenter's file. In the young animal most of the crown lies below the gum, but erupts gradually as the crown is worn away. In a very old horse, for example, very little of the crown will be left. This gradual reduction of crown height is useful in archaeology to estimate the approximate age at death of an animal.

Hares, rabbits and rodents have overcome rapid tooth wear by continuously adding enamel and dentine to the base of some or all of their teeth. This kind of tooth is described as 'open-rooted'. The root becomes converted to new crown. Most mammal teeth, however, 'close' their roots soon after eruption, which means that no further addition of enamel to the crown can occur.

Tooth histogenesis (see fig. 2.17)

In the early stage of embryological development, the epithelium (an ectodermal layer) which lines the mouth forms small infoldings in areas where teeth will form. These, together with some of the underlying mesenchymal (mesoderm) tissue, are known as tooth buds or germs. The tooth germs of reptiles and amphibia remain throughout life and successive germs are continuously budded off. But in the mammals (which are mostly diphyodont), only one germ is produced at each tooth site, and the permanent-tooth germs are budded off from the corresponding deciduous tooth germs.

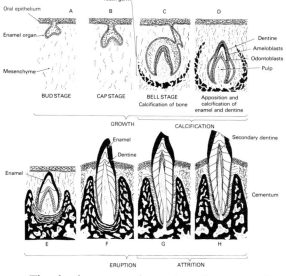

2.17 The development and eruption of a mammalian tooth—in this case a human deciduous (milk) incisor. Bone and enamel are black. *From Bloom and Fawcett, 1975*

The tooth bud develops a dent beneath which a concentration of cells (of mesodermal origin) form the dental papilla (fig. 2.17c). It is from these cells that the odontoblasts (dentine secreting cells) will form, while the ectodermal layer of cells of the tooth bud— the enamel organ—become the ameloblasts which secrete the outer enamel layer of the tooth. A tooth, embryologically speaking, is of dual origin: enamel-ectodermal and dentine-mesodermal.

Both papilla and enamel organ gain height and assume the approximate shape of the tooth to be. The cells of the papilla commence dentine secretion, and as the dentine grows thicker, the odontoblasts retreat, leaving cytoplasmic processes within the dentine. Calcification of the dentine follows soon after deposition of the fibrillar organic matrix, as in bone. At this time the cells of the enamel epithelium become tall and commence secretion of enamel. Mammalian enamel is composed of prisms—each made up of enormous numbers of closely packed crystallites. The general direction of these prisms is from the dentine surface to the tooth outer surface. Enamel is largely inorganic, being formed from calcium salts in the form of large apatite crystals and it is the hardest substance found in the body. Soon after tooth eruption, the superficial layer of ameloblasts disappears and so no further enamel can be laid down. Dentine, however, may be continually deposited as secondary dentine by the odontoblasts within the pulp cavity, so that the latter becomes smaller. Secondary dentine is important as it compensates for loss by abrasion and disease.

The cells which form the third bone-like substance, cementum, are called cementoblasts. Secondary deposits of cementum may be deposited throughout life, and the rate of cementum deposition, and hence its opacity, may vary seasonally to produce bands rather like annual tree rings (fig. 2.18). This has potential use in archaeology to determine the season

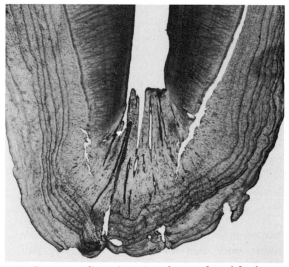

2.18 Cementum lines. A sectioned root of a red fox lower canine tooth from Denmark. Nine incremental lines are visible in the cementum. *Photograph courtesy Helen Grue*

in which an animal was killed (Chapter 4). In some groups of mammals such as horses, artiodactyls and rodents, which develop deep infolding of their enamel, an extensive covering of cementum extends over the enamel too. Their teeth have both root cementum and crown cementum. Crown cementum helps protect the enamel folds which suffer extensive pounding during chewing.

HORNS AND ANTLERS
(see Modell, 1969; Halstead, 1974)

Other mammalian skeletal structures which are commonly found on archaeological sites are antlers and horn cores. In the course of their evolution many ungulates have developed complicated outgrowths on their heads: horns and antlers. These are quite different in their structure and development, but both function as display and defence organs. Horn and antler shape is generally characteristic for each species, so their presence will help the zoo-archaeologist in making a correct identification. Basically horns are composed of a dead horny sheath around a bone core, while antlers are bone protuberances. Most horns are not shed, while antlers are shed annually. Both horn and antler, as well as bone, have long served as the raw material for making a wide range of implements. A full account of this technology since Roman times is given in Arthur MacGregor (1985), *Bone, antler, ivory and horn.*

Horn (fig. 2.19)
Horns consist of an outer keratinous sheath (finger nails and hair are composed of keratin) which grows out from the skin and which surrounds a bone core. While the horn itself is dead, the enclosed bone core is well supplied with blood and is living tissue. In most horned mammals, the male's horn is larger than the female's, and in some species females may be hornless. Horn is not usually shed, although the pronghorn antelope of North America is an exception: it sheds the outer horny sheath annually. Rhinoceros horn too, is exceptional, in that it does not contain a bony core, and it is not shed.

Horn is relatively soft, fibrous and flexible. If soaked in water it can be split into thin translucent sheets, once used for example in making lantern windows (Hodges, 1976 and see Chapter 8). But horn, unlike the horn-core, is rarely preserved in the archaeological record.

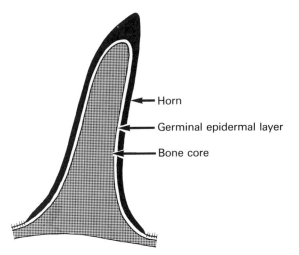

2.19 Horn. Diagrammatic section through a bovid horn. The epidermal horn (black) encloses a bone core (stippled). The latter is often penetrated by sinuses.

Antler (fig. 2.20)
The possession of antlers is a characteristic of the deer family (Cervidae). Antlers are usually produced by the male only but in the reindeer (or its North American equivalent, the caribou) both sexes have them. Antlers are shed annually and at a specific time of the year; a characteristic much used in archaeology to try and determine at what time of year a particular antler or cervid skull could have been collected or slaughtered.

Antler is living bone tissue, and except for a short period just before shedding is well supplied with blood. Growing antler is covered with a hairy skin, the 'velvet'. Antler growth is a modified endochondral process in which cartilage at the growing tip of the antler (the so-called zone of proliferation) grows, is subsequently calcified and finally after chondroclasis is replaced by bone tissue (Banks and Newbrey, 1983). Unlike limb bone ossification, antler growth occurs by apposition at the *tip* in a manner similar to the apical meristem of a growing plant root. No remodelling can occur. Antlers grow very rapidly—by as much as one centimetre per day. This rate of development has been compared to the kind of growth which occurs in cancerous bone (Modell, 1969). When antler is fully grown, the velvet dies and peels or is rubbed off and the deer (after a pause of a few weeks) becomes sexually aggressive. This is the beginning of the rut or breeding season. At the end of the rut, osteoclasts

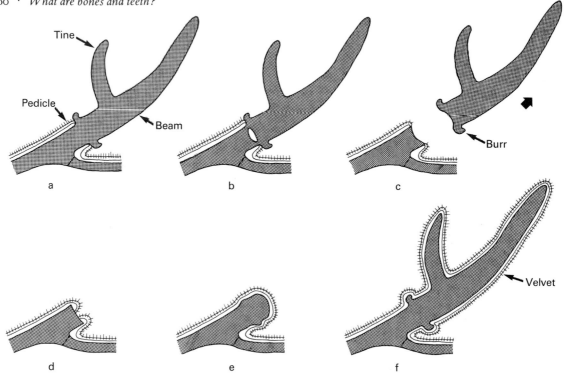

2.20 Antler development in deer. Diagrammatic sections to show the growth cycle of an antler. (a) Mature antler. (b) Resorption commences at the base which results in the formation of a sinus between pedicle and basal burr. (c) Antler is shed. (d) Skin now covers the scar on the pedicle. (e) Regeneration of new antler commences. (f) New antler is now fully grown and velvet is about to be shed. *From Schmid, 1972 after Weber*

resorb the base of the antler at its junction with the pedicle—a bony knob or outgrowth of the frontal bone of the skull—and the antler drops off. Skin then covers over the scar on the pedicle and in due course regeneration of a new antler begins (fig. 2.20).

Freshly shed antler and antler cut from a recently slaughtered animal is relatively soft, but rapidly becomes hard. Antler can be temporarily softened by prolonged soaking in water and it becomes comparatively easy to carve (Hodges, 1976). In Europe the tradition of antler working has been traced back to the Upper Palaeolithic.

FISH, MOLLUSCS ETC.

Besides mammals, two other groups of animals have not only been widely exploited in antiquity as a source of food, but are often preserved in the archaeological record. They are fish and molluscs. Unlike most bone tissue in mammals these two groups, one vertebrate, the other invertebrate, do not generally remodel their hard tissue, but continue its growth throughout life. Moreover seasonal variations of factors like temperature and/or food availability, tend to influence the rate at which hard tissue is deposited. This variation is often visible as series of rings or lines of different opacity referred to as growth increments. And in the absence of remodelling, a complete record is left of the animal's life. Counting or measuring seasonal rings can provide an estimate of the individual's age at death and close inspection of the nature of the last increment can sometimes reveal the season when death occurred. In some intertidal molluscs very fine growth lines reflect individual tides. Use of tidal lines on archaeological molluscs may even provide a time of death, accurate to within a few weeks (Chapter 4).

Bird bones, and even egg-shell, and sea urchin shell, are sometimes found on archaeological sites. Bird bone is easily distinguishable from mammalian bone, since it contains large cavities which in life are filled with air. Insects, crustaceans and even parasite eggs too (Chapter 3) have been found on archaeological sites. But their identification requires very specialist knowledge.

CHAPTER THREE

On reconstructing past environments

Archaeofaunal remains may provide clues as to what kind of environment existed in the past. The basic assumption is that an animal's present-day dietary and climatic preferences were the same in prehistory. Animal remains may indicate whether the environment was forested or open grassland; whether it was hot or cold, whether the seashore was nearby or not, and even how sanitary conditions were.

The methods used to reconstruct past environmental conditions from archaeofaunal remains, which I shall discuss in this chapter, come under four headings:

(a) The presence or absence of animals with well defined ecologies.

(b) Their abundance within an assemblage and the diversity of the assemblage.

(c) Body size.

(d) Body shape.

On a somewhat medical note, occasional finds of cesspits and coprolites (fossil stools) can provide a more intimate picture of the environment in antiquity.

PRESENCE/ABSENCE OF SPECIES

In mid-latitude Europe species such as the extinct straight-tusked elephant (*Palaeoloxodon antiquus*), the extinct woodland rhino (*Dicerorhinus mercki*), the hippo (*Hippopotamus amphibius*), wild boar, fallow and roe deer usually characterise faunal assemblages from the last interglacial period (Butzer, 1971:258).

As conditions became colder during the last Ice Age some or all of these species may be found further south in the Mediterranean region. Typical tundra species like reindeer, musk ox, arctic hares, lemming and arctic fox; and alpine species like ibex, chamois, alpine marmot and alpine vole extended beyond their tundra and mountain haunts. Animals usually associated with very cold climates such as woolly mammoth (*Mammuthus primigenius*), woolly rhino (*Coelodonta antiquitatis*), steppe bison and giant elk (*Megaceros giganteus*) all had an extended range during the Ice Ages.

At the height of the last Ice Age the woolly mammoth extended from northern Spain across Europe and Asia, into Alaska and eastward into new England and even as far south as Florida!

Françoise Delpech and Emile Heintz (1976) have summarised all known occurrences of deer and bovids on French Pleistocene sites. The reindeer would appear to be the best indicator of really cold conditions. It is found in various assemblages dated to all three European Ice Ages (Mindel, Riss and Wurm) and it was apparently absent from France in the interglacials. Indeed in the last Ice Age it was so abundant in France that the term 'Reindeer Age' is often applied by prehistorians to this period.

In the Upper Pleistocene of Britain glacial periods were characterised by herb and grass vegetation; consequently grazing animals like horse and woolly rhino were common. Interglacial periods were characterized by the expansion of broad-leaved forests and by species preferring this kind of vegetation, hence fallow deer and wild boar were common in interglacial periods (Stuart, 1982).

One specific British example where the fauna was

used not only to date a cave sequence but also to determine the kinds of climate correlated with each level is Tornewton cave in Devon (Sutcliffe and Zeuner, 1962; see Chapter 8). The mammal remains indicate a climate cycle. Reindeer and glutton in the bottom layer signify glacial times. The layer above this contains neither reindeer nor glutton, but a southern form of the woolly rhino, hippo and hyaena. Sutcliffe and Zeuner thought that it represented an interglacial period. And above this was a level containing reindeer again, horse and woolly rhino, signifying a return to cold (glacial) conditions.

Lemmings too are good indicators of very cold conditions. Today these animals are restricted to Arctic regions in Russia, Scandinavia and North America (fig. 3.1; Yalden, 1982). Lemming bones have been found in several southern English late Pleistocene deposits. In France Jean Chaline (1976) has reconstructed a palaeoclimatic 'curve' for the Pleistocene using rodent finds. Especially indicative were the two genera of lemmings, *Dicrostonyx* and *Lemmus*. They appear to have migrated into France during many of the cold periods. In the USA too lemming bones are reported south of their present arctic distribution. For example Kurtén and Anderson (1972) found them in the lowest cultural level at Jaguar cave, Idaho, dated to 9600 bc, suggesting former tundra conditions there.

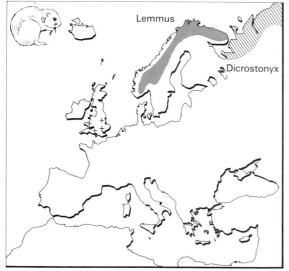

3.1 Modern distributions of the varying lemming, *Dicrostonyx torquatus* in the tundra of Russia and the Norway lemming, *Lemmus lemmus* in Scandinavia. Remains of these two rodents occur frequently in Younger Dryas (9–8000 bc) faunas in England. *From Yalden, 1982*

RELATIVE ABUNDANCE OF SPECIES

Using the presence or absence of, say, cold- or warm-loving animals to infer past climatic conditions is somewhat crude. A refinement of this method is to make counts of the remains of different species. A succession of several archaeological strata each containing large samples of fauna will provide a series of plots, which may have some palaeoenvironmental (such as vegetation and climate) significance. An early pioneer of this approach was Dorothea Bate in the 1930s. She studied the animal bones from Dorothy Garrod's excavations of the Mount Carmel caves in Israel, undertaken in the 1920s. These caves contained a succession of Upper Pleistocene levels. She plotted the frequencies of fallow deer and gazelle in each of these levels (Bate, 1937). Her implied assumption was that an alteration in the frequencies of species of animals hunted by early man reflects naturally occurring changes. This assumption, however, was subsequently questioned by a number of palaeontologists who suggested that varying percentages of different species merely reflect the particular hunting habits of ancient man at specific times. The fossil sample therefore represents a selection by man of specific animals from the environment, and not one which necessarily offers any clue as to the nature of that environment (Howell, 1959).

Eric Higgs (1967), in defence of Bate, suggested that changes in hunting fashion do occur, but are restricted to short time spans and are normally associated with peoples who had agriculture as an alternative source of food. In his opinion the relative proportions of the different species represented in an archaeofaunal assemblage are correlated with the relative proportions of the species living in the area at that time. Assemblages which accumulate through human agency should reflect whatever man was able to collect from the environment, and while proportions may be distorted by the fortunes of a single hunt or season, an accumulation of faunal remains over, say, several millennia should override this distortion.

The two most common large mammals in the Mount Carmel caves were the Mesopotamian fallow deer and the gazelle. Gazelle, like their close relatives the goats and sheep, have very high crowned teeth (Chapter 2) well adapted to grazing abrasive grass. Moreover they have a physiology particularly well suited to heat and aridity. The fallow deer, however, has low crowned teeth, and prefers to browse on leaves. Its teeth are not well suited to abrasive grasses, neither is it well adapted to hot arid conditions—it is a typical woodland animal. The resulting series of plots which Bate obtained should therefore reflect the proportion of woodland habitat to grassland, in turn a reflection of the amount of rainfall.

Bate obtained a most interesting increase of gazelle compared to deer in the uppermost levels (the Natufian, in el Wad level B, dated to *c*10,300–8500 bc; see table 6). Fallow deer had decreased from between 20–50 per cent of the deer + gazelle complement to a mere 'few' per cent. Her conclusion was that the Natufian represented a dry period in this part of the Levant, perhaps contemporary with post-glacial warming up in Europe.

The Natufian is a period of great interest since it heralded the domestication of animals like sheep and goat (Chapter 6). Aridification at this time would appear to corroborate Gordon Childe's (1928) 'Oasis theory' of domestication—the theory that man and animal came into closer contact around shrinking water resources, and that the relationship developed from one of hunting to one of husbanding.

Since the days of Garrod, several other archaeological excavations in Israel have revealed long sequences of fauna. Some of these include fauna from the Natufian period. Archaeologists have also been able to refine the chronology of the Natufian, and are able to divide it into early and late stages. I have studied these faunal assemblages and my results confirm Bate's (Davis, 1982). It would appear that the fallow deer became rare towards the end of the Natufian (fig. 3.2). But it did not become extinct, since historical records report its presence in Palestine as late as the eighteenth century. This late Natufian faunal change coincides with a size decrease in many species of mammals in the Levant (see end of this chapter).

The Natufians were culturally more sophisticated than their predecessors. They were the first people in the region to live in circular, constructed dwellings: possibly representing the earliest permanently settled villages. They may have been the first widely to exploit wild cereals. If indeed it did get drier *c*10,000 bc and grasslands expanded at the expense of the forests, then the increased exploitation of cereals as well as gazelle would be easier to understand. While agreeing that increased numbers of gazelle implies an expansion of grasslands, Andrew Garrard (1982)

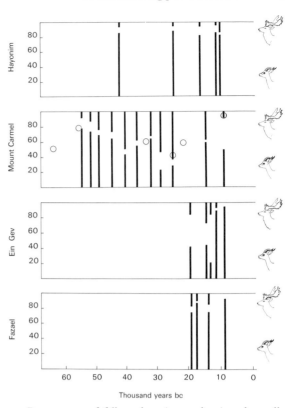

3.2 Percentages of fallow deer (upper bars) and gazelle (lower bars) in three archaeofaunal sequences in northern Israel—Hayonim, Kebara (Mount Carmel), and Ein Gev; and a sequence in the central Jordan valley—Fazael. Bate's (1937) data from Tabun and el Wad (Mount Carmel) are shown as circles and are similar to the Kebara data. Note the decrease in numbers, or disappearance, of fallow deer at Mount Carmel, Ein Gev and Fazael by 9000 bc (Natufian period) perhaps reflecting a decrease of woodland. *From Davis, 1982*

offers an alternative explanation: it was man, rather than the arid climate, who cleared the trees in order to allow wild cereals to expand.

What do other sources of evidence show? According to Aharon Horowitz (1979), a geologist specializing in the Pleistocene, the period after *c*9000 bc was indeed much drier. Similarly another geologist, Paul Goldberg (1982), has found evidence for lakes dating to 12–10,000 bc, in parts of the now arid Sinai peninsula. Both he and the archaeologist Ofer Bar Yosef (1982) suggest, on the basis of site distribution patterns, that aridity increased 10–9000 bc—when ancient levels of the Dead Sea also indicate drier times (Neev and Hall, 1977).

In the Dordogne valley, southwest France,

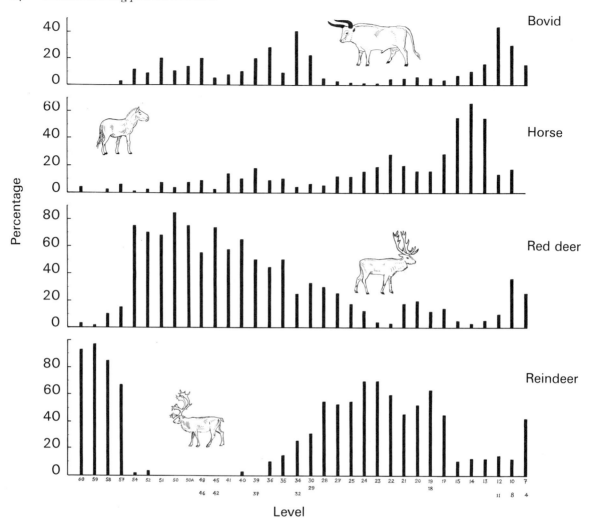

Bovid

Horse

Red deer

Reindeer

Percentage

Level

3.3 The faunal succession at Combe-Grenal, France. Bordes and Prat's (1965) analysis of numbers of large bovid, horse, red deer and reindeer in an Upper Pleistocene cave. Percentages of these four animals are plotted in each of the major levels in the cave—oldest on the left, youngest on the right. The two reindeer peaks (levels 60–57 and levels 34–17) are correlated with the last-but-one Ice Age (Riss) and the second stadial of the last Ice Age (Wurm II) respectively.

François Bordes and Prat (1965) studied the animal remains from 13m of deposit (64 layers in all) in the cave of Combe–Grenal with their associated Acheulean and Mousterian artefacts. They counted the relative abundance of animals typical of cold environments in each layer. A succession of layers with a 'cold' fauna could be assigned to a Glacial period. And they were able to correlate the whole sequence of layers to the two last Ice Ages of the

generally accepted sequence of European Ice Ages: a combined use of faunal remains for chronology and climatic interpretation.

In the early levels there is a predominance of reindeer (levels 60–57; fig. 3.3). They suggest that these levels belong to the Riss (last but one) Ice Age. The abundance of red deer in levels 54–35 as well as the presence of wild boar and roe deer all suggest forested conditions. Bordes and Prat date these levels to the first and early second stadials (these being short warmer intervals) of the Wurm (last) Ice Age (i.e. Wurm I and Wurm II). After which (layers 34–17), a return to severe cold conditions of Wurm II is suggested by the dominance of reindeer again. Finally, horse, and afterwards bovids in layers 15–13, may signify the development of steppe at the end of Wurm II.

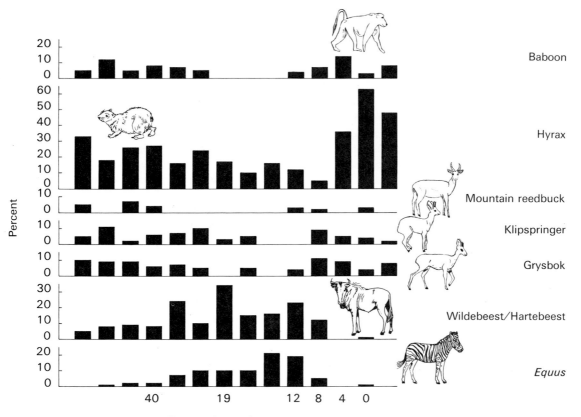

Percent

Baboon

Hyrax

Mountain reedbuck

Klipspringer

Grysbok

Wildebeest/Hartebeest

Equus

Thousand years bc

3.4 Remains of large mammals from Boomplaas cave, South Africa. The lowermost and uppermost strata contain a predominantly woodland and bush fauna and date to the last Interglacial and present Interglacial (Holocene) respectively. Levels dating between 20,000 bc and 10,000 bc contain a fauna which is more typically grassland, and which Klein correlates with the maximum glaciation of the last Ice Age. *From Klein, 1983*

Françoise Delpech (1983) has examined bones from numerous other sites in the Dordogne region and provides a continuation of the Bordes–Prat scheme. Broadly, she finds evidence, in the form of further reindeer peaks, of the cold periods: Wurm III and Wurm IV. In the early part of Wurm III milder humid conditions may have existed as suggested by red and roe deer, and wild boar. At the end of Wurm IV woodland animals replace the earlier cold species.

Further to the south, in the upper Pleistocene deposits in the Cueva del Toll 50km north of Barcelona, Kurtén (Donner and Kurtén, 1958) too was able to correlate faunal with climatic changes. A change of climate had already been deduced from the pollen record. Spain, unlike the Dordogne, was

further away from the severe influence of the ice caps. Instead of typical glacial animals, such as the reindeer, the 'main Wurm' levels at Cueva del Toll were characterized by woodland animals such as red deer, hippo, *Rhinoceros mercki*, wild boar, beaver, etc. In the interstadial period separating the 'early' and 'main Wurm' a fauna comprising grazers such as bison, aurochs, horse, and ibex, suggests an open, warm and dry environment.

The last 15 years have seen the publication of several studies made on archaeofaunal sequences from the southern hemisphere which contribute to our understanding of climatic change in southern Africa and Australia.

Richard Klein has been analysing faunal remains (especially large mammals) from numerous prehistoric sites in South Africa. Most are situated near the coast, some inland. Several contain long sequences which include deposits dated to the post-glacial and last Ice Age. Some are dated as early as the last Interglacial. Klein recognizes certain trends in the South African faunal succession which are best explained as being the result of environmental factors—particularly rainfall and sea level change. Gratifying confirmation of Klein's climatic interpretations comes from Avery's (1982) study of the small mammals (shrews and rodents). I shall discuss some of her results later (pp. 66–67). Perhaps the richest and longest sequence which both Klein and Avery studied is from the inland site of Boomplaas cave (Klein, 1983). Boomplaas is in the Cango valley, Oudtshoorn district, roughly 80km north of the present coast. It has deposits which range from c80,000 years ago to c500 AD.

The most significant change in frequencies of large mammals that Klein found in the southern Cape is a cyclical change from bush and woodland animals to grassland animals and back (fig. 3.4). Klein correlates this with changes in the vegetation resulting from a high to low to high rainfall sequence. The lowermost strata at Boomplaas, which Klein dates to the last Interglacial, contain a fauna which is very similar to the topmost bush and woodland fauna, indicating that conditions there then were similar to what they are in the present postglacial (i.e. today). In levels which date between 20,000 and 10,000 bc the fauna is heavily dominated by grassland species such as equids: quagga (a zebra which became extinct in historical times), mountain zebra or both, and large alcelaphine antelopes: wildebeest, hartebeest or both (bones of some of these closely related species are difficult to distinguish). After 10,000 bc, bush and forest animals such as grysbok, steenbok, klipspringer, mountain reedbuck, hyrax and baboon, gradually become more abundant, and by 4–3000 bc dominate the faunal spectrum. This latter bush-fauna is the one known to have been there in recent historical times. Analysis of charcoal remains from Boomplaas also indicates that the vegetation between 10 and 4–3000 bc was different from vegetation both before and after. Broadly then, grasslands were progressively replaced by bush and forest after 10,000 bc, and by 4–3000 bc, bush and forest had completely taken over.

At Nelson Bay cave situated on the present-day coast between longitudes 23° and 24° (Robberg peninsula) Klein (1975) had a shorter faunal sequence extending from c16,000 bc (i.e. the latter part of the last Ice Age) into the Holocene. Klein found that between 16,000 and 12,000 bc the animals consisted overwhelmingly of grazing species such as wildebeest, hartebeest, springbok, giant buffalo and quagga. Here too, as at Boomplaas, was a fauna quite unlike the one which would be expected given the known local vegetation in recent historical times— closed evergreen forest—in which none of these animals could live. Furthermore absence of marine elements in the fauna was a surprise since Nelson Bay cave is close to the sea today. Klein (1975) suggests that these faunal anomalies reflect the vast coastal grassland plain which would have existed there during the last Ice Age when sea levels were as much as 120m lower. According to bathymetric maps a sea level drop of this magnitude would have put the coastline some 80km away: too far for fishing forays. By 10,000 bc, rising sea levels would have drowned this vast coastal plain, and brought the seashore closer to Nelson Bay. In the levels dated to c10,000 bc, the remains of shellfish, sea birds and fish first appear in the deposits, and are thereafter present in enormous quantities. The grazing animals which characterized the earlier levels disappeared. Their place was taken by such historically recorded species as bushbuck, bushpig and grysbok—all indicating that closed vegetation had replaced the open grasslands.

In her study of Upper Pleistocene small-mammal remains (which are no doubt accumulations of owl pellets) from South African sites, Margaret Avery (1982) has adopted two approaches. She calculated, for each level, (a) the species diversity of the community of small mammals and (b) the mean size of each species.

Her 'species diversity' approach utilizes a biological fact that more mammalian species are found in areas with mild climates than in areas with harsh ones. This is an extension of the observation that animal life in the tropics is more abundant and varied than in temperate climates. Thus it should follow that changes in species diversity in one place at different times in the past should reflect climatic variation. Avery calculated the 'Index of General Diversity; H'. This index takes into account both aspects of diversity: species richness and 'evenness of importance' of each species.

She was able to recognize considerable differences in the structure of small-mammal communities of different ages both at Boomplaas and at coastal sites. The general diversity index, H, conformed to known general climatic trends, H being much higher in postglacial than in glacial communities. Her interpretation is that conditions during glacial times were harsher than postglacial and interglacial conditions.

Avery does point out that low indices would be expected in a desert or other harsh environment today, so that changes in the past could have been towards increased diversity (reflecting, say, higher rainfall)—a pattern opposite to that observed in the southern Cape.

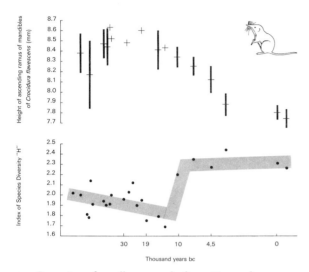

3.5 Remains of small mammals from Boomplaas cave, South Africa. Both a low species diversity, and the larger size of shrews, correlate with cold conditions of the last Ice Age. For the shrew samples, the mean (horizontal line) ±95 per cent confidence limits of the mean (thick vertical bar) are portrayed. *From Avery, 1982*

At Boomplaas A, Avery reports (fig. 3.5) a striking difference between the high indices for the postglacial samples and low indices for the glacial samples. The lowest diversity occurs in samples from the last glacial maximum. After the latter a major climatic improvement is interpreted which is maintained throughout the Holocene (the present post-glacial period).

Both Avery and Klein assumed that the faunas they were studying in these cave sequences were accumulated by single agents: owls and man respectively. Turning to an important site in another part of the southern hemisphere, Tasmania, we find a very much more complicated picture.

Sandra Bowdler's (1984) faunal sequence is in many ways analogous to Klein's coastal one. She has suggested that the predominant influence on a 23,000-year-long faunal sequence was the rise of sea level at the end of the last Ice Age. Bowdler studied the fauna and artefacts from Cave Bay cave on a small island (Hunter island) off the northwest coast of

Tasmania. She has found evidence for human occupation there at least as early as 21,000 bc until 16,000 bc. The site was then unoccupied (except for one brief visit *c*13,400 bc) until 4600 bc when the site was occupied by people with a well-developed coastal economy. The site was finally abandoned within the last 1000 years, but before European contact.

During this 23,000 year sequence the situation of the cave changed from that of inland site to one located on the coast of a small island. The faunal remains seem to confirm this major change in the local geography in three ways: (a) the presence of animals which indicate a certain kind of environment, (b) the proportion of macropod mammals (kangaroos etc) versus rodents and birds (fig. 3.6) and (c) the abundance of different species.

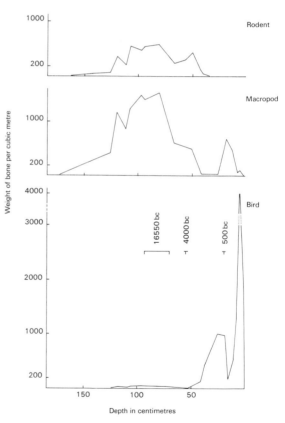

3.6 Faunal frequencies at Cave Bay cave, Hunter island, Tasmania. A plot of the abundance (expressed as bone weight in grams per volume of deposit) of the three main groups of animals in the main levels of trench II of this cave. Oldest levels are at the left and youngest levels at the right. *From Bowdler, 1984*

(a) In the Pleistocene deposits remains of animals which prefer an open environment are represented. One such animal is the barred bandicoot, abundant in the lower deposits, and absent from post-terminal Pleistocene levels. The brown bandicoot, which prefers denser vegetation, becomes more common in the post-4600 bc layers. (It probably survived until recent times.) A rodent (*Pseudomys higginsi*) is found today exclusively in the Tasmanian rainforest. It too is more abundant in the recent deposits at Cave Bay cave.

(b) The lower levels of the cave were deposited when it was an inland site. It was located on a small hill on the Bassian plain. Low sea levels in the Pleistocene meant that the huge Bassian land shelf was uncovered and connected Tasmania to the southeast Australian mainland. Macropods such as the wallaby and Tasmanian pademelon and rodents form the bulk of the Pleistocene faunal remains. After 4600 bc sea level had risen, the Bassian plain drowned, leaving Tasmania an island. Hunter island was now at least partially cut off from the Tasmanian mainland. Also Cave Bay cave was situated close by the sea. Macropods and rodents became rare. Their place was taken by large numbers of birds, mainly sea birds; many if not most were probably remains of ancient man's meals.

(c) It is well known that island faunas tend to be poor in terms of numbers of species (though not individuals). 'No island has nearly the number of species it would have if it were part of the mainland' (MacArthur, 1972:79). Part of the decrease in mammal species is explained by Bowdler as being the result of 'islandization'. Hunter island is too small to support a great many species of land mammals.

Generally it is assumed that man is the main agent responsible for accumulating large mammal bones in a cave, and owls the rodents. But at Cave Bay cave man and owls were not the only predators and bone accumulators. Bowdler mentions peregrine falcon and Tasmanian devil as two candidates. She suggests that in the Pleistocene man and devils were the main agents which hunted the large mammals. Man probably hunted the wallaby and perhaps pademelon, while the devil's diet may have been more eclectic, and their prey bones could be identified as they tended to be reduced to a uniform small size. Owls accumulated the rodent bones. In the Holocene, however, man and peregrine falcon were the dominant carnivores. Devils were absent, and owls

may now have preferred to roost in the trees rather than the cave as the area became more thickly vegetated towards the end of the Pleistocene. Owls will roost in caves in treeless areas.

With long faunal sequences and abundant samples, analysis can often be taken a stage further—beyond simple identification and counting. For example, mammalian body size often varies with climate. Knowing just how size and climate are related today provides a method for deducing climatic conditions in antiquity. Thus fossil mammal bones and teeth measurements can serve as 'palaeothermometers': a technique for reading off the temperature at any time in prehistory.

BODY SIZE

Zoologists have long known that individuals of many species (or groups of closely related species) of mammals and birds are large in cold climates and small in warm climates. This is known as the Bergmann effect, after the zoologist who first documented this phenomenon in 1847. For example, mammals tend to larger body size as latitude increases. Scandinavian wolves are larger than Arabian ones, the woolly mammoth was larger than its relatives, the Indian and African elephants, and the puma decreases in size from northern North America and southern South America towards the equator (Kurtén, 1973).

Consideration of basic geometry provides a plausible explanation. Volume, which produces heat, increases to the power 3. Surface area, which dissipates heat, only increases to the power 2. Hence a large body has relatively small surface area and should be a better conserver of heat in a cold environment. For example, physiologists Herreid and Kessel (1967) showed that, by doubling body weight, birds and mammals can lower heat loss per unit weight by 30 per cent. A large body also has the added strength to carry more fat and longer hair.

The Bergmann effect is not a rule, for there are many exceptions. Other factors, especially food availability, also influence body size. Nevertheless, a change in body size is one of several strategies whereby an animal can adapt to different temperature regimes (Mayr, 1956).

Pioneering work using fossil mammals to chart temperature fluctuations in the Pleistocene was car-

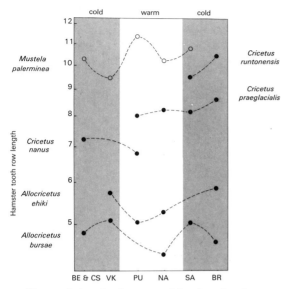

3.7 Size variation in the stoat, *Mustela palerminea*, and various hamsters (*Cricetus* and *Allocricetus*) from a series of Pleistocene sites in Hungary. Kurtén correlates small size in the stoat and large size in the hamsters with two cold periods (shaded) and large size in the stoat and small hamsters with warmer conditions. Tooth measurements in millimetres are plotted for the following sites: BE & CS = Beremend and Csarnóta, VK = Villány Kalkberg, PU = Püspökfürdo, NA = Nagyharsányberg, SA = Sackdilling, BR = Brassó. *From Kurtén, 1960*

ried out by the palaeontologist Björn Kurtén (1960). He measured stoat and hamster teeth from a series of Pleistocene sites in Hungary (fig. 3.7), and obtained a series of oscillations in tooth size through time. The hamster (*Allocricetus bursae*) exhibited an undulation spanning $1\frac{1}{2}$ wavelengths. However, stoat oscillations were opposite to those of the hamsters: stoats would get smaller as hamsters got larger.

Kurtén then measured modern stoats and hamsters. He found that both animals display a north-south size gradient (cline); one the inverse of the other. Northern hamsters are larger than their southern relatives. Northern stoats are smaller than their southern relatives. Kurtén was therefore able to infer a series of cold and warm oscillations of the Pleistocene climate in Hungary.

He also attempted to calibrate his data. Modern hamsters show a 20 per cent size difference across 10 degrees of latitude. Put another way, hamsters in Stockholm or Riga are 20 per cent larger than hamsters in Nuremberg or Budapest respectively. Since Hungarian Pleistocene hamsters oscillated in

size by the same amount, Kurtén concluded that temperature changes in central Europe during the Pleistocene were quite considerable. Further south, in another study (Kurtén, 1965), he demonstrated that many carnivores had undergone size decrease after the last glacial period in the Levant.

I did something similar to Kurtén in my study of Israeli late Pleistocene-Holocene large mammals (Davis, 1981). Intensive prehistoric investigations in Israel during the last 20–30 years have uncovered a sequence of well-stratified and often accurately dated archaeofaunal remains.

Which animals underwent a post-glacial size decrease, and by how much? How can this be related to size variation of the same species today over a wide geographical range? I had carefully to separate these size changes from those associated with man's direct influence (i.e. domestication; Chapter 6).

Many mammals in Israel, such as gazelles, aurochs, foxes, wolves, wild boar and wild goats were larger during the late Pleistocene than they were during the Holocene, or today. An exception to this observation is the fallow deer, which did not apparently alter in size. In archaeological sites whose dates span the very end of the Pleistocene of Israel (Epipalaeolithic culture periods) I had enough specimens of fox teeth and gazelle teeth and bones to be able to determine accurately just when size reduction (for these two animals at least) occurred (figs. 3.8 and 3.9). This happened between 10,000 and 12,000 years ago, probably during the early Natufian, 9500 bc.

Today wolves, foxes and wild boar increase in size as environmental temperature decreases. For example, Scandinavian wolves and foxes are much larger than their relatives in the Levant and Arabia. (Modern gazelles and wild goat do not extend into Europe, so I could not examine their size-temperature behaviour over a wide geographical range.) Fallow deer appear to contradict the 'Bergmann effect' as the European fallow is smaller than the Mesopotamian fallow of the Near East. In sum, then, most of the animals which altered in size after the last Ice Age in Israel do so today as the environment becomes colder.

Besides a present-day inverse correlation between size and temperature, the time of size decrease of foxes and gazelles in antiquity very closely coincides with the global rise of temperature at the end of the last Ice Age: c9–10,000 years bc (fig. 3.8). A correlation between two variables does not necessarily mean

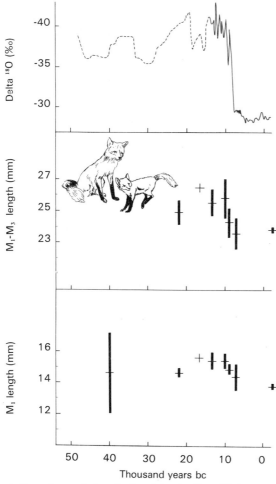

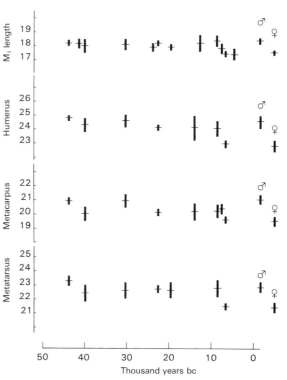

3.9 Late Pleistocene-Holocene size variation of the gazelle, *Gazella gazella*, in northern Israel. Plots of lower third molar length, distal humerus width, distal metacarpal width, and distal metatarsal width in millimetres. Sample means (horizontal lines) ±95 per cent confidence limits of the mean (vertical bars) are shown. On the far right are modern male and female gazelles. Note the size decrease *c*9000 bc. *From Davis, 1981*

3.8 Fox size variation in Israel in the Late Pleistocene-Recent. A plot of molar tooth-row (M_1–M_3) lengths and carnassial tooth (M_1) size in millimetres against time. Sample means (horizontal lines) ±95 per cent confidence limits of the mean (thick vertical bars) are portrayed. Note the size decrease 10–9000 bc. At the top Dansgaard *et al*.'s (1969) delta Oxygen 18 graph from the Greenland ice sheet is shown which indicates the probable time of the post Ice Age temperature increase. *From Davis, 1981*

one causes the other. But it was tempting to conclude that temperature alone in this case was the main factor selecting for large or small individuals of these mammals in the late Pleistocene and Holocene respectively.

In the next stage of my investigation, and like Kurtén, I tried to calibrate the size-temperature relation. Museums and published data provided tooth measurements of modern foxes, wolves and wild boar from Europe and the Near East. These I plotted against environmental temperature (mean· January

value, for example) taken from metereological records. I now had an idea of how much each of these animal's teeth was likely to vary with respect to the temperature of the environment (fig. 3.10). In Israel at the end of the Pleistocene, fox and wolf carnassial (M_1) teeth decreased by about 1.7mm and 4.3mm respectively, and wild boar lower third molars by 5.9mm. Today, a dental size difference of this magnitude is equivalent to an environmental temperature difference of 15° centigrade for the wild boar, and 16° centigrade for wolf and fox. That all three animals should provide so similar a result was a surprize, and strongly suggests that all three animals were reacting in a similar way to the same environmental factor(s) in antiquity.

This result raised my hopes that here we had a kind of 'palaeothermometer'. Alas perusal of the literature as well as commonsense made me realize that my

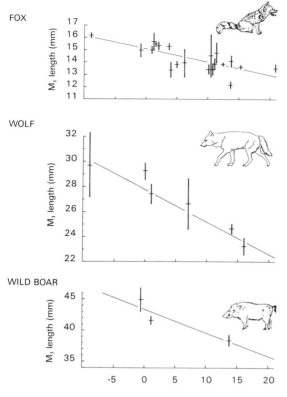

FOX

WOLF

WILD BOAR

Mean January temperature °C

3.10 Some mammals are larger in colder regions. A plot of tooth size (sample mean ±95 per cent confidence limits are portrayed) against environmental temperature (mean January temperatures from meteorological reports) for modern foxes, wolves and boars. *From Davis, 1981*

estimated Near Eastern temperature change 12,000 years ago is far too drastic. It would suggest that conditions there in the late Pleistocene were like those in southern Sweden today. Most geologists estimate that the Near East was a mere 5° centigrade colder in the late Pleistocene. Presumably other factors (perhaps rainfall) were also responsible.

A similar approach has been made by both Avery and Klein working on small and large mammals from the Late Pleistocene-Holocene in South Africa.

Avery (1982) investigated the variation in size of small mammal remains from South African Upper Pleistocene sites. She also obtained modern samples of the same species and was able to investigate how their size alters with environmental temperature today. For example, the shrew *Crocidura flavescens* is larger in colder climates, whereas another shrew *Myosorex varius* is smaller in colder climates.

In the Upper Pleistocene deposits at Boomplaas cave (fig. 3.5) *Crocidura flavescens* was larger, while *Myosorex varius* was smaller. By assuming that their present-day size-temperature relationship was the same in the past, both species suggest colder conditions in South Africa during the last glacial maximum.

Klein and Cruz–Uribe (1984), encouraged by Avery's results, analysed mean individual size in several species of South African carnivores and small herbivores—both modern and fossil. Like Avery's *Crocidura flavescens*, they found that mean size in carnivores increases with decreasing temperature. However, the situation in the small herbivores is more complex, with size increasing with rainfall in browsers, and decreasing with rainfall in grazers. Klein and Cruz–Uribe suggest that this reflects the increase in browse relative to grass under moister conditions.

Klein and Cruz–Uribe's results for the black-backed jackal, *Canis mesomelas* (fig. 3.11) are interesting. Modern black-backed jackals conform to the Bergmann effect: the largest occur farthest from the equator, in the Cape Province of South Africa, at the southern tip of the African continent. The smallest

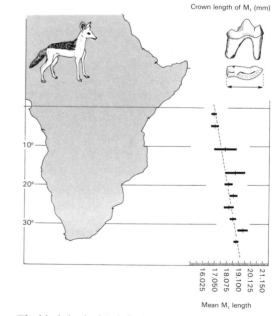

Crown length of M₁ (mm)

Mean M₁ length

3.11 The black-backed jackal, *Canis mesomelas*, is larger in higher latitudes. Basal crown length in millimetres of jackal carnassial teeth are plotted against latitude in the southern half of Africa. Vertical line is the sample mean, horizontal bar the 95 per cent confidence limits of the mean. *Courtesy Richard Klein*

ones are found in equatorial East Africa at the northern limit of this animal's range. Jackals from areas in between such as the Transvaal, are on average intermediate in size. What does the fossil record in South Africa show? Klein and Cruz–Uribe report that this jackal was indeed larger when climatic conditions supposedly were colder. They too suggest that fossils of certain species of mammals should provide the zoo-archaeologist with a useful tool for constructing detailed curves of climate change.

BODY SHAPE — THE DOGWHELK

The dogwhelk *Nucella lapillus* is a slow-moving carnivorous gastropod mollusc which feeds mainly on barnacles and mussels. It is common on north Atlantic rocky shores, and unlike many molluscs it has no planktonic dispersal phase. The female lays her eggs in capsules attached to the rock surface, from which the young hatch directly. The species thus probably exists in innumerable discrete breeding populations, each of which may evolve in response to local habitat selection pressures (Crothers, 1978).

The malacologist John Crothers (1978) made the interesting observation that the dogwhelk's shape varies according to the degree of exposure to wave action. Animals from exposed shores have short squat shells, while those from sheltered localities are characteristically elongated. By dividing shell-length (L) by aperture height (Ap)—to give a ratio of shell-shape—Crothers obtained a precise correlation between this ratio and the degree of exposure of rocky shores in south Wales. He recommended the use of this ratio to determine the exposure grade of a given shore.

During the 1970s Paul Mellars excavated five large Mesolithic (*c*3300–2600 bc or 4100–3400 BC) shell-middens on the Inner Hebridean island of Oronsay off the west coast of Scotland (fig. 3.12; see also Chapter 4). Among the shells (mostly limpets), crustacea, and bones of fish, bird and mammal were many dogwhelk shells, unfortunately mostly broken. However, in several of the middens there were sufficient complete shells for Andrews *et al.* (1985) to take up Crothers' recommendation and use his ratio to determine whether conditions around the coasts of Oronsay were as rough then as they are today. Evidence from other sources suggest that this was not

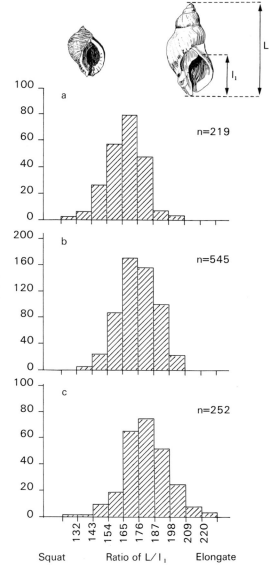

3.12 Shell shape and exposure. The dogwhelk, *Nucella lapillus*, a mollusc of North Atlantic rocky shores, varies in shape according to the degree of exposure. On the top left is a squat shell from an exposed locality, on the top right an elongate shell from a sheltered locality. The graphs show frequencies of shell-shape categories. (a) From the west (exposed) coast of Oronsay, Scotland, today. (b) From the east (sheltered) coast of Oronsay, Scotland, today. (c) From Mesolithic shell-middens on the east coast of Oronsay, which suggest that conditions were calmer 3300–2625 bc (4100–3400 BC). *From Andrews* et al., *1985 ($l_1 \simeq Ap$)*

so: for example the presence of forests growing nearer the Atlantic coast in northwest Scotland indicates a period of more tranquil seas (Lamb,

1977:416). Andrews *et al.*'s, study would indeed appear to corroborate this palaeobotanical evidence.

Modern dogwhelks collected on shores around Oronsay varied according to the degree of exposure from 'sheltered' to 'very exposed'. Thus the values of a (slightly modified) Crothers' ratio were $c1.8$ in sheltered localities (such as southwest from Cnoc Sligeach), $c1.7$ in exposed localities and $c1.6$–1.7 in very exposed localities (the western coast facing the Atlantic Ocean). The average values for this ratio in whelks from modern east coast localities range from sheltered to moderately exposed. What of the fossil dogwhelks from the middens?

Unfortunately the sample from the west coast at Priory Midden was too small, but the overall ratio for the east coast middens (there was no difference between them) gave a value which is slightly (and statistically significantly) higher than modern east coast whelks. In other words, Mesolithic whelks were more elongate. Andrews *et al.* conclude that maritime conditions 5–6000 years ago off western Scotland were a little calmer than they are today.

PARASITES

So far we have discussed the palaeoenvironment at a somewhat gross level. Work, at a microscopic level, is also revealing something about humans' very immediate environment in the past—the state of sanitation.

Many parasitic worms in the gut of vertebrates (including humans) produce resistant eggs or cysts at some stage of their life cycle which have a hard chitinous covering. These pass out with the faeces. In areas with poor sanitation the eggs may contaminate food, or be accidentally ingested by children playing on the ground. Under certain conditions parasite eggs and cysts may preserve in archaeological deposits. Eggs of trematodes (flukes), nematodes (roundworms) and cysts and eggs of cestodes (tapeworms) have been recorded from many archaeological sites in Europe (Jones, 1982).

Andrew Jones is currently investigating soil samples from Roman, Viking and medieval levels at York in northern England for evidence of parasite infestations. His findings are mildly horrifying. York was a prosperous city from Roman times until the mid fourteenth century, but was not very clean. In 1322 King Edward II claimed that that city stank

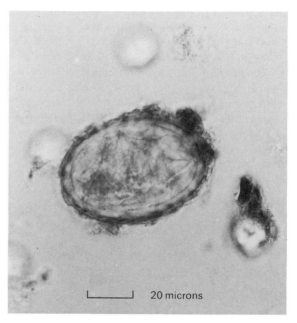

3.13a and **b** An ascarid (a) and trichurid (b) egg from the 'Lloyds Bank 6–8 Pavement stool' from Anglo-Scandinavian York. They are respectively 67 and 52 microns in length. Scale is 20 microns. *Photographs courtesy Andrew Jones*

more than any other town in the kingdom (Jones, 1982). Jones has some evidence which corroborates Edward II's opinion.

During excavation at one site 'Lloyds Bank 6–8 Pavement' in York, an almost complete coprolite, considered to be of human origin, was unearthed from an Anglo-Scandinavian layer. In the laboratory Jones examined samples taken from this coprolite. He identified large numbers of eggs of *Trichuris trichiura*, the human whipworm, and eggs of *Ascaris lumbricoides*, the maw-worm (fig. 3.13). He counted 66,000–68,000 *Trichuris* eggs per gram of faecal matter and 9000–12,000 *Ascaris* eggs per gram. These counts have to be doubled for estimating their original concentration in fresh faeces. Comparing these calibrated counts with examinations made on present-day patients, Jones stated that '... the individual who passed the Pavement coprolite was parasitized by at least a small number of maw-worms and several hundred whipworms. Such an infestation today would certainly be classed as a heavy one, although well within the limits of human tolerance' (Jones, 1983). Other workers are scanning similar material from archaeological sites.

From the few examples given in this chapter, it can be seen how the archaeofaunal record can often preserve evidence for all kinds of environmental data, from Ice Ages to the sanitary conditions of our ancestors.

CHAPTER FOUR

In what season was a site occupied?

One question which a prehistorian asks of a site is 'in which months of the year was it occupied'. A small site is often suspected of having served as a temporary location for the exploitation of some seasonally available resource. A large site, with substantial architectural remains and storage pits, for example, could have been a base camp or permanent, year-round occupation. Certain sites may have been used in winter and others in summer. Some sites may have been permanently occupied with outlying stations being visited for short periods, the last a scheme which Peter Rowley-Conwy (1983) proposes for Danish Mesolithic hunter-gatherers of the Ertebølle culture.

At a more general level: did our prehistoric ancestors lead a nomadic existence, and, if so, when did they first establish permanent settlements? A change from nomadism to sedentism may have important demographic repercussions: settling down may result in a population increase (see below), which, through the threat of starvation, may stimulate technological changes like the adoption of animal and plant husbandry. How then can faunal remains contribute towards studying the seasonal aspect of our ancestors' way of life?

Faunal remains sometimes indicate at what time of the year a particular resource was exploited and, by extension, when a site was occupied. However, while evidence for occupation in a particular season may be forthcoming, proving that a site was *not* occupied for the rest of the year is difficult: absence of proof is not proof of absence. Also, positive evidence for date of death of an animal in a particular site does not necessarily mean that the animal was eaten by the inhabitants of that site at that particular time. Animals may have been cured, dried and traded. For example in the Maori culture of New Zealand, although present locally between October and April, *dried* mutton-birds were traded in quantity over considerable distances (Coutts and Higham, 1971; quoting ethnographic records). Northwest American Indians were known to smoke shellfish and fish for winter food (Vancouver, 1798).

In this chapter I shall describe some of the methods used to pinpoint the season (and sometimes even the month) of death of animals in antiquity. But first, why are prehistorians so interested in seasonality, nomadism and sedentism?

SEDENTISM AND BIRTHRATE

Richard Lee (1972) made an extensive study of the !Kung Bushmen in Botswana, southern Africa, in the 1960s—a time when many were in the process of settling down and establishing permanent villages. He detected a rise in the birthrate as nomadism was abandoned: the spacing between births was reduced from an average of four years among nomadic bushmen to three years or less among their settled relatives.

Lee suggested two principal factors responsible for population control among Bushmen. Firstly, women on the move have to carry their young. Secondly, the diet of nomads tends to lack soft 'mushy' food, so infants have to be breast fed for as much as three and a half years. It is well known that lactation suppresses ovulation, so continued breast feeding results in births being well spaced apart, in this case by about four years. Once people are permanently settled the transport constraint no longer exists, and settled Bushmen who keep goats and grow soft vegetables can wean their infants at a younger age. And the birth interval may drop to 33–36 months.

Many archaeologists believe that people (in the Near East at any rate) who first domesticated plants and animals had already been leading a sedentary life for one or several millennia. If this was the case, then we can explain *why* man began animal and plant husbandry when he did, both of which produce more calories per unit area of land but require a much greater work input than hunting and gathering. Man was forced to become technologically innovative as a result of a population increase and the threat of starvation.

POTENTIAL SEASONAL INDICATORS

The kinds of animal remains which provide seasonal evidence group within the following four categories.

(a) Animals (or stages in their life-cycle) which are only present in a given location at a specific time of year such as migratory birds and insect pupae.

(b) Parts of the skeleton which undergo some kind of identifiable change in a particular season such as antlers, developing limb-bones, and erupting teeth.

(c) Hard tissues which are deposited incrementally such as the growing edge of sea shells, fish vertebrae and otoliths (ear stones), and mammalian tooth-cementum.

(d) Hard tissues which are 'worn down' at a known rate, such as mammalian deciduous teeth.

For tooth wear, and to some extent eruption too, we are unfortunately limited to the juvenile dentition; eruption and wear of the adult teeth—especially M3—varies by many months, so that any single tooth in a particular eruption/wear stage could just as easily indicate an animal that died in winter as one that died in summer.

Many seasonality methods depend upon the occurrence of a single well-defined birth season, and the presumption of a rate of change (be it tooth eruption and wear, or accretion of hard tissue) little different from its modern relatives.

I shall now describe several studies which have made use of these seasonally varying factors.

AN INDIAN BURIAL IN SOUTH DAKOTA — INSECTS

It is only in rare instances that insect remains are found among archaeological debris. One exception is Gilbert and Bass' (1967) investigation of Arikara Indian burials in South Dakota (Leavenworth site in Corson County) which date between c1802 and 1832. Gilbert and Bass found traces of fly pupae (the pupa is the fly's equivalent of the butterfly's chrysalis) in the eye sockets and abdominal cavities of some of the skeletons. The flies were identified as either Calliphorid or Sarcophagid (blue/green bottle and flesh) flies. They have a lifespan of 24 days and produce several generations per season, and appear in South Dakota by late March and disappear by mid-October. Thus Gilbert and Bass were able to infer summertime death and burial of these particular skeletons.

MEIENDORF—BONE GROWTH, ANTLERS AND BIRDS

One of the first examples where archaeofaunal remains were used to infer the season in which a site was occupied was Meiendorf in northern Germany. This Upper Palaeolithic site (dated to c15,000 bc), now a suburb of Hamburg, was excavated in the 1930s by Alfred Rust. In Late Pleistocene times it must have been situated in the tundra at the edge of the north European ice sheet. Karl Gripp studied the bones (most were of reindeer) from Meiendorf, and Rust (1937) was able to conclude from the faunal remains—in particular measurements of reindeer sacra, growth stages of antlers, and the presence of aquatic birds like ducks and geese—that Meiendorf was occupied during the brief Arctic summer for 2–3 months between June and October. Rust suggested that Meiendorf was the final northern destination of reindeer hunters' summer migration from central Germany. A migratory pattern which he likened to that undertaken by Lapp, Inuit and Siberian peoples in modern times.

STAR CARR YORKSHIRE, ENGLAND—ANTLERS AND TEETH

The early Mesolithic site of Star Carr (*c*7572 bc; Chapter 8) is one of the best known Mesolithic sites in Europe (Clark, 1972). Fraser and King (in Clark, 1954) suggested that Star Carr was occupied in winter and spring. Their findings were based on the presence of shed or unshed antlers of roe deer, red deer and elk. These deer shed their antlers at specific times of the year: elk in January, red deer in April and roe deer in October. Fraser and King noticed that 65 out of 106 red deer antlers had been 'broken out' of skulls while there were only three stag crania and two frontlets from which antlers had been shed. They therefore inferred that the main period of settlement coincided with winter when stags carried their antlers (from September through to March). The presence too of numerous shed red deer antlers suggested collection in April when antlers are shed. A similar line of reasoning was applied to the other two species of deer. However, as Grigson (1981:119) and others have pointed out, it is dangerous to use antlers in making seasonality interpretations. Antlers can be collected and stored from one season to another, which was no doubt the case since antler was a favourite raw material for manufacturing tools. Moreover Grigson (1981) noticed the bones of crane, which suggests summer occupation at Star Carr, as this bird is a summer visitor to Britain.

Since the original study of the Star Carr fauna our understanding of the development of cervid teeth has improved. Legge and Rowley-Conwy (1986) have made a complete re-examination of the fauna of Star Carr, and have come to different conclusions regarding the seasonal evidence from that site. Their results suggest summer occupation.

They noticed that roe deer jaws divide clearly into two major groups. Thirteen mandibles and one maxilla either have very heavily worn deciduous teeth (with the permanent premolars in some cases visible beneath them), or have the permanent premolars in early eruption after shedding of the deciduous teeth. By comparing this series of jaws to modern reference material, they found that the youngest of these jaws corresponds to animals killed in April at the earliest and that the whole series of jaws indicates a restricted kill period—a few months at the most. There follows a gap in the roe deer tooth eruption sequence which is considered good evidence for the seasonal killing of roe deer. There are no jaws with permanent premolars and M_3s in the later stages of eruption or coming into wear. Modern comparative specimens at this stage are derived from animals aged one and a half years old (i.e. killed in their second winter). All older Star Carr jaws have premolars and all cusps of M_3 well in wear—coming from animals aged two years and above. Unfortunately after the second year variability in tooth wear is too great to permit accurate seasonal dating from dentition.

While red deer and elk antlers were obviously important raw material for making tools, and showed much evidence of working, this was not the case for roe deer antlers, probably due to their small size. Roe deer antlers showed no signs of working. Legge and Rowley-Conwy suggest that they can legitimately be taken as seasonal indicators. With 77 unshed roe deer antlers, April–November occupation is indicated.

Additional finds at Star Carr also indicate summer occupation. They include:

(a) Neonatal bones of elk and red deer. An elk maxilla for example contains deciduous molars which are completely unworn. Since these teeth come into wear very early in life and since elk are born mid-May to mid-June, the Star Carr elk must have died in summer.

(b) Two red deer skulls with antlers shed. Since red deer shed their antlers in April, these two skulls must have come from animals hunted soon afterwards before new antler growth would have commenced.

(c) Several red deer mandibles with deciduous molars. Two of these have deciduous M_3s about to be shed, and one has M_3 erupting, and indicates a probable age of two years, giving a kill date of late spring or summer.

Most of this seasonal evidence points to a late spring/summer occupation of Star Carr. If correct the unanswered question of where the inhabitants of Star Carr spent their winters remains, and Legge and Rowley-Conwy speculate upon other regions such as the sea coast.

ABRI PATAUD, FRANCE—REINDEER ANTLERS, FOETAL BONES, ERUPTING TEETH AND CEMENTUM BANDS

The Abri Pataud, a rockshelter in the Dordogne valley of southwestern France, served as a habitation for Upper Palaeolithic man between *c*35,000 and 20,000 years ago. Arthur Spiess (1979) has analysed the faunal remains from this site. He paid particular attention to the reindeer remains which constituted the bulk of the fossil fauna: reindeer was the most important species. Spiess was well qualified to study this material since he had gained much experience from studying caribou (the North American name given to reindeer) in North America. One assumption he had to make, however, was that the time of the rut (around 15 October), date of calving (mid May) and rate of development of modern Canadian reindeer is similar to late Pleistocene reindeer in southwestern France. Among the Abri Pataud faunal remains were juvenile reindeer mandibles and long bones from foetal individuals. Spiess obtained evidence for late autumn, winter and early spring culling of the large mammals at this site.

Spiess found only one specimen of reindeer antler (of an adult male). Although still attached to its skull, it showed signs that it was about to be shed, and the animal must therefore have been killed around November/December. Sixteen foetal long bones, however, provided rather more useful seasonality data. Spiess assumed these all belonged to reindeer. By plotting graphs of the growth of museum specimens of aged reindeer foetal bones, Spiess could determine a relation between foetal long-bone length (he measured the ossified portion of the diaphysis) and age in months. These ages could then be converted to calendar months. For example a foetal femur of 3.99cm corresponds to a most likely age of 110 days, suggesting death occurred in late January or early February (i.e. October 15 + 110 days). His results indicated foetal deaths occurring from December through to February.

Spiess applied a similar line of reasoning to a small collection of mandibles of very young reindeer with deciduous dentition, whose first and/or second molars were in the process of erupting. Data for Canadian reindeer show that M_1 commences eruption at 3–5 months of age. M_2 commences eruption between 10 and 15 months. The juvenile mandibles from Abri Pataud could be 'grouped' into a 5–10 month age class: many had M_1 half erupted (i.e. well into the 3–5 months class) or M_1 fully erupted but with M_2 still in its crypt (i.e. before the 10–15 months age class). Again, assuming French reindeer calved in mid-May the 5–10 month age class corresponds to a winter time of death. Three other specimens from Abri Pataud 'grouped' into a second, older class, with M_2 one quarter or less erupted, suggesting death in the early stages of the M_2 eruption span at 10–11 months of age which corresponds to death between mid-March to mid-April. None was found with M_2 half or three-quarters erupted—i.e. say 12+ months old, or summer kills. Despite the very small samples that he had, Spiess thinks that the mandible-age data indicate October–March or winter killing of reindeer.

A similar kind of analysis was carried out by Jane Richter (1982) on juvenile aurochs mandibles from the Maglemosian (*c*6100 bc) site of Ulkestrup Lyng Øst in Denmark. Several mandibles showed slight wear on their deciduous teeth suggesting that they derived from individuals of 4–10 weeks of age. And since aurochs probably calved in March or April, these aurochs calves at Ulkestrup probably died in late spring. Patrick Munson (1984) has applied the same reasoning to juvenile woodchuck mandibles in a study of fauna from an Indian site in Indiana. He suggests that many other large North American rodents such as prairie dogs and marmots could also be utilized in this way.

A laboratory technique, developed mainly by game biologists over the last few decades, ages mammals by counting their dental cementum bands (Grue and Jensen, 1979). Cementum is a bony tissue deposited throughout a mammal's life as thin layers around the roots of its teeth (Chapter 2). When sectioned and examined under a microscope, these layers appear as a series of alternate light and dark bands analogous to tree-rings. They correspond to seasonal variation in food abundance. Usually two bands, one dark and one light, are accreted each year. If one knows to which seasons the dark and light bands correspond, then identification of the outermost band (i.e. the one being formed just before death) should indicate at what time of year death had occurred. The technique is difficult to carry out on fragile archaeological material. Nevertheless, Spiess did find 6 reindeer, 2 red deer and 2 horse teeth whose outermost cementum bands, he felt, could be reliably 'read'. These all showed that the outermost band was a dark one. Today in Arctic and sub-Arctic reindeer, a dark band, corresponding to a period of slower metabolism, forms between December and April. If we assume that this seasonality pattern was similar in southwestern France in the late Pleistocene, then these animals must have been hunted in winter, which confirms the dates documented by foetal long bones and tooth eruption.

At another upper Palaeolithic (belonging to the Aurignacian culture) site in southwestern France, La Quina, 80km west north west of the Abri Pataud, Guillen and Henri-Martin (1968) studied the state of dental eruption in juvenile reindeer jaws. Their M_1 and M_2 eruption data also suggested seasonal occupation, but from mid-May to October—a period complementary to that of the Abri Pataud's supposed October to April occupation. It is tempting to imagine that these two sites were respectively winter and summer camps of nomadic hunters belonging to the same culture, but a lot more seasonality analyses have to be undertaken in southwestern France before this kind of interpretation can be seriously considered.

ISRAEL—JUVENILE GAZELLES AND DECIDUOUS TEETH

In my study of late Pleistocene–early Holocene archaeofaunal assemblages from north and central Israel, I discovered that during (or just before) the Natufian culture period (10,300–8500 bc) the percentage of young gazelle bones (i.e. those with unfused long-bone epiphyses) increased from *c*26 to 33 per cent (Davis, 1983). It was not possible to explain this as resulting either from increasingly intense hunting, as Elder (1965) had for Indian deer-hunters in North America (Chapter 5), or from domestication. I therefore sought another explanation.

I assumed that gazelle breeding patterns have remained constant throughout the Mousterian–Natufian, with a birth peak in the spring. My explanation for the increase of juveniles in the Natufian assemblage at Hayonim terrace (Natufian, *c*9000 bc) is based upon a seasonal variation in the juvenile count of gazelle in the wild. Counts of the age composition of modern herds of gazelle in Israel reveal a higher proportion of juveniles in the summer than in winter. This is due to a birth peak in the spring, and high juvenile mortality in winter.

In the assemblages which precede Hayonim terrace, I suggest that the age profile of young gazelles culled is roughly equivalent to their *winter* proportion in nature, while on the terrace an increased cull of young might be equivalent to a mean *annual* proportion of the young in nature. This latter increase is due to the inclusion of the summer juveniles. Indeed a number of the gazelle bones found on the terrace probably belonged to new-born individuals. The next stage in my investigation was to look closely at the mandibles of juvenile gazelles.

A study of the eruption and wear of modern gazelle teeth from northern and central Israel (Davis, 1980) showed that *Gazella gazella* sheds its deciduous teeth by *c*13–15 months of age.

Besides having high-crowned adult teeth to cope with abrasive grasses, young gazelles have high-crowned deciduous teeth too, especially the last deciduous molar, m_3. Its crown wears down with age from *c*7–10mm 'crown height' at birth before wear commences, to a mere 2–3mm by the age of 13–15 months when it is shed and replaced by the P_4.

From three large archaeofaunal assemblages I had enough juvenile gazelle mandibles to attempt a seasonality study based on their deciduous teeth. The assemblages were: Mousterian (50–40,000 bc) levels at Kebara cave Mount Carmel, the Aurignacian (*c*24,000 bc) levels at Hayonim cave in the western Galilee, and the Natufian (*c*9–10,000 bc) site at Hayonim terrace, outside Hayonim cave.

I measured the crown heights of all the gazelle deciduous m_3s from these three assemblages. The plotted results (fig. 4.1) represent an approximate age profile of the young gazelles hunted by early man in Israel. The small samples and unresolved problems of preservation make my interpretation speculative. Nonetheless I suggest that the rather narrow 'peaking' of the Hayonim Aurignacian and Kebara Mousterian m_3 crown heights (most are between 4–6mm, which may correspond to 8 and 12 months old) argues for a relatively short period when the young gazelles were killed, probably during the winter. However, the distribution of Hayonim terrace Natufian m_3 crown heights is markedly different. Here 'peaking' is less marked, m_3s of all wear stages are well represented, not just the 4–6mm ones. This may signify that at Hayonim terrace gazelle had been hunted all seasons of the year—summer included.

Here then we have evidence, if tenuous, that prehistoric man may have changed from nomadism

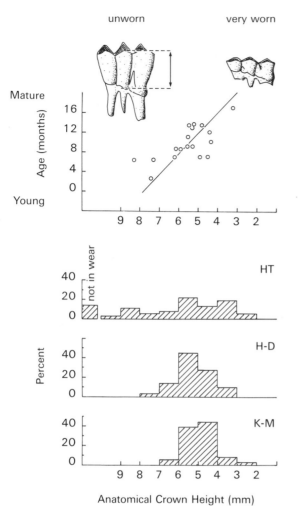

unworn   very worn

Anatomical Crown Height (mm)

4.1 Prehistoric seasonal hunting of gazelles in Israel: a study of modern and archaeological gazelle, *Gazella gazella*, deciduous molar teeth. *Above*: plot of m_3 crown height in millimetres against age in months of 18 modern aged gazelles from the eastern Galilee: older juvenile gazelles have shorter crowns. *Below*: percentages of gazelle m_3 teeth of different crown heights from three archaeological assemblages.

(1) HT = Hayonim terrace, Natufian (9000 bc) n = 37
(2) H–D = Hayonim cave, Aurignacian (24,000 bc) n = 58
(3) K–M = Kebara cave, Mousterian (50–40,000 bc) n = 36

The K–M and H–D plots show a restricted grouping of age, while HT plots have a wide dispersion of ages which includes some unworn m_3s. Were K–M and H–D gazelles hunted in winter and HT gazelles hunted throughout the year? *From Davis, 1983*

to sedentism in the Natufian some 11,000 years ago. Hunting and gathering was still the basis of the Natufian economy. Apart from a very sophisticated tool kit consisting of flint microliths, and art, the Natufian is characterized by the remains of solid stone-walled dwellings—the earliest evidence for permanent architecture in the Levant. And archaeologists have long considered the Natufians to have been the first people in the Levant to live in permanently settled villages. Natufian sites are fewer in number than those of preceding cultures, but are usually much larger, also suggesting that some kind of reorganization of society may have taken place.

If this reconstruction of events in the Natufian is correct, then, given Lee's studies of the !Kung Bushmen, we can explain why food animals and plants were domesticated in the subsequent Neolithic culture period. Early Natufian bands of hunters formed permanently settled villages perhaps 11–12,000 years ago. This was also the time of post-Pleistocene climate-change, and one wonders whether this did not have some influence. The adoption of sedentism may have led to reduced spacing of births and so to a population increase. By Neolithic times higher levels of population and the threat of starvation forced an economic change, and man undertook the domestication of plants such as wheat and barley and food animals such as the goat and sheep (Chapter 6).

CALIFORNIAN FISH

The archaeologist confronted with the remains of certain 'cold-blooded' animals such as fish and molluscs will probably have more success trying to determine season of exploitation than his colleague will with terrestrial mammals. Fish, like most animals which cannot regulate their body temperature, grow with characteristic periodicity (Nikolsky, 1978:190). Growth is rapid when food is abundant which may be during the warmer months, and slow when certain food may not be available. Moreover, unlike mammals, bone-growth in fish is not accompanied by any re-modelling or resorption (Chapter 2). The net result of these two characteristics is that scales and most bones of fish keep a permanent record of this inequality in the growth rate within their own structures as alternating zones of wide and narrow rings. The wide rings are dark in reflected light and pale in direct light, and narrow rings are pale in reflected light and dark in direct light. They correspond to periods of accelerated and retarded growth respectively. The Dutch naturalist Leewenhoek in 1684 first suggested that these rings could be used to 'read' the age of a fish. Thus, as with cementum bands, by observing the nature of the outermost zone of a fish scale or bone the season of death may be established. In warmer tropical and sub-tropical waters other factors besides temperature, such as gonad maturation, may complicate the pattern. Among Californian fish, spawning stress between March and June is the most likely cause of narrow-ring formation (Casteel, 1972).

With a knowledge of seasonal variation in Californian fish bone growth, Richard Casteel analysed the large numbers of fish vertebrae in four concentrations of fish bone associated with two burials in a burial complex in California (French Camp, south of Stockton). There was some uncertainty on the part of the excavator as to which concentrations were associated with which of the two burials; however, it did seem that three belonged with one burial, while the fourth was associated with either burial. Casteel then attempted to (a) determine in what season the fish had originally been killed, and (b) use these seasonality data to link the fourth fishbone concentration with its rightful burial. (This of course could only be possible if the two burials occurred in different seasons, and assumes too that the fish were freshly caught when interred with the burial.)

Casteel analysed 596 vertebrae whose margins were intact, and made three categories with their respective time of death:

(1) Vertebrae with the narrow-ring present on the margin: March–June;

(2) Vertebrae with a small amount of growth after the narrow-ring: July–October;

(3) Vertebrae with much growth after the narrow-ring: November–February.

His results (fig. 4.2) show that most specimens in samples b, c, and d did show the same season of kill (July–October) suggesting that they did indeed belong to one and the same burial. Most of the specimens, however, in the fourth sample (a) indicated a November–February kill, and therefore were probably originally interred with the other burial. Casteel was therefore able to suggest not only when

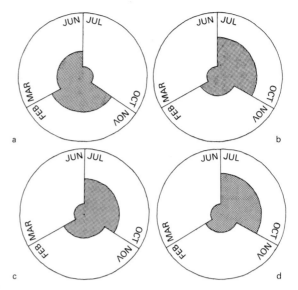

4.2 Casteel's (1972) analysis of fish vertebrae from four burials in a burial complex in California. The plots show 'season of fish-death' data read from vertebrae associated with four samples: burial (a) n = 445, burial (b) n = 41, burial (c) n = 89, and burial (d) n = 21. Most specimens in (b), (c) and (d), were fished in the same season. Specimens in (a) were probably fished in November–February.

fishing was being carried out, but also that here were two burials whose interment had occurred at different times of the year.

ORONSAY OTOLITHS

A most remarkable example of the use of fish remains to determine seasonal exploitation is Mike Wilkinson's (Mellars and Wilkinson, 1980) study of saithe (or coalfish—*Pollachius virens*) otoliths from Mesolithic sites on the island of Oronsay: 3300–2600 bc (*c*4100–3400 BC) in the Inner Hebrides, off the west coast of Scotland (Chapter 8). In the course of wet sieving, Wilkinson recovered numerous saithe otoliths during excavations at four sites on this island.

Otoliths or 'ear-stones' are calcareous nodules found in the inner ear of most vertebrate animals. They are concerned mainly with balance. In bony fish (teleosts), unlike other vertebrates, they are quite large (figs. 4.3 and 4.4) and grow by daily accretion. The largest and most distinctive (to species and sometimes even to population) of the three pairs are

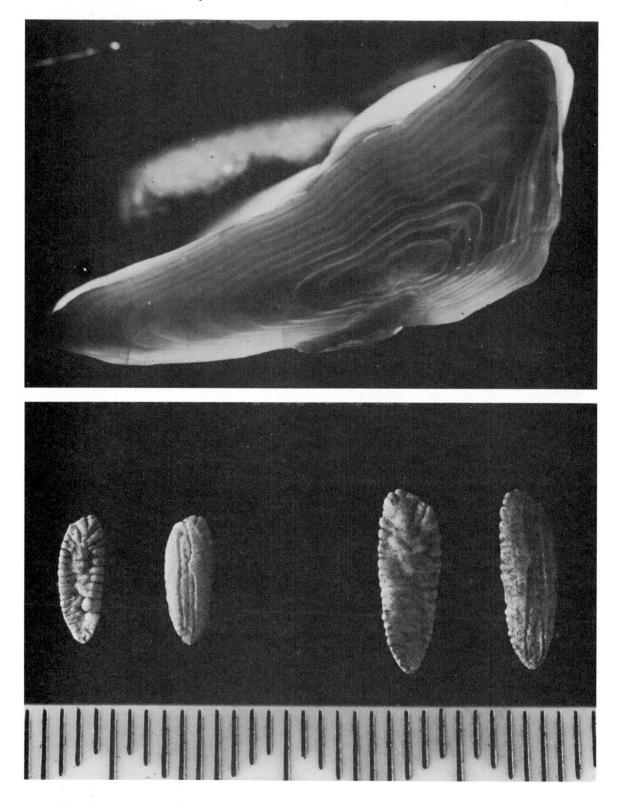

the sagittae otoliths. These have the greatest potential as an archaeological indicator of seasonality.

During the first three years of life saithe grow very rapidly, as do their otoliths (fig. 4.5). Otolith size during this period will therefore be approximately proportional to age. Like most fish, saithe have a well-defined spawning season, so a random catch at one particular time should therefore contain two or three otolith size-classes, each representing a different age group.

At the two sites, Cnoc Sligeach and Cnoc Coig, the otolith length distributions exhibit a bimodal pattern. The one from Priory Midden shows a unimodal distribution. A fourth histogram, from Caisteal nan Gillean II, shows an intermediate pattern in which otoliths are distributed more evenly over the whole range of lengths. In a fascinating piece of detective work, Wilkinson has interpreted these patterns of otolith length distributions as signifying seasonal fishing in antiquity.

Wilkinson fished saithe off Oronsay at different times of the year and obtained a plot of otolith growth rate (fig. 4.5, top left). By assuming that (a) the growth rate and (b) the time of spawning of saithe 5000 years ago was the same as it is today, he could 'read off' the time of year to which a particular otolith size is equivalent, and hence the time the fish was caught.

Wilkinson suggests that fishing at Cnoc Sligeach was during the summer months of July and August, and at Cnoc Coig a little later, from September to November. Note (fig. 4.5, bottom left) how both modal sizes at Cnoc Coig are consistently to the right by about 1mm of those recorded in Cnoc Sligeach. Supporting evidence for autumn occupation of Cnoc Coig is provided by hazel-nut shells found there and the predominance of grey-seal bones, some very young. Seals form breeding colonies on land during the early autumn, and then make easy targets for human hunters.

At Priory Midden, a site which is in a sheltered location, otolith length measurements exhibit a strong unimodality suggesting that fishing was carried out there between the beginning of the winter and early spring, and that first-year fish only were taken. Supporting evidence for winter occupation of Priory Midden comes from the abnormally low recovery of saithe bones compared to shells. Modern saithe of the older age classes are known to retreat into deep water during mid-winter, and would therefore be inaccessible to the fishing techniques employed in antiquity. However first-year fish remain within the inshore zone for longer into the winter and would therefore have remained more accessible. This would explain the predominance of first-year fish. It is not until the later part of the winter that the main offshore movement of first-year fish occurs. After this all age classes of saithe would have been most difficult to obtain. Furthermore a low measure of dispersion of Priory Midden otolith length measurements could reflect fishing at a time when the overall rate of growth is low, i.e. during winter.

At the fourth midden, Caisteal nan Gillean II, fishing was carried out over a longer period of the year, perhaps with a major emphasis during June–July.

Oronsay is a small island, and the archaeological findings have not so far provided all the answers. For example, were these middens occupied by the same group of people both hunting and gathering different resources and changing location seasonally, or was the island visited for short periods during the year by people from one of the nearby islands such as Jura?

MOLLUSCAN CALENDARS

Besides fish, another group of cold-blooded animals, the molluscs, may leave some clue as to the season in which they died. Like fish, molluscs do not remodel or resorb their hard tissue once it has been deposited. The shell therefore remains as a record of the pattern of the animal's life history. And, like fish with their bones, many molluscs produce more shell during the summer than during the winter. Shell growth may even cease altogether in winter.

GROWTH-LINE ANALYSIS

Certain molluscs such as some intertidal bivalves, when sectioned and examined under the microscope,

---

4.3 A sectioned otolith (ear stone) from a 110cm cod caught off the Norway coast in January 1963, and estimated to have been 12 years old. Note the annual incremental growth lines. *Photograph courtesy A.R. Margetts. Crown Copyright, Ministry of Agriculture, Fisheries and Food*

4.4 Saithe (coalfish) otoliths. Scale in millimetres. *Photograph courtesy Paul Mellars*

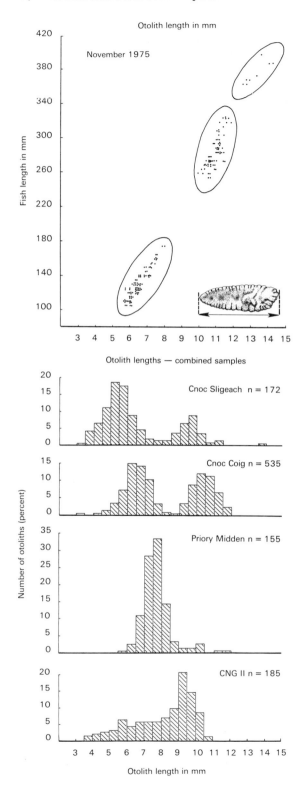

Otolith length in mm

November 1975

Fish length in mm

Otolith lengths — combined samples

Cnoc Sligeach n = 172

Cnoc Coig n = 535

Priory Midden n = 155

CNG II n = 185

Number of otoliths (percent)

Otolith length in mm

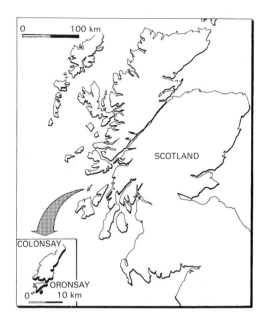

SCOTLAND

COLONSAY

ORONSAY

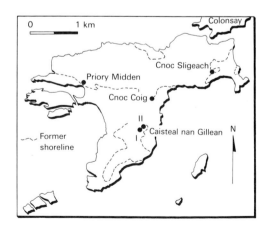

Colonsay

Cnoc Sligeach

Priory Midden

Cnoc Coig

Caisteal nan Gillean

Former
shoreline

N

reveal narrow increments of growth separated by very thin dark lines. These are now known to be formed during high and low tides respectively. As many as several hundred of these may be counted per growing season. In 'growth-line analysis', the first step is to subdivide the microscopic increments of shell deposited within this growing season into a 'tide count' and then, if the date of commencement of the summer growing season is known, this 'tide count' may be converted to a calendar date. One basic assumption which has to be made is that the month when summer growth commences today is approximately the same as it was in antiquity. (Time of commencement will, of course, vary with latitude as will length of growing season.) Seasonal interpretation of a fossil species of mollusc then, requires a thorough knowledge of its modern growth characteristics in the same region.

With a view to understanding the time of year that cockles had been collected in the Scottish Mesolithic site of Morton in Fife (*c*4432 bc), Margaret Deith (1983) made a careful study of modern Scottish specimens of the common edible cockle, *Cerastoderma edule*. In order to understand shell-fishing habits of prehistoric coastal Japanese, Hiroko Koike (1975) studied the clam, *Meretrix lusoria*.

SHELL GROWTH

In molluscs, new shell is deposited by the secretory mantle around its growing edge. In intertidal molluscs such as the common edible cockle, Richardson *et al.* (1979) demonstrated in a series of experiments that an increment of new shell is deposited while the animal is submerged during high tide. Growth ceases

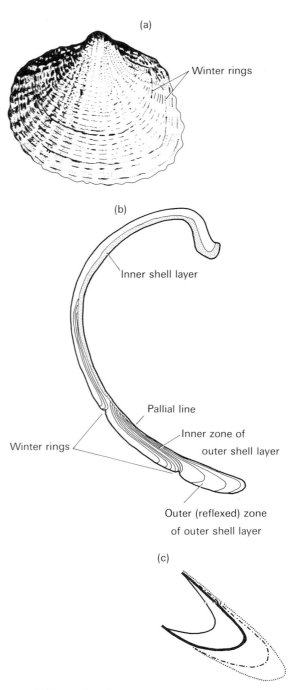

4.5 Wilkinson's study of saithe otoliths on Oronsay, Inner Hebrides, Scotland. *Above left:* relationship between modern fish length and otolith length of saithe caught in November 1975. Note the grouping into 'first', 'second' and 'third and older', year age groups. *Below left:* numbers of saithe otoliths in different size classes on four Mesolithic sites on Oronsay. Wilkinson's seasonal interpretations are as follows:

July–August fishing at Cnoc Sligeach
September–November fishing at Cnoc Coig
Winter fishing at Priory Midden

and (?) a longer period of fishing with possible emphasis during June–July at Caisteal nan Gillean II (CNG II). *From Mellars and Wilkinson, 1980, 1978*

4.6 Shell growth and seasonality. (a) Valve of the common cockle, *Cerastoderma edule*, with two winter rings. (b) A section of the same valve to show the grooves formed by these winter rings. (c) Growing edge of (b) with the positions of the next two growth increments indicated by dotted and dashed lines. *Drawings by Sue Wanek, courtesy Margaret Deith*

during low tide emersion as the mantle is withdrawn and the shell valves close; a dark line then forms. These growth bands, laid down tidally, are visible under the microscope when the shell is sectioned (figs. 4.6, 4.7 and 4.8).

In temperate latitudes, shell growth slows down and less material is added as winter approaches. Koike measured the width of the increments in her specimens of *Meretrix*. These measured 50 microns (the diameter of human hair ranges from approximately 50 to 70 microns) in summer, 15 microns in December and a mere 12–5 microns in February, the time of minimum sea temperature in Japan. In very cold waters—as Deith found in Scotland—increments gradually become reduced in size to a point where they are indistinguishable from one another; and shell growth ceases completely during winter.

This reduction or cessation of growth in winter results in the formation of a groove in the shell surface which is visible to the naked eye—the 'growth recession ring'. A shell's last winter ring thus serves as a reference point from which any subsequent growth may be measured and converted to a calendar date.

In order to make seasonal interpretations from fossil shells it is necessary to know how long each growth increment takes to form, and the date when the growth season commences. An example is Margaret Deith's study of cockles collected from the shores of Fife in eastern Scotland. She collected shells at different times during the summer growing season over a period of three years, 1979–81, and was able to 'calibrate' her molluscan calendar. In cockles collected in May she counted an average of 90 lines and those collected in September 283 lines (each line separating two increments). In other words 193 lines had formed in 101 days. During this time the shores were covered by 195 tides. The correlation between number of tides and lines is excellent and clearly confirms that increment formation is tidal. By working back, Deith could then calculate the approximate date when incremental growth commences: around 22 April (i.e. 45 days before 31 May). The total number of lines laid down in any one growing season is rather variable and is *c*300, equivalent to about 21.5 weeks, i.e. from 22 April to 25 September. Deith points out that both dates are 'average estimates' and will probably vary slightly from year to year according to weather conditions, so the accuracy with which resolution of a cockle's date of death can be made is no greater than about a week—this of

course for cockles which died during the five summer months' growth season. Cockles collected during the winter can only be designated as 'winter collected'— a major limitation of the use of cockles in Scotland for seasonal analysis.

Deith then examined cockles from the Mesolithic shell midden at Morton in Fife. Between two winter growth-recession bands she counted an average of 298 lines, very close to the modern count of 300, which indicates that cockles 7000 years ago grew for the same length of time per year. At Morton 79 per cent of the cockles were winter collected, but 21 per cent did have 'summer edges' indicating summer collection. The number of lines from the last 'winter recession ring' to the growing edge of these 'summer shells' when converted to a calendar date gave dates of collection in late June/early July. Given the error factor, they could all have been gathered on the same day. Deith concludes that Morton represents a 'field camp' type of site occupied during brief sporadic episodes, but not a permanently occupied one, nor one which was occupied for the specialized seasonal exploitation of some resource. Indeed, besides molluscs, the remains from Morton—which include deer, boar, cattle, fish and sea-bird—suggest a broad-based economy.

In Japan Koike (1975) suggests that, in seven successive layers at Miyamotodai, a late Jomon period site (2000–825 bc or 2500–1000 BC, in Chiba prefecture) *Meretrix* shells were gathered from late winter to spring. However, at Natsumidai, a late Kofun period site (*c* AD 500–700, on the east bank of the Edo river, 3km from Tokyo Bay), *Meretrix* shells indicated collection throughout the year, with marked peaks in late winter and spring. Very few were collected in late autumn and early winter (Koike, 1979).

Deith, and Koike have demonstrated the potential of growth-lines; but some shells without obvious discrete growth increments are not amenable to this kind of analysis.

OXYGEN ISOTOPE ANALYSIS

For molluscs such as limpets and top shells with no well defined tidal growth lines, Nicholas Shackleton and Margaret Deith have used another approach. Their method uses oxygen isotope variation to measure the temperature of the water when the

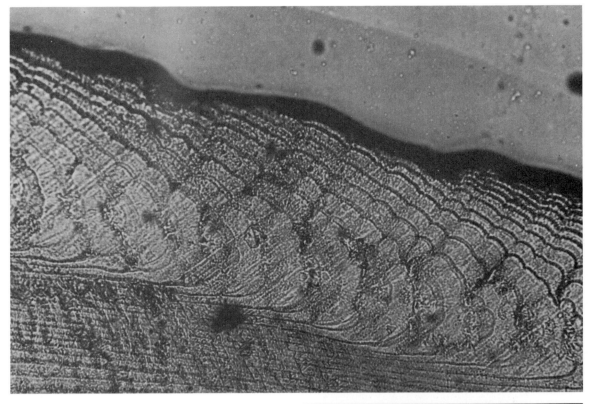

4.7 A section of the common cockle, *Cerastoderma edule*, shell collected from Eden in Fife, Scotland. This shows tidally deposited increments. Photograph of an acetate peel using transmitted light, approximate magnification is ×750. *Courtesy Margaret Deith*

4.8 A section of the common cockle, *Cerastoderma edule*, shell collected from Stiffkey in Norfolk, showing tidally deposited increments. Scale is 20 microns (1 micron = 1/1000th of a millimetre). *Scanning electron microscope photograph, courtesy Margaret Deith*

growing edge of the shell was being produced.

Most elements of the earth's crust are made up of two or more 'kinds' of atoms which have the same chemical properties but which differ in their atomic weights. These are known as isotopes. For example carbon consists mainly of atoms with an atomic weight of 12 but also a very small quantity of carbon with atomic weight 13 (in an approximate ratio of 90:1) and an even smaller amount of the unstable (radioactive) isotope of atomic weight 14 (written ^{14}C). It is this isotope which has proved so useful in archaeology for dating organic substances.

The two stable isotopes of oxygen are of interest in

geology and archaeology. They are the lighter oxygen 16 and heavier oxygen 18. On average there are 5000 ^{16}O atoms per ^{18}O atom in the constituents of the earth's crust, the oceans, the atmosphere and living matter. Variation in their ratio is of interest to us here.

Substances of different density vary in their thermodynamic properties. Harold Urey (1947) first suggested that the ratio of these two oxygen isotopes should vary according to temperature, and that by measuring this ratio in geological specimens of carbonates (i.e. oxides of carbon formed by living organisms) an estimate of palaeotemperatures could be made. This is because during the calcification process, a slight bias which is temperature dependent may favour one isotope over the other during the uptake of oxygen atoms from the environment and their incorporation within the crystal lattice of the shell. The warmer the water, the lighter or more depleted in ^{18}O the carbonate will be. A mollusc which lays down shell material throughout the year is thus recording the changes in the temperature of sea water through the annual cycle. If this continuous record is sampled at suitable intervals, the resulting graph should parallel the sea temperature curve and the isotopic value of the carbonate taken from the growing edge will indicate the time of year when the shell was collected.

The technique of measuring oxygen isotope ratios using a mass spectrometer is sufficiently sensitive to detect seasonal variation of temperature. By applying the same principle as in 'growth line analysis' to archaeological shells, Shackleton (1973) was able to determine when a mollusc had been collected by measuring the oxygen isotope ratio of its growing edge in relation to the ratio in material laid down earlier. A 'warm' ratio will indicate summer collection and a 'cold' ratio winter collection.

In Shackleton's method a series of small samples of shell (0.2–0.5mg) is drilled across the shell back from the growing edge. Each sample is treated and examined in a mass spectrometer for its ^{18}O abundance ratio. In this way an 'oxygen isotope profile' may be plotted.

This method works only for molluscs that deposit calcium carbonate throughout the year—a species that does not deposit any shell in winter will not register a winter temperature at its edge even if it did die in winter. The method will only work if the original oxygen atoms incorporated in the shell remain there (no subsequent recrystallization occurring). Shackleton collected modern limpets (*Patella tabularis*) in the winter (July) of 1971 in South Africa. He cut the shells in half and drilled micro-samples spaced at regular 2mm intervals along the face of the cut surface (fig. 4.9a). Their growing edge did indeed show evidence of winter collection (fig. 4.9b) in that the outermost samples' oxygen isotope reading was 'cold'. Microsamples derived from further up the shell fluctuated first to 'warm' (the preceding summer) and then 'cold' again (the winter of 1970), then 'warm' and finally 'cold' again (winter 1969). The overall range in isotopic composition was 1.4 per mill, equivalent to about 7°C, and about two years growth was covered. During this two-year period, average sea temperatures varied from about 13°C to 20°C. Thus the 'oxygen isotope profile' is closely related to the sea temperature fluctuation, and *P. tabularis* provides a reliable record of the seasons.

Shackleton then examined limpets of the same species from the 'Wilton' culture (c7000–3000 bc) of Nelson Bay cave, 530 km east of Cape Town, South Africa. Two profiles (fig. 4.9c) indicate winter collection. One limpet, from midden J, may have lived right through the winter and could therefore have been collected in November. Taking whole profiles is expensive. A short-cut method permitting large numbers of shells to be analysed quickly is simply to file a small sample from the growing edge of the shell. Shackleton examined 'edge samples' from 15 limpets from Nelson Bay cave (fig. 4.9d). All gave oxygen isotope readings in the 'cold' end of the spectrum indicating winter collection. Did South African hunter-gatherers resort to shellfish in winter only as other sources of nourishment became hard to find, or were they leading a semi-nomadic existence, spending winters near the shore and summers inland?

Deith (1983) is applying the same method in Cantabria, northern Spain. She has analysed top shells, *Monodonta lineata*, from three Asturian or Mesolithic (6700–4850 bc) sites: Penicial, La Riera and Mazaculos. 'Edge samples' from top shells from all three sites gave oxygen isotope ratios which mainly fall within the range of winter values. Deith suggests that they were collected at some time between December and April, although some were collected in autumn. None, however, is in the summer end of the spectrum.

Deith suggests that the most likely interpretation of the Asturian shell data is that shellfish were simply

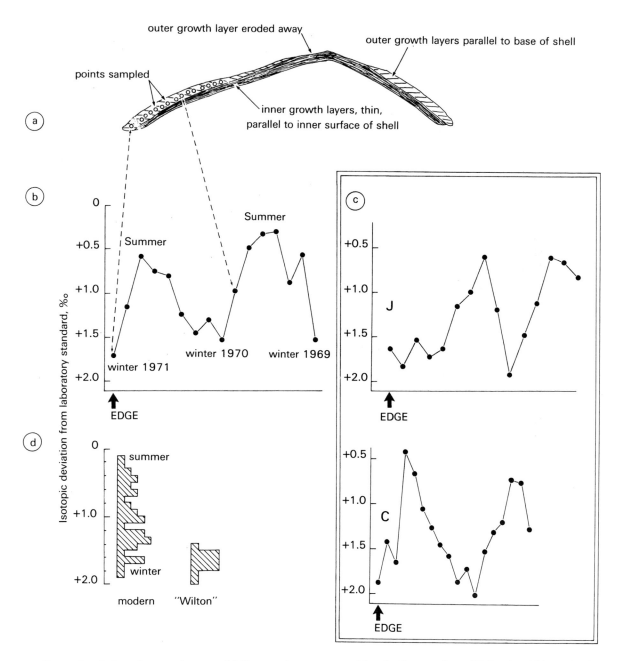

4.9 Seasonal variation of oxygen isotopes. (a) Cross section of the South African limpet, *Patella tabularis*, whose outer growth layer Shackleton sampled in order to obtain an oxygen isotope profile. (b) This particular limpet was collected in winter (July) 1971 in South Africa, thus the outermost sample's isotopic deviation suggests cold conditions. (c) (in box) Similar 'oxygen isotope profiles' from two prehistoric limpets from 'Wilton' middens. Both specimens (from midden J above, and midden C below) have edge isotope contents suggesting winter collection. (d) Analysis of samples taken from the edge only of 15 limpets from 'Wilton' middens (shown on the right) all fall within the winter range of modern *Patella tabularis* (42 analyses; left histogram). *From Shackleton, 1973*

not eaten in summer, as other resources were available. This, however, does not preclude several other possibilities: (1) the area was not occupied in summer, (2) the *pattern* of shellfishing varied seasonally (in summer the empty shells were left near the shore where the soft parts were consumed, instead of being brought back to the warm environment of the base camp) and (3) sites within clusters of sites were used sequentially.

These alternative interpretations highlight the problem of using one resource alone to draw seasonality inferences. A single species only tells us when it was collected and not whether the site was occupied at other times of the year.

To date, the best seasonality indicators are provided by aquatic animals—fish and molluscs. But large-scale exploitation of aquatic resources may not have begun, in the Near East, Africa and Europe at least, until 12,000 years ago. So we are limited as to the archaeological periods when shells and fish may be used for seasonality analysis.

CHAPTER FIVE

Our hunting past

This chapter focuses on the interaction between 'early humans', including our Australopithecine ancestors, and animals. The period discussed began several million years ago and ended when people began husbanding animals.

What was the nature of the relationship between the earliest humans and animals and who dominated whom? Did humans eat meat, and, if so, was it hunted or scavenged? Given that people hunted, how intensively did they hunt, how adept were they and what techniques did they use? And finally, were humans responsible for the extinction of innumerable species of large animals towards the end of prehistoric times, particularly in Australia, America, Madagascar, New Zealand and on various Mediterranean islands? The answers to most of these questions are far from being solved.

I shall therefore be dealing with several million years of hominid-animal relations. In order to understand the evolutionary context let me briefly summarize the main aspects of this evolution from *Australopithecus* to *Homo sapiens*. In brief, our ancestors may be arranged in an evolutionary lineage from *Australopithecus afarensis* to *Homo habilis* to *Homo erectus* to Neanderthals and finally modern human. (The last two both belong to different sub-species of *Homo sapiens*.)

The fossil record of mankind's earlier evolution (from Miocene proto-hominids to *Australopithecus*) is poor and therefore little understood. Nevertheless it appears that our own earlier evolution was restricted to Africa. Our hominid ancestors were descended from a primate which probably lived by clambering among trees of the great forests of that continent. Most palaeontologists consider that this ancestor was

a fruit eater, although some (e.g. Teleki, 1975) suggest that it may have been an omnivore. Its descendants, the Australopithecines, moved out of the forests and into the grasslands. Just when this relocation occurred is still a mystery, but it probably happened between 10 and five million years ago. Certainly around three million years ago in Africa *Australopithecus* was bipedal. (Just over two million years ago another group—the robust Australopithecines—evolved. They were probably herbivorous, and may have been an evolutionary side-branch, perhaps becoming extinct one million years ago.)

While *Australopithecus* undoubtedly used stones and sticks as tools, the earliest evidence we have so far for the manufacture of tools (the first were made from pebbles) goes back 1.75–2.2 million years and is associated with his descendant *Homo habilis*. *H. erectus* (otherwise known as 'Peking man' or 'Java man') represents the next step towards humans and was the earliest of our ancestors known outside Africa. *Homo erectus'* tool kit was more developed and included hand-axes—the so-called Acheulean tradition. *Homo erectus*, then, not only walked upright and made tools, but inhabited the two Old World landmasses, Eurasia and Africa. *Homo sapiens* (modern human) evolved from *H. erectus* between 100,000 and 300,000 years ago. An early form (?race or subspecies) of *H. sapiens* was Neanderthal known mainly from Europe and the Near East. Neanderthals were short and stocky and are associated with flake-tool or Mousterian stone tools. They were possibly the first to practise burial rites. From then on the rate of humans' cultural development exceeded human biological evolution. By 40,000 years ago modern people with their more sophisticated blade tool (or Upper Palaeolithic) industries had evolved. Their cultural sophistication (tools, art, and no doubt clothing too) enabled them to colonize hitherto uninhabited parts of the world such as Australia and later America. As we shall see this was to have dire consequences for many of the larger animals in those regions.

Richard Lee and Irven DeVore (1968) have estimated that of the 80,000,000,000 people who have ever lived on earth, over 90 per cent have lived as hunter-gatherers, about 6 per cent have lived by agriculture, and the remaining few per cent have lived in industiral societies.

What do the archaeofaunal remains tell us about human–animal relations during these earlier stages in hominid evolution? In outline, they suggest that the following changes may have occurred:

(1) Our Australopithecine ancestors in Africa, whose diet may have consisted mainly of fruit, were themselves hunted by large carnivores.

(2) The evolution some two million years ago of tool-making *Homo* coincided with his ascendancy over the rest of the animal kingdom. Perhaps too at that time the hominid diet came to include more meat.

(3) At some stage during the *Australopithecus–Homo erectus* lineage a change occurred from scavenging to hunting.

(4) People's expansion and colonization of new territories coincided with (but did not necessarily cause) the extinction of many large animals.

(5) The final major change in peoples' relation with animals is the advent of husbandry, which will be discussed in the next chapter.

In very early sites we cannot assume that animal bones found with early hominids represent the leftovers of their meals, nor even that hominids dominated other large mammals or ate meat. Alan Walker (1981), analysing scratch marks on the surfaces of robust Australopithecine teeth, suggests that their diet was based upon a preponderance of fruit. And according to Charles Brain, *Australopithecus*, far from killing other large animals, was itself being predated: carnivores rather than hominids were the main agents responsible for accumulating the animal bones.

Brain (1981) has studied animal bones associated with remains of *Australopithecus* and early *Homo* in southern African caves. In particular he has analysed breakage patterns of bones, carnivore-ungulate

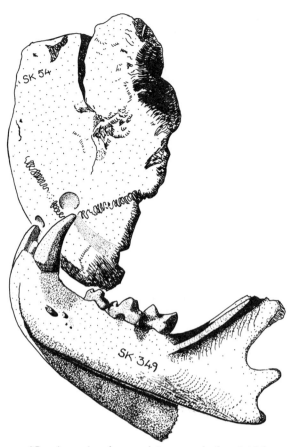

5.1 'Carnivore involvement' in an early hominid bone assemblage from Swartkrans, South Africa. Two holes in a skull bone of an Australopithecine child (SK 54) match closely the spacing of a leopard's lower canine teeth. *From Brain, 1981 fig 221*

ratios, and the presence of carnivore tooth-marks. Carnivores usually leave characteristic chewing marks on bone, and are also known to consume a higher proportion of other carnivores than people do. His conclusions are that these caves originally served as carnivore lairs, and that the accumulated animal and hominid bones are the debris not from *Australopithecus'* meals but from those of large carnivores. The main culprits may have been hyaenas and various cats such as leopards and the extinct false sabretooth— *Dinofelis*. So, far from being a hunter, *Australopithecus* was being hunted. (Lawrence Straus; 1982, similarly using the carnivore-ungulate ratio, also suggests a carnivore role for Spanish Mousterian assemblages associated with Neanderthals. Neanderthals were apparently more dependent upon scavenging and opportunistic hunting than was modern human.)

The data from two Transvaal caves, Sterkfontein and Swartkrans, are especially interesting. Many of the hominid and antelope bones in these caves exhibit tooth marks and other signs of chewing, suggesting at the very least some degree of 'carnivore involvement'. The spacing of holes (33mm apart) in the parietal bones of an Australopithecine child's cranium (SK 54; fig. 5.1) at Swartkrans matches closely the spacing of the lower canine teeth of a leopard. Brain suggests that this damage could have been caused when a leopard (or juvenile of a larger carnivore) picked up by the head the child it had killed and dragged it to a secluded place.

Besides overall carnivore influence, Brain found some interesting changes occurring within these sites which point to the developing ascendancy of

5.2 Hominids versus carnivores as accumulators of bones. Brain's analysis of faunal remains from three layers at Sterkfontein, South Africa. Bones in layer 4 are associated with *Australopithecus africanus*, and bones in layer 5 with (?) *Homo*. The percentage composition of different groups of animals suggests that a change occurred between layers 4 and 5: *Australopithecus* may have been hunted, while *Homo* may have had greater control of the environment. *From Brain, 1981 fig 171*

hominid over animals. At Sterkfontein (fig. 5.2) Brain discovered important differences between level 4 and the much later (by 0.5–1 million years) overlying level 5. Besides fauna, level 4 contains an abundance of *Australopithecus africanus*, a gracile (i.e. with slender limb bones) form of the Australopithecine lineage. Only a few identifiable hominid fragments are known from level 5, and these are tentatively assigned to *Homo*, although numerous chopping tools are known from this layer. No tools have been reported from level 4. By comparing the faunal remains of levels 4 and 5 at Sterkfontein, Brain has drawn some interesting conclusions. Faunal changes seem to coincide with the disappearance of *Australopithecus* and the arrival of early tool-making *Homo*. For example, one significant change was the carnivore-ungulate ratio. This ratio is 48 per cent in level 4 of Sterkfontein—a relatively high value. (It is 37 per cent at Swartkrans level 1; inhabited by *Australopithecus robustus*.) According to Brain this value suggests carnivore hunting and scavenging. The ratio falls to 15 per cent in the overlying level 5 of Sterkfontein. (It is 12 per cent in level 2 at Swartkrans; which was also inhabited by *Homo*). This

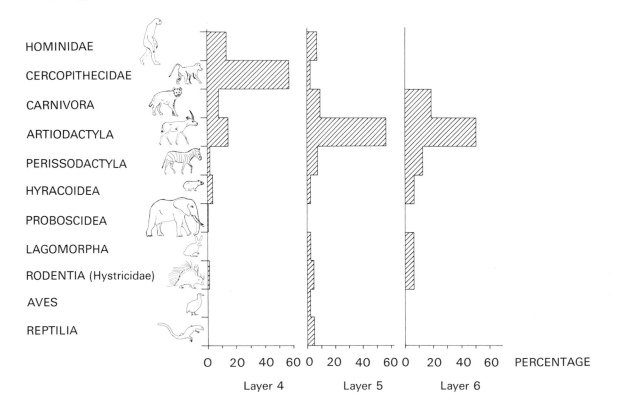

HOMINIDAE
CERCOPITHECIDAE
CARNIVORA
ARTIODACTYLA
PERISSODACTYLA
HYRACOIDEA
PROBOSCIDEA
LAGOMORPHA
RODENTIA (Hystricidae)
AVES
REPTILIA

0 20 40 60 0 20 40 60 0 20 40 60 PERCENTAGE

Layer 4   Layer 5   Layer 6

much lower ratio suggests that hominids (i.e. *Homo*) had appropriated the dominant position previously held by carnivores.

The Sterkfontein level 4 antelopes (mostly medium to large individuals) are predominantly juvenile, suggesting they had been predated (Vrba, 1975, and see below), presumably by large carnivores. In the overlying level 5, the proportion of juveniles is much lower, and antelopes were derived from a wide range of weight classes. At least one bone piece in the level 5 collection shows indisputable chop marks caused by a sharp-edged tool. This would make it likely that *Homo* was utilizing these animal bones for food. Was *Homo* hunting or scavenging? I shall discuss this difficult question below when I deal with some of the research carried out in East Africa.

Taken together the differences between lower and upper levels at Sterkfontein and Swartkrans suggest that, while scavenging carnivores such as large cats were mainly responsible for the bone accumulations in earlier times, *Homo*, now capable of manufacturing tools, was the primary agent in the later levels: *Homo* had become master of his security, previously threatened by the large carnivores. Increased intelligence and the possession of crude weapons may, Brain suggests, have tipped the balance of power in *Homo*'s favour. Despite this mastery over danger, these first people were still dependent upon the kills of other carnivores before they themselves could scavenge a meat meal.

So much for South African early hominids. Much work is also being undertaken in East Africa, where six different regions have now yielded altogether over 40 early Pleistocene sites (Isaac, 1983). They are in Olduvai gorge in Tanzania, Chesowanja, Olorgesailie and Koobi Fora in Kenya, and Melka Kunture and Gadeb in Ethiopia. They contain stone artefacts and significant concentrations of bones (?food debris) of the large African mammals. In several cases detailed studies of the associated animal bones have been undertaken—particularly at Olduvai, Olorgesailie and Koobi Fora.

The beginning of meat-eating, like the adoption of bipedality, is shrouded in mystery. Vegetable remains are scarce in the archaeological record, especially in the very early sites, so we have no means of quantifying their importance versus that of animals. A common assumption in archaeology is that the quest for meat played a dominant role in shaping the course of human evolution. But we still do not understand how and when meat-eating began (Klein, 1979). In late Pleistocene and recent sites animal bones are easily identified as food refuse. They are clearly associated with human activity such as hearths, shelters, discarded artefacts and so on. But, as one goes back to earlier stages of hominid development, the association with animal bones becomes less clear. As Richard Klein has pointed out to me, many early (Lower and Middle Pleistocene) sites are lakeside or streamside localities where the stratigraphic association between bones and artefacts could be merely coincidental.

Was meat being eaten? And given that it was, what was the nature of the hominid–animal relation— hunter or scavenger? So far we cannot answer these two questions for sure. In general, abundant remains of artefacts with bones of large mammals are strong evidence, but not proof, of a gastronomic association between early human and animals.

While it is difficult to discover whether the actual killing of these animals was done by early hominids, some research has considered what was being done (and how) with the resulting carcasses. Here (as in the southern African caves) the possible influences of both hominids and large carnivores such as lions and hyaenas have to be considered.

Several researchers working on East African material (Bunn, 1981; Potts and Shipman, 1981, for example) and using scanning electron microscopy have demonstrated that scratch marks found on large mammal bones were caused by stone tools. This is strong evidence for an association between stone artefacts and bones, rather than some kind of accidental, post-mortem association.

Pat Shipman (1983), however, cautions against taking cut-marks on animal bones as proof of meat-eating. In her opinion, cut-marks merely demonstrate that our hominid ancestors were using stone tools to remove tissues from carcasses. Cut-marks do not tell us what the hominids did with these tissues afterwards. For example early human's primary interest could have been in extracting sinews and skin for making bags. Henry Bunn's (1981) findings, however, include evidence not only of cutting, but of hammer-induced smashing of marrow bones, suggesting a gastronomic use.

More direct evidence for meat eating in those early times is hard to find, but two lines of investigation, admittedly tenuous, have been brought to bear on this matter. They are pathologies which derive from meat eating, and microwear studies of the associated stone tools.

Walker *et al.* (1982) microscopically examined sections of bones from a nearly complete *Homo erectus* skeleton from Koobi Fora dated to *c*1.6 million years. It showed signs of having suffered a chronic disorder typical of a diet too rich in vitamin A (hypervitaminosis). This can occur when excessive amounts of liver—especially carnivore liver—are eaten. Hypervitaminosis of this kind was encountered by early polar explorers who ate polar bear and husky dog liver.

Keeley and Toth (1981) examined the wear patterning on stone implements dated to *c*1.5 million years also from Koobi Fora. In their opinion patterning resembles that experimentally produced by cutting meat (as well as other substances). Both these studies suggest then that a dietary shift may have occurred by 1.5 million years ago from the Australopithecines' predominantly fruit diet to one which also included some meat (i.e. an omnivorous diet) in *Homo erectus*. But was this meat scavenged or hunted?

EARLY MAN: HUNTER OR SCAVENGER?

Elizabeth Vrba (1975) and Shipman (1983), generalizing from other mammals, have proposed criteria for differentiating bone assemblages acquired by hunting from those acquired by scavenging: age, prey size and prey species habits.

Many of the animals which are hunted are juveniles. But carcasses of animals being scavenged, by hominids say, are less likely to include so many juveniles, as many of the young animals are rapidly consumed by predators, before hominids could have arrived at the scene of the kill.

Hunters are more likely to concentrate upon a restricted range of prey size. Since scavenging implies random, opportunistic sampling, animals scavenged are likely to vary in size, but tend towards the larger end of the size scale. This is because smaller prey (like juveniles) caught by hyaenas for example, are completely consumed and disappear in a very short time (Kruuk, 1972:126).

Early hunters would have 'targeted' on a single type of animal, while scavengers are more likely to exploit prey derived from a broad range of habits.

Shipman looked at the age and size composition of the animals represented in the collections of animal bones with cut-marks from Olduvai. The animals there showed a broad range of sizes from small bovid to giraffe, but skewed towards the large sizes (what are termed size class III or larger). They include bovids, equids, and giraffids—which have varied habits and come from a variety of habitats. There were very few juveniles, although the problem of small samples, and poor preservation of juvenile bones makes it difficult to apply the 'age' criterion. None the less, Shipman suggests that 'scavenging as a dominant mode of meat procurement seems highly probable' among the early hominids at Olduvai. What do the cut-marks tell us about carcass treatment?

The cut-marks on Olduvai animal bones were mostly on midshafts rather than around joints—a distribution suggesting that hominids were removing meat from the carcasses as rapidly as possible. Disarticulating a leg (which would leave cut-marks around the joint), and running off with it, would have put hominids at great risk from predators. Fire is the best way to keep other predators such as hyaenas and lions at bay. Lack of it must have had serious implications for early hominids processing carcasses and storing meat.

The earliest possible (and controversial) evidence for fire comes from Chesowanja dated to 1.4 million years ago, and consists of lumps of baked clay associated with Oldowan artefacts (see Gowlett *et al.* 1981). The next earliest evidence does not occur for another million years—at Zhoukoudian (Chou Kou Tien) half a million years ago. In Africa, secure evidence for fire comes from numerous Middle Stone Age (*c*200,000–30,000 years ago) sites and consists of fossil hearths (Klein, 1983). Cooking, then, was perhaps a later invention.

To summarize work in South and East Africa: *Australopithecus* (who may have scavenged carcasses) was himself often subjected to predation by canivores like large cats (and ?hyaenas too). In later periods, tool-making hominids were no longer predated, but were able to defend themselves. Food procurement at this early stage in the evolution of our ancestors was probably by scavenging.

Working in East Africa, Pat Shipman (1983) has postulated a shift from scavenging to hunting. This shift may have occurred between one and two million years ago. The contemporary fossil record then reveals three striking changes which took place:

(1) *Homo erectus* appeared with its larger, more complex brain, and bigger body.

(2) Fire may have come under hominid control.

(3) The more sophisticated and varied Acheulean stone-tool industry was developed.

These changes would have improved hominids' ability to keep a carcass once it was obtained, and may therefore have triggered the shift to hunting. But in truth we still have little knowledge of precisely when early humans started hunting. A guess would be some time after one million years ago (see also Blumenberg, 1979).

Hunting must have placed a great premium on cooperation among humans. It is difficult to imagine the killing of large mammals without highly coordinated, cooperative action among people (Washburn and Lancaster, 1968).

One of the earliest East African sites studied with a view to establishing whether hominids, rather than other carnivores, hunted and butchered is Olorgesailie in Kenya. This Acheulean hand-axe site is about 60km southwest of Nairobi. It was first discovered by Louis and Mary Leakey, and subsequently excavated by Glyn Isaac (1977), who dates it between 700,000 and 400,000 years ago. Despite the absence of hominid bones, it was probably inhabited by *Homo erectus*. Animal bones and artefacts were found in a horizon interpreted as a small watercourse or channel. The dominant animal present in the faunal assemblage is the extinct giant gelada baboon, *Theropithecus oswaldi*, a primate which must have weighed about 65kg (about the size of a female gorilla). Shipman, Bosler and Davis (1981) have studied the Olorgesailie *Theropithecus* bones and have bravely addressed the difficult question of whether the hominids there were responsible for hunting and butchery.

Primates are rare in the fossil record, so such an abundance of primate bones already suggested to Shipman *et al.* that they had been hunted (but by whom?), and representation of all parts of the body further ruled out the possibility that these bones had accumulated via water currents. The question they then asked is who hunted and butchered these remains?

Study of the abundant teeth provided an age 'profile' of the *Theropithecus* remains. Of the 90 individuals represented only 14 were adults (that is with the third molar in wear). Such an abundance of

juveniles is yet another hint that *Theropithecus* was hunted.

To determine whether the Olorgesailie bones had been butchered by hominids or by carnivore activity, Shipman *et al.* examined bone frequencies and the manner of breakage of Olorgesailie bones, and compared them with bones from earlier sites in East Africa where non-hominid carnivores were assumed to have been responsible. First, the frequencies of different parts of the skeleton in these two kinds of assemblage were quite different, and second, certain kinds of breakage pattern were observed at Olorgesailie. One particularly impressive breakage feature was damage to the anterior surface of the proximal femur in the form of 'oval pits'. As many as 92 per cent of the Olorgesailie *Theropithecus* femora had suffered this kind of damage. Another breakage feature they observed was one in which the inferior surface of the calcaneum had been removed.

Despite the absence of cut marks on the Olorgesailie *Theropithecus* bones, Shipman *et al.* seem fairly certain that hominids there were dismembering carcasses using hand axes. Parts of the anatomy which are consistently absent were presumably smashed into unidentifiable fragments. The hominids while not using their tools with 'surgical precision' were butchering the baboon carcasses effectively.

Having established that hominids probably butchered the *Theropithecus* carcasses, evidence for hominid, rather than non-hominid hunting rests on evidence which they admit is slender—that all parts of the body are represented. Modern carnivores are known to destroy body parts differentially, and the body-part frequencies of *Theropithecus* from earlier East African sites (presumed not to have been hunted by hominids) showed a different pattern to that shown by the Olorgesailie collection.

If within the last one million years our ancestors were hunting large mammals, can we deduce something about how they performed this activity: did our ancestors become more adept in the course of time? We now have to jump from the Middle to the Late Pleistocene of Africa for archaeofaunal evidence of human's hunting capability.

Richard Klein has studied faunal assemblages in South Africa, dating from 130,000 years ago to the present. This is one of the few regions in the world with a long and continuous archaeofaunal sequence. It spans two major culture periods known in South African archaeology as 'Middle Stone Age' and 'Late

Stone Age'. The Middle Stone Age began about 200,000 years ago. Middle Stone Age assemblages are characterized by large stone flakes and blades. Ornaments are unknown and bone tools rare. Late Stone Age assemblages contain smaller implements, items of personal adornment and bone tools—in brief a more sophisticated tool kit. The Late Stone Age probably first appeared between 30,000 and 40,000 years ago, and people making Late Stone Age artefacts were still living in South Africa when Europeans arrived there in the sixteenth century. Klein suggests that people's hunting capability became more effective during this 130,000 year period. Two aspects of his work are revealing: (a) the relative abundance of different species and (b) the age composition of each species culled.

SPECIES ABUNDANCE

Some especially dangerous species (the ferocious warthog or bushpig, or both) are better represented in Late Stone Age sites, while less dangerous species (the docile eland in particular) are relatively more common in the earlier Middle Stone Age ones. And there is no evidence for any change in the environment which could have brought about this faunal change. Klein suggests that Late Stone Age people in South Africa possessed the technology to kill from a distance—perhaps they used sophisticated snares, bows and arrows or a spear thrower. For example, Klein (pers. comm.) cites some artefactual evidence to support this thesis. Artefacts interpretable as parts of composite arrows are known only in the Late Stone Age.

AGE-RELATED MORTALITY PATTERNS

Besides listing the different species in his late Pleistocene-Holocene sequence, and counting how common each species was (Chapter 3) for several of the more abundantly represented species, Klein has reconstructed their mortality patterns. This he did by measuring dental crown heights (Chapter 1). Zoologists who have made detailed studies of predators and their prey now understand what the probabilities of survival are for each age group in a herd of animals. These data constitute 'life-tables'. For example,

juvenile and senile ungulates are most vulnerable to predation, while the prime adults are better able to defend themselves against predators. Klein's work suggests an interesting analogy between this situation in the animal world and early hunting peoples.

He (Klein, 1979) recognized two basic patterns (fig. 5.3). The first was one in which Stone Age hunters concentrated upon young animals, less than one year old, and older adults towards the end of their lifespan, and took few prime adults. This pattern, which is termed an attritional one, characterized the blue antelope, roan antelope, Cape buffalo, and recently extinct giant buffalo (*Pelorovis antiquus*). The second pattern was one in which hunters took relatively fewer young and more prime adults. This was observed in the bastard hartebeest and especially the eland. This second pattern closely reflects the age structure of the live herds—with a greater proportion of young adults of reproductive age, and is termed a catastrophic pattern.

How does Klein interpret these two very different age-related hunting patterns?

The first pattern closely resembles that observed for animal predators such as lions preying on Cape buffalo (Sinclair, 1977). Adult buffaloes are very large. A herd can be quite aggressive and will charge attacking predators like lions, which are usually deterred as a result. Hence the scarcity of prime-age buffaloes in lion kills. Very young buffalo are small, slow and ungainly and are therefore particularly vulnerable, as are the very old. The very young and old are therefore taken in numbers out of proportion to their representation in the living herd. The similarity between lion kill samples and human kill samples from Middle and Late Stone Age assemblages suggests, according to Klein, that Stone Age hunters were 'constrained by the same factors that constrain lions when they prey upon buffalo', i.e. they were hunting mainly very young and very old adults. Buffalo and blue and roan antelope were presumably hunted individually by stalking.

What of the second (i.e. catastrophic) pattern observed for the eland and bastard hartebeest? Their mortality pattern closely reflects the age structure of complete living herds; that is, with a majority of prime adults. Klein's explanation is that herds of these animals were driven over a cliff. The bastard hartebeest and eland are known to be especially amenable to driving, and whole groups might easily be trapped in this manner. Klein also cites pictorial evidence for

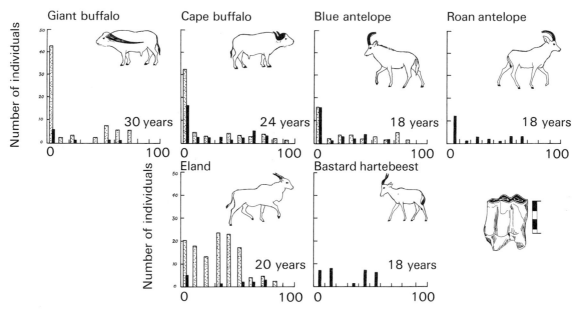

5.3 Age classes of bovids culled by Middle Stone Age people at Klasies River Mouth (stippled) and Late Stone Age people at Nelson Bay Cave (black). These age distributions are deduced from dental crown heights and calculated as a percentage of lifespan. There are two main categories: (1) For buffaloes, blue and roan antelope—relatively few prime adults were culled. (2) For eland and bastard hartebeest, a higher proportion of prime adults were culled. Klein suggests that the differences between these two categories reflect different hunting strategies. *From Klein, 1979*

this kind of hunting strategy: a Later Stone Age rock-painting in the Transkei which depicts eland being driven over a cliff by aboriginal hunters.

Similar interpretations have been made of natural (i.e. non-cultural) assemblages in palaeontology. Voorhies (1969) studied a faunal assemblage containing an extinct pronghorn antelope *Merycodus furcatus* from a late Miocene (c12 million years old) locality in Nebraska. Its age-profile closely resembled that of a living herd of antelope. Voorhies' interpretation was that the herd had died suddenly in some catastrophe such as a flash flood.

FORAGING INTENSITY

Apart from large mammals, South African prehistoric people exploited marine resources such as shellfish, fish and flying sea birds. Klein (1979) has some evidence that limpets were exploited more intensively in Late Stone Age than Middle Stone Age times.

The limpet, a common inhabitant of rocky shores, grows like most molluscs by accreting calcareous matter to the edge of its shell. Older limpets have larger shells. Assuming that people prefer larger limpets, continuous heavy foraging will lead to a decrease in the average size of the limpets.

The coastal sites of Sea Harvest and Hoedjies Punt are 120 km north of Cape Town and probably date to the end of the last Interglacial c70,000 years ago. Klein found that fossil limpet shells (*Patella granatina*) at these two sites were large—similar in size to limpets found today on the relatively unexploited coast (fig. 5.4). However fossil limpets from the Late Stone Age sites of Elands Bay cave and Paternoster, which date between 8000 and 1000 years ago, were considerably smaller. This, Klein suggests, indicates more intensive limpet exploitation in Late Stone Age times, perhaps the result of an increased human population.

Clark and Straus (1983) also found a probable relation between foraging intensity and limpet size at the northern Spanish site of la Riera; here numerous edible sea shells, mostly limpets, were recovered. During the Solutrean and early Magdalenian periods (18,000–13,000 bc) the 'average maximum diameter'

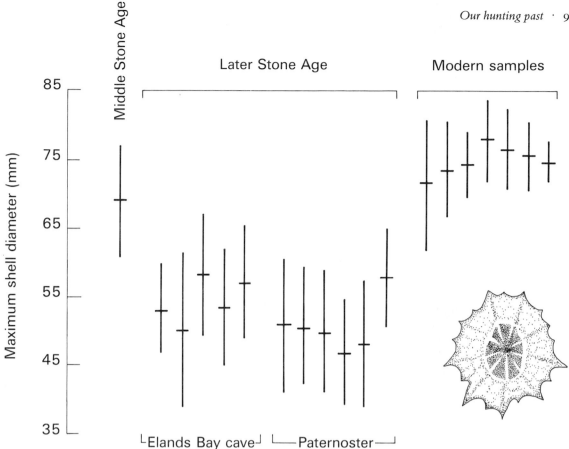

5.4 Foraging intensity at coastal sites in South Africa. Limpets, *Patella granatina*, from the Middle Stone Age (Sea Harvest Midden) were larger than limpets from the Later Stone Age (Elands Bay Cave and Paternoster). People at Sea Harvest were collecting shellfish less intensively. Horizontal line = mean, vertical line = one standard deviation either side of the mean. *From Klein, 1979*

of the limpets was *c*38–46mm, and the ratio of shell-weight to mammal-bone weight was relatively low. By the Azilian and Asturian periods (*c*12,000–5000 bc), limpet 'average maximum diameter' had fallen to a mere 22–28mm, but the ratio of shell to bone had become very high. Both limpet size and shell abundance suggest increased exploitation of molluscs. But during these later times, the rise in sea level would have brought the sea shore nearer to the site (perhaps from a distance of 10km to 2–3km). Whether the increased exploitation of marine resources (sparid fish, and the smaller coastal species of limpet, *Patella intermedia* too) simply reflects this changed proximity to the coast or whether it was due to population increase (or perhaps both?) is a matter of debate (see for example Bailey, 1983).

EVOLUTION OF MODERN HUMANS: THEIR IMPACT UPON THE ENVIRONMENT

So far we have discussed early humans and their hominid ancestors of the Pliocene and Pleistocene periods. During this time people evolved both biologically—for example, brain size increased—and culturally: they became better tool-makers. According to Klein's faunal evidence from South Africa these changes are reflected in the game species they hunted: they became more sophisticated hunters.

THE PEOPLING OF NEW WORLDS

After Africa and Eurasia, Australia was the first major landmass to be peopled. This settlement happened at least 30,000, perhaps 45,000 years ago, and involved a sea-crossing of some 70km. The Americas were next.

While early humans lacked the necessary cultural sophistication to colonize the harsh regions of north-eastern Siberia, modern people *Homo sapiens sapiens* (around 40–50,000 years ago) had the cultural and intellectual wherewithal to colonize successfully Siberia—the land adjacent to Alaska. From Siberia they were able to cross the Bering straits, exposed as dry land during the last glacial maximum. While Alaska may have been populated before 10,000 bc, peopling of the rest of America had to await the opening of an ice-free corridor east of the Rockies between the Cordilleran and Laurentide ice sheets. Some scholars, however, suggest that the Americas may have been peopled earlier—a subject which is still hotly debated. Who was it that settled the New World?

The earliest and best-dated human remains in North America belong to the 'Clovis Fluted Point' culture, with its characteristically shaped projectile points (Haynes, 1980). This is dated to between 9500 and 9000 bc, and is followed by the Folsom culture with its 'Folsom points' of 9000–8000 bc. Clovis assemblages are remarkably similar, with few local variations in tool types, suggesting their rapid spread. Cultural diversity in the New World did not increase until after 9000 bc, when early Americans were presumably settling down to a more sedentary way of life. A close link is proposed between the Clovis culture and its Old World antecedents—there are similarities to sites in Siberia (Haynes, 1980). Within a millennium or two both North and South America were inhabited by humans.

In the Mediterranean, the first evidence of peopling of islands such as Cyprus, Crete, Malta, Corsica and the Balearics does not come until after 7000 bc (see the end of this chapter).

Madagascar was peopled *c* AD 500, and New Zealand, which was the last Pacific ocean island to become inhabited by humans, was settled by Polynesians between AD 750 and 1000 (Bellwood, 1978).

THE COLONIZATION OF NEW LANDS: PLEISTOCENE EXTINCTIONS

The discovery and settlement by Stone Age people of hitherto uninhabited lands, in particular Australia and America, leads us to a most controversial subject in Quaternary palaeontology—the apparently sud-den extinction of so many species of large animals—mostly large mammals and large flightless birds. (Those whose estimated body weight exceeded 44kg are often classed as 'megafauna'.)

WHAT WAS LOST AND WHERE

As long ago as 1839, Charles Darwin reflected on the near-recent quadrupeds of America. He wrote that that continent must formerly

> have swarmed with great monsters, like the southern parts of Africa, but now we find only the tapir, guanaco, armadillo, and capybara; mere pigmies compared to the antecedent races. The greater number, if not all, of these extinct quadrupeds lived at a very recent period; and many of them were contemporaries of the existing molluscs. Since their loss, no very great physical changes can have taken place in the nature of the country. What then has exterminated so many living creatures? (Darwin, 1839:210)

The extinct North American animals (figs. 5.5 and 5.6) included the Shasta ground sloth (*Nothrotheriops*), well known for its dung deposits. When fully grown it probably weighed between 135 and 180 kg. The larger Jefferson's ground sloth (*Megalonyx jeffersoni*) was about the size of an ox. Remains of this animal were first discussed at a meeting of the American Philosophical Society in 1797, an event which marked the beginning of vertebrate palaeontology in North America (Kurtén and Anderson, 1980). Sabre-tooth cats, scimitar cat (*Homotherium*), giant beaver (*Castoroides*) the size of a black bear, various horses, peccaries, the North American camel (*Camelops*), a long-legged llama (*Hemiauchenia*), a mountain deer (*Navahoceros*), several pronghorned antelopes (*Capromeryx*, *Stockoceros* and *Tetrameryx*), mastodont (*Mammut*) and mammoth (*Mammuthus*)—these are just some of the 34 genera of large mammals which became extinct by 9,000 bc at the close of the Wisconsinian (last) Ice Age. This represents two-thirds of North America's large mammal genera.

Extinctions had of course occurred in earlier periods in North America (as elsewhere), and some authors have pointed out (e.g. Webb, 1984) that the late Miocene extinctions were even more extensive than the final Pleistocene ones. However, we cannot accurately date these Miocene extinctions and so the rate at which they occurred is unknown. Within the Pleistocene, however, the extinctions which occurred

5.5 Artists' reconstructions of some of the North American Late Pleistocene mammals which may have become extinct as a result of overhunting by Palaeoindians. (a) New World sabretooth, *Smilodon*; (b) long-nosed peccary, *Mylohyus*; (c) a four-horned Pronghorn antelope, *Stockoceros*; (d) flat-headed peccary, *Platygonus*; (e) giant beaver, *Castoroides*; (f) horse, *Hippidium*; (g) Shasta ground sloth, *Nothrotheriops*; (h) mastodont, *Mammut*; and (i) the North American camel, *Camelops*. The scale for each animal is one metre. From drawings in Martin and Guilday in Martin and Wright (1967) and from drawings by Peter Murray in Anderson in Martin and Klein (1984). *Courtesy Paul Martin and the University of Arizona Press*

5.6 Artist Charles Knight's reconstruction of a Pleistocene scene around a waterhole at Rancho la Brea, Los Angeles, USA. The animals included are giant ground sloth, sabretooth tiger, vulture, mammoth and dire wolf. *Courtesy Department Library Services, American Museum of Natural History. Neg. No. 39442*

*c*11,000 years ago (i.e. in the Rancholabrean period) were drastic compared to those which had occurred in the preceeding 3 million years. Compare the loss of these 34 genera to the 10 genera lost during the Blancan age, 7 during the Irvingtonian, and 3 during the pre-Wisconsinian Rancholabrean (Spaulding, 1983).

In South America some 46 genera became extinct at around the same time. This was nearly 80 per cent of its large mammal fauna. South America lost animals like *Glyptodon*, a heavily armoured and clumsy edentate (the order of mammals which includes sloths, armadillos and anteaters) whose body and upper limbs were encased in an immense turtle-like armour plating covered with horny scales, and *Megatherium*, a giant ground sloth, which attained a length of 6m. (This was first described by Cuvier in 1795.) Some other South American animals included a New World sabretooth cat, *Smilodon*; a giant capybara, *Neochoerus*; South American horses, *Hippidion* and *Onohippidium*; the elephant-like gomphothere *Cuvieronius*, and *Toxodon*—sometimes described as a giant guinea pig built like a short-legged rhinoceros with hippo-like habits.

In Australia by the end of the Pleistocene, 19 genera, or 86 per cent of the megafauna (comprising large marsupials, reptiles and birds) became extinct (fig. 5.7). Most were probably slow-moving and therefore vulnerable to newly arrived hunters. Many

belonged to the kangaroo and wallaby family (Macropodidae). *Protemnodon*, a giant wallaby, was larger than any living kangaroo. *Procoptodon* was a massive 3m tall kangaroo with short, broad face. With its upturned lower incisor teeth, and huge furrowed molars, it probably browsed on shrubs and trees. The rhino-sized *Diprotodon* was the largest. The Diprotodons were browsers with the build of wombats. Most marsupial families lost at least one giant form. There was, for example, a giant wombat *Phascolonus gigas*—twice the size of a modern wombat and weighing half a ton or more. There was a giant echidna *Zaglossus*. A predator *Thylacoleo*, or marsupial lion, was as big as a leopard, had big powerful teeth and an enormous claw on each front foot. There were huge reptiles and birds too. A massive goanna, *Megalania*, was 6–9m long, larger than any living lizard in the world; and a flightless bird *Genyornis* was probably similar to the extinct moa of New Zealand. About one third of the large Australian animals that existed 50,000 years ago were extinct by 13,000 bc, or perhaps even earlier: according to Murray (1984) the Australian fauna was essentially 'modern' by 30,000 years ago.

New Zealand lost its giant flightless moas, and Madagascar its elephant birds and giant lemurs. Seven genera of primates disappeared from Madagascar. They were all quite large and probably diurnal (Dewar, 1984). The largest was *Megaladapis edwardsi* with an estimated male body-weight of between 50 and 100kg. The smallest extinct species overlapped the size range of the largest living species, but all other extinct forms were larger than the surviving lemurs. Some of the extinct ones had locomotor patterns unknown among living lemurs, such as 'terrestrial

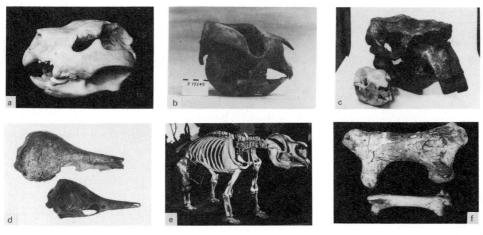

5.7 Some Pleistocene animals of Australia. (a) Skull of the carnivorous Marsupial lion, *Thylacoleo carnifex*. (b) Skull of the giant short-faced kangaroo, *Simosthenurus occidentalis* (Late Pleistocene, southern South Australia: scale in cm). (c) Skulls of the giant wombat, *Phascolonus gigas*, compared with the living hairy-nosed wombat, *Lasiorhinus latifrons*. (d) Skulls of the giant echidna, *Zaglossus ramsayi* (Pleistocene, South Australia), and the living echidna, *Tachyglossus aculeatus*. (e) Mounted skeleton of the largest known marsupial, the rhino-sized herbivorous, *Diprotodon optatum*. Specimen from the Pleistocene at Lake Callabonna, South Australia. (f) Femora of the living emu, *Dromaius novaehollandiae* (left), and the extinct *Genyornis newtoni* (right) from the Pleistocene of South Australia. *Photographs by Neville Pledge and R. Ruehle, courtesy South Australian Museum*

quadrupedalism' and 'ponderous vertical climbing' like the koala bear. These would have been particularly vulnerable to human hunting. Those that survived are generally nocturnal or small diurnal tree-livers. Other animals which Madagascar lost include two genera of large flightless 'elephant birds' (the largest resembling an ostrich), a pygmy hippopotamus, a local form of aardvark, and giant tortoises.

Northern Eurasia lost only a few genera: the woolly rhinoceros, woolly mammoth, straight-tusked elephant, giant deer, bison and hippopotamus. Similarly, Africa lost only seven genera.

THE CAUSE: PEOPLE OR CLIMATE?

Early nineteenth-century speculations on the causes of Pleistocene extinctions invoked events like Noah's flood and glaciers. Today, opinions still differ as to the cause of these extinctions. This lack of consensus partly reflects twentieth-century views of early people: 'noble savage' or 'nature's sole mistake'. Some hold people alone responsible. Some implicate changes in the environment resulting from the last Ice Age and its abrupt termination. Others suggest that both humans and climate affected the Pleistocene faunas: an already stressed ecosystem being suddenly set upon by sophisticated hunters.

The evidence varies in both quantity and quality. While North America and Europe have long been scrutinized, serious archaeofaunal research in South America and Madagascar is only just beginning.

Just how great either factor was depends on which region is considered. Humans probably played a dominant role in the demise of New Zealand's moas, and of Madagascar's giant lemurs and flightless birds. But extreme dry conditions may well have brought about the extinction of Australia's giant marsupials.

In both Australia and North America it is difficult to choose between the two sides in the human versus climate debate. This is because both climatic change and peoples' entry into these continents probably occurred simultaneously with the megafaunal extinctions. Radiocarbon dates so far available in North America suggest that the arrival of humans and the final Pleistocene extinctions were synchronous processes (Meltzer and Mead, 1983). But reliable dates are all too rare, so it is still impossible to determine whether or not extinctions coincided precisely with peoples' appearance in North America. Correlation is one thing, cause and effect quite another. Indeed, in North America, it was ultimately climate—lowered sea level, followed by final Pleistocene warming—that permitted people (a) to cross the Bering land bridge and (b) to traverse southwards through the ice-free corridor east of the Rockies. *Quaternary Extinctions* edited by Paul Martin and Richard Klein (1984) brings together a wide spectrum of opinions on this subject.

MEGAFAUNAL EXTINCTIONS: THE CASE AGAINST CLIMATE

Dale Guthrie (1984) argues that late- and post-Pleistocene climatic change was sufficiently great to have caused widespread extinctions of many land animals. In his opinion the last glacial-postglacial warming up resulted in present relatively severe conditions, quite unlike any which existed before in the Pleistocene. (He was referring primarily to North America.) The change was very abrupt; it acted as an 'unparalleled jolt' on the fauna. The vast North American grasslands with their reduced diversity of plant species developed—perhaps for the first time. These grasslands provided ideal conditions for animals like the bison, whose post-Pleistocene range expanded considerably. However, animals like elephants, ground sloths and equids, which have less advanced digestive systems (they do not ruminate) need a more diverse diet. They were unable to cope on a diet of few species of grass, and so became extinct. Guthrie also suggests that increased seasonality in the Holocene led to a more restricted growth season. Besides causing extinction, worsening of the environment would also explain why a number of lineages of large mammals not only became smaller, but also exhibit a decrease in the size of their antlers, tusks and horns. (Chapter 3).

While climatic change began earlier and continued later, Guthrie cites evidence that the main shift occurred with great rapidity between 10,000 and 9000 bc (the very same millennium which saw the intrusion of the Clovis culture into North America). King and Saunders (1984) link the dwarfing and ultimate extinction in North America of the mastodont (*Mammut*) with the collapse of the spruce forests between 10,000 and 8000 bc. King and Saunders believe that the mastodonts could not adapt to these environmental changes, because unlike previous Pleistocene vegetation changes, the one of 10,000 bc was too sudden, and it occurred at a rate that mastodont adaptability just could not tolerate.

David Horton's (1984) 'arid expansion model' seeks to explain the severe wave of extinctions in Australia as having resulted from the outward expansion of the central Australian desert. People probably first arrived in Australia in 31,000 bc, perhaps even 45,000 bc. But the peak of large-mammal extinction does not, according to some evidence which Horton cites, appear to have occurred until *c*24–13,000 bc, when a period of extreme aridity hit Australia. Water holes would have dried up—a situation reminiscent of African droughts. Horton reckons that no areas in Australia or even Tasmania were left where the majority of large Pleistocene marsupials could have found refuge, and those that did were able to do so only after undergoing a reduction of body size. The whole continent became one vast dry desert. However, the red kangaroo, well adapted to dry conditions, not only survived, but expanded its range. While admittedly rather meagre, there is some evidence for a possible catastrophe having occurred to the fauna in Australia.

A bone-bed containing the remains of 10,000 giant extinct animals was found at 'Lancefield swamp' in southeastern Australia (Gillespie *et al.*, 1978). Most belonged to *Macropus titan*, a kangaroo which must have been twice the size of the living grey kangaroo, and 7 per cent belonged to *Protemnodon anak*. Analysis of the state of eruption and wear of the teeth revealed that 80 per cent of the *Macropus* were over 7 years old and only 8 per cent less than 2 years old. The scarcity of young animals suggests a population in which breeding had ceased for several years, owing to drought conditions. Interpretation of the Lancefield swamp site is conjectural. But there are two points that are most important for the extinction debate: (a) the swamp contains associated stone artefacts and (b) it has provided two ^{14}c dates of 24,000 bc—7000 years after the earliest record for people in Australia. If the artefacts (and there are only two of them) really are associated with the assemblage and if the dates are correct, then extinction by 'overkill' along the lines Martin proposes for America would seem unlikely.

MEGAFAUNAL EXTINCTIONS: THE CASE AGAINST HUMANS

The great nineteenth-century palaeontologist Sir Richard Owen first studied the Pleistocene mammals of Australia. He (Owen, 1877) could find no evidence for climatic change to account for the disappearance of the large Australian marsupials, and wrote that the hostile agency of man must have brought about

> the final extinction . . . of all the characteristic mammals which happened to surpass in bulk the still existing, swift retreating, saltatorial and nocturnal kangaroos.

Paul Martin has long argued that people were responsible for late- and post–Pleistocene land-animal extinctions. During the last 20 years he has developed a model whereby the large Pleistocene mammals in regions previously uninhabited by humans were suddenly subjected to heavy and very efficient predation by a rapidly growing population of hunters. This is his overkill-by-'blitzkrieg' hypothesis (fig. 5.8). His case is based upon the following seven observations:

(1) The mammals which became extinct at the end of the Pleistocene had all survived preceding climatic changes—there were at least six cold-warm or arid-wet cycles. An unresolved question is whether these earlier fluctuations were as drastic as the final Pleistocene one. In Martin's opinion some at least were (although Guthrie maintains that they were not). If Martin is correct, then the latest Pleistocene fauna (i.e. the Rancholabrean fauna of North America) should have been well adapted to such environmental perturbations. Why then, Martin asks, did the last glacial-postglacial climatic change but not the previous climatic changes bring about such drastic changes in the fauna? The only event unique to the period around 9000 bc in North America, when extinction occurred, was the arrival of prehistoric big-game hunters with their 'Clovis' culture (fig. 5.9).

(2) Examine the last 3.5 million years of North American palaeontology, and it is plain that extinction was not across the board. Larger mammals tended to suffer extinction at a much higher rate than smaller ones such as rodents at the end of the Pleistocene. For example, in North America losses include three genera of elephants, six of giant edentates (ground sloths for example), 15 of ungulates and various giant rodents and carnivores. Two-thirds of the Rancholabrean (final Pleistocene) fauna disappeared leaving bison, musk-ox, wapiti, moose, mountain goat and sheep, deer and pronghorn antelope to represent the 'native' fauna of the continent (Mosimann and Martin, 1975). Vance Haynes (1984) has studied several faunal sequences in

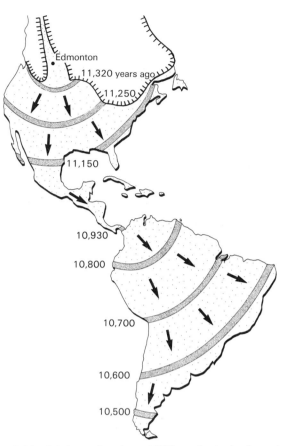

5.8 Martin's 'megafaunal overkill' hypothesis. At the end of the last Ice Age, hunting peoples arrived in North America, and soon attained a critical density. This led to the extinction of many species of large animals. A 'front' of hunters advanced southwards. This advance commenced at the southern end of the ice-free corridor near present-day Edmonton and by one to three millennia later had reached southern South America. *From Martin, 1973*

the American south west, and notes that megafaunal extinction between 9500 and 8500 bc coincides very closely with the age of the Clovis culture, which is dated to the period between 9500 and 9000 bc. In Haynes' words, 'the stratigraphic coincidence of the first visible evidence of hunters and the last skeletons of the . . . megafauna is intriguing'. Mead (1986) has produced two radiocarbon dates of 9210 bc and 9068 bc for the disappearance from Arizona of Harrington's mountain goat and the Shasta ground sloth—both of these dates coincide very closely with the Clovis culture.

There are a dozen or so well documented cases of such an association between skeletons of extinct

5.9 Palaeoindians hunting *Camelops*, the North American Pleistocene camel. *Painting by Jay Matternes, courtesy National Geographic Society (c)*

animals and cultural debris of their supposed destroyers. Eleven southwestern and western US localities are known where mammoth remains are in firm association with human artefacts dated between 9200 and 9000 bc (Saunders, 1980). Saunders suggests that single family units of mammoths in North America were 'confronted, contained, and catastrophically cropped by Clovis hunters'. Clovis people were clearly subsisting on big game with a marked emphasis on mammoth and bison. Where animal remains are present, all Clovis sites have mammoth, and many Clovis bone tools are made from bone and ivory of that animal. At kill sites, mammoth carcasses are only partially disarticulated and only a few limbs removed, indicating only partial utilization. Bison carcasses were often more dismembered suggesting more thorough butchering and utilization of meat (Haynes, 1980). One example is Naco in southern Arizona. Bones of a mammoth were found associated with eight Clovis Fluted points (possibly spearheads; Haury *et al.*, 1953). The points were located between the skull base and fore-part of the rib cage. Perhaps this was a mammoth that got away only to die shortly afterwards? (Haynes, 1980).

At the nearby Lehner Ranch site, 13 projectiles (mainly Clovis Fluted points), eight butchering tools and charcoal from two fires were found among the remains of nine immature mammoths, and bones of horse, tapir and bison (Haury *et al.* 1959). One of the Clovis points was lodged between the ribs of a young mammoth. The Lehner assemblage rests on a fossil stream bed, and has provided a date of 9–10,000 bc. The stream may have served as a mammoth trap. Indeed, most of the mammoth kills took place in low ground at springs, along a creek, or in a pond, suggesting ambushing at a watering place (Haynes, 1980).

Larry Agenbroad (1984) has collated some 48 dated localities of late mammoth finds in North America. He shows that from a centre of earlier successful mammoth kills (more or less coincident with the supposed point of entry of humans into North America), kill sites of younger date diffuse outwards in all directions from that centre.

(3) In Africa, Europe and Asia—continents which had a long history of man-animal relationships—megafaunal extinction appears to have been much less marked in terms of numbers of genera disappearing. In temperate parts of Europe and Asia four late glacial genera of large mammals were lost: mammoth (*Mammuthus*), woolly rhinoceros (*Coelodonta*), giant deer (*Megaceros*), and musk-ox (*Ovibos*). Animals there would have had time to adapt to peoples' improvement of hunting techniques. This improvement would, in the course of the Eurasian Pleistocene, have had a gradual selective effect on the fauna there. Species unable to withstand human predation would have had a million years or more to adapt or go extinct.

The animals which did survive in North America such as bison, deer and musk-ox, were Eurasian in origin. They were conditioned to people and are characterized by erratic migratory movements and gracile build—both attributes favouring their ability to withstand onslaught by human hunters.

(4) In Madagascar and New Zealand, where there is no doubt that humans arrived late, faunal extinctions coincide with or follow the arrival of humans. Extinctions occurred quite suddenly, at a time when there is no evidence for any natural (i.e. environmental) change.

Radiocarbon dates from sites in Madagascar show that extinctions there were completed by 900 years ago. Pastoralists are thought to have first arrived, probably from Borneo, certainly no earlier than the first century AD, perhaps a few centuries later. Robert Dewar (1984) suggests that it was some hunting and forest-burning, but mainly competition from introduced livestock (cattle, sheep and goats) which was responsible for extinctions.

In New Zealand, midden remains of moa bones suggest people were voracious predators of the moas. Radiocarbon dates from sites in South Island show that they were occupied earlier in the north than in the south. Trotter and McCulloch (1984) envisage a 'moving peak' of moa hunting 800 years ago gradually becoming more recent to about 500 years ago in the far south (fig. 5.10). This would, if on a smaller scale, fit in well with Paul Martin's prehistoric overkill model for North America, although the longer time of 300 years is easily explained. Unlike the Palaeoindians, prehistoric New Zealanders also grew crops and exploited the abundant coastal resources. They did not need to move so rapidly.

(5) Extinctions were not simultaneous (fig. 5.11). They happened at different times in different regions: mammoths have not been recorded in China after 18,000 bc (Liu and Li, 1984) but in North America we know they survived until 9000 bc. In other words mammoths became extinct in northern Europe and China before they did so in North America; the wave of mammoth extinctions followed people. Pleistocene-Holocene climatic changes, however, were synchronous (at least in the northern hemisphere) and if they were the cause, then extinctions should have been synchronous too.

Murray (1984) also points an accusatory finger at early people. He finds evidence for diachrony; extinctions follow the arrival of humans in Australia and then in Tasmania. While more specialized animals became extinct by *c*28,000 bc, in Tasmania extinction was delayed by some 10,000 years; which coincides with the date of 18,000 bc when people were able to cross the Bass straits. Similarly in areas such as the Willandra lakes and the Perth region, where the earliest occupations have been found, the megafauna apparently disappeared first (Flood, 1983).

Extinctions in western New South Wales (Flood, 1983:155), occurred before 25,000 bc (and probably before 30,000 bc), during a period when, according to geological evidence, the Willandra lakes there had high water levels. This is hardly consistent with the hyper-aridity model. The only event occurring before or during the period of extinctions in New South Wales was the arrival of humans (see Flood, 1983:155).

Two medium-sized carnivores, the Tasmanian devil and the thylacine, were the victims of a later and separate phase of extinctions in mainland Australia (Flood, 1983:153). This second phase is correlated with the introduction by people into mainland Australia of a more efficient carnivore—the dingo—some four or more millennia ago. The absence of the dingo from Tasmania suggests a post-9000 bc date (when Tasmania became isolated from mainland Australia by rising sea levels) for its introduction. Moreover, the absence of dingo from Tasmania explains how both thylacine and Tasmanian devil were able to survive until very recent times there (the Tasmanian devil still survives). The dingo's ancestry and affinities remain enigmatic (Macintosh, 1975). Dingos are pets and suppliers of warmth: at night they serve as blankets. In the outback a cold night

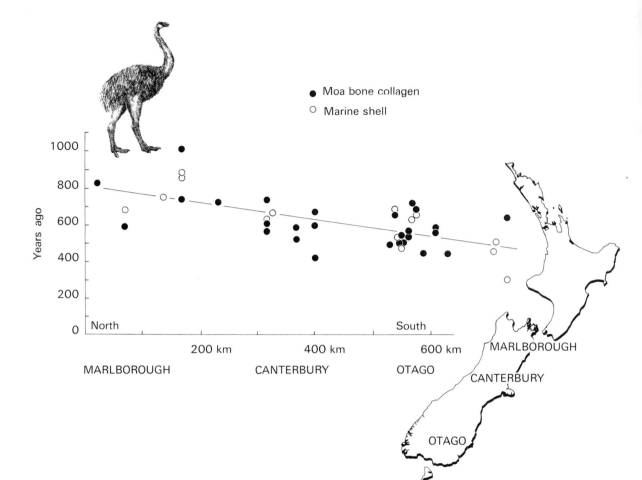

5.10a Artist's reconstruction of the extinct flightless moa, *Dinornis giganteus*, of New Zealand. Its total height was 2.5–3m. *Drawing by Cristina Andreani, courtesy Augusto Azzaroli*

5.10b The extinction of the moa in New Zealand. Dates of moa-hunter sites on the east coast of South Island show that within approximately 300 years a 'front of moa extinction' had moved from north to south. Dates are from radio-carbon analyses made on moa bone and marine shell. *From Trotter and McCulloch, 1984. Courtesy University of Arizona Press*

may still be referred to as a 'five-dog-night' (Manwell and Baker, 1984).

Another anthropogenic factor sometimes invoked as a cause of extinction in Australia is fire. Kershaw (1984), working on a sequence of sediments from Lynch's crater in north-eastern Queensland, has found palaeobotanical evidence (from the pollen spectrum) of a replacement of the rainforest by fire-adapted eucalypts between 40,000 and 24,000 bc. Support for his fire hypothesis comes from the dramatic increase of charcoal particles c38,000 bc. Charcoal concentrations are known from other sites too, and aboriginal peoples' use of fire is well known. Kershaw suggests that the habitat changes induced by fire may have been sufficient to bring about extinctions of the megafauna—perhaps already under stress from other environmental changes.

(6) Extinctions occurred without replacement, or if replacement did occur, then the new species were those introduced by people—such as the dingo in Australia.

(7) The archaeology of extinction is obscure. Martin terms this 'low archaeological visibility'. How does he account for this? Both he and Mosimann (Mosi-

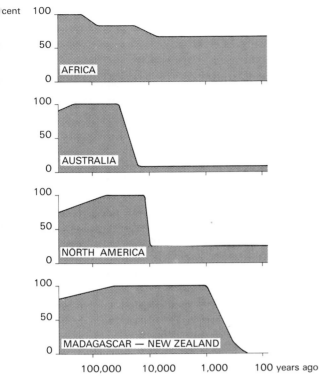

5.11 Martin's 'megafaunal overkill' hypothesis. Percentage survival of large animals on three continents and two large islands during the last 100,000 years. Extinction was less severe in Africa where only seven genera have disappeared over the last 100,000 years, while in Australia, 19 genera became extinct within the last 40,000 years, and in North America, 70 genera became extinct, most, perhaps all, within the last 15,000 years. Madagascar and New Zealand also suffered heavy losses. *From Martin, 1984*

mann and Martin 1975) have elaborated the Pleistocene overkill model. Using a computer, they simulated what could have happened following the arrival in Edmonton, western Canada, from Siberia across the Bering land bridge 9500 bc of 100 hunters, and their subsequent invasion of the whole American continent (fig. 5.6). These invaders would have come from a long lineage of 'skilful hunters with hundreds of thousands of years of Palaeolithic experience behind them'. But the American megafauna had never experienced such predation before. Hence for a brief period until they learned fear, such large animals would have been easy prey. (It is well known that animals which have evolved on uninhabited islands are 'naive'. On meeting humans for the first time, they are easily approached, and can even be touched. This would explain the rapid demise of prey species in

regions previously uninhabited by people—particularly islands such as New Zealand, Madagascar, Fiji and Hawai (Cassels, 1984).)

Mosimann and Martin considered factors like the amount of megafauna before invasion, rates of megafaunal replacement and the rates of human population growth. By varying their input parameters they simulated year by year growth of hunters, their rate of advance across the continent of America, their population density within what they termed a 'front' of advance, the numbers of units of prey they must have consumed and the time it would take for the megafauna to become extinct. Mosimann and Martin assumed that this new and favourable habitat would have provided a major sitmulus to population growth among the hunters—an annual growth rate as high as 3.5 per cent being feasible.

Their results were remarkable. Using modern data from East Africa, they assumed an initial megafaunal biomass as high as 150 million animal units (1 unit being 450kg of biomass). In one of their simulations for example, they introduced 100 Palaeoindians at Edmonton. One person in a family of four does most of the killing at an average rate of one animal unit per week—with about half being wasted. They take an average of 13 units per person per year. Such easy hunting results in the tribe's doubling every 20 years and the depletion of local herds, and necessitates expansion into fresh territory. Eventually a dense population front develops which moves southwards radially from Edmonton and behind which the megafauna is exterminated. In 220 years this front has reached Colorado, and after another 73 years the front covers the remaining 1000 miles of North America. In 293 years some 300,000 prehistoric hunters could have wiped out 100 million large animals.

This then is the basic scenario for North American overkill which Mosimann and Martin have proposed. Other simulations vary the parameters, but most result in rapid depletion of the megafauna. The amount of cultural debris (such as flint tools) left by the brief but devastating passage (they use the word 'blitzkrieg') of the hunters across America would be very limited and would result in 'low archaeological visibility': very little would be preserved as evidence.

Mosimann and Martin suggest that with the hunters' front advancing 10 miles per year with a population density of one person per square mile, it would pass through localities in about 12 years. To find evidence of this passage archaeologists 'would have to detect 11,000-year-old artefacts discarded by one person per square mile within an interval of 12 years only', and these artefacts must be discriminated from all others left in the ensuing 11,000 years by all later cultures.

The probability that any latest Pleistocene (i.e. Rancholabrean) bone comes from a slaughtered animal is about one in one thousand. While an archaeologist searching latest Pleistocene outcrops may have a good chance of finding extinct animals, he has a poor chance of finding one that might have been destroyed during the brief period of overkill. The likelihood of such a finding would be further reduced by the hazards affecting preservation of bones and associated artefacts. Mosimann and Martin emphasize this expected low visibility of megafauna-man associated finds. The rarity of such finds is one of the main arguments against their overkill model in North America.

McDonald (1984) explains extinction—and survival too—of different genera of the North American megafauna in terms of their reproductive capacity (table 5.1). Extinct taxa were usually larger than their closest surviving relatives (just as in Australia)—and therefore presumably slower reproducers. Take the case of the peccaries, a good example of size-selective extinction. Of five species, the two largest (*Platygonus* and *Mylohyus*) became extinct, leaving the three smaller species, the Chacoan, white lipped, and collared peccaries (Sowls, 1984). Why did equids and elephants become extinct while bison and deer survive? Today *Equus* females produce offspring only

at 18–24 month intervals while bison do so annually. Bison produce between 2.3 and 16 times the biomass of *Equus*. In 25 years a single female *Odocoileus* (deer) could potentially generate 1000 times the biomass that a single female elephant could generate (McDonald, 1984).

In smaller-bodied forms age-indiscriminate hunting would have removed individuals from all age classes, stimulating increased reproduction and hence accelerating the actual birth rates (McDonald, 1984). Larger-bodied animals need more time to reach sexual maturity, and continued culling of individuals would have rapidly reduced population size. Human hunting efficiency would therefore have affected these slower reproducers, imposing great demands on their limited reproductive potential. This demand would have rapidly passed beyond their recovery threshold, leading to total collapse. The large flightless moas of New Zealand are thought to have had a low rate of reproduction. If depleted, their population recovery would have been slow at best (Trotter and McCulloch, 1984). Only fast reproducers (these are termed by ecologists as 'r-strategists') could have withstood the onslaught.

The huge musk-ox and the large tapir are exceptions to this explanation. According to McDonald, they survived because they inhabit relatively impenetrable regions: the Arctic far north and central American tropical forests respectively.

In my opinion, people played the dominant role in bringing about the extinctions of many Pleistocene large animals. Climatic changes, particularly at the end of the Pleistocene, may have put certain species under stress, and reduced their areas of distribution.

	Female age at sexual maturity (years)	Gestation period (days)	Birth interval (years)	Potential number of young per year	Age at decline of fertility	Number of young/25 years/female	Potential number of descendants/25 years/ female	Approximate body weight (kg)	Potential biomass of descendants (kg)	Biomass relative to Elephas
Elephas	18	640	4	0.25	>25	2	2	3080	6150	1
Equus	2	330–360	2	0.5	15	7	198	265	50930	8
Bison	2	275	1	1.0	15	13	1361	675	813700	132
Odocoileus	0.5	200	1	1.8	10	16	74502	80	5905890	960

Table 5.1 The reproductive potentials of elephant, horse, bison, and North American deer. These data show how the sudden arrival of an efficient and voracious predator may have affected animals with a slow turnover like mammoths and horses, but deer and bison with their huge reproductive capabilities could have survived.
From McDonald 1984: table 18.5.

5.12 The Gull-Lake bison drive, Saskatchewan, Canada. An artist's reconstruction of how it might have functioned. *From a drawing by Robert Frankowiak, courtesy Thomas Kehoe*

This is no doubt what happened during the earlier Ice Ages. But it was late Pleistocene peoples' advanced hunting technology and wider distribution which acted as the last straw in bringing about megafaunal extinction. In regions such as Africa and Eurasia with a long man-animal record, species of large animals had time to adapt, and a sudden wave of extinctions did not occur.

BISON HUNTERS IN NORTH AMERICA

Following the extinction of the slow-reproducing North American megafauna 11 or 12 millennia ago, native Americans continued to live by hunting and gathering. The most widespread large animal left in quantity on the North American plains, until Europeans brought the horse, was the bison (or buffalo). Records of early European explorers show that native Americans had become adept at specialized bison hunting. Most spectacular are the bison drives which were of two kinds: pounds and jumps. Operating these drives was a communal affair, and

may have happened only once a year when single or multifamily groups would come together. October was probably the favoured time (Frison, 1971), though they took place at other times too.

In bison pounds, herds were driven through a funnel 0.5 to 4 miles long into an enclosure where they would be slaughtered (fig. 5.12). In bison jumps, herds were driven to their death over a cliff. The explorer, Henry Hind, while visiting the Plains Cree Indians in 1857, wrote a vivid account of how the Indians 'bring in the buffalo':

> When the skilled hunters are about to bring in a herd of buffalo from the prairie, they direct the course of the gallop of the alarmed animals by confederates stationed in hollows or small depressions, who, when the buffalo appear inclined to take a direction leading from the space marked out by the 'dead men', show themselves for a moment and wave their robes, immediately hiding again. This serves to turn the buffalo slightly in another direction, and when the animals, having arrived between the rows of 'dead men', endeavour to pass through them, Indians here and there stationed behind a 'dead man', go through the same operation, and thus keep the animals within the narrowing limits of the converging lines. At the entrance to the pound there is a strong trunk of a tree placed about one foot from the ground, and on the inner side an excavation is made sufficiently deep to prevent the buffalo from leaping back when once in the pound. As soon as the animals have taken the fatal spring they begin to gallop round and round the ring fence looking

for a chance of escape, but with the utmost silence women and children on the outside hold their robes before every orifice until the whole herd is brought in; they then climb to the top of the fence, and, with the hunters who have followed closely in the rear of the buffalo, spear or shoot with bows and arrows or fire-arms at the bewildered animals, rapidly becoming frantic with rage and terror, within the narrow limits of the pound. A dreadful scene of confusion and slaughter then begins, the oldest and strongest animals crush and toss the weaker; the shouts and screams of the excited Indians rise above the roaring of the bulls, the bellowing of the cows, and the piteous moaning of the calves. The dying struggles of so many huge and powerful animals crowded together, create a revolting and terrible scene, dreadful from the excess of its cruelty and waste of life, but with occasional displays of wonderful brute strength and rage; while man in his savage, untutored, and heathen state shows both in deed and expression how little he is superior to the noble beasts he so wantonly and cruelly destroys.

(Hind, 1860:358–9)

Archaeological evidence in North America for these so-called 'bison procurement complexes' goes back as early as the end of the Pleistocene to the Palaeoindian period. I shall briefly mention a few of the well-known bison-kill sites which have been investigated by archaeologists in North America over the last few decades.

George Frison (1982:2) believes that these sites represent 'patterned human behaviour rather than fortuitous encounters with animals in a favourable location'. The majority were probably large-scale communal kills, and occurred in streams and dry *arroyos* (stream beds).

One of the earliest is Agate Basin in eastern Wyoming, dug by Frison, which has yielded numer-ous projectile points and bison bones. The earliest culture level at Agate Basin is Clovis (*c*9500 bc) and includes several remains of extinct animals such as mammoth and camel. In a later level dated to *c*8000 bc (the Agate Basin culture period) careful analysis of the state of dental eruption of the bison skulls suggested that they had been killed in winter. If so, short-term preservation and storage of meat may have been done by freezing.

Joe Ben Wheat (1972) has excavated the Olsen-Chubbuck bison-trap site in Colorado. It is dated to 8200 bc and contained the remains of over 190 bison which may have met their death in a single event when stampeded into a narrow *arroyo*. Of a mere 47 artefacts found among the bones at this remarkable

site, 27 are projectile points—most leaf-shaped. Wheat describes the general disposition of the skeletal remains. These formed three layers: whole animals at the bottom, nearly whole animals on top of these, and finally, piles of bones composed of segments of skeletons, with scattered disarticulated bones overly-ing both of the lower layers. Wheat suggests that they represent one massive deposition resulting in part from the bison drive itself, and in part from sub-sequent butchering operations.

Another bison-drive site is Gull Lake in south-western Saskatchewan which was excavated by Tom Kehoe (Kehoe, 1973). Here bison were probably stampeded into a natural corral. Kehoe excavated nearly seven metres of deposits which extended laterally across several hundred feet, and date from *c*AD 50 to *c*1400. Of 1885 stone artefacts found, just

5.13 Excavation of bison bones from the Gull-Lake bison drive site. *Photograph courtesy Thomas Kehoe*

5.14 Bison bones from the excavation of Casper site in Wyoming. *Photograph courtesy George Frison*

over half were flaked triangular, side-notched projectile points. Nearly all the bone is bison, present in a 'staggeringly large amount' (fig. 5.13). For example, in the first bone layer Kehoe estimates that some 900 individuals are represented. Earlier layers probably contained fewer bison, perhaps 300 per layer. Many of the limb bones were whole, some were semi-articulated, and spinal columns were often intact. This suggests mass killings and substantial waste.

George Frison (1974) excavated Casper Site, the site of another important early bison kill on the high plains of east central Wyoming. It is dated to around 8000 bc and on the basis of the associated projectile points (some 60 were recovered) Frison concludes that it belongs to the so-called 'Hell Gap' culture period.

Frison uncovered the remains of over 70 bison (fig. 5.14) in what was a natural 'parabolic sand dune'—in effect, a sandy bowl—which undoubtedly served as a trap. There are many such 'dunes' today in that area and their sides, especially towards the top, can be

quite steep—difficult for large ungulates to negotiate (fig. 5.15).

Charles Reher, who analysed the state of eruption and wear of the bison teeth, was able to determine at what time of year the slaughter took place. For example, most of the 34 calf mandibles' first molar teeth showed moderate wear on the first cusp and little or none on the second cusp. In modern bison this eruption/wear stage is reached at an age of 6–7 months. Since bison calve in spring, the Casper Site, like most bison kill-sites, must have been exploited in the autumn (probably November). Reher also plotted M_1 crown-heights of older (5–12 year old) mandibles from Casper and two other sites and found that crown heights break down very approximately into discrete age groups: 5.6 years, 6.6 years and so on.

In the autumn, after the rutting season, most bulls congregate by themselves. Hence, according to Reher, the overwhelming predominance of cows and young at Casper Site. In fact only three bulls could be accounted for. The general picture which emerges from the Casper Site bone and tooth analysis is this: a herd of cows with their young were driven

5.15 A 'parabolic sand dune' in Wyoming of the type thought to have been exploited by Palaeoindians as bison traps. *Photograph courtesy George Frison*

to their death in the autumn. Frison (1974:107) hypothesises that every autumn people would come together for the communal kill and subsequently break up into smaller bands. This pattern of behaviour lasted from the Palaeoindian period until the introduction of the horse by Europeans. In historic times there was a spring kill too, as larger human groups exhausted the winter meat supply.

These bison drive sites are especially widespread on the Northern Plains of the USA and Canada. Most Northern-Plains bison drives took place in the autumn, and cows rather than bulls were the preferred sex. This is when cows are in their prime, but bulls, as a result of the autumn rut, are in relatively poor condition. (The cows' period of poor condition is in the spring when calving takes place.) This seasonal variation in their condition explains why cows were preferred in autumn kills. At Garnsey-site, however, in southeastern New Mexico, John Speth (1983) found in a series of late-fifteenth-century AD bison kills that bulls were the preferred sex and that according to the dental evidence killing occurred in spring.

When it came to closer examination of the sex ratios as revealed by each separate part of the skeleton Speth found some rather surprising results. While low meat-yielding elements such as skulls gave a sex ratio of 60:40 in favour of males (which he took to represent the original sex ratio of bison culled), some of the high meat and fat-yielding limb bones showed sex ratios as high as 70:30 in favour of females. Moreover for such higher-yielding elements he noticed that female bones tended to be less thoroughly broken by butchery than their male counterparts. His interpretation of these findings is that bull carcasses—especially their high-yielding body parts—tended to be preferentially butchered and exported from the Garnsey kill-site. Why the discrimination against cows?

By springtime, Indians would have exhausted most of their stored sources of 'plant energy' (carbohydrates) from the previous summer. Obtaining energy by eating large amounts of meat is not efficient, and can lead to disorders such as protein poisoning. Fat, however, is a highly concentrated source of energy, and Speth quotes many ethnographic references which highlight its importance to human hunters. He suggests that Indians at Garnsey were primarily interested in bulls in their peak condition with relatively higher fat yields, and so most of the bones left behind at the site were from cows—lean and fat-depleted as a result of the spring calving season.

The introduction of the horse along with other European goods brought a change to Plains Indian culture and the eventual demise of the bison there (Frison, 1971). Indians who traded with newly arrived Europeans could have offered *pemmican*—a long-lasting mixture of pounded dried meat, en-riched with fat and dried fruit which keeps for a long time. *Pemmican* was especially favoured by European traders in the far north.

The expanding European settlement of North America brought with it commercial opportunities: a market for meat and hides. Firearms too were introduced which led to increasing pressure on American wildlife. Evidence for the presence of Europeans in North America (the so-called 'post-contact' period) on sites, is often manifest in the form of horse teeth, guns and metal tools. William Elder (1965) has archaeofaunal evidence which probably reflects the American Indian trade with European settlers.

INCREASED HUNTING OF DEER BY INDIANS

Elder examined deer jaws from three prehistoric and two 'historic' Indian sites in Missouri. Using dental eruption and wear criteria, he plotted the deer age distributions. At the prehistoric sites occupied be-tween 1000 bc and AD 1750 the age distributions of the culled deer were similar to those of stable populations of ungulates (fig. 5.16). They included moderate numbers of old and senile individuals. However most of the bones from the two 'historic' or 'post-contact' sites occupied between AD 1725 and 1780 derived from young adults, with very few old and senile individuals represented. This kind of age distribution is typical of a population undergoing rapid turnover, as might be induced by heavy predation.

Elder suggests that a lucrative trade in venison and more efficient hunting with firearms and horses were the two main factors responsible for higher popul-ation turnover of deer in later times.

BONE RUINS IN EASTERN EUROPE AND UKRAINE

Let me digress briefly here into a field perhaps better termed 'osteo-architecture'. Archaeologists, especi-ally in the Ukraine, and as far west as southern Poland (Kubiak, 1977), have uncovered many late Pleisto-cene sites containing huge quantities of mammoth bones (figs. 5.17, 5.18, 5.19, and 5.20). Mammoth

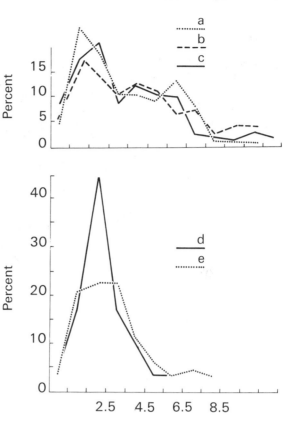

5.16 Increased hunting of deer following the growth in demand for venison in the USA. Age composition, in years, of deer culled by Indians in Missouri during prehistoric periods (above) and historic periods (below).

(a) Arnold research cave   (1000 BC–AD 1000, n = 95)
(b) Tick Creek cave   (AD 800–1200, n = 280)
(c) Utz site   (AD 1500–1750, n = 92)
(d) Gumbo Point site   (AD 1750–1777, n = 29)
(e) Brown site   (AD 1725–1780, n = 153)

From Elder, 1961

bones are even termed 'the hallmark of Ukrainian early man sites' (Klein, 1973:52; Klein provides a useful English summary of the Russian literature). Many of these sites date to the very end of the last Ice Age, or even post-glacial times, when mammoth had become extinct. None of them, however, represents clearly a place where mammoth were killed. Instead, most of these mammoth bones occurred in patterned arrangements suggesting ruins—they seem to have served as constructional material. This idea is suppor-ted by the strongly disproportionate representation of certain parts of the skeleton.

5.17 Uncovering the remains of a Late Palaeolithic settlement of mammoth hunters in Cracow, southern Poland. *Photograph courtesy Henryk Kubiak*

5.18 Reconstruction by G. Zakrzewska of a Late Palaeolithic dwelling of mammoth bones. *Photograph courtesy Henryk Kubiak*

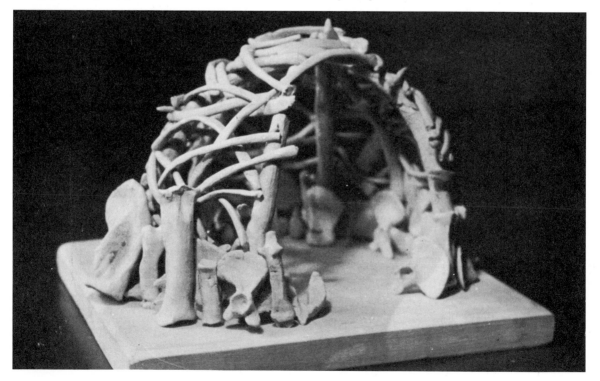

5.19a The mammoth-bone dwelling at Mezhirich (Ukraine). Pidoplichko's reconstruction of how mammoth skulls and their tusks were probably used to make the main supporting structure of this dwelling.

5.19b Excavation of the Mezhirich dwelling in plan view. *From Pidoplichko, 1976*

Most of these bones were probably scavenged from the skeletons of animals that had died naturally. Supporting evidence for this comes from chemical analysis of the bones. At the late Palaeolithic site Mezin (Chernigov region of the Ukraine) mammoth bones of different geological age and deriving from at least 116 individuals were found in a single mammoth bone 'ruin'.

One early example of such a mammoth bone dwelling is Molodova I, some 380km northwest of Odessa. This Mousterian site was excavated by A.P. Chernysh. An oval arrangement of large mammoth bones 10m × 7m enclosed an area containing 29,000 pieces of flint, hundreds of animal bones (food remains) and 15 hearths. Chernysh suggests (Klein, 1973:69) that the large bones were used as weights to hold down skins stretched over a wooden framework. If correct, his ring of bones would constitute a very early example of a 'ruin' known from any site.

Ivan Pidoplichko (1969, 1976) excavated some of the most spectacular bone 'ruins' so far found in the Ukraine. At Mezhirich, in the Cherkassy Region for example, he found a 'ruin' consisting of 385 mammoth bones covering a circular area 4–5m across (figs. 5.19 and 5.20). Beneath these bones Pidoplichko

5.20 A mammoth-bone dwelling at Mezhirich in the Ukraine. (The late I.G. Pidoplichko is standing to the left.) *Photograph courtesy N.K. Vereshchagin*

found 4600 flint artefacts and an ash–filled circular pit (?hearth).

In Pidoplichko's reconstruction the building was shaped like a beehive, similar to a Chukot Yaranga or 'skin tent' of today. The base of the structure consisted of a circle of some 25 mammoth skulls, each arranged so that its frontal bones faced inwards (this was how he found them). Other elements which made up the foundation were 20 mammoth pelves and 10 long bones embedded vertically in the ground. On top of these and the skulls were 12 more skulls, 30 scapulae, 20 long bones, 15 pelves and segments of seven vertebral columns. Still higher—and presumably for holding down skins over a wooden framework—there were 35 tusks. Ninety-five mammoth mandibles, piled up in columns around parts of the foundation, may have served as a peripheral retaining wall (Klein, 1973:96).

MEDITERRANEAN ISLANDS — A CASE STUDY

It is rare for a terrestrial animal accidentally to reach an oceanic island. For a species to succeed in establishing itself, a breeding pair (or pregnant female) would have to arrive. Therefore, in terms of numbers of species, oceanic islands have impoverished faunas, especially islands which are far from the mainland.

Subsequent evolution of the colonists would occur in an environment quite unlike the mainland in terms of competing species. And, as we shall see below, the results are often quite bizarre. Evolutionary biologists, beginning with Charles Darwin and Alfred Wallace, have taken a keen interest in oceanic island biology: such islands may be viewed as 'natural laboratories'.

Much of the Mediterranean sea is so deep that even with the lowering of Pleistocene sea-level, many islands like the Balearics, Corsica, Sardinia, Sicily, Crete and Cyprus must still have remained isolated. Many would have coalesced to form 'super-islands' such as Mallorca-Minorca-Ibiza, Corsica-Sardinia, Sicily-Malta, a central Aegean land-mass (the Cyclades), and a south Aegean arc (Crete-Karpathos-Kasos). Others, like many of the north Aegean islands, are not surrounded by particularly deep sea, and must have been joined to the mainland.

Palaeontological exploration of the Mediterranean islands began in 1647 when Giovanni Francesco Abela, archaeologist and commander of the Knights of Malta, discovered large bones of a four-legged creature on Malta. Since then many palaeontologists have taken a keen interest in Mediterranean island mammals. I too have been studying the history of the Cypriot fauna in association with an archaeological expedition directed by Alain le Brun.

Before human colonization (6000 bc), the inhabitants of many of the Mediterranean islands (those which had been islands for a very long period) were rather bizarre 'endemic' animals. They had undergone marked changes—large mammals such as ungulates and elephants became small, and small ones, like rodents and insectivores, became large, even, in some cases 'giant'. Some examples are the small antelope, *Myotragus* ('mouse-goat') in the Balearics (fig. 5.21; Waldren, 1982) and a close relative *Nesogoral* (the Sardinian 'goat') in Sardinia (Gliozzi and Malatesta, 1980); pygmy elephants (fig. 5.22) the size of a labrador dog (as little as 90cm high), and pygmy hippopotami (fig. 5.23) in Sardinia, Sicily, Malta,

5.21 Artist's reconstruction of the extinct 'mouse-goat', *Myotragus balearicus*, from Mallorca. Shoulder height was 40–50cm. *Drawing by Cristina Andreani, courtesy Augusto Azzaroli*

5.22 Artist's reconstruction of two of the extinct pygmy Mediterranean island elephants. These are compared with the ancestral *Elephas* (=*Palaeoloxodon*) *antiquus* of Middle and Late Pleistocene continental Europe which had a shoulder height of 3–3.5m. On the right is *Elephas mnaidrensis* of Middle and Late Pleistocene Sicily and Malta with a shoulder height of 160–180cm. On the left is *E. falconeri* of the Late Pleistocene of Sicily and Malta with a shoulder height of 90–100cm. *Drawing by Cristina Andreani, courtesy Augusto Azzaroli*

5.24 Artist's reconstruction of two of the dwarfed Mediterranean island deer. These are compared with the ancestral *Megaceros* (=*Praemegaceros*) *verticornis*, of early Middle Pleistocene continental Europe, which had a shoulder height of 145–160cm. In front is *Megaceros algarensis* of Middle to Late Pleistocene Sardinia with a shoulder height of 80–100cm. On the left is *Megaceros cretensis* of Late Pleistocene-Holocene Crete with a shoulder height of 55–65cm. Sondaar *et al.* (1986) suggest that the Sardinian deer was not as small as deer on other Mediterranean islands due to the exceptional presence of Palaeolithic humans on Sardinia. *Drawing by Cristina Andreani, courtesy Augusto Azzaroli.*

5.23 Artist's reconstruction of the pygmy hippopotamus, *Hippopotamus creutzburgi*, of Late Pleistocene Crete, smaller than the Sicilian pygmy hippo but larger than the modern Liberian *Choeropsis liberiensis*. *Drawing by Cristina Andreani, courtesy Augusto Azzaroli*

Crete and Cyprus (some as small as a pig). Other bizarre members of this Mediterranean island fauna, all now extinct, included dwarf deer (fig. 5.24), giant mice, giant dormice (fig. 5.25), large shrews, and *Prolagus*, a 'rat-like' hare (figs. 5.26 and 5.27; Petronio, 1970; Boekschoten and Sondaar, 1972; Symeonides and Sondaar, 1975; Dermitzakis and Sondaar, 1978; Azzaroli, 1981 and 1982; Zammit Maempel and de Bruijn, 1981).

The extinct faunas of most Mediterranean islands lacked large ground predators, and on some islands even small predators too. This and the typically low diversity of species may explain the peculiarity of island animals.

Besides the Mediterranean islands, other islands with bizarre extinct faunas are known too. Some examples are the small elephant descended from the North American mammoth, on the Santa Barbara Islands off the coast of California and the giant murid rodent *Canariomys* of the Canary islands. On the Malay islands palaeontologists have found remains of a small elephant and giant rats; and on Madagascar lived *Megaladapis*, a giant lemur. (See also Sondaar, 1987.)

How did the ancestors of the bizarre endemic species first arrive on Mediterranean islands? The following three routes have been envisaged:

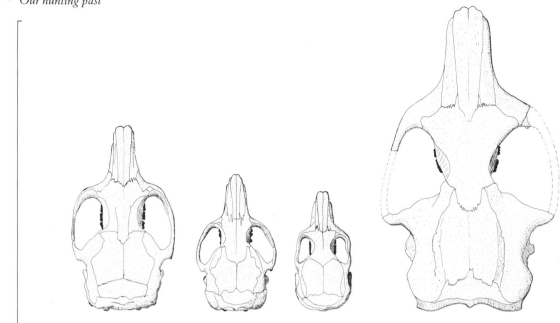

10 cm

Glis glis
(Edible dormouse)

Eliomys quercinus
(Garden dormouse)

Dryomys nitedula
(Forest dormouse)

Leithia melitensis
("Giant" dormouse)

from Spinagallo cave, Sicily.

5.25 Skull of a 'giant' dormouse, *Leithia melitensis*, from Spinagallo cave, Sicily, compared with skulls of three modern dormice from mainland Europe. *From Petronio, 1970*

5.26 The rat-like hare, *Prolagus sardus*, of Pleistocene and Holocene Corsica and Sardinia. Mounted specimen in the Museum of Archaeology, Corsica. *Photograph courtesy Jean-Denis Vigne*

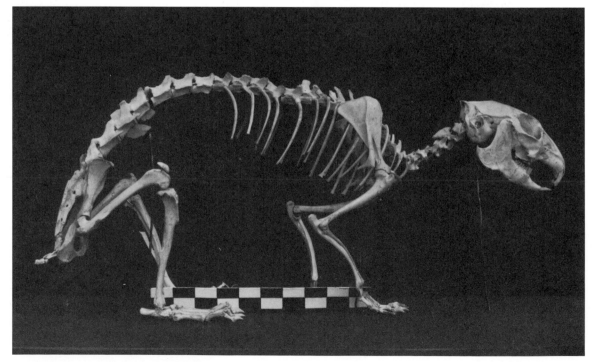

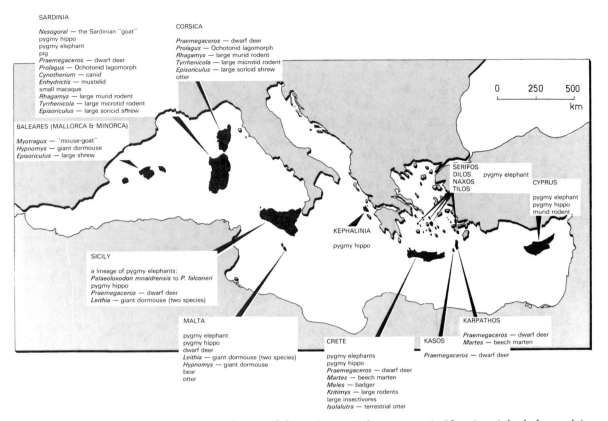

SARDINIA

Nesogoral — the Sardinian "goat"
pygmy hippo
pygmy elephant
pig
Praemegaceros — dwarf deer
Prolagus — Ochotonid lagomorph
Cynotherium — canid
Enhydrictis — mustelid
small macaque
Rhagamys — large murid rodent
Tyrrhenicola — large microtid rodent
Episoriculus — large soricid sfhrew

CORSICA

Praemegaceros — dwarf deer
Prolagus — Ochotonid lagomorph
Rhagamys — large murid rodent
Tyrrhenicola — large microtid rodent
Episoriculus — large soricid shrew
otter

BALEARES (MALLORCA & MINORCA)

Myotragus — "mouse-goat"
Hypnomys — giant dormouse
Episoriculus — large shrew

SERIFOS
DILOS
NAXOS   pygmy elephant
TILOS

CYPRUS

pygmy elephant
pygmy hippo
murid rodent

SICILY

a lineage of pygmy elephants:
Palaeoloxodon mnaidrensis to *P. falconeri*
pygmy hippo
Praemegaceros — dwarf deer
Leithia — giant dormouse (two species)

KEPHALINIA

pygmy hippo

MALTA

pygmy elephant
pygmy hippo
dwarf deer
Leithia — giant dormouse (two species)
Hypnomys — giant dormouse
bear
otter

KARPATHOS

Praemegaceros — dwarf deer
Martes — beech marten

CRETE

pygmy elephants
pygmy hippo
Praemegaceros — dwarf deer
Martes — beech marten
Meles — badger
Kritimys — large rodents
large insectivores
Isolalutra — terrestrial otter

KASOS

Praemegaceros — dwarf deer

0   250   500
km

5.27 Map of the Mediterranean and lists of some of the bizarre endemic mammals—many dwarfed or giant forms—once present on islands there before Neolithic people arrived 8000 or 9000 years ago. Incompletely understood geological sequences on many islands means that some species listed here may be earlier forms which underwent subsequent evolutionary changes. Many were probably encountered by the early human settlers, and some managed to survive with them for some time. (For more detailed information on the Greek islands see Dermitzakis and Sondaar 1978.)

(1) Some like *Myotragus*, and *Nesogoral*, the giant dormouse, and large shrew *Episoriculus* of the western islands (Azzaroli, 1981) may date back to the time $5\frac{1}{2}$ million years ago when the Mediterranean dried up (Hsu, 1978).

(2) Some, and this may include the deer and hippos, may have crossed temporary land-bridges formed as a result of sea-level lowering during the Ice Ages. Azzaroli suggests that this may have happened in Corsica, Sardinia and Sicily. Crete also may have been joined to mainland Greece during the Pleistocene, and tectonic factors may have played a role

there (Malatesta, 1980). If so it might help explain why the Pleistocene fauna of these islands is relatively rich, compared with Cyprus which was always an island.

(3) A third route could have been by swimming. Elephants are known to have successfully swum as far as 40km (Johnson, 1978). Dermitzakis and Sondaar (1978) cite recorded examples of the swimming abilities of deer and hippos too, though perhaps deer are not such good swimmers as elephants and hippos are. This may explain why deer never managed to make the crossing to Cyprus—an island just too far from the mainland—while elephants and hippos did.

The limb bones of several of these island mammals have now been studied in detail (Leinders and Sondaar, 1974; Sondaar, 1977; Houtekamer and Sondaar, 1979; Waldren, 1982). The pygmy hippo moved its limbs mainly in the fore-aft direction but could not move them sideways. This kind of movement suggests that it had forsaken an aquatic habitat for a life on dry land where, in the absence of predators, it could live quite safely.

Both *Myotragus* and the Cretan dwarf deer (but not

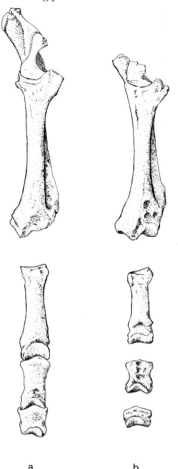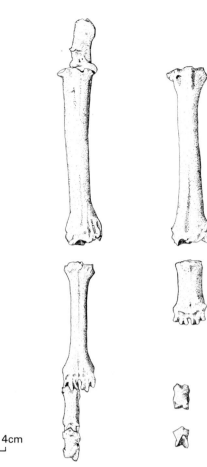

0 2 4cm

a   b   c   d

5.28 'Low gear' locomotion in island mammals. Fore-limb bones (radius, metacarpal and phalanges 1 and 2) of two island mammals compared with their mainland relatives. (a) The small recent hippo from West Africa, *Choeropsis liberiensis*, and (b) the pygmy Pleistocene hippo of Cyprus, *Phanourios minor*. Note the relatively short metacarpal and phalanges of *Phanourios* indicating slow locomotion. (c) A recent goat and (d) the endemic extinct bovid, *Myotragus balearicus*, of Mallorca. Again note the very short metacarpal and phalanges of *Myotragus* indicating slow locomotion in the insular animal. *From Sondaar, 1977*

the Sardinian 'goat' *Nesogoral*) exhibit a shortening (fig. 5.28) and fusion of several of the bones in their feet. These characteristics indicate a gait reduced to a mere amble ('low-gear' locomotion), unusual in antelopes and deer, which normally rely upon speed to escape from predators. The Sardinian 'goat' *Nesogoral* did not have shortened metapodials (Gliozzi and Malatesta, 1980), and one wonders whether this did not have something to do with the exceptional presence on Sardinia of two species of small carnivore, a mustelid and a canid. Furthermore, judging from the structure of its skull, the eye orbits of *Myotragus* were directed forward, which would restrict its lateral vision and its ability to sense potential enemies lurking in the rear. But according to Waldren, frontal vision gave *Myotragus* better stereoscopic focusing and hence improved its ability to forage among the rocky Mallorcan terrain. He also reports cases of healed bone-fractures in individuals which, under normal circumstances, would have fallen prey to carnivores.

What of the giant dormouse? Rodents usually escape predators by hiding in crevices; hence their small size. So the absence of carnivores on Mediterranean islands would permit the survival of larger individuals, which could compete more successfully for limited food resources. Thus dormice of 'giant' proportions would evolve.

From studies of island squirrels in southeast Asia,

Lawrence Heaney (1978) showed that limited food supply and competition between species are also important in determining size. Paul Sondaar (1977) noticed that most of the dwarf deer bones from one Pleistocene locality in Crete were fragile and deformed, suggesting a diseased condition, osteoporosis, resulting from chronic malnutrition. Absence of predators may have led to recurrent population explosions followed by mass starvation. Thus for large mammals such as elephants and deer, selection might favour smaller individuals which needed less food. On islands with few species larger rodents may have evolved to exploit a wider range of food.

About 6000 bc, people began to colonize most of these islands (Cherry, 1981). As a general rule the early period of colonization belongs to the Neolithic culture period (Sicily is an exception in this respect, as it was probably connected to the mainland and colonized earlier). People introduced (table 5.2) several species of livestock (most presumably domesticated) and agriculture. Why was settlement delayed for so long? After all, prehistoric people had navigated across 80–100km of sea and reached Australia some 30,000–40,000 years earlier. Yet colonization of the Mediterranean islands occurred a millenium or more after the advent of agriculture and animal husbandry in the Near East. Human populations probably increased greatly during the Neolithic, perhaps creating a stimulus for migration. John Evans

(1977) suggests that island colonization represents a quest by the Neolithic peoples for more farmland.

But there is evidence that people *did* visit at least one island before the Neolithic. Archaeologists excavating at Franchthi cave in the southern Argolid peninsula of Greece (we shall discuss the faunal sequence at Franchthi in Chapter 6), which has a sequence of levels from 23,000–3000 bc, recovered obsidian, a highly valued volcanic glass used for making tools, in layers dated to c7500 bc. Trace-element analysis of this obsidian by J.E. Dixon (Dixon and Renfrew, 1973) reveals that it must have come from the island of Milos, some 130km to the southeast. Dixon and Renfrew state that Milos was an island even in late Pleistocene times, so boats probably crossed to Milos before 7000 bc and may therefore be the earliest clear documentation of seafaring in the Mediterranean. These obsidian finds coincide with discoveries of large fish bones in the same Mesolithic levels at Franchthi, which, according to Payne (1975), may indicate seagoing activity— possibly correlated with the supposed early obsidian trade.

What happened to the bizarre endemic fauna? The Neolithic people who arrived on these islands brought with them a range of domestic livestock which eventually replaced much of the earlier fauna. The endemic pygmy elephants, pygmy hippos, pygmy deer, *Myotragus*, giant rodents and so on

Pleistocene	Aceramic Neolithic (Khirokitia and Cape Andreas Kastros)	Wild mammals in Cyprus Today
pygmy hippo pygmy elephant	pygmy hippo—live or fossil?	
	Mesopotamian fallow deer (probably survived until the Middle Ages)	
	mouflon/sheep	mouflon
	goat	
	pig	
	dog	
	fox	fox
	cat	
mice (two species)	mouse (house mouse)	house mouse spiny mouse rat
shrew	shrew	shrews (two species) long-eared hedgehog hare bats (seven species)

Table 5.2   The mammal fauna of Cyprus at various times.

vanished, and today the only 'wild' mammals are feral descendants of imported livestock: 'wild' boar on Corsica and Sardinia, 'wild' goat on Crete, Gioura and Antimilos, and mouflon on Corsica, Sardinia and Cyprus, as well as foxes, rats, mice and so on.

The fate of many of the earlier endemic mammals remains unclear. So far, only Mallorca and Corsica provide clear evidence of human overlap with these endemic mammals. William Waldren (1982) who studied the fauna of Muleta cave on Mallorca, found an overlap between humans and *Myotragus* lasting some 2800 years. According to earlier opinion, *Myotragus* became extinct over 20,000 years ago, but Waldren found it in layers as late as 2200 bc. The earliest human inhabitants of Mallorca must have relied mainly upon *Myotragus* and fish for their supply of meat, for Waldren finds no evidence of domestic animals from the mainland such as sheep, goat, pig and cattle until shortly after 3000 bc.

In early Neolithic (sixth millenium bc) levels at the rock-shelter of Araguina-Sennola in southern Corsica, Jean-Denis Vigne *et al.* (1981) found clear evidence that the ochotonid (pikas), *Prolagus sardus*, had been hunted and eaten by people. In level 17 of this site Vigne found that many of the *Prolagus* limb bones were broken and burnt at one end (fig. 5.29), suggesting that this animal had been roasted and eaten by the Neolithic colonists of Corsica. Vigne (1983) suggests too that *Prolagus* along with an endemic shrew (*Episoriculus*) and two giant rodents (*Rhagamys* and *Tyrrhenicola*) continued to co-exist with people in Corsica for several millennia, finally becoming extinct only 2000–3000 years ago.

Pierluigi Ambrosetti (1968) studied a very large assemblage of dwarf elephants from Spinagello cave near Syracuse in Sicily and found that some of their bones were blackened, perhaps by burning. This provides tenuous evidence that people were present in Sicily at the same time as the dwarf elephants.

In Corsica, Vigne (1983) suggests two factors which helped to bring about the extinction of the endemic animals: (a) predation by people and introduced dogs which brought about the demise of the large rodents, the insectivores and *Prolagus* and (b) the introduction of competing species of small mammals such as *Crocidura* (shrew), *Apodemus* (field mouse), house mouse and rat. In Cyprus, the demise of the pygmy hippo and pygmy elephant probably resulted from a combination of direct predation by people and competition with the new ungulate arrivals,

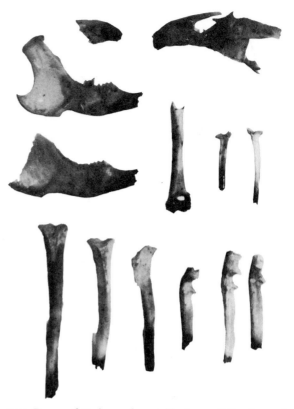

5.29 Bones of *Prolagus*, the rat-like hare of Corsica and Sardinia, from the Early Neolithic at Araguina-Sennola, Corsica. Note the burn marks at the ends of the bones: evidence that it was eaten by early human settlers there. *Photograph courtesy Jean-Denis Vigne*

some of which probably escaped to give rise to feral populations. Both pig and hippopotamus are classified within the suborder Suinae, and are in fact ecologically similar; the pygmy hippo's closest competitor must accordingly have been the feral pig. And the feral pig triumphed. Thus hippo, and in a similar way elephant, were supplanted by the new imported mainland fauna. But until 1984 we had no osteological evidence to support this hypothesis. No pygmy hippo assemblages (there are over a dozen known on Cyprus) contained any evidence for humans in the form of cut-marks on the bones or stone tools, and no Neolithic archaeological site contained the remains of the Pleistocene endemic animals. Then during the summer of 1984, we were lucky to discover a foot-bone (the distal half of a metacarpus; fig. 5.30) of a pygmy hippo among the faunal remains from le Brun's excavation at the Aceramic Neolithic site Cape Andreas Kastros, one of the earliest occupations

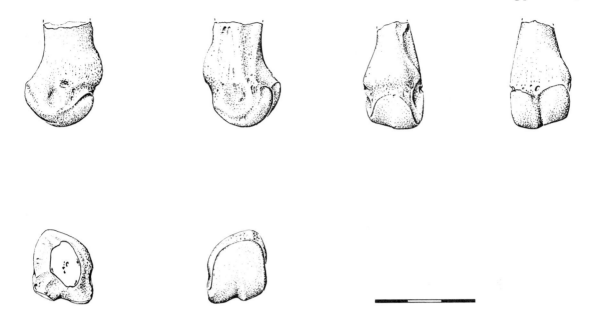

5.30 The fossil pygmy hippo metacarpal from the Neo-lithic site, Cape Andreas Kastros in Cyprus. From left to right, top to bottom: lateral, medial, anterior, posterior, superior and plantar views. Scale is 3 cm. *Drawing by Odile le Brun.* Is this evidence that Neolithic Cypriots hunted the pygmy hippo, or were they interested in palaeontology?

on Cyprus. This may be the first, admittedly tenuous, evidence that humans and pygmy hippo co-existed 8000 years ago. But we cannot jump to the conclusion that Neolithic people actually hunted live hippos: this bone might have been collected as a fossil by some keen Neolithic palaeontologist.

With luck, forthcoming excavations of the earliest levels at Khirokitia (the other Cypriot Aceramic Neolithic site being dug by le Brun) may reveal more clues to the enigma of the extinct pygmy animals of that island.

Recently Paul Sondaar and his team (Sondaar *et al.*, 1986) have discovered some intriguing remains of Palaeolithic humans at Corbeddu cave in Sardinia. These consist of an aberrant hominid temporal bone, deer bones with V-shaped scratches, cuts and polish on them. Sondaar thinks that people may have arrived in Sardinia as early as the Middle Pleistocene. We may have to rethink some of our ideas concerning the early settlement of Mediterranean islands.

By 8–10,000 years ago hunting and gathering peoples had expanded into the major continental land-masses. This expansion then set the stage for a fundamental change in the relationship between many of these peoples and the animals and plants in their environment: this leads us to discuss the subject of animal domestication.

CHAPTER SIX

From hunter to herder:
the origin of domestic animals

From the very beginning of hominid existence several million years ago in Africa until relatively recent times, our ancestors subsisted by scavenging, hunting and gathering. In several parts of the world, there are peoples such as the Australian Aborigines, the Bushmen of southern and southwestern Africa, the Amazonian hunters of South America, and the Inuit of North America, who still live primarily by hunting and gathering. Animal and plant husbandry, however, extend back a mere 10,000 years (possibly longer for plants), according to available evidence. This is less than one per cent of hominid existence. The major part of the history of human civilization—the growth of population, social change, urbanization, and such mundane things as cheese, and the clothes we wear—stems from domestication (and agriculture). Domestication represents a crucial move to control nature rather than merely take from it. It is an innovation that ranks in importance alongside the discovery of fire and tools.

Why did people domesticate animals? Which animals were first domesticated, when and where?

The quest to answer these questions undoubtedly represents the most exciting challenge to zoo-archaeology. How, faced with bits of fragmented bones and teeth from an archaeological site, can we determine the status—wild or domestic—of a particular fossil species? In this chapter I shall discuss some of the important palaeontological criteria whereby the remains of domestic animals can be distinguished from their wild forebears.

First what do we mean by domestication? A domestic animal (or plant for that matter) is one whose breeding is largely controlled by humans. Evolution of a domesticated species therefore results mainly from artificial selection, with natural selection playing only a subsidiary role. The process of domestication implies the separation (partial or complete) of a breeding stock from its wild forebears. Richard Meadow (1984) has defined domestication as a process in which humans have shifted their attention from the *dead* animal to securing and selectively maintaining the most important product of the *living* animal—its offspring.

Within the Old World we can recognize several phases in the history of domestication. These are closely linked with the social and economic development of our ancestors. First there was the dog, presumably domesticated by hunting peoples. Next to be domesticated were the most economically important of our domestic animals: the four farm-yard species—sheep, goat, cattle and pig. They were probably domesticated initially for their primary or slaughter products (meat, hides, etc). Horses, donkeys and camels did not appear until much later and were no doubt mainly used for carrying people and goods, and for traction. This third phase was a time when people commenced exploiting animals for their secondary products such as power, milk, wool and dung, and will be discussed in the next chapter. (Transition from one phase to the next was not necessarily abrupt.)

The ancient Egyptians tamed several animal species, like the oryx and hyaena (Zeuner, 1963), which are not known to have been domesticated. Of all the animals which were known to mankind 5–15,000 years ago, only a handful of species have been successfully domesticated. Table 6.1 lists the most important ones; many are large mammals. Why then, of all the species of large mammal known

Dog	wolf	*Canis lupus*	Near East	c. 10,000	bc
Sheep	Asiatic mouflon	*Ovis orientalis*	Near East	7000	bc
Goat	Bezoar goat	*Capra aegagrus*	Near East	7000	bc
Cattle	Aurochs	*Bos primigenius*	Near East	6000+	bc
Pig	Wild boar	*Sus scrofa*	Near East	6000+	bc
Donkey	Wild ass	*Equus asinus*	Near East	3500	bc
Horse	Tarpan	*Equus ferus*	southern Russia	c. 4000	bc
Cat	Wild cat	*Felis silvestris*	Near East	c. 6000	bc
Camel	Wild camel	*Camelus ferus*	southern Arabia	c. 3000	bc
Llama	Guanaco	*Lama guanicoe*	Andean puna	by 4000	bc
Alpaca	Guanaco	*Lama guanicoe*	Andean puna	by 4000	bc
Ferret	Western polecat	*Mustela putorius*	NW. Africa/Iberia	?	
Guinea-pig	Cavy	*Cavia aperea*	Peru	? 5–1000	bc
Rabbit	Wild rabbit	*Oryctolagus cuniculus*	Iberia	? 1000	bc
Chicken	Red jungle fowl	*Gallus gallus*	India–Burma	? 2000	bc
Turkey	Wild turkey	*Meleagris gallopavo*	Mexico		

Table 6.1 Some of our more important domesticated animals, their supposed wild ancestors, and the region and possible date of their first domestication.

to humans in antiquity were only a few like the sheep, goat, and wolf, selected for domestication? Other species like deer, antelope, and jackal were never, as far as we know, successfully domesticated. Important clues towards an answer to this question can be found by considering their behaviour. Juliet Clutton-Brock (1978) points out several important differences between animals which were successfully domesticated and those which were not, and cites some modern experimental attempts (apparently unsuccessful so far) to herd animals like the oryx and the eland (both antelopes) in East Africa.

Antelopes are independent and have a strong sense of territory, particularly during the rut. When feeding they range over large areas and maintain high inter-individual distances. This makes it difficult to round them up and herd them. Sheep and goats, however, are not markedly territorial. Their social structure is based upon well-defined dominance hierarchies, particularly among the males, which are established by visual cues such as body and horn size. They are gregarious, maintain short inter-individual distances and bunch together. These factors make it easy to herd and domesticate sheep and goats.

Most of the animals domesticated by man are social. One of the characteristics of the behaviour of social animals (first investigated by Konrad Lorenz—pioneer of animal behaviour) is a prolonged juvenile period when social bonding occurs between young and mother, or young and other herd members. This social bonding process Lorenz termed 'imprinting'. By removing the natural mother he was able to imprint himself upon newly hatched ducklings to the extent that they would follow him rather than their natural mother. Wolf cubs can be similarly imprinted into a man-animal bond. In New Guinea today, a similar process goes on—wild piglets are often suckled by women. The pig's omnivorous diet makes it an ideal companion for humans. Pigs also seek bodily contact with other members of their family groups and like to huddle together.

Solitary animals like the jackal have no need for the development of strong social ties with other members of their own species, and such bonding as exists tends to be weak. Hence it is difficult or even impossible for humans to include themselves artificially within these animals' network of social ties.

An exception to such generalizations is the cat. Cats are relatively solitary animals. Instead of relating to one another, they are fiercely territorial and form a strong association with their domain. A 'domestic' cat therefore is bonded to people's habitation rather than to humans themselves. In transferring odour from its scent glands by rubbing up against its owner's legs the cat is simply including them within its territory.

WHERE WERE ANIMALS FIRST DOMESTICATED? THE HEARTH IDEA

In his search for the origin of our domestic herd animals, the nineteenth-century economic geographer Eduard Hahn (1896) thought that Mesopotamia

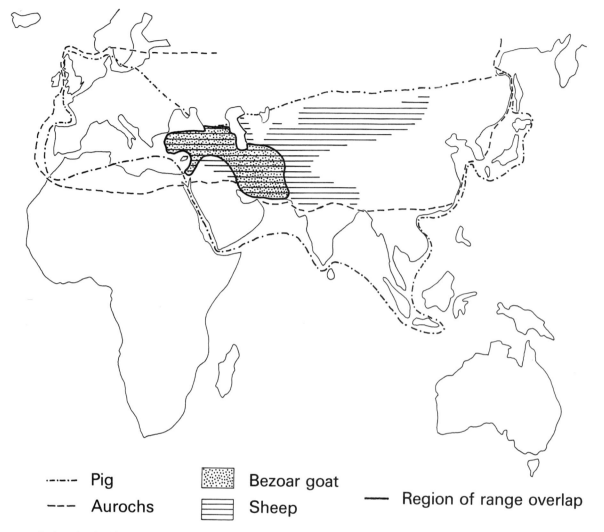

	Pig		Bezoar goat		
	Aurochs		Sheep		Region of range overlap

6.1 The hearth of Old World domestication. The original distributions of the potential ancestors of our four main domestic animals overlap in the Near East. *Redrawn after Isaac, 1970 fig 7*

and the 'fertile crescent' formed the earliest centre or hearth of seed agriculture, and that herd animals were an integral part of that endeavour. Indeed, a plot of the early Holocene distribution of the wild progenitors of our main domestic livestock species (sheep, goat, cattle and pig) shows that they all overlap in that region (fig. 6.1).

Initially, Near Eastern agriculture relied upon sheep, goat, wheat and barley. Farther east, in China and southeast Asia, pigs and (perhaps later) some of the large bovids (buffalo, zebu and banteng), chicken, rice and millet were the staple food sources. The current view is that rather than a single Old World hearth, animal domestication may have commenced more or less simultaneously in the Near East and in east Asia. A separate focus of domestication occurred in America.

Most of the animals of the New World are quite different from those of the Old. The three main species which the early Americans domesticated were in South America a camelid, the guanaco (from which both llama and alpaca are thought to be derived), and a rodent, the guinea-pig; and in North America a bird, the turkey (fig. 6.2). The history of these animals is still very imperfectly understood. Perhaps there were two main centres of animal domestication, one in Mexico and the other in the Andes. Some have conjectured that the early Amer-

Rio de las Balsas

6.2 Domestication in the Americas. Map to show the probable original distributions of the guanaco, prior to AD 1532 (light stippling), guinea pig (hatched) and wild turkey (heavy stippling). *From Wheeler, 1984 and Crawford, 1984*

ican civilizations were predominantly plant-based, unlike their counterparts in the Old World who relied to a greater extent upon animals.

Zoology provides important clues to where an animal was originally domesticated. First, the correct identity of the wild progenitor and its original distribution have to be ascertained. For some animals there can be little confusion: goats come from the wild bezoar goat *Capra aegagrus*; cats from the wild cat *Felis silvestris*; pigs from the wild boar *Sus scrofa*, and so on. But as we study wild animals more closely, we find significant variation between populations from different regions. Let me examine in depth an example of the way that zoology can tell us where an animal was originally domesticated. A particularly promising line of investigation is cytogenetics, the study of the number and form of a species' chromosomes (its karyotype; Hsu and Benirschke, 1967–1977).

Chromosomes are thread- or arm-like structures situated in the cell nucleus which contain DNA, the hereditary material. At one time it was thought that they were absolutely constant within, and therefore diagnostic of, a species, but it is now clear that they vary like any other biological character. The chromosome complement of the body is said to be diploid since the nuclei contain one paternal and one maternal set. Since the 1950s it has become technically feasible to study chromosome form and structure (Berry, 1977; John, 1976).

Another laboratory technique, electrophoresis, examines the speed with which different tissue enzymes migrate across an electric field. Minor variants in the same enzyme, supposedly reflecting genetic mutants, can be separated. By determining the frequencies of different variants of a variety of enzymes, different populations of the same species may be compared. This technique has already proved useful in the quest for the closest wild relative of one or two of our domestic animals.

Sheep

Today there are six recognized species of wild sheep found across the Near East, Asia and western North America (fig. 6.3). (The mouflon of Cyprus, Corsica and Sardinia is not strictly speaking a wild animal, but a feral one. It is now thought to be descended from domesticated sheep introduced in the early Neolithic; Poplin, 1979.) But from which of these six species is our domestic sheep derived?

A joint Soviet-American team has studied the cytogenetics and geographic distribution of Old World sheep such as the mouflon, urial, and argali (Nadler *et al.*, 1973). It found that the karyotype of the Asiatic mouflon of Anatolia, western and south-western Persia is the same as in the domestic sheep with 54 chromosomes. This is the only wild sheep with this chromosome number. The neighbouring urial of northeastern Persia has 58, and the argali further east has 56.

This is strong evidence that modern domestic sheep are descended from the Near Eastern mouflon, and casts doubt on the idea that urials from the Aralo-Caspian basin were somehow involved.

Pigs

The distribution of the wild boar extends from Europe across to east and southeast Asia: a very large area from anywhere within which the pig could have originated. Some work has been carried out by different laboratories on wild boar and pig chromosomes (Popescu *et al.*, 1980; Bosma *et al.*, 1984). All domestic pigs examined so far have 38 chromosomes. However, wild boar vary from having 36 chromosomes in western Europe (France, Switzerland, Holland, Germany, and Austria) to 38 in Asia and the Far East (Azerbaijan, the Amur region of the USSR, Java and Japan; some individuals were also found with 37). In Israel too, wild boars have 38 chromosomes (Wahrman, pers. comm.) as do boars in Yugoslavia. Assuming the modern distribution of boar karyotypes was similar in antiquity, then the domestic pig probably originated somewhere between Yugoslavia in the west and the Far East.

Equids

Another family of mammals whose cytogenetics has been fairly extensively studied is the equidae: horses, asses, onagers and zebras (Jones and Bogert, 1971; Ryder *et al.*, 1978). Unfortunately the horse and wild horse karyotypes do not help us very much. The only wild horse living today is the Mongolian *Equus przewalskii*. While it has the same 'total number of major chromosome arms' as the domestic horse (94) these chromosome arms are arranged as 66 chromosomes. All breeds of domestic horses have only 64 chromosomes. The equids are notable for their rapid chromosome (i.e. karyotypic) evolution. (This contrasts with the cats, for example. Nearly all species of cat have the same number of chromosomes.) Either

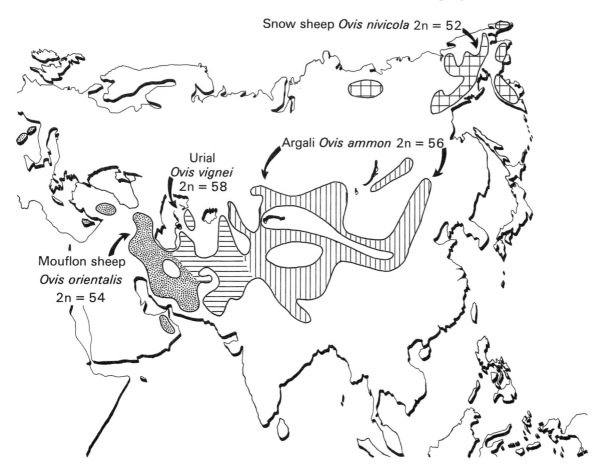

Snow sheep *Ovis nivicola* 2n = 52

Argali *Ovis ammon* 2n = 56

Urial
Ovis vignei
2n = 58

Mouflon sheep
Ovis orientalis
2n = 54

6.3 Chromosomes and the origin of domestic sheep. Karyotype analysis of various Asiatic wild sheep has shown that only the south-west Asian mouflon has the same number of chromosomes as present-day domestic breeds of sheep. *From Nadler et al., 1973; and Bunch et al., 1976*

the 66–64 change from wild to domestic horse occurred since domestication or, as is more likely, the horse is derived from a wild forebear which possessed 64 chromosomes and which has since become extinct. Some authorities believe that this was the south Russian tarpan, a wild horse that became extinct in the late nineteenth century (Bökönyi, 1978). Perhaps the tarpan had 64 chromosomes. Will we ever know?

Similarly, and not surprisingly, while the Mongolian wild ass, the Persian onager (*Equus hemionus*), and the donkey (*E. asinus*) all have the same 'total number of major chromosome arms', *E. hemionus* has them combined as 56 chromosomes and the donkey as 62. The donkey probably originated from a wild ass in the Near East or northeast Africa.

Cattle

The last of the aurochs (*Bos primigenius*), the cow's supposed ancestor, died in a Polish forest in 1627 (Zeuner, 1963). However a small karyotypic difference (of the y chromosome's morphology) has been reported (Hsu and Benirschke, 1967–77) among domestic cattle: between domestic humpless and humped (zebu). This supports the suggestion that the zebu originated separately from a south Asian progenitor, the now extinct *Bos namadicus*.

Dogs

Chromosomes do not help us much in elucidating the origin of the dog. The two Old World wild canids which most closely resemble it, the wolf and the jackal, both have similar karyotypes (with 78 chromosomes). Tissue extract and enzyme electrophoresis, however, has revealed small differences between dog and wolf on the one hand and jackal on the other. Wolves and all the different breeds of dogs are similar (Seal, 1975; Simonsen, 1976). These findings support the theory (although they do not prove) that the dog originated from the wolf.

Goats

In the Middle East there are two wild goats: the ibex (*Capra ibex*), an animal of the arid regions of Sinai, eastern Egypt and southwestern Arabia, and the bezoar goat (*Capra aegagrus*), of Turkey and Persia (Harrison, 1968). It is believed that the latter was the ancestor of our domestic goat. Domestic goats and ibex, however, can easily be crossed to produce fertile offspring; indeed they have the same number of chromosomes.

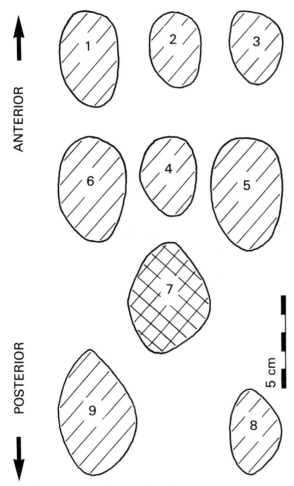

6.4 Ibex—*Capra ibex*, and wild goat—*Capra aegagrus*, horn cores. Cross sections of the base to show the difference between these two species. 1–6 are ibex, 8–9 are wild goats. 7 is a *Capra* horn core from Ein Gev 1, northern Israel, dated *c*14,000 bc.

Close study of the horn cores (the bone interior of the horn) indicates that the domestic goat is closer to the bezoar than to the ibex. Bezoar and domestic goats both have horn cores with a sharply developed anterior keel, while the ibex horn core has a flat anterior surface (fig. 6.4). The ability to distinguish these two species of goat on skeletal material has proved useful in archaeology.

South American camelids

There is much dispute over the relationship between the four 'species' of South American camelids: guanaco, vicugna, llama and alpaca. The first two are wild, and the other two are domestic. The guanaco is considered by many authorities to be the forebear of both llama and alpaca (Novoa and Wheeler, 1984). The llama, the larger of the two, is basically a beast of burden, and its wool is used for coarse fabrics. The alpaca produces wool with a long fine fibre. Both animals also provide meat, hides, dung and bezoar stones. (Bezoar stones are calculi found chiefly in the stomach and intestines and used in various medicinal preparations.)

All four 'species' have the same karyotype with 74 chromosomes and all will interbreed to produce fertile offspring. Llama and alpaca may be crossed to produce the huarizo (when the male parent is a llama) or misti (when the male parent is an alpaca). Moreover, the bones of all four 'species' are difficult to distinguish, and, as we shall see later, Jane Wheeler, a student of camelid domestication, has had to treat them as a single entity in her Peruvian archaeofaunal assemblages.

Conclusion

Human population increase, parallel expansion of farmland, and overhunting, have diminished the natural habitats of many mammals. Some, like the aurochs, have become extinct. The wild relatives of our other farmyard animals have modern distributions that generally bear little relation to what these must have been at the dawn of animal husbandry 5–10,000 years ago. Consider the fragmented distribution of Asiatic wild sheep (fig. 6.3) which at one time must have extended continuously across a far greater range. Wild sheep were probably once present in the Levant too; their bones have been found on Mousterian and Epipalaeolithic sites in Syria and the northern Negev of Israel respectively (Payne, 1983; Davis *et al.*, 1982). One of the tasks of zoo-archaeology in its quest for the place of origin of domestication is to map out such former distributions.

ARCHAEOLOGICAL CRITERIA FOR RECOGNIZING DOMESTICATION

Turning now to the archaeofaunal record, how is it possible to differentiate the bones of a domestic animal from the bones of its wild forebear? Put another way, how can we recognize the advent of this change in peoples' relationship with certain animals in the archaeological record? Broadly, the criteria used by zoo-archaeologists may be grouped under six headings. They are (1) presence of a foreign species, (2) morphological change, (3) size differences, (4) species frequency change within a succession of faunas, (5) cultural factors and (6) sex and age-related culling.

Besides domestication there are other factors, such as an alteration of the environment, which may bring about changes in many of the above six variables. These other factors have to be accounted for, so great care is required. But when several of these variables change, it may be safe to make the wild-domestic distinction.

Import of a foreign species

The sudden arrival of a new species is often a sure sign that it was introduced as domestic stock by humans. Examples are sheep in southern France, Corsica, and South Africa, sheep and goats in Greece and Britain, horses in the Levant, cats in Cyprus, dogs in South America and turkeys in Mesoamerica.

Wild sheep and goats did not exist in Britain, western Europe and Africa. David Geddes (1985) found that sheep appear in southern and southeastern France in the late Mesolithic. These finds are firmly dated to between 5300 and 6000 bc well before the appearance of other domesticated animals, cultivated plants, pottery and the establishment of settled villages there. He suggests that the introduction of sheep represents an early step in the adoption of animal husbandry by hunter-gatherer societies in the western Mediterranean. Similarly Jean-Denis Vigne (1984) found sheep bones dated to 6570 bc in layer 18 of Araguina-Sennola in Corsica—an island where no sheep had existed in earlier times. (Dates for the early

occurrence of sheep in the Swiss Neolithic are somewhat later—2940 bc; Higham, 1968.)

Richard Klein (1984) records the introduction of sheep into southern Africa between AD 50 and 250, which roughly coincides with the introduction of pottery. The appearance of sheep in the Cape (cattle too may have been introduced soon afterwards) heralded a situation observed and reported by early European travellers in parts of South Africa. They wrote that the land was shared by Stone Age hunter-gatherers known as Bushmen and Stone Age pastoralists known as Hottentots. This is reminiscent of Natufian/Mesolithic hunter-gatherers and Pottery Neolithic sheep-goat herders in the Near East.

Aurochs did not exist in Ireland. So finds of cattle in Irish sites must signify their shipment across the Irish sea. According to Caroline Grigson (1984), the earliest British sites discovered so far with cattle, sheep or goats are the earthen barrows of Lambourn in Berkshire (*c*3400 bc), and Horslip (*c*3240 bc) and Fussell's lodge (*c*3200 bc), both in Wiltshire.

6.5 The cat mandible (Kh 83 3025) from the Neolithic site (*c*6000 bc) of Khirokitia in Cyprus. Bottom: internal view, top: external view. This could be an early domestic cat. *Photographs by Odile le Brun*

Culture period/Age	^{14}C date	Historical date
Iron Age	975 – 500 bc	1200 – 586 BC
Late Bronze Age	1250 – 975 bc	1550 – 1200 BC
Middle Bronze Age	1800 – 1250 bc	2200 – 1550 BC
Early Bronze Age	2400 – 1800 bc	3100 – 2200 BC
Chalcolithic	3650 – 2400 bc	4500 – 3100 BC
Pottery Neolithic	6000 – 3650 bc	6000 – 4500 BC
Pre-Pottery Neolithic B	7300 – 6000 bc	
Pre-Pottery Neolithic A/Khiamian	8500 – 7300 bc	
Natufian	10,300 – 8500 bc	
Geometric Kebaran, Mushabian, etc	12,500 – 10,300 bc	
Kebaran	17,000 – 12,500 bc	
Upper Palaeolithic	40,000 – 17,000 bc	
Mousterian	>75,000 – 40,000 bc	

Table 6.2 The archaeological periods of the Levant from the Mousterian to Iron Age, with approximate dates before the Christian era. Courtesy Ofer Bar Yosef.

A picture is beginning to emerge of the gradual diffusion of livestock husbandry out of the Near East and Mediterranean basin into Europe and Africa. In 1983 Alain le Brun uncovered a well-preserved cat mandible (figs. 6.5 and 6.6) at the Neolithic (see table 6.2 for chronology of the Levant) site of Khirokitia in southern Cyprus (c6000 bc). It belongs to the species known to have been domesticated, and in view of the absence of wild cats from Cyrpus, it probably belonged to a domestic cat—an early find for this animal in the Near East.

The horse may have become extinct in the Near East towards the end of the Pleistocene. The sudden reappearance of horse bones in an Early Bronze Age site (Arad; in a level dated to 2280–2080 bc or 2950–2650 BC, fig. 7.12) presumably marks the spread of domestic horses beyond southern Russia/Ukraine at that time.

According to Crawford (1984) the range of the wild turkey never extended south of the Rio de las Balsas valley (near Mexico City). Hence turkey bones found to the south must have come from traded (and therefore perhaps domesticated) birds. Similarly the appearance of chicken bones and artistic representation of chickens in Europe in the latter part of the first millennium BC must signify the spread of chickens into Europe from southeast Asia—probably by way of Persia where in the religion of Zoroaster the cock was sacred. The Greeks are presumed to have brought them across, perhaps after the Persian wars. In ancient Greece the cock was called the 'Persian bird' (Hehn, 1888: 241,244).

The wolf, perhaps the ancestor of the domestic dog, is not known to have ever inhabited South America. Since remains of dogs are reported from very early sites there, dogs probably accompanied humans during their early migration into South America.

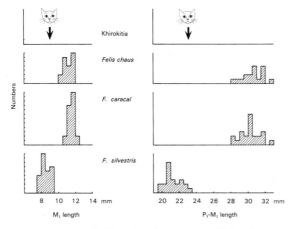

6.6 Identification of the Khirokitia cat mandible. There are three common species of wild cats today in the eastern Mediterranean, no wild cats on Cyprus. The measurements of the Khirokitia specimen (carnassial tooth length, and tooth row length) given in the top row suggest that it is *Felis silvestris*—ancestor of the domestic cat, perhaps even a domestic cat.

Morphological change

This criterion was at one time considered to be the most reliable indicator of a fossil animal's wild or domestic status. Today, many (but not all) of our domesticated animals differ markedly from their wild ancestors in a number of ways, for example, general body proportions, horn shapes, colouring, hair and fleece, and body size. Some of these characters are reflected in the skeleton.

Most modern domestic goats have helically twisted horns, while the wild goat *Capra aegagrus* has scimitar-shaped horns. Many dog breeds possess either an excessively shortened or an elongated skull compared with that of the wolf. The domestic pig's forehead is concave, while that of the wild boar is flat. And some breeds of domestic animals are dwarfed, a character seldom found among their wild relatives.

Many of these changes, however, may not have occurred until the later stages of animal husbandry, and are associated with the development of highly selected breeds. For example, domestic goats from the Near Eastern Chalcolithic and Bronze Ages had twisted horns. Neolithic goats, which on the basis of other criteria (see below) were almost certainly domestic, have horn cores which are essentially 'wild-type'. Specialized breeds of dogs with their bizarre body- and head-shapes like the mastiff and greyhound types are depicted on bas-reliefs in ancient Mesopotamia and Egypt (Zeuner, 1963), but there is little evidence for such breeds in earlier periods. Moreover, bones from most of the earlier deposits are usually very fragmented. Most remains of Mesolithic dogs consist of mandible fragments, which are hardly

6.7 Many domestic animals are smaller than their wild ancestors. Artist's reconstruction of the aurochs or wild ox and Celtic and modern domestic cattle. Bulls above and cows below. *Courtesy Joachim Boessneck*

different in terms of shape from those of the wolf. Similarly whole pig skulls are rare, especially in Mesolithic and early Neolithic assemblages. Differentiating 'domestic' from 'wild' in the later periods (when we can usually be sure, from other sources, what we are dealing with) is less problematic than recognizing the very beginnings of domestication.

Size

The skeletal and dental remains of some of our domestic animals may be distinguished from those of their wild ancestors on the basis of a size difference: cattle are smaller than aurochs (fig. 6.7), pigs are smaller than wild boar, sheep are smaller than mouflon, many breeds of dog are smaller than the wolf, and domestic guinea pigs are larger than wild *Cavia*. In many cases, then, a size change accompanied the process of domestication. (But here too, size-change may have lagged behind initial domestication.) For animals like cattle and pigs, Joachim Boessneck (1978) has suggested, diminution was due to early peoples' preference for large numbers of small and probably therefore more easily managed animals, over a few large intractable ones. Alternatively, in their initial attempts at capturing and taming wild animals like the boar and the aurochs, people may have preferred to select smaller individuals. This explanation is not entirely satisfactory (Jarman and Wilkinson, 1972) since many mammals display an inverse relationship between body size and

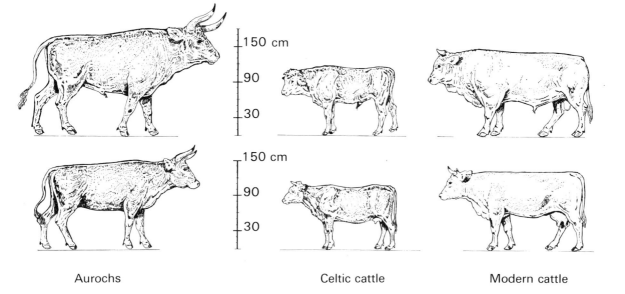

Aurochs   Celtic cattle   Modern cattle

ferocity. Small bulls, for instance, can be extremely dangerous if annoyed.

In the early stages of the domestication of bovids and pigs the areas in and around human settlements would have become increasingly overgrazed. Elsie Widdowson (who pioneered nutrition research in besieged Britain during the Second World War) has suggested that this would have meant poorer nutrition levels resulting in smaller adult size (see for example Widdowson and McCance, 1975). In her work on human nutrition, she points out that nutrition can influence foetal growth by slowing down the growth rate in the last part of gestation when appetite centres in the brain are developed. This leads to the setting of reduced appetite after birth, and the already small infant takes less food than its larger counterpart and shows no sign of 'catch-up growth' normally characteristic of rehabilitation after undernutrition at older ages. Whatever may be the reasons for changes in size associated with domestication, the size criterion is possibly the most widely used means of separating domestic animals from their wild relatives in archaeofaunal remains. For example Charles Higham (1968) has demonstrated significant size differences between pigs and cattle on the one hand and their wild ancestors on the other in Danish and Swiss prehistoric sites. He too is of the opinion that poor nutrition, especially in winter, was the major cause of a size reduction.

In Britain domestic and wild cattle bones are easily distinguished. They usually fall clearly into separate size categories: large for aurochs, small for domestic breeds (figs. 6.8a and 6.8b). Sometimes specimens of intermediate size are found, and it is tempting to take these as evidence for incipient domestication. However, this overlooks the possibility that domestic animals were (actively or accidentally) crossed with their wild relatives. This must have occurred at least occasionally.

Since the mid-nineteenth century zoologists have known that for any particular species or group of closely related species of mammal or bird, individuals are larger in cold climates. For instance, Scandinavian wolves are larger than Arabian ones. A similar body-size—climate relationship must have existed in the past (Chapter 3).

There is still no consensus among palaeoclimatologists as to how great a climate change occurred at the end of the last Ice Age in regions like the Near East which were far away from the Alpine and Scandi-

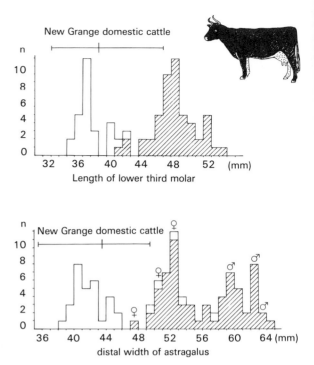

6.8 Separation of wild from domestic cattle bones in Britain and Scandinavia. Wild cattle bones and teeth are much larger (shaded) than those of domestic cattle (English Neolithic cattle shown unshaded). *From Grigson in Evans* et al., *1983*

navian ice sheets. Most would agree, however, that around 9–10,000 bc it became considerably warmer in the Near East.

Since the domestication of certain animals was probably underway soon after the end of the last Ice Age in the Near East the zoo-archaeologist must exercise great care not to confuse two variables, both of which can affect mammalian body size: human interference (i.e. domestication) and environmental change (i.e. temperature increase).

In the Israeli archaeofaunal sequence I have been able to separate these two size-change events (fig. 6.9; Davis, 1981). Intense archaeological activity during the last 30 years in Israel has provided sufficient data for several animal species. These data indicate that many mammals (such as foxes, gazelles and aurochs) did indeed get smaller 9–10,000 bc. I have correlated this size-change event with the temperature increase of that period (Chapter 3). But, in addition to a Pleistocene-Holocene size decrease, *Canis*, *Bos* and *Sus* underwent another size decrease which is relevant to the study of domestication.

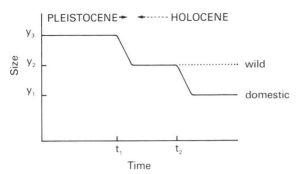

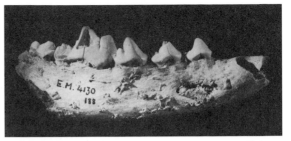

6.9 Size, climate and domestication. For some animal species it has been possible to recognize two temporally separate factors which brought about a size-decline: an environmental factor (perhaps temperature increase) at the end of the Pleistocene at time t_1, and a cultural factor (domestication) at time t_2. For the wolf-dog t_1 may have coincided with t_2.

6.10 Aurochs-cattle (*Bos*) size, climate and domestication. These are measurements (individual specimens shown as circles, samples by their mean ±95 per cent confidence limits) of *Bos* astragali from archaeological sites in Israel and the surrounding countries, during the last 90,000 years. Note that Pre-Pottery Neolithic (PPN) *Bos* at Jericho was smaller than earlier *Bos* in the Pleistocene. *Bos* of later periods such as Pottery Neolithic (PN), Chalcolithic, Bronze and Iron Ages was similar in size to domestic cattle. *From Davis, 1981*

6.11 The small wolf-dog mandible from Ein Mallaha, a Natufian site in northern Israel. It was found in a level dated to *c*9600 bc, and is similar in size to a dog mandible, but considerably smaller than modern Israeli wolves. Scale in centimetres. *Photograph by Abraham Niv*

During the Neolithic, *Bos* bones and teeth became as small as those of Iron Age (fig. 6.10) and modern unimproved breeds of domestic cattle, and by the Chalcolithic (*c*4000 bc) *Sus* teeth had become equivalent in size to those of the domestic pig (fig. 6.13a). At two Natufian sites in Israel (Hayonim terrace in the western Galilee, and Mallaha in the Hula basin; dates approximately 9–9500 bc) we have found a *Canis* mandible (fig. 6.11) and a lower carnassial (M_1) tooth. Both of them are *smaller* than modern (i.e. Holocene) Israeli wolf mandibles and teeth (fig. 6.13b). These

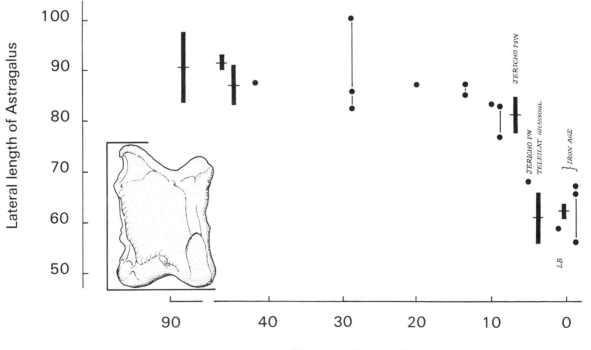

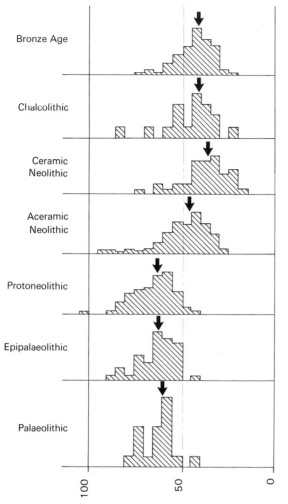

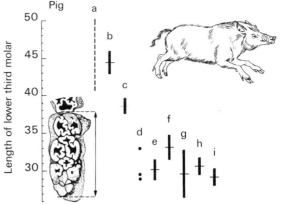

6.13a Wild boar-pig (*Sus*): size, climate and domestication. Measurements of the lower third molar of wild boar and pigs. Individual measurements are represented by circles, samples by their mean ±95 per cent confidence limits. (a) and (b) are Late Pleistocene wild boars from the Levant, (c) are modern Israeli wild boar. The difference in size between a+b and c suggests a Pleistocene-Holocene size reduction of wild boar. A further size reduction associated with domestication is suggested by a comparison of the measurements of pigs (d–i) from the eastern Mediterranean with modern wild boar (c). *From Davis, 1981*

6.12 Hans-Peter Uerpmann's (1979) plots of size indeces of sheep bones from sites in the Near East. A size decrease between Protoneolithic (10–7500 bc) and Aceramic Neolithic (7500–6500 bc) probably reflects the domestication of sheep before, or during, the latter period.

Natufian canid remains are in fact the same size as a large domestic dog mandible and they have therefore been identified as belonging to the dog. Thus on the basis of a size diminution, there is some evidence that dogs, cattle, and pigs may have been domesticated by 9500, 5000 and 4000 bc respectively.

Hans-Peter Uerpmann's (1978; 1979) general survey of sheep bones from Near Eastern archaeological sites indicates that (a) recent wild sheep are slightly smaller than late Pleistocene ones and that (b) in the eighth and seventh millennia bc smaller 'domestic-sized' sheep appeared, suggesting that this animal was domesticated by 7700–6500 bc (fig. 6.12).

Priscilla Turnbull and Charles Reed (1974) de-

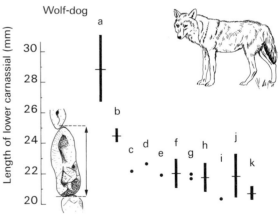

6.13b Wolf-dog (*Canis lupus-familiaris*): size, climate and domestication. Measurements of the lower carnassial tooth (M_1) of wolves and dogs. Individual measurements are represented by circles, samples by their mean ±95 per cent confidence limits. (a) is a small sample of Late Pleistocene wolves from the Levant. (b) is a sample of modern wolves from Israel. The difference in size between (a) and (b) indicates possible Pleistocene-Holocene size decrease. A further size decrease associated with domestication is indicated by the dog measurements (f–k) for example. Early wolf-dog teeth which fall in this smallest size category are specimens (c) from the Natufian of Hayonim terrace, Israel; and (d) the Natufian of Ein Mallaha, Israel; and (e) from the Zarzian of Palegawra, Iraq. *From Davis, 1981*

scribed a *Canis* mandible from Palegawra cave in northeastern Iraq. Palegawra was excavated in 1955 by the Chicago Oriental Institute's Iraq-Jarmo project. This cave is in the southwest foothills of the Zagros mountains east of Kirkuk. The deposit, which belongs to the Zarzian culture, and from which the *Canis* mandible came, is dated to about 10,000 bc. Turnbull and Reed note its small size (fig. 6.13b) compared with wolves from the Zagros and its general similarity to modern local Kurdish dogs, and suggest it belonged to a dog rather than a wolf. It may therefore be the earliest domestic dog so far found. However, while most agree that the Palegawra *Canis* mandible is dog, some doubt has been expressed about its stratigraphic provenance. Uerpmann (1982) believes that the layers in the upper 80cm of the cave are contaminated with material from later periods, and this could date the Palegawra dog as late as the seventh millennium bc.

An archaeological mission to Pakistan under the direction of Jean-François Jarrige is excavating the site of Mehrgarh, located on the Bolan river in the Kachi district of Baluchistan. At this site it is possible to follow the course of cultural development from *c*6500 bc to *c*2000 bc (= 2500 BC) without any apparent time gap, In the strata uncovered at Mehrgarh, Richard Meadow has been able to examine changes in frequency (see next section) and size of the common animals in the course of the site's occupation. The most abundantly represented animals are cattle (probably *Bos indicus*), sheep, goats and gazelles. Mehrgarh is one of the few sites in Asia where the shift from hunting to domestication of animals can be documented.

Meadow (1984) has compared the sizes of his archaeological specimens with those of a 'standard animal' (fig. 6.14) following a method devised in part by Hans-Peter Uerpmann. He has done this because the numbers of individual measurable elements were too small.★

Meadow's 'standard *Bos*' is a large male zebu, his 'standard sheep' a modern medium-sized wild female from western Persia, his 'standard goat' the average

★The technique provides plots along the same axis of the dimensions of different elements. All measurements are compared with the analogous dimensions of a 'standard' whose size is represented on the graphs by the central o line. The dimensions of the various bones from this animal along with the corresponding ones from the archaeological specimens are converted into logarithms and then one value is subtracted from the other for each comparison. In this way the varying sizes of different elements are taken into consideration.

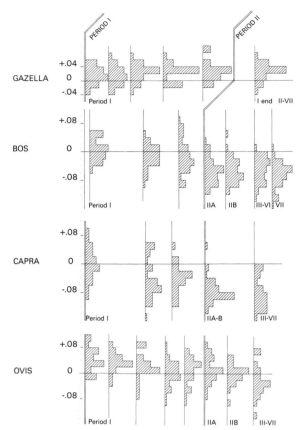

6.14 Size variation of gazelle, cattle, goat, and sheep bones at Mehrgarh, Baluchistan, plotted according to the difference of logarithms method. Measurements above the zero line are larger than the standard animal, and below smaller. Time progresses from left to right. Notice that gazelles remained more or less constant in size, while cattle, goats and sheep became smaller. *From Meadow, 1984*

of a wild male and a wild female from the Taurus mountains, and his 'standard gazelle', the average between a male and a female southeast Persian *G. dorcas*.

Within the Aceramic levels of period 1 Meadow notes an increase in cattle, sheep and goats relative to gazelles. Moreover sheep and cattle dimensions show the following: (1) the presence of very large, presumably wild forms in the earlier Aceramic levels, (2) the absence of very small animals in these same levels and (3) an overall size decrease of the cattle by the beginning of period II and of sheep by the end of that period, but no size decrease of the gazelle, an animal not known to have ever been domesticated. The absence of any diminution of the gazelle suggests that size change in the sheep and cattle was not due to some overriding environmental factor.

For the goats of Mehrgarh, Meadow thinks that the situation is quite different from that of either cattle or sheep. Even in the earliest levels at Mehrgarh small goats are present. While some size reduction does occur there, Meadow believes that domesticated goats had already been introduced—perhaps from the Baluchi highlands—by the time of the earliest levels. This means that the goat may well be the first husbanded animal in the region. It could have been the mainstay of the Early Aceramic economy, but once cattle and sheep breeding got underway its importance diminished.

Further support for the view that goats were domesticated during the Aceramic Neolithic comes from two tombs, each containing, besides a human skeleton, the complete carcasses of five infant goats (see below).

To turn briefly to the Americas, Jane Wheeler (1984) has studied camelid remains from archaeological sites in the Andes. Fragmented bones of alpaca and llama are extremely difficult to distinguish. She has used the size difference between them to try to trace their biological history. Faunal samples from early periods in Andean valley sites do not include many camelids. Those which Wheeler has studied come from large animals (presumably guanaco) and are not highly variable. She found that many of her samples from later periods, however (particularly those from 1000 bc to Inca times), were characterized by their very high coefficient of variation. These coefficients were so high (ranging from 8–21) that the samples could not be considered to have come from a single uniform interbreeding population.

The earliest indication of domestic lamoids in her valley sites is from the Chihua period of 3800–2400 bc(= 4600–3150 BC), at Pikimachay cave in the Ayacucho valley. The few skeletal elements she was able to measure included both large and small individuals, suggesting, if tenuously, a domesticated state.

The domestication of the guinea pig *Cavia* was accompanied by increased size. Among the various domestic characteristics (coat colour and various cranial characters) size is the most easily measured, and changes resulting from selection for large size can be traced. Elizabeth Wing (1978) has studied *Cavia* remains in several areas in the Andes. She admits that the wild ancestry of this animal is still poorly understood. She has found that samples which date from about 2300–830 bc (= 3000–1000 BC) are relatively small and cannot therefore include the stages of

initial domestication. Samples from the Ayacucho valley (Pikimachay cave, for example) show a general increase in size and a greater coefficient of variation. This had probably occurred by 830 bc (= 1000 BC) and Wing suggests it is evidence for the process of domestication.

Species spectrum change

Like size, the 'species spectrum change' method of identifying the advent of husbandry depends upon recognizing a change within an archaeofaunal sequence: a shift in the frequencies of different species. Such a sequence should derive from a limited geographical area in order to eliminate the possibility of geographical variation. The method assumes that: (1) late Pleistocene people were opportunists and exploited any large mammals they could trap or spear; hence the mammal bones associated with human remains would, with the possible exception of excessively large and ferocious species, represent the complete spectrum of larger mammals in the environment at that time. (2) The animals first domesticated were those we know today as domesticated animals, such as sheep, goats, cattle, pigs, llamas and alpacas.

With these two assumptions in mind, let me illustrate how this method can be applied to a series of archaeofaunal assemblages spanning say the last 50,000 years. A shift from an earlier spectrum of species which includes many animals not known to have ever been domesticated to a later spectrum which includes 'prodomesticates' should reflect an economic shift from hunting to husbandry. (In the Old World 'prodomesticates' includes animals such as sheep, goats, cattle and pigs, and in the New World includes the camelids.)

Perhaps one of the most striking archaeofaunal changes is the shift in frequencies of ungulate species about 8–10,000 years ago in Israel (Davis, 1982). This appears to have occurred (fig. 6.15) between the Natufian and the PPNB, probably between the PPNA and PPNB (i.e. about 7300 bc). In archaeological sites dated to pre-Neolithic times, deer and gazelle predominate. From the Chalcolithic onwards, sheep, goat and cattle dominate the faunal spectrum. The numerical importance of the goat is already manifest in the seventh millennium bc: in the Pre-Pottery Neolithic B sites of Beisamoun, Abu Gosh and Jericho. Sheep, which are not found in northern Israel before the Neolithic, may appear in small numbers soon after the PPNB.

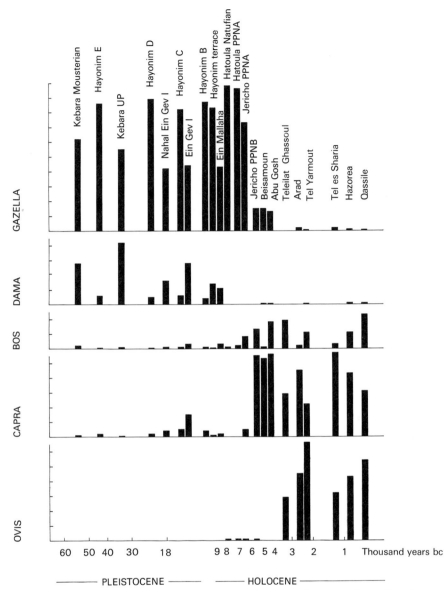

6.15 Species spectrum change and domestication. The major Late Pleistocene-Holocene faunal assemblages in Israel in chronological order from left to right. The percentages of gazelle, fallow deer (*Dama*), cattle-aurochs (*Bos*), goat (*Capra*) and sheep (*Ovis*) are shown. A major faunal shift occurred from deer + gazelle to goat + sheep + cattle in the Neolithic. This shift probably reflects a change from hunting to husbanding.

It is unlikely that this Neolithic change represents a replacement due to extinction of deer and gazelles, since both these species are found, if only in small numbers, in post-Neolithic sites. The fallow deer was present in Israel as recently as the nineteenth century and the gazelle survives to this day. With this objection removed, on what basis can it be argued that the Neolithic faunal shift reflects a change from hunting to husbanding?

First, neither gazelles nor fallow deer are known to have ever been domesticated. The gazelle—a rather nervous animal, particularly in the rutting season—is not considered by zoologists to be a potentially domesticable animal. Secondly, we know from historical records that the sheep and goats from the later periods (Late Bronze Ages, for example) were domesticated, as indeed they are today. It therefore seems logical to assume that the shift from deer and gazelles to sheep and goats is strong evidence for the advent of caprine husbandry.

In addition the data show that the change towards an increase of domesticable species was not a sudden transformation. In PPNB times there was still much hunting of gazelles. This decreased but continued presence of gazelle bones suggests that older patterns of reliance on the hunt for animal protein had not yet disappeared. Perhaps these gazelles point to man's reluctance to abandon a way of life he had pursued for countless millennia. (I found a similar reliance upon gazelles in the Neolithic in a sequence of faunal assemblages from western Persia.) Alternatively, one can easily imagine that during this early phase in man's experiment to control animal breeding and behaviour, fluctuating success necessitated continued reliance upon hunting as a supplementary source of animal protein, and this is reflected in the continued presence of gazelle bones in the assemblages.

It is only in the Chalcolithic (fourth millennium BC) that products of the hunt cease being a major component in the diet of the people inhabiting the Israel region. In this period, as well as those which follow, the concentration upon sheep, goat, and cattle no doubt signifies an essentially modern animal husbandry economy.

Sebastian Payne (1975) has found a similar switch to prodomesticates at Franchthi cave in the Argolid, southern Greece. Excavations there by Thomas Jacobsen (1976) have revealed a rich sequence of occupations, from the late Palaeolithic through the Mesolithic and Neolithic, up to the end of the late Neolithic. The sequence is dated by 32 radiocarbon dates from *c*23,000 bc to *c*3000 bc. Payne recognizes 11 main faunal phases, and his results are shown in fig. 6.16. In economic terms, the Palaeolithic and Mesolithic deposits reflect the traditional hunter-gatherer picture: resources include a wide range of animals—smaller mammals, birds, fishes and molluscs—and also nuts and seeds. Bones of large fish suddenly appear at the beginning of D2, which with the contemporary increased frequency of obsidian (probably from the island of Milos, 130 km to the south east) suggests the use of seagoing boats and perhaps improved fishing techniques. We have discussed this important finding in Chapter 5.

The most striking aspect of the Franchthi faunal succession, as in that of northern Israel, is the change from red deer (*Cervus elaphus*) to caprines (sheep,

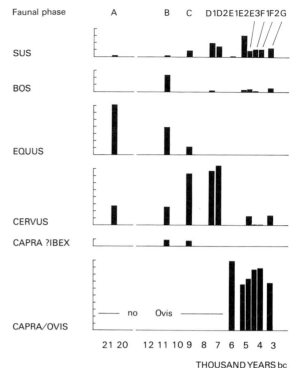

6.16 Species spectrum change and domestication. The faunal sequence at Franchthi cave, Greece. Percentages of the six common large mammals—wild boar-pig (*Sus*), aurochs-cattle (*Bos*), equids, red deer (*Cervus*), large goat (?ibex), and sheep/goat. The main faunal phases are given in the top row. *From Payne, 1975*

Ovis and goats *Capra*) during the seventh millennium bc. Quite suddenly, in phase E1 sheep and goats make up more than 90 per cent of the larger mammals. Sheep do not occur prior to the seventh millennium bc in the Franchthi sequence, and wild sheep were undoubtedly absent from southeastern Europe, just as they were from northern Israel. There is little evidence for an occupational break between Mesolithic and Neolithic at Franchthi. The suddenness of this faunal switch argues, according to Payne, in favour of the view that the Neolithic was intrusive rather than a local development. Perhaps Neolithic farmers invaded from the east?

Not only do the sheep represent an introduced species, but Payne noticed that the Neolithic *Capra* bones are much smaller than the Upper Palaeolithic *Capra* bones from this site. Despite their scarcity, the Upper Palaeolithic *Capra* bones seem consistently great in size, suggesting that they may be ibex bones.

In this case the Neolithic *Capra* may also represent an introduced species. A further noteworthy point is the reversal in abundance between equids and deer, a change which Payne correlates with climate and local vegetational change.

Further to the north and west, in Switzerland, Charles Higham studied archaeofaunal remains from that country. A late Swiss hunting culture was the 'Late Tardenoisian', an example being the site of Birsmatten which has a radiocarbon date of *c*3390 bc. Its fauna is predominantly red deer, wild boar and

6.17 Species spectrum change and domestication. The faunal sequence at Mehrgarh, Baluchistan. Percentages of large mammals at Mehrgarh and Sibri Damb. The animals are: wild mammals such as deer and nilgai, gazelle, sheep (*Ovis*), goats (*Capra*), and cattle (*Bos*). Notice the increased importance of cattle in the Ceramic Neolithic, and decreasing importance of wild animals and gazelle. *From Meadow, 1984*

beaver. The earliest known Swiss Neolithic site with associated remains of sheep/goat is Egolzwil 3 which has a radiocarbon date of 2940 bc. This date compared with dates from Franchthi and Britain indicates that it may have taken 3000 or more years before Alpine and northwest European peoples adopted livestock husbandry.

To return to Meadow's Neolithic and post-Neolithic assemblages from Baluchistan, Pakistan. Besides measuring the bones of the common species of animals at Mehrgah, Meadow (1984) has also calculated their relative abundance. Figure 6.17 shows these as percentages in the 13 divisions of the archaeological sequence there, and at the nearby site Sibri Damb. These span the period from Aceramic Neolithic through to the third millennium BC. Like the sequences at Franchthi and northern Israel, that from Mehrgarh shows a decrease of wild animal exploitation, indicated by remains of wild caprines,

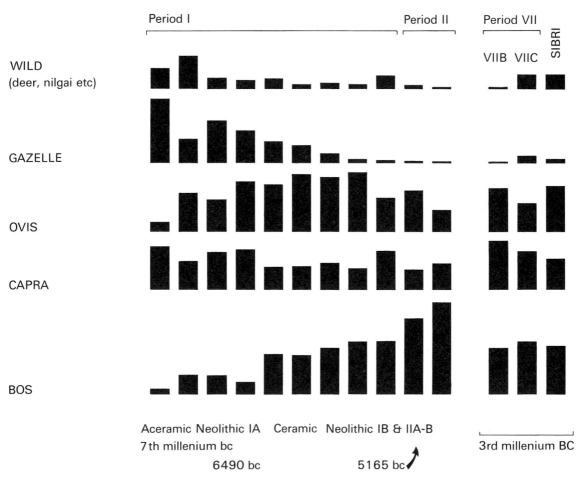

deer, nilgai and gazelles, and an increase of pro-domesticates: sheep, goats and especially cattle.

By the end of period I the majority of the faunal remains derive from the three prodomestic animals. The change is most marked for cattle, whose numbers increase from a mere 4 per cent in the earliest levels to 38 per cent by the end of period I and to 65 per cent by period IIB. In the late fourth millennium BC at Balakot—another Pakistani site, 90km NNW of Karachi—cattle remains constitute as much as 75 per cent of the mammalian remains.

We may accept that the greater reliance upon cattle, sheep and goats in the course of period I at Mehrgarh reflects increasing dependence upon animal keeping and herding. The question which Meadow asks is: were these animals domesticated in the Mehrgarh area from locally available wild stock, or were they imported (already domesticated) from abroad, as was probably the case for the goat? The gradual size decrease in the case of *Bos* argues for local domestication. Gradual size decrease in the sheep, however, is more difficult to understand. Today (but not necessarily in antiquity) Baluchistan is inhabited by the urial (wild sheep) and is outside the distribution of the mouflon. This, however, does not preclude the possibility that the urial was domesticated at Mehrgarh and later replaced by sheep of mouflon ancestry imported from the west.

Putting all this together, the evidence so far retrieved from Mehrgarh suggests that the goat was introduced—already domesticated—at the beginning of the sequence (c6500bc) and cattle were probably domesticated locally towards the end of period I (?by 5500 bc). The location and timing of sheep domestication, however, remain enigmatic. These dates are as early as those for caprine and *Bos* domestication further to the west in the 'fertile crescent'. This supports Gordon Childe's idea that agricultural developments in Baluchistan took place before archaeologically detectable evidence for any influence from the west.

To return again to the Americas, several prehistoric sites have now been excavated in the Puna (high Andean plateau) of Junin and the nearby Puna of Lauricocha in the central Peruvian Andes. This is an area more than 4000m above sea level with an abundance of natural pasturage for camelids. It remains verdant throughout the year. Wheeler (1984) has synthesized the archaeofaunal data from these sites, and these data help to clarify our understanding

of animal exploitation since the end of the Pleistocene. She believes that this was the area where the process of camelid domestication was carried out. By way of comparison, a lower altitude 'valley' site, Guitarrero cave, has provided a faunal sequence spanning the same time. Faunal changes reported by Wing from this site are similar, although possibly a little later.

The Puna faunal assemblages come from Uchcumachay cave, Panaulauca cave, Pachamachay cave, Acomachay and Telarmachay rock shelter, all in the Puna of Junin, and Lauricocha cave in the Puna of Lauricocha. Preceramic assemblages can be assigned

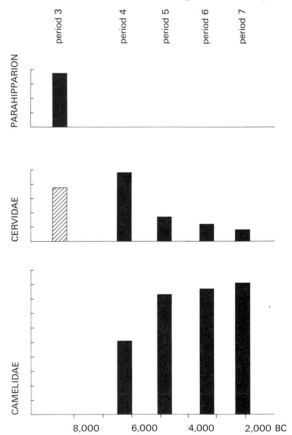

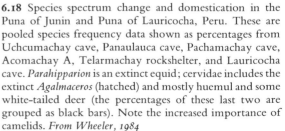

6.18 Species spectrum change and domestication in the Puna of Junin and Puna of Lauricocha, Peru. These are pooled species frequency data shown as percentages from Uchcumachay cave, Panaulauca cave, Pachamachay cave, Acomachay A, Telarmachay rockshelter, and Lauricocha cave. *Parahipparion* is an extinct equid; cervidae includes the extinct *Agalmaceros* (hatched) and mostly huemul and some white-tailed deer (the percentages of these last two are grouped as black bars). Note the increased importance of camelids. *From Wheeler, 1984*

to five periods of the proposed 'central Andean chronology' and I have pooled Wheeler's frequency data accordingly in figure 6.18. This shows a gradual decrease of deer remains and increase of camelids from 7–2000 bc. Prior to the arrival of camelids to this area around 7000 bc (they are known in earlier contexts in Ecuador to the north and Bolivia to the south), the presence of a few bones of the extinct Pleistocene equid *Parahipparion peruanum* and an extinct Pleistocene deer *Agalmaceros blicki* associated with human artefacts in the Uchcumachay cave suggest that man was hunting these beasts for food.

Wheeler correlates the appearance of camelids in the Puna of Junin about 7000 bc with the disappearance of the Pleistocene equid and deer, and thinks this might have been the result of climatic change between 10 and 7000 bc. But there is little evidence from other disciplines to support this contention. Could not man have been the agent responsible? If so are not the camelids of 7000 bc early domesticates? Supporting evidence for this second speculation is going to be even harder to find given the difficulty of distinguishing between bones of the four 'species' of camelids.

Guitarrero cave (site PAN 14–102), located in a high intermontane valley in the Callejon de Huaylas in northern Peru, 2580m above sea level, is at a much lower altitude than the Puna sites. It was excavated by Thomas Lynch, and Elizabeth Wing (1980) studied the faunal remains. She too found a change in the relative abundance of camelids and deer. Deer remains are very abundant—over 80 per cent—in the earliest level. Thereafter their numbers steadily decline (77, 59 and 24 per cent) and camelids, absent from the earliest sample dated to before 8600 bc, steadily increase (10, 33 and 35 per cent). A comparison of Guitarrero cave's sequence with that from the Puna of Junin shows that the magnitude of this change is different. In the valley sites camelids range from 0–50 per cent while in Puna sites, during the same time span, they range from 57–96 per cent. Moreover, the increase in intensity of camelid use probably appears earlier in the Puna than in the valley sites. If Wheeler and Wing are correct, camelids were first domesticated in the high altitude Puna, and only later brought down into the Andean valleys.

Wheeler (1984) postulates a three-stage development in the Puna of Junin. The first is in 'period 4' (7–5500 bc) in which there was hunting of all Puna ungulates. In the second period from 5200–4000 bc

hunting was more specialized, concentrating more upon guanaco and vicugna. The period between 4000 and 3500 bc marks the appearance of early domestic camelids. Evidence comes from Telarmachay rock shelter and consists of alpaca type incisor teeth which make their first appearance then (in layer 'lower v-1'). These teeth can apparently be distinguished from the other camelid incisors by their being intermediate in form between those of guanaco/llama and vicugna: 'exhibiting a non-spatulate rectangular cross-section, with enamel only on the labial (internal) surface and root formation occurring only at advanced age' (Wheeler, 1984). Further evidence for domesticated camelids in layer 'lower v-1' of Telarmachay is the increase of foetus/neonate remains. We shall discuss this later.

Cultural signs

There are a number of rare finds which show some kind of close relationship between man and animal. These include deliberate burial of whole animals, evidence for the wearing of bits, the occurrence of pathological specimens, partially digested food bones and finds of shed milk teeth. Wall paintings and figurines of animals may also tell us something about their relationship with ancient man.

Burial. Striking support for Meadow's hypothesis that goats at Mehrgarh were herded as early as the eighth millennium bc comes from two graves. These were unearthed in the earliest Aceramic occupation (top of MR3s 8). Two burials were uncovered, each containing the articulated skeletons of five kids (fig. 6.19; Lechevallier, Meadow and Quivron, 1982). These had been arranged in semi-circular fashion around the contracted legs of a human skeleton, and, judging by their largely unworn milk teeth, they were less than three months old when killed.

In 1977, François Valla unearthed a tomb while excavating the Natufian site of Ein Mallaha in the Hula basin, northern Israel (Davis and Valla, 1978). The tomb, H.104, is situated in a level which has provided three radiocarbon dates: 9350, 9650 and 9750 bc, as well as the small dog-sized *Canis lupus/familiaris* mandible shown in fig. 6.11. The tomb revealed the skeleton of a senile human (probably a woman, although the pelvis is too badly damaged to confirm this). Beneath her left hand (fig. 6.20) were the fragmentary remains of an animal. This turned out to be a wolf/dog puppy (the two are

6.19 Cultural signs of domestication from Mehrgarh, Baluchistan. Five kids buried in a grave (MR3 tomb 287, layer 7) dated to the eighth millennium bc. See Lechevallier *et al.*, 1982. Drawing by Gonzague Quivron. *Courtesy Richard Meadow and Jean-François Jarrige*

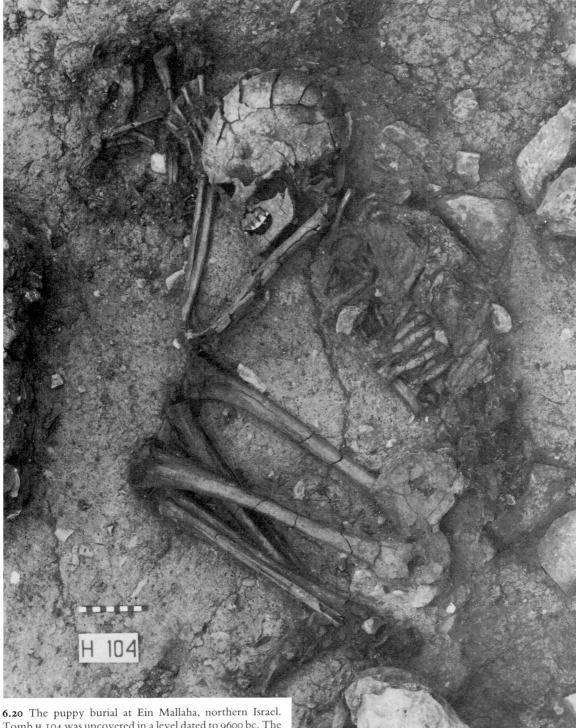

6.20 The puppy burial at Ein Mallaha, northern Israel. Tomb H.104 was uncovered in a level dated to 9600 bc. The puppy skeleton, identified as either dog or wolf, is under the senile human's left hand. See Davis and Valla, 1978. *Photograph Alain Dagand*

difficult to distinguish) which, judging by the state of its milk dentition, had died at the age of 3–5 months. Clearly there was some close association between the old woman and animal—an affectionate rather than gastronomic relationship.

This cultural evidence along with the biometric evidence (p. 138) and the identification of possible dog-digested bones (p. 149) makes it clear that Natufian people possessed a domestic animal, not one which they ate (otherwise dog bones would be common on Natufian sites, which they are not) but one which perhaps hunted with them—the earliest known case of man-animal symbiosis.

From Missouri in the USA comes more evidence, again in the form of a burial, for some kind of special relationship between ancient man and dog. R. Bruce McMillan (1970) describes a complete dog skeleton from Rodgers shelter in Benton county, in a zone dated to *c*5500 bc. The skeleton belonged to an adult dog about the size of a fox-terrier. It was found in a shallow basin-shaped prepared pit under a small tumulus of dolomite stones. It represents one of the earliest finds of canid interment recorded for North America.

Bone corrosion. Besides a reduction of size and the puppy burial, there is more evidence to corroborate the early domestication of the dog. This takes the form of partially corroded animal bones in the Neolithic period of Greece and Natufian period of Israel.

Payne and Munson carried out a series of dog-feeding experiments (Chapter 1). Dogs will swallow bones which are less than about 2.5cm long. Those that survive the action of stomach acid and digestive juices are recognizably corroded. Payne has found corroded sheep/goat carpals, tarsals and phalanges in the Neolithic levels at Franchthi cave. The absence of such corrosion on larger sheep/goat bones and cattle bones rules out the possibility that acids in the soil had caused this corrosion. Payne's conclusion is that Neolithic people at Franchthi kept domestic dogs.

In 1983, while studying the Natufian faunal remains from Hatoula, a site in central Israel, I found numerous corroded small bones (about 5 per cent of the bones were affected in this manner; see fig. 6.21). These reminded me of the ones Payne and Munson had recovered from their dog-feeding experiments in America. The importance of this discovery prompted me to re-examine the Mousterian-

Natufian archaeofaunal material from Hayonim in western Galilee, Israel. I could find no trace of this phenomenon among the large faunal samples dated to the end of the Pleistocene (i.e. in levels which preceded the Natufian). However, several corroded gazelle bones were found in the smaller sample from the Natufian (level B). Clearly, some agent arrived during or just before Natufian times and was responsible for the partial corrosion of certain animal bones in these Epipalaeolithic sites (Davis, 1985).

Does the appearance of corroded bones 8–10,000 bc in the Israeli archaeofaunal sequence signify canine activity and therefore man's possession of dogs at Hatoula and Hayonim? This interpretation is one which I favour, the more so in that it corroborates the other evidence of man's domestication of the dog in the Natufian 8–10,000 bc.

Milk teeth, pathology, bit wear and bone breakage. Thanks to careful recovery techniques, shed caprine milk teeth—recognizable by their extensive wear and resorbed roots—have now been reported in early Neolithic contexts. Payne has found them from the Aceramic Neolithic onwards at Franchthi cave. Daniel Helmer (1984) found them in Early and Middle Neolithic sites in southern France. Both cases are interpreted as signifying sheep and goat penning.

In nature wild animals which suffer sickness or bone fracture are soon killed by predators. The chance that such an animal would have been trapped by man and that its remains would appear in an archaeological assemblage is small. Indeed diseased and fractured bones are uncommon on early (pre-Neolithic) sites. Animal husbandry implies some degree of protection of the domesticated species from its natural enemies, and one might then expect the remains of animals with fractured limb bones, maloccluding teeth and joint diseases to end up among the archaeofaunal debris. A higher percentage of animals with such pathological signs is indeed found in many post-Neolithic assemblages. However, this method has not been explored much as yet as a means of identifying early domestication.

One interesting case of obvious man-induced 'pathology' comes from the ancient fortress of Buhen in northern Sudan, where a stallion skeleton was found and dated to the sacking of Buhen in 1375 bc (=1675 bc). (The horse is not native to ancient Egypt.) It was studied by Juliet Clutton-Brock (1974), who reports oblique wear on the lower first

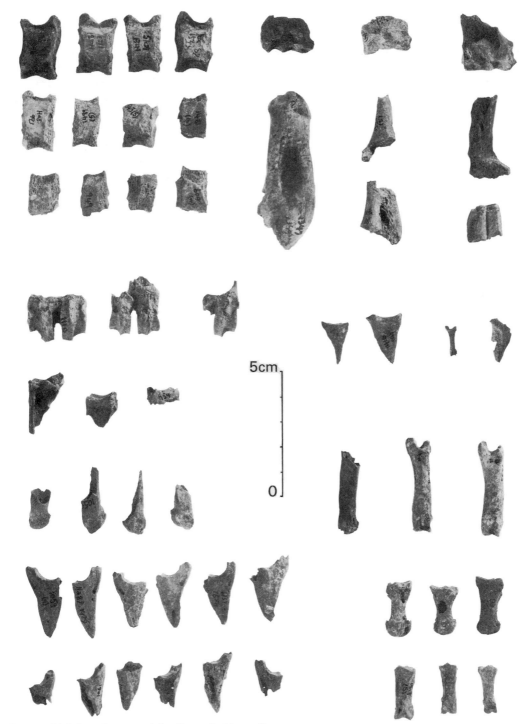

6.21 Bones which have been partially digested. Most of these are gazelle bones and come from Natufian levels at Hatoula, central Israel. See Davis, 1985. *Photograph Marjolaine Barazani*

premolar tooth (P_2)—the probable result of wearing a bit. This therefore provides evidence for riding and hence domestication of the horse some time before 1375 bc.

A rather tenuous clue to understanding when food animals were first domesticated in the Levant is provided by the pattern of bone breakage. Bones from Mousterian to Epipalaeolithic (90,000–8500 bc) sites in Israel were heavily fragmented, presumably to extract the nourishing marrow. This contrasts with bones found in Chalcolithic and later sites, which show little evidence of deliberate fragmentation. The earliest site in the Israeli sequence with complete long bones is Beisamoun (PPNB; 7300–6000 bc). There are several possible reasons for this change—an alteration of cooking habits for example. I have suggested, however, that it is related to food availability and domestication. In a hunting economy, man was likely to exploit the animal carcass to the full. Domestication of ungulates, however, provided an assured source of animal protein, which ended the need to exploit the carcass fully: man could now afford to be wasteful. This too is possible supporting evidence for man's possession of domestic goats in the PPNB in Israel.

Age and sex

Another way to determine the wild or domestic status of an animal species in an archaeological context, but which requires a large sample, is through its age and sex composition. In nature several factors influence an animal's population structure. Disease, adverse climatic conditions, lack of food, predation and sometimes even old age, all take their toll, particularly of the very young and old. Under severe conditions few young may survive, and the population goes into decline. Conversely, a relaxation of these constraints, especially predator pressure, means that more young will survive. This may lead to a population explosion. The age structure of a herd, which may be summarized as a 'life table', will therefore be of prime interest to game ranchers investigating a herd's health and stability. Age and sex composition will fluctuate from year to year but over a long period will exhibit certain consistent characteristics. The gazelle remains found on late Pleistocene Israeli sites indicate that about 30 per cent were juveniles (i.e. less than $c13$ months old)—a figure which is more or less what one would expect in a stable population of wild herbivores. In other

words, people in antiquity were probably not exercising a preference for either the juveniles or the adults as far as these small antelopes are concerned (but see Chapter 4).

Domestication implies some protection from predators. The mortality pattern of a herd of domesticated animals is mainly dictated by their human owners. Since the growth rate of an animal decreases as it gets older it becomes increasingly uneconomical to keep it in terms of fodder. A maximum return (of carcass weight) on feed is obtained by slaughtering shortly before an animal reaches maturity. For sheep and goats this may be between 6 and 12 months, and the juveniles slaughtered are often predominantly the males not required for stud purposes, the females (mostly) being kept longer for reproduction, milking etc. A preponderance of juvenile bones usually indicates this kind of economy. Among the many examples is the typical Late Bronze Age site Tel es Sharia in the northern Negev, Israel, where the proportion of young domestic goat and sheep is $c60$–70 per cent (fig. 7.3). A present-day example is that of domestic goat mandibles collected around Bedu encampments in the southern Sinai, Egypt; these were mostly from individual goats aged between 6 and 12 months. An increase in the proportion of juveniles might therefore signify the inception of a domestic economy. Other economic factors too have to be taken into account as we shall see in the next chapter.

Carleton Coon (1951) studied the fauna from Belt cave on the southeastern border of the Caspian Sea in Persia. It contained both Mesolithic and Neolithic levels. Apart from a shift from gazelles in the Mesolithic to goats in the Neolithic, and despite the rather small sizes of the samples, he found that (1) the percentage of immature gazelles was low and (2) the percentage of immature sheep and goat rose dramatically between layers 8 and 10 (16–20 per cent immature) and layers 1–7 (59 per cent immature). Coon was therefore one of the first to apply age-structure analysis to the zoo-archaeological investigation of early domestication.

In another part of Persia, the Deh Luran plain of Khuzistan, Kent Flannery (1969) studied the faunal remains from a sequence of sites spanning the seventh to fourth millennia bc. He examined the age profile of the goats. Even in the earliest of these assemblages only two-thirds reached an age of one year, and less than a third reached 3.5 years. This kind of age profile indicates, according to Flannery, that the goats were domesticated rather than wild and hunted.

The faunal sequence from Shanidar-Zawi Chemi Shanidar in Iraqi Kurdistan is often quoted as providing evidence for the presence of domestic sheep in the proto-Neolithic. At these sites Perkins (1964) suggested that the high proportion of young sheep bones proved that domestication had occurred there by about 11,000 years ago. However, it has been pointed out that Perkins' data show a similarly high proportion of juveniles in the Mousterian level, perhaps due to a small sample size (Bökönyi, 1969). Neither the age nor the species spectrum data from this sequence convince me that there is much evidence for the advent of sheep husbandry. Uerpmann's (1978) measurements of the sheep bones from these sites did not reveal any evidence for a size reduction associated with domestication. The case for domesticated sheep at Zawi Chemi Shanidar should be regarded as unproved.

Mortality rates among newborn wild camelids in South America are reported to be relatively low (below 5 per cent). In contrast llamas and alpacas suffer high neonatal mortality. This is apparently caused by an intestinal infection (*enterotoxaemia*)

which may assume epidemic proportions as a result of close confinement in dirty corrals—especially during the rainy birth season (December–April). Today llama and alpaca herders consume the neonates which die. In her study of animal remains from Puna sites in the Andes, Jane Wheeler has linked the occurrence of large numbers of neonate camelid bones (after 3500 bc) with their close confinement, and hence domestication, in antiquity.

SUMMARY

To summarize briefly what archaeological evidence there is for when and where domesticated animals were first husbanded. The oldest domesticated animal seems to be the dog, perhaps descended from the wolf. Early reliably dated finds derive from a

6.22 A hypothetical scheme (based on a small amount of evidence) to illustrate the suggested rate of spreading of animal husbandry into Europe from the Near East. The dates refer to the introduction of domestic livestock such as sheep and goats (or the 'idea' of animal husbandry): (a) after 5000 bc, (b) between 6000 and 5000 bc, (c) between 7000 and 6000 bc, (d) before 7000 bc.

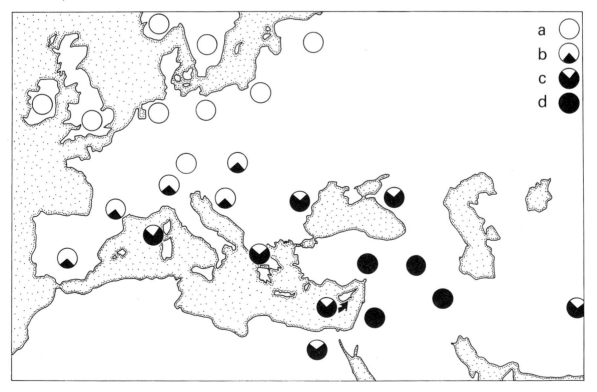

hunting-and-gathering culture-period in northern Israel. Other early finds also come from hunter-gatherer cultural contexts such as the Mesolithic site of Star Carr in Yorkshire, England (Degerbøl, 1961), and various North American sites. The dog would have been the only domestic animal that the early native Americans possessed. The dog was also introduced into Australia, and gave rise to the dingo. Its absence from Tasmania puts a limit of 10,000 bc to our estimate of when the dog first reached Australia since Tasmania became separated from mainland Australia at that time by the post-Pleistocene sea level rise.

Sheep and goats were domesticated some 2–3 millennia later. This probably occurred in the Near East during the eighth or seventh millennium bc (fig. 6.22). We cannot yet determine for certain whether goat herding began in the western part of the Near East (e.g. the 'fertile crescent') and sheep herding further east, though this is quite possible. Pigs and cows appear to have been first domesticated, probably in the Near East, very soon afterwards, perhaps during the seventh millennium bc. Cattle may have had two or even more separate centres of domestication, one in the Near East, the other in India. It is likely too that the pig was independently domesticated in China, but we still have very little evidence from that part of the world. According to Chow Ben-Shun (1984) there is evidence for domestic pig and dog in prehistoric China in the seventh millennium bc followed by chicken (?6000 bc) and water buffalo (3835–2240 bc). He compares north with south Chinese sites. In the north the main animals were pig, dog and chicken, while in the south they were pig, dog and water buffalo. In general then, early husbandry in east Asia relied upon the pig, early west Asian husbandry relied mainly upon sheep and goat, and perhaps south Asian husbandry relied on the large bovids (zebu, buffalo etc).

Animals like the donkey, the horse and the camel were probably not domesticated until the third or second millennium BC. Their geographical origins remain obscure—perhaps the Near East, southern Russia/central Asia and Arabia respectively. Llama and alpaca were probably domesticated by 3000 bc in the higher regions of the central Andes. The origins of the domestic rabbit, chicken, turkey etc are more recent, and lie partly within the realm of ancient history.

WHY DOMESTICATE ANIMALS IN THE FIRST PLACE?

Perhaps the most difficult question to address is why man domesticated animals in the first place. No doubt there were different reasons for different animals. The dog, a social carnivore like man, was perhaps exploited for its hunting ability. Caprines and bovids were presumably viewed as transportable sources of meat and so were domesticated for eating. Animals like the horse, donkey and camel were a source of power and transport and were domesticated to carry people and ever-increasing loads of produce (see next chapter).

Two somewhat fanciful suggestions as to why man first domesticated animals are Isaac's (1962) 'religious hypothesis' and Zeuner's (1963) 'crop robbers' hypothesis. Erich Isaac, a geographer, suggested a link between the shape of animal horns and the shape of that ancient deity— the moon. Frederik Zeuner saw animal domestication as following on from that of plants. Capture and domestication of animals like cattle was a necessary step to control and prevent them from stealing man's crops. An excess of grain would have been necessary to supply winter fodder. Plant-husbandry may indeed have preceded animal-husbandry.

For a long time it was believed that the transition from hunting to husbandry was a move from a precarious existence to one providing assured sustenance. The idea that hunting and gathering required high expenditure of energy with little return in the form of food and that a major labour saving is obtained by a switch to farming is probably wrong. Richard Lee (1968), studied the !Kung Bushmen, hunter-gatherers in the Kalahari of southern Africa. He discovered that Bushmen enjoy a plentiful and balanced diet, and only spend an average of 2.5 days per week in their quest for food. Similarly, Australian Aboriginals in Arnhem land spend an average of 3.5–5 hours per day food gathering and this activity is not particularly arduous. It is now realized that farming and husbanding animals are much more arduous than hunting and gathering, and require a higher input of labour.

The transition from hunting and gathering to farming in Denmark provides an interesting example. Peter Rowley-Conwy (1984) suggests a direct link between reduced food supply resulting from environmental change and the 'need' to adopt farming. Bandkeramic farmers reached north central Germany by *c*3700 bc (= 4500 BC), but the Danes with their Mesolithic Ertebølle culture did not adopt agriculture for another thousand years (2475–2400 bc). Most Ertebølle people were permanently settled, and coastal resources played a large role in their subsistence. Rowley-Conwy suggests that foraging was at least as attractive as farming, with oysters filling a vital gap in the seasonally available resources in springtime. So why the sudden appearance of agriculture *c*2400 bc in Denmark?

Towards the end of the fourth millennium bc, sea-level and coastline changes in Scandinavia led to a fall in the salinity of the sea in western Denmark, below that tolerated by the oyster. Ertebølle hunter-gatherers would have had to contend with intermittent ecological crises. And these led to the eventual adoption of farming.

Despite their lower efficiency, animal and especially plant husbandry are more intensive. A given area of land will support a larger number of people. Today many scholars believe that population pressure and cultural/economic change are closely if not causally linked. This belief takes its origin from the writings of the economist Thomas Malthus (1798), who also profoundly influenced Darwin's thought. Malthus thought of population levels as being dependent upon the availability of food resources, rather than population pressure directly stimulating economic change.

In the 1930s Gordon Childe suggested that domestication—the 'Neolithic' or 'food-producing revolution'—occurred soon after the last Ice Age when areas like the Near East became drier. Water sources and oases were therefore shrinking. The environment could no longer support as many animals and people as previously: its carrying capacity was reduced.

Mark Cohen (1977) has synthesized many anthropological and archaeological data. He suggests that an increase of the human population (population pressure) was the main factor which stimulated people to cultivate crops. Food-animal domestication would have followed hard on the heels of this first agricultural innovation.

Childe, Cohen, and Rowley-Conwy all see domestication as an adaptation to meet a crisis: the upsetting of a delicate balance between peoples' needs and what the environment could produce. Perhaps there is truth in their claims: added to the continuous population increase at this time a sudden reduction in the productivity of the environment—due to post-Pleistocene climate change—may have brought matters to a head.

The cultural period preceding the Neolithic food-producing revolution is characterized by a sophisticated technology (microliths, early traces of architecture, art, etc) and, in the Near East at any rate, 'villages' may have become permanently inhabited (Chapter 4).

Seasonal nomadism creates logistic problems in having children. The establishment of permanent settlements in the Mesolithic period would have solved some of these problems and given an additional spurt to the birth rate (Sussman, 1972). Localized pockets of dense population would have resulted. Indeed Near Eastern Mesolithic sites are generally larger than those from preceding periods.

Most archaeologists would agree that the world's human population had been steadily increasing for countless millennia. Cohen's evidence, mostly archaeological, shows that population had probably increased to a critical level by early Holocene times. The area of the globe inhabited by people had expanded and peripheral regions such as northeastern Asia had become colonized. In many regions there was an overall increase in the density of sites. Besides big game, other food resources were now exploited, such as the less desirable smaller mammals, fish and molluscs—and these ever more intensively. Pestles and mortars, common on Old World Mesolithic sites, suggest the use of foods requiring much preparation. Cohen argues that in the Near East a deterioration of climate at the end of the last Ice Age, while similar in degree to earlier climatic changes (such as the one of 70,000 years ago), might have coincided with a critically high level of human population.

Global climate change probably had a more marked effect upon peripheral regions such as those bordering the deserts of the Near East. A change in the human economy was therefore necessary in those regions above all. Unlike previous occasions, when population levels were lower and cultures more primitive, people were now intellectually better equipped to confront these problems, and they decided to husband crops and domesticate animals. I use the word 'decided' advisedly. Remember that Epipalaeolithic people were biologically no different from us, and were as intelligent as we are. Millennia of dependence upon hunting and gathering would have provided Epipalaeolithic people with a knowledge—in some ways better than our own—of the plants and animals on which they depended.

The Hatoula faunal sequence

It is clear that in the Levant food-animal domestication began in the PPNB period (7300–6000 bc). Therefore, a knowledge of man-animal relations during the preceding PPNA (8500–7300 bc) is important to understand why domestication occurred just when it did.

Some intriguing zoo-archaeological data have been uncovered from Monique Lechevallier and Avraham Ronens' excavation at Hatoula in central Israel. (The discovery, in 1982, of 'Digested' bones from the Natufian levels at this site is discussed on page 148.) The 1984–1986 seasons at Hatoula increased the sample of PPNA animal bones, so that a comparison with the bones from the underlying late Natufian (c9500–8500 bc) levels is now possible.

Joelle Pichon (a specialist in bird remains) and I noticed two quite striking differences between the Natufian and PPNA faunal assemblages:

1) Relative to large animals, there are many more birds, fish and small mammals such as hares and foxes in the PPNA than in the Natufian.

2) The age profiles of the gazelles indicate a higher proportion of juveniles in the PPNA than in the Natufian.

These differences between Natufian and PPNA culture periods may be reflecting an increase of the human population during the ninth and eighth millennia bc. By eighth millennium bc times, the increased population meant that people were forced to exploit sources of food such as small animals which are less rewarding in terms of meat obtained per unit of energy required to procure them. Gazelles were subjected to more intense hunting, which led to a higher turnover of gazelles (a downward shift of their age pyramid, as Elder had found for the deer in 'post-contact' North American Indian middens; see page 115). Later, during the seventh millennium bc (PPNB period) and perhaps resulting from further demographic pressure, an entirely new economic strategy had to be adopted: sheep and goats were domesticated.

CHAPTER SEVEN

Later domesticates and the secondary uses of animals

We have now established that sheep, goats, cattle and pigs were domesticated by *c*5000 bc in parts of the Old World. Once domesticated these animals must have been subjected to ever increasing artificial or man-induced selection. Different breeds have appeared.

Breeds largely reflect the various uses to which livestock are put by different peoples in different regions. Take cattle and sheep, for example; today in Britain the Aberdeen Angus is raised primarily for beef, while the Jersey is favoured for its rich milk; and in Persia there are three main breeds of sheep, one for wool, one mainly for meat, and one for lamb skins. Their common ancestors, the aurochs and wild sheep respectively, would have been hunted for their carcass products alone; you cannot milk wild animals.

Milk and wool brings us to the subject of this chapter—the exploitation of livestock for their so-called secondary products: milk, fibres, dung and muscular power. Andrew Sherratt (1981) suggests that the shift to secondary products separates two stages in the development of Old World agriculture: an early stage of hoe cultivation in which technology and transport were based upon human muscle power and in which animals were kept primarily for their slaughter products such as meat and hides, and a later stage with plough agriculture, pastoralism and a technology based upon the harnessing of animal power.

However the archaeological evidence is too scarce to determine whether such a shift in emphasis to secondary products was rapid or gradual. In this chapter I shall discuss what little evidence there is for when and where this shift may have first occurred, and the part it may have played in the rise of civilizations, particularly in the Near East. In brief, it appears that in that region for some time following domestication, sheep and goat continued to be regarded as mobile reserves of meat and hides. But several millennia later the new emphasis was upon exploiting the *living* animal in a continuous manner, rather than the *dead* animal. This must have been a significant development in animal husbandry.

MILK — ADVANTAGES AND PROBLEMS

From an economic point of view an enterprise based on milk production (sheep, goat and cattle being the most commonly milked animals) is often more efficient in terms of protein and energy output than one geared solely towards meat production. For example 4–5 times the amount of energy and protein are yielded in milk compared to meat per unit of feed. (Meat is still obtained from surplus males and old females.) From a dietary point of view milk is a good source of calcium as well as fat, protein, sugar, and vitamin D. Moreover, milk is easily converted to transportable and storable products such as yoghurt, butter and cheese. For some people, like the Reguibat camel nomads of the Sahara, milk may be the main source of nourishment (Gauthier–Pilters and Dagg, 1981).

Wild mammals do not produce milk in excessive quantities like some of the modern highly bred dairy animals of northern Europe do today. Breeding up milk livestock must have taken many generations of selection and so occurred some time—perhaps even millennia—after the initial domestication of livestock in the Near East. But where did this occur?

Geography and origin

A tenuous clue is provided by our own milk-consuming habits today. Milk is hardly drunk by most of the original inhabitants of west Africa, China, southeast Asia and the Americas. After weaning, most people from these regions are unable to digest 'milk-sugar' (lactose), since their digestive systems lose the ability to produce the enzyme lactase. Drinking milk results in diarrhoea, cramps and flatulence (Simoons, 1979; 1980). Most northern Europeans, Indians, Africans such as the Fulani and Maasai, and some Near Easterners are able to digest milk, however, which forms an important part of their diet. Milk contains vitamin D, which prevents rickets but which is also produced in our skin through the action of sunlight. The lack of sunlight in northern Europe could have conferred a selective advantage upon early farmers there who were able to utilize milk. A similar selective advantage for milk drinkers in the Middle East where cholera is prevalent has been hypothesized for the Bedouin (Simoons, 1979), as people afflicted with this disease need to drink large amounts.

Did milking originate therefore in the Near East/Europe? Many Mediterranean peoples (such as the Greeks and Cypriots) are lactose-intolerant, yet commonly practise milking. By the process of converting the lactose of fresh milk to lactic acid, as happens when yoghurt is prepared (using bacterial cultures), or further removing the lactic acid to produce cheese, these milk products become digestible even to the lactase-deficient. For example, over 80 per cent of the milk produced in Greece and Cyprus is converted to cheese, while the figure in Finland and Britain is 10 per cent or less (McCraken, 1971).*

WOOL BIOLOGY

The coats of wild sheep and goat consist of fairly short, thick, bristly hairs known as kemps, which obscure an even shorter undercoat of fine thin wool fibres (fig. 7.1). The Neolithic domestic caprines

*It is interesting to note that Strabo in his 'Geography' (IV, 5.2) wrote in 7 BC that the men of Britain, 'although well supplied with milk, make no cheese'.

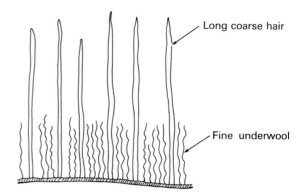

7.1 Wool versus kemp. Structure of the double coat in wild sheep. The long coarse hairs or kemps are about 6cm long. *From Ryder, 1969*

almost certainly had similar coats to their wild ancestors. Thus the 'wild' mouflon sheep of Corsica, Sardinia and Cyprus, and the Agrimi goat of Crete—both now thought to be feral descendants of livestock introduced by Neolithic man—have wild-type kempy coats. If included in clothing, kemp would make it rough and uncomfortable to wear: it has harsh 'handle'.

The fleeces of modern highly selected wool sheep have little or no kemp (fig. 7.2). This reduction in the hair diameter of the outer coat and the frequent elimination of kemp must have resulted from a long period of human selective breeding. The major changes from the coat of the wild sheep were (1) the development of a fleece, (2) the loss of the natural black and brown colour of the wild ancestor and (3) the disappearance of the annual spring moult, a change which prevented the loss of wool and allowed sheep to be shorn when the fleece is required (Ryder, 1969).

Among goats, unlike sheep, there has been little development of the coat for textile use. Ordinary goat hair has long been woven into coarse cloth, as in the tents of nomads. Cashmere is the underwool combed from a moulting goat with a coat little changed from that of the wild ancestor. Only the mohair grown by Angora goats resembles the fleece of a sheep. (Mohair is in fact superior to sheep's wool.)

Camel and llama hair and alpaca wool also make an important contribution, although little is known archaeologically of when camelid fibres were first used.

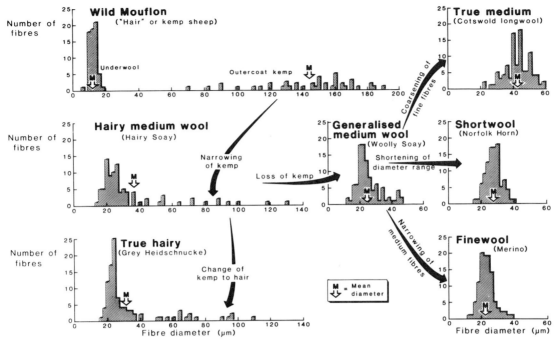

7.2 Fleece development in sheep. A plot of the frequencies of different diameter fibres in the coats of wild mouflon and several breeds of domestic sheep. 1μm (micron)=one thousandth of a millimetre. *From Ryder and Gabra-Sanders, 1985. Courtesy Michael Ryder*

ARCHAEOLOGICAL EVIDENCE FOR MILK AND WOOL

There is very little archaeological evidence for the beginning of dairying. Milk does not fossilize, although Zaky and Iskander (1942), who undertook a chemical analysis of the contents of jars from Saqqara in Egypt dated to 2400–2230 bc (3100–2890 BC), thought they might have contained cheese. And dairy breeds, like breeds generally, are hardly distinguishable on the basis of bone fragments. (It is difficult enough separating sheep bones from goat bones.) So an indirect approach is required. The most promising line of inquiry is a careful consideration of species frequencies and the ages at which animals were slaughtered in antiquity.

In a meat-producing economy it makes sense to slaughter near the end of an animal's immaturity (Payne, 1973). The kind of slaughter pattern that results from this strategy is exemplified by the modern Bedu goats from Deir el Arbaein in southern Sinai (fig. 7.3). They had mostly been slaughtered

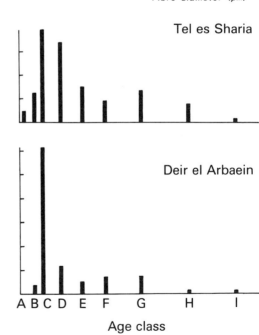

7.3 Age-related kill-off patterns of goats. Percentages of mandible age classes from Late Bronze Age levels at Tel es Sharia, northern Negev, Israel; and modern goat mandibles collected from an abandoned Bedu encampment at Deir el Arbaein in the southern Sinai, Egypt. The age classes are those of Payne (1973). Both patterns show a predominance of young, suggesting that meat was the prime objective.

between the age of 6 and 12 months. So too the age distribution of the caprines (mainly goats) at the Late Bronze Age site of Tel es Sharia (northern Negev, Israel) is thought to indicate a primarily meat-producing economy. Milk and wool production among sheep and goat does not significantly decline until they are several years of age (4–7 years was the age suggested to me by villagers in western Persia).

Thus, careful examination of the age distribution of sheep and goat mandibles from an archaeological site may provide some clue as to the kind of economy they represent. A predominance of juveniles may signify a meat economy. An abundance of older animals, greater than say five years of age, may indicate an economy emphasizing secondary products like milk and wool (besides meat). Let us turn to one faunal sequence where the possible beginning of secondary product exploitation may be recognized.

The Kermanshah faunal sequence

In 1978 Louis Levine carried out a series of small-scale excavations of 'village' sites (they were small mounds) near Kermanshah in western Persia (table 7.1). I was invited to study the faunal remains from his excavations at the four villages of Sarab, Siahbid, Choga Maran and Jammeh Shuran. The excavated levels spanned the period from the Ceramic Neolithic of c6000 bc to historic times (around 500 BC). In addition, Philip Smith had already excavated the nearby Aceramic Neolithic site of Ganj Dareh, whose fauna was studied by Brian Hesse (1978). So I had at my disposal a Neolithic-Historic faunal sequence from a restricted region of the Near East, which gave me an opportunity to consider economic development at a time—the fourth millennium BC—when the Near East was to become an important centre of

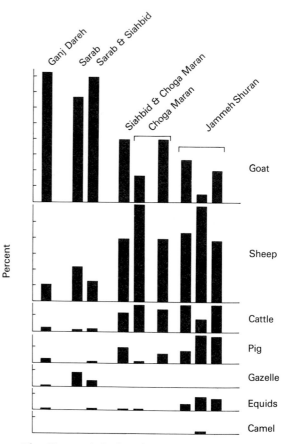

7.4 The Kermanshah faunal sequence. Percentages of different animals from sites and layers are plotted in chronological order from left to right: Ganj Dareh (Hesse, 1978), Aceramic Neolithic; Sarab, early Ceramic Neolithic; Sarab and Siahbid, late Ceramic Neolithic; Siahbid and Choga Maran, early Chalcolithic; Choga Maran, middle Chalcolithic; Choga Maran, Early Bronze Age; Jammeh Shuran 10–5, Iron Age III and I; Jammeh Shuran 4–3, Achaemenid; Jammeh Shuran 2–1, early Parthian. *From Davis, 1984*

Site	Period	^{14}C date	Historical date
Jammeh Shuran 2–1	Early Parthian		250 – 100 BC
Jammeh Shuran 4–3	Archaemenid		550 – 250 BC
Jammeh Shuran 10–5	Iron Age I–III		1200 – 550 BC
Choga Maran	Early Bronze Age	2200 – 1900 bc	2800 – 2500 BC
Choga Maran	Middle Chalcolithic	4100 – 2900 bc	5000 – 3600 BC
Choga Maran	Early Chalcolithic	5000 – 4100 bc	5800 – 5000 BC
Siahbid	Early Chalcolithic	5000 – 4100 bc	5800 – 5000 BC
Siahbid	Late Ceramic Neolithic	5500 – 5000 bc	
Sarab	Late Ceramic Neolithic	5500 – 5000 bc	
Sarab	Early Ceramic Neolithic	6000 – 5500 bc	
Ganj Dareh A–E	Aceramic Neolithic	8500 – 7000 bc	

Table 7.1 Sites excavated by Levine and Smith in the Kermanshah region, western Persia: levels and chronology.

civilization. My results, however, are little better than speculations since our samples are generally rather small.

But I did have sufficient material to analyse (a) the frequencies of different animals and (b) the age composition of the caprines (sheep and goat) and pigs.

First the species frequencies (fig. 7.4): these suggest a diversification of the animal economy from a reliance mainly on goat (and some gazelle—presumably hunted) in the Neolithic to a reliance on a more mixed spectrum of goat, sheep, cattle and pigs in the subsequent periods. By the first millennium BC (at Jammeh Shuran) equids too are well represented, and even camel is present.

The caprine age compositions proved to be most interesting (fig. 7.5). The majority of the caprines (mostly goat) culled in the Neolithic (Ganj Dareh, Sarab, and Siahbid) were aged 2–3 years and younger: presumably kids slaughtered for meat. A meat-producing economy is similarly suggested by data from several other Near Eastern and eastern Mediterranean Neolithic sites. For example, in a survey of Greek archaeological sites, Payne (1985) notes that a high proportion of the caprines from Neolithic sites had been slaughtered young. Over 60 per cent of the caprines slaughtered in the Neolithic period at Knossos in Crete were younger than two years. In the Neolithic levels at Franchthi cave in the south Argolid peninsula, most of the sheep and goats were young, and at the Aceramic Neolithic site of Nea Nikomedia in northern Greece the caprines were all killed before approximately four years of age, and many in their first year (Payne, pers. comm.). Further east at another Aceramic Neolithic site, Aşıklı Hüyük (Payne, 1985) in Nigde province, Anatolia (early seventh millennium bc), most of the sheep and goat had been slaughtered between the ages of one and four years. At Gritille Hüyük (also seventh millennium bc), in the Karababa basin of southeastern Anatolia, Stein and Wattenmaker (1984) found that most of the caprines were slaughtered before the age of two. They concluded that the Neolithic was 'an autonomous village based economy which relied predominantly on domesticated sheep and goats as a source of meat, rather than for secondary products', which they suggest accords well with the subsistence economy of a non-stratified society.

To return to my sequence from Kermanshah. The age composition of caprines from the later periods

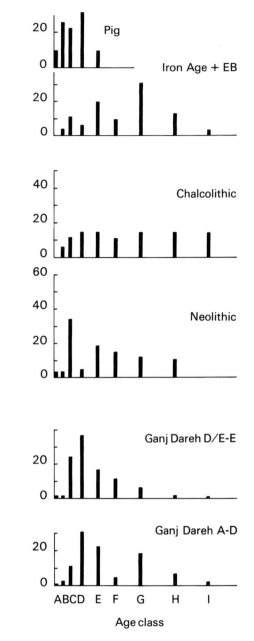

7.5 Age-related kill-off patterns of sheep/goat in the Kermanshah archaeofaunal sequence. The percentages of mandible age-classes are given. Pigs from Jammeh Shuran are also included. These patterns suggest a primarily meat economy in the Neolithic, and a subsequent shift in emphasis—perhaps in the Chalcolithic—to secondary products such as milk and wool. The Iron Age pigs were very young and were probably an important source of meat. Data from Ganj Dareh are from Hesse, 1978. *From Davis, 1984*

(when sheep predominate over goat), especially at Jammeh Shuran, shows a much higher proportion of older individuals. This kind of age distribution suggests that the sheep, prior to their slaughter, were exploited for products other than just meat. In contrast, the pigs culled at Jammeh Shuran—now obviously an important part of the animal economy—were mostly juvenile; i.e. pigs may have partially replaced kids as a source of meat. Despite the rather small samples from the Chalcolithic at Siahbid and Choga Maran, I am tempted to suggest (Davis, 1984) that the change from a caprine meat economy to a secondary products economy occurred during that period *c*5000–3000 bc in western Persia. In Europe there is some evidence (though perhaps as tenuous as my own from Persia) for the advent of secondary product exploitation, somewhat later, in the fourth and third millennia bc (see below).

Outside the Near East

Margaret Sakellaridis (1979) has summarized numerous reports of Mesolithic and Neolithic prehistoric excavations and their faunas in Switzerland. Approximately 3500 bc saw the replacement of a Mesolithic culture—based upon hunting red and roe deer, aurochs and boar—by a Neolithic one. The Neolithic saw the introduction of sheep and goat, both species foreign to that land and therefore presumably domestic. Sakellaridis discusses the age-related culling data of the cattle, sheep and goat. For example the percentages of mature (over 2–3 years) cattle at the early Neolithic sites of Eschen-Lutzenguetle and Eschen-Borscht (in the Alpine-Rhein valley) were between 50 and 80 per cent. At Ossingen-Hausersee (Pfyn and Corded ware cultures, *c*3000 bc) 80 per cent of the cattle had attained

maturity and most of these were female, but 85 per cent of the culled swine were below 2 years—not an atypical age for meat (i.e. pork) production. At the Neolithic (late Cortaillod culture, *c*2800 bc) sites of Seeberg-Burgaschisee Sud and Sudwest in western Switzerland the percentages of adult cattle were 50 and 61 per cent, a high proportion of the goats were adult and all of the adult goats and cattle were female. Thus cows and goats may have been milked. These data then suggest that milking could have been practised as early as 3500 bc in Switzerland. But many of these faunal samples are small and derive from excavations carried out by different archaeologists some time ago. Therefore any conclusions regarding secondary exploitation must be viewed with caution.

In the Middle Bronze Age, *c*850 bc (*c*1000 BC) at Grimes Graves, Norfolk, England, Tony Legge has interpreted the ageing and sex data of cattle as indicating a dairy economy. He found (Legge, 1981) that the majority of the males were killed while young, leaving a female:male sex ratio among adult cattle of between 4:1 and 6:1 (Chapter 8).

OTHER EVIDENCE FOR EARLY DAIRYING

Is there any other evidence to support the contention that milking began almost 7000 years ago? The answer is: not much. According to Simoons (1971) and Sherratt (1981), the earliest pictorial evidence for milking comes from an Uruk period (*c*2500 bc) cylinder seal from Iraq. It depicts reed-built byres with calves and jugs—possibly for milk. More impressive evidence comes from the temple of Ninhursag at al 'Ubaid (*c*2000 bc), Iraq (fig. 7.6). It is

7.6 Frieze from the temple of Ninhursag at al 'Ubaid, Iraq, dated to *c*2300–1600 bc (third millenium BC). Human figures appear to be milking cows. See Hall and Woolley, 1927. *Photograph courtesy the Trustees of the British Museum*

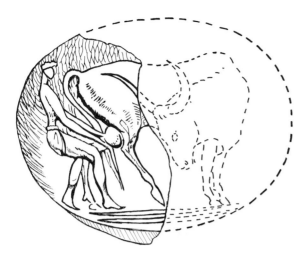

7.7 Late Bronze Age seal impression from the palace of Minos at Knossos, Crete, which depicts a human milking a cow. *From Evans, 1935 (By permission of Mark Paterson on behalf of the Sir Arthur Evans Trust)*

an inlay frieze of limestone figures milking (from the back) what appear to be cows. A series of human figures and large jars suggest milk being processed (Hall and Woolley, 1927). A seal from Sir Arthur Evans' (1935) excavation at Late Bronze Age Knossos (Crete, fig. 7.7) also shows milking.

Widespread and radical changes in the kinds of pottery vessels in Europe and the Near East may also reflect this dietary innovation. These new kinds of vessel occur in the Ghassulian of the Levant, and the Early Bronze Age of Anatolia, Bulgaria and Cyprus, and the Baden culture (*c*2500 bc) of central Europe. In Italy they are referred to as 'milk boilers' and in Cyprus as 'milk bowls' (Sherratt, 1981).

OTHER EARLY EVIDENCE OF WOOL

The history of textiles is a discipline unto itself. For a long time in Europe flax was probably the main source of fibres and was woven into linen textiles. Preserved textile fragments from the fourth and early third millennia BC in Swiss lakeside villages are all linen. Cotton did not diffuse westwards out of India until classical times (the late fourth century BC) and its use was relatively limited until the Roman conquests of the second and first centuries BC (Mazzaoui, 1981).

The earliest evidence for wool is from literary and pictorial records in the Near East and seems to coincide with the beginning of urbanization in Mesopotamia (Sherratt, 1981). But an archaeological record of wool fibres has only so far been traced in Europe. Michael Ryder, a wool biologist, has devoted many years of study to the fleece changes evident in archaeological remains of textiles which are only rarely preserved (see for example Ryder, 1969; 1983).

In certain European waterlogged archaeological deposits, a transition from linen to wool appears to have occurred as a result of the introduction of wool into north-central Europe in the Corded Ware and Early Bronze Ages (fig. 7.8). The earliest European find of wool is the wrapping from a flint dagger handle belonging to the late Neolithic 'Dagger

7.8 A wool blanket from the Danish Early Bronze Age period II. This comes from the burial mound of Trindhoj in south Jutland. *Photograph courtesy Elisabeth Munksgaard, National Museum, Copenhagen*

period' beginning *c*1900 bc (2400 BC). It came from a peat bog at Wiepenkathen in northern Germany (Sherratt, 1983). Sherratt (1981) also notes that in the Early Bronze Age, pins suitable for fastening loose woollen weaves became common, replacing the buttoned leather clothing of the Neolithic.

Ryder suggests that a fleece did not develop until the Bronze Age in Europe, and that white sheep began to become more common during the Iron Age, which was also when the breeding of sheep with continuous wool growth may have begun. In Egypt, however, there is little evidence of fleeced sheep before the New Kingdom (*c*1290 bc; 1570 BC), and he (Ryder, 1984) suggests that flax was the primary fibre there for much longer than in Europe.

ANIMAL POWER

Another change which occurred in man's perception of animals was the idea of harnessing their muscular power to carry burdens across long distances, and to pull ploughs, wheeled carts and even chariots of war. The use of pack animals must have eased the problems of transporting harvest, etc. Both domestic ass and camel no doubt enabled many Near Eastern peoples to adopt a nomadic way of life. Animal-drawn ploughs would have made exploitation of difficult soils possible and may have been a major factor in the expansion of settled parts of the Near East in post-Neolithic times.

Cattle were probably the first of the large animals to be exploited as beasts of burden and traction, and are still an important source of power in many parts of the world (Zeuner, 1963). Dogs, sheep and goats also may serve to pull and carry small loads, but there is little archaeological evidence for their use in this respect.

Archaeological evidence
Only through very careful analysis of sex-ratios, and pathologies induced by mechanical stress and castration, can we hope to discover when cattle were first used as a source of power rather than as a source of meat, etc (fig. 7.9).

Armour-Chelu (Chapter 8) has found possible evidence for stress-induced pathology of cattle bones from a Neolithic site in England.

From Vadastra, a late fifth-millennium bc site on the lower Danube and other sites in Rumania,

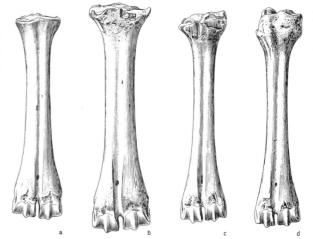

7.9 Pathology which may have been induced by excessive strain. (a) Normal cattle metatarsal, (b) metatarsal with exostosis (extra bone deposition) at the proximal end, (c) and (d) metatarsals and one of the tarsal bones have fused. These examples are from the fourteenth- to sixteenth-century AD site of Dokkum in Holland. *From Gelder-Ottway, 1979. Courtesy Anneke Clason and Sheila van Gelder-Ottway*

Corneliu Mateescu (1975) noticed that the proximal and distal articulations of cattle radii were 'more developed in transverse direction' compared with modern cattle not used for traction. The cattle, therefore, may have been subjected while still young to great physical effort, and resistance to stress at the joints had resulted in remodelling of the bone. Mateescu speculates that cattle were used at Vadastra for ploughing, transport and threshing, and cites the abundant remains of cereals in pits, etc as evidence for large-scale cultivation of cereals in the Middle and Late Neolithic on the lower Danube.

Reports of articular pathologies in early (e.g. Neolithic, Bronze and Iron Age) material are rare. Studies of stress-induced osteological changes are certainly a worthwhile avenue of research. What is needed is a properly controlled experiment in which animals today are subjected to varying degrees of mechanical stress. A start could be made by collecting recent skeletons of retired work animals, and as a first step John Baker and Don Brothwell (1980) recommend a study of draught buffalo used in rice paddies.

Sherratt (1981, and 1983) cites cultural evidence for the use of cattle power. Some of the examples he gives are Sumerian pictograms and cylinder seals from Uruk in southern Mesopotamia which date to

7.10 Cattle power. Impression of a cylinder seal of the Uruk period, 3200–2700 bc (first half of the fourth millennium BC). *Drawing by Ann Searight, courtesy Andrew Sherratt*

7.11 Cattle power. Impression of a cylinder seal of the Akkadian period, *c*1850 bc (2300 BC), from southern Mesopotamia which shows a two-handled plough (ard) with sowing funnel. *Courtesy the Ashmolean Museum, Oxford*

the end of the fourth millennium bc (fig. 7.10), and copper models of yoked oxen from Bytyn near Poznan in Poland which date to c2750 bc (3500 BC).

The earliest plough marks have been found under long barrows in Britain, Denmark and Poland dated to c2625 bc (3400 BC; Sherratt, 1981). These are assumed to signify animal traction, but the possibility of man-drawn ploughs should be considered. The earliest evidence for the use of wheeled carts comes from Archaic Sumerian pictograms from Uruk (Sherratt, 1981 and fig. 7.11 for a later example). Sherratt suggests that both plough and cart were developed in northern Mesopotamia by c3200 bc and within half a millennium or so spread as far as northwestern Europe.

The spread of plough and cart heralded a major alteration of the economy and settlement patterns. It marks the beginning of the Early Bronze Age in Anatolia, the Aegean and the Balkans, the Baden culture in central Europe, the Middle Neolithic in northwestern Europe and the Chalcolithic in southwestern Europe.

Perhaps the major handicap facing the zooarchaeologist, trying to trace the use of animals like the horse, ass and camel for power, is the scarcity of their bones in the archaeofaunal record. This is hardly surprising since few animals need be kept for this purpose, compared with the numbers of animals such as sheep and goats kept for food. There is also little to differentiate the bones and teeth of domestic horse from wild horse, donkey from ass and onager, and wild camel from domestic camel. Much of the evidence for the harnessing of animal power therefore comes from cultural finds such as plough marks, bas-reliefs, ceramic models, appurtenances such as bits and even (in the second and first millennia bc) texts. It is most likely that animals such as the horse, donkey and camel played a major role in the growth of Near Eastern trade and civilization from the fourth millennium bc on.

THE EQUIDS— HORSE AND DONKEY

Horse

One source of animal power that had a great impact upon civilization was the horse. The horse is an animal of speed and has been harnessed as an engine of war. In the Near East the chariot is associated with newcomers, Kassites, Hittites and Hurrians—peoples who dominated western Asia in the mid-second millennium bc (Drower, 1969). The horse is often implicated in the expansion of Indo-European speaking peoples (Piggott, 1952:273; Epstein, 1972). Superior understanding of the use of stirrups by William's mounted soldiers led to King Harold's defeat at Hastings in 1066, and to the Norman conquest of England (Chapter 8).

Most authorities believe that the horse was domesticated from the tarpan, the wild horse of the steppes of eastern Europe, southern Russia and the Ukraine, which finally became extinct in the Ukraine by the end of the nineteenth century (Bökönyi, 1978). Horse remains are known from the late Pleistocene of the Levant and many regions of Europe: it probably became extinct there in the early Holocene before the Neolithic. Among more than 100,000 animal bones from several dozen Neolithic sites in the Carpathian basin Bökönyi failed to find a single horse bone.

The presence of antler bits from the fourth-millennium bc Chalcolithic settlement of Dereivka on the Dnieper river (Bökönyi, 1978) may be considered as the earliest possible evidence for domestic horse in the southern Russia/Ukraine region.

At Norşun Tepe in eastern Anatolia, small numbers of horse remains were identified from the first half of the third millennium bc (Chalcolithic) by Boessneck and von den Driesch (1976), who consider them to be derived from wild horse. Bökönyi (1978), however, suggests that the Norşun Tepe horse may have been domesticated. I have identified horse bones from the Early Bronze Age at Arad in the northern Negev of Israel (c2280–2080 bc; 2950–2650 BC; Davis, 1976, fig. 7.12), but cannot state with any certainty that these were from domestic horses. However, horse has not been found in Israel in Mesolithic, Neolithic or Chalcolithic sites, so it is tempting to consider the Arad horse as domestic.

Horses do not appear in quantity in northern and central Europe until the Early Bronze Age (Beaker) period, c2000 bc, and they are associated with the Bell Beaker people. In Ireland too the horse first appeared c2000 bc in the Beaker period (Wijngaarden-Bakker, 1974) and by 1600 bc the horse had become quite common in central Europe. A little later still, before the thirteenth century BC (in the Early Yin period of King Wu Ting's reign) domestic horse first appeared in China (Chow Ben-Shun, 1984).

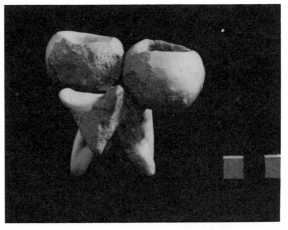

7.13 Model of an animal (?donkey) carrying two containers on its back from the Chalcolithic of Giv'atayim, Israel. *Courtesy J. Kaplan*

7.12 The domestication of the horse. A horse metacarpal (on the left), compared with two ass or onager metacarpals (on the right), from the Early Bronze Age site of Arad, northern Negev, Israel. (See also **1.12**.) *Photograph Abraham Niv*

Donkey

The wild ass was once widely distributed in the arid regions of the Near East and northeastern Africa. I have identified ass bones and teeth from the Chalcolithic (3660–2400 bc) at Teleilat Ghassoul in Jordan and from the Early Bronze Age at Arad in the northern Negev of Israel (Davis, 1980). However, since Arad and Ghassoul are situated on the desert's edge where wild ass was once common, and since the teeth and bones of domestic ass and wild ass are virtually impossible to distinguish, the Arad and Ghassoul finds could well derive from wild ass.

Sherratt (1983), however, has brought together several interesting items of archaeological evidence from these same periods in Israel, suggesting the use of pack animals. They consist of an animal figure carrying two containers on its back (fig. 7.13; Kaplan, 1969), a bull carrying 'churns' from Chalcolithic contexts and a pack donkey from the Early Bronze Age I. An Early Bronze Age III pottery model of a donkey carrying baskets from Cyprus (Sherratt, 1981) reinforces the theory that this animal was being harnessed in the Near East by the early second millennium bc.

The question of whether the Persian onager had previously been harnessed to pull carts has not been satisfactorily resolved. It is only with difficulty that certain bones (the metapodials) of ass and onager may be distinguished (Chapter 1).

THE IMPACT OF EQUIDS

How does the appearance of donkeys and horses in the Near East in the fourth/third millennia bc tie in with what is known about the rise of civilizations and the growth of trade? The possible use of pack animals at that time can be linked with an expansion into the Negev and Sinai, and increasing trade, metallurgical activity, and the formation of trade links with predynastic Egypt. These trade routes are said to have become increasingly important during the period of formation of the Egyptian state. Traded objects appear, though bulk trade by sea apparently took over from the fifth dynasty onwards (Sherratt, 1983).

As for horses, they became widespread in the Near East in the first half of the second millennium bc when the earlier forms of solid-wheeled carts were refined by way of the cross-bar and spoked wheels into the horse-drawn chariot (Sherratt, 1983). Chariotry was further developed on the steppes, and thence reached Europe c1620 bc, where models of spoked wheels are found in the Otomani culture of eastern Hungary and Rumania, and by 1300 bc in Mycenae, Greece. Thus chariotry, horse-rearing expertise and its technical vocabulary may have developed in a wide arc around the older civilizations of the Near East in the middle second millennium bc (Sherratt, 1983).

THE CAMEL

Both camel and donkey are associated with dry climates. However, the camel has certain advantages over the donkey. The camel can carry twice the load of a donkey, moves faster, and needs less frequent feeding and watering. Once domesticated, the camel allowed man to traverse and exploit the vast desert belt which stretches from Morocco in the west, across north Africa and Arabia to central Asia in the east. Camels are closely linked with desert nomadism such as is practised by the Tuareg and Bedouin today, the development of caravan trade on a more 'international' scale, and in later times the Arab domination of the Sahara (Gauthier-Pilters and Dagg, 1981). Camels even came to supplant wheeled transport throughout much of the Near East, especially when many of the Roman roads fell into disrepair (Bulliet, 1975).

Today there are two sub-species of camel: the desert-adapted one-humped dromedary of Arabia and north Africa, and the more robust, short-limbed, longer-haired, two-humped bactrian of central Asia. Apart from feral herds, the dromedary no longer exists in the wild; a population of wild bactrians may still exist in Mongolia. When mated, dromedary and bactrian produce vigorous offspring (Zeuner, 1963). Both must have been independently domesticated, the dromedary perhaps in southern Arabia (Hadramaut for example, where it may initially have been exploited for its milk; Bulliet, 1975) and the bactrian in Asia (perhaps in Persia). As with horse and donkey, evidence for early camel exploitation is sparse too.

Textual references to the camel and actual finds of this animal are rare in the Middle East before the end of the second millennium bc. The ancient Egyptians named everything they saw, including even fleas, but their texts remain silent with regard to the camel (Midant-Reynes and Braunstein-Silvestre, 1977). This makes the early Biblical account of camels somewhat anomalous: the account of the ten camels used by Abraham's servant bringing Rebecca, Isaac's future wife, from Mesopotamia (*Genesis*, 24: Abraham lived in the sixteenth century bc or nineteenth century BC). Perhaps, as Richard Bulliet (1975:64) suggests, the domestic dromedary was known 'on an occasional basis' between 1950 and 1100 bc.

According to Bulliet's hypothesis, towards the end of the second millennium bc camels came to be widely exploited and bred in parts of the Middle East. He links this spread of the camel with the increase in the incense trade, a trade which was probably in the hands of Semitic peoples and which led eventually to the rise of Petra. Semites probably arrived in southern Arabia, where camels were possibly already domesticated, between 1030 and 980 bc. The substances in demand, frankincense and myrrh, are gum resins found in southern Arabia which were very highly prized in antiquity, and valued like gold. They were used in offerings and cosmetics, and they figured among the classical materia medica (Van Beek, 1969).

Archaeology
Paula Wapnish (1981) studied the animal bones from Tel Jemmeh in the northern Negev, Israel (near the ancient port of Gaza). She speculates on a link between the military use of the camel (probably dromedary) as a pack animal and the development of the incense trade. Most of the 500 camel bones that she found at Jemmeh (only a very small proportion of the faunal remains) came from the Assyrian (675–600 BC) and neo-Babylonian/Persian (c600–332 BC) periods. Those from the Assyrian period may derive from camels used as pack animals by Assyrian soldiers, under Esarhaddon and later his son Ashurbanipal, who invaded Egypt. The first historical references to camels in Egypt date to this time (Midant-Reynes and Braunstein-Silvestre, 1977). Jemmeh is situated at the end of a great trunk route connecting Israel with Egypt, as well as the great spice route into southern Arabia—the source of frankincense and myrrh. Wapnish suggests that these camel bones may derive from lame and other unwanted camels sold off by desert traders using them as pack animals along the spice routes.

Some further intriguing evidence for pre-second-

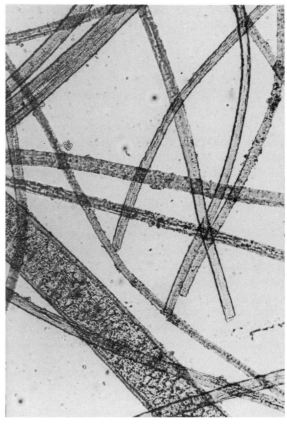

7.15 The camel and its secondary products. A microscopic examination of wool fibres from fragment 4234 (see **7.14**). According to Compagnoni and Tosi (1978) the thick camel hair seen here is easily distinguishable from fibres of sheep or goat. Magnification is approximately × 185. *Photograph courtesy Giovanna Vallauri, ISMEO, Rome*

7.14 The camel and its secondary products. An 8cm long fragment of wool (no. 4234 from room ccxiiia of phase 6) from Shahr-i Sokhta, Seistan, eastern Persia dated *c*2000 bc (2700–2500 BC). Scale in centimetres. See Compagnoni and Tosi, 1978. *Photograph courtesy Giovanna Vallauri, ISMEO, Rome*

millennium bc camel, through not necessarily domestic, comes from the site Shahr-i Sokhta in Seistan, northeastern Persia. Here Bruno Compagnoni and Maurizio Tosi (1978) have uncovered and identified camel hair (figs. 7.14 and 7.15), dung and bones which date *c*2120–2000 bc. Several of the bones may have belonged to the bactrian camel. The camel dung was found in a jar. On the basis of the size of the

dung, it probably derived from a young animal. Camel hair too was identified—woven together with a much larger quantity of sheep or goat fibres.

During a re-examination of the photographic archives from Sir Mortimer Wheeler's excavation of Mohenjo-Daro in the Indus valley (Harappan culture, *c*1850 bc; 2300 BC), Richard Meadow (1984) identified a photograph of a one-year-old camel skeleton; it had probably been buried on purpose. Camel bones and figurines of two-humped camels were found at Pirak in the northern Kacchi plain in second- and first-millennium bc deposits (Meadow, 1984). Pirak, near the foot of the Bolan pass, is on one of the major trade routes connecting Sind with the Afghan highlands, the Persian plateau and central Asia. Meadow links the introduction of this animal into the Indus valley in the second millennium bc with the onset of long-distance trade with peoples in the highland regions.

SOME GENERAL CONSIDERATIONS

Let me conclude this chapter by speculating upon the possible interaction between man-animal relations and the rise of human civilization based upon the admittedly scant archaeological and faunal evidence from the Near East.

During the ninth, eighth and seventh millennia bc, Neolithic society was organized in small tribes or villages with relatively simple societies; that is, no complex hierarchies existed. Villagers were probably living more or less at subsistence level, growing just enough crops to feed themselves and their livestock. Animals (mainly sheep and goat) were probably raised primarily for their slaughter products, i.e. meat and hides. Some hunting supplemented this source of meat.

After 6000 bc, during the sixth-fourth millennia bc, the following economic changes may have occurred:

(1) Sheep and goat began to be exploited for their milk and wool.

(2) Animal power (as from oxen) harnessed to ploughs permitted settlement of marginal lands.

An initial step towards the rise of Near Eastern civilizations may have been the production of agricultural surpluses which could in turn be traded. Surpluses would have included not just crops and beasts, but also milk products, wool, and even locally manufactured textiles. Trade was a crucial factor in the process of urbanization (Crawford, 1973), fostering the development of market centres, each serving a hinterland of small agricultural villages.

Trade requires transport; hence the need for pack animals and (when the terrain is not too mountainous) animal-drawn wheeled vehicles. This need to transport goods may be correlated in the Near East with the presence of domestic ass and horse as early as the Chalcolithic. Trade, especially across long distances, implies the existence of a merchant class, the accumulation of wealth, and the stratification of society. Moreover, these trading centres (cities) served as meeting places for traders from foreign lands, and became foci for the cross-fertilization of different cultures and ideas (Leemans, 1977).

Archaeology suggests that by the third millennium bc the great proto-urban centres were carrying on a vast amount of trade. Beale (1973) cites the example of southern Mesopotamia which was then a great argicultural country offering products such as cereals, fish, beasts, oils, textiles and leather articles. In return it could receive cedar, various metals and precious substances such as lapis lazuli and steatite. He suggests that there was a balanced relation between Mesopotamia and Persia and that the development of cities was taking place at the same time in at least four culturally distinct areas east of Mesopotamia—this largely thanks to long-distance trade. However, none of these changes (trade, accumulation of wealth and urbanization) would have been possible without domesticated beasts of burden. So careful consideration of faunal remains from post-Neolithic sites in the Near East is vital in trying to understand these economic developments.

Trade required keeping of accounts and hence the invention of writing. Centres of wealth would inevitably have asserted their power over expanding amounts of territory, giving rise to the 'city state'. This implies a governing class, perhaps aided by a military whose deployment required horse-drawn vehicles and pack animals.

Further improvement in trade might have come in the second millennium bc with the domestication and widespread use of the camel. This animal was probably important in the development of a new lifestyle in the Near East—desert nomadism. Nomads themselves probably undertook much of the long-distance trade, or at least controlled it as it passed through their territory.

By this time the Near East was divided up among several powerful civilizations whose power was to some extent clearly the result of successful harnessing of animals like the horse and camel.

CHAPTER EIGHT

Britain: a zoo-archaeological case study

Many British archaeological sites were dug in the nineteenth and early twentieth centuries, when the complexities of stratigraphy were less well understood and digging techniques more primitive than they are today. Many valuable data like fossil animal bones were unfortunately lost as a result. One of the richest Pleistocene sequences, at Cresswell crags in Derbyshire, was 'uncovered' (if that is the right word) in the 1860s in just three days—using dynamite!

However, some invaluable findings emerged: finds of man-made tools associated with remains of extinct animals helped to vindicate the pioneers of evolutionary biology, like Charles Darwin, in their efforts to demonstrate the antiquity of man. In this connection, remember Frere's (1800) late eighteenth-century finds at Hoxne, Suffolk (see Introduction). In this chapter I shall discuss many of the major relevant sites in the British Isles one by one.

For most of the Pleistocene, Britain was strongly influenced by the severe climate of the glacial periods or 'Ice Ages' (fig. 8.1, and table 8.1). There were many of these, separated by warm interglacials, each probably lasting between 10,000 and 20,000 years. During the coldest parts of the Ice Ages most of Britain was covered by an ice cap (fig. 8.2).

So much water was frozen in the North American and Scandinavian ice caps during glacial periods that sea levels were considerably lower than they are now. This is known as 'Eustatic sea-level lowering'. It uncovered a broad land-connection between Britain and the continent across the North Sea and English Channel from Denmark south to northern France.

Glacials and interglacials may be characterized by their respective cold and warm faunas. Indeed much Pleistocene palaeontology has tried to match successions of cold and warm faunas with the conjectured sequence of glacial and interglacial periods.

When conditions became warmer after the last Ice Age (the Devensian; see fig. 8.4 and table 8.1 for British Pleistocene terminology) there was a period during which Britain was still connected to the continent. This allowed the replenishment of the British fauna by warmth-loving species. Once Britain became an island again, any further arrival of new species, apart from bats and birds, could only have occurred by boat through the agency of man. The British Late Pleistocene-Holocene faunal succession reflects both the natural climatic variation and the migration of man and his animals—both food-stock and commensals.

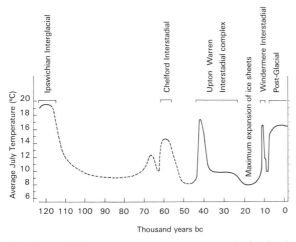

8.1 Upper Pleistocene summer temperatures in lowland central Britain since the last Interglacial, based on evidence from fossil beetles. *From Coope, 1977*

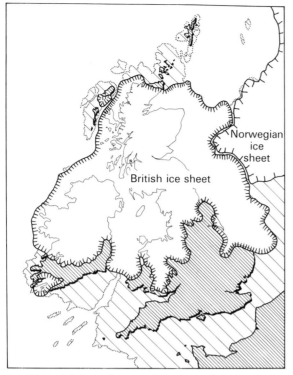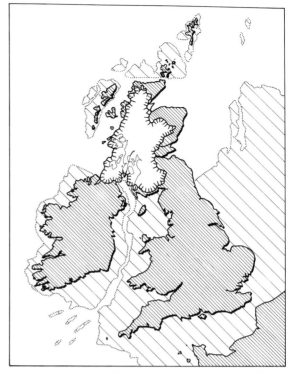

8.2 Map of Britain showing the extent of the ice during maximum glaciation (left) and during the late last Glacial (right). Obliquely hatched areas represent ice-free land. *From Campbell, 1977*

Apart from a period at the end of the Devensian, man was absent from these Isles during the main Ice Ages themselves. Presumably it was too cold. We catch 'archaeological glimpses' of him only during the relatively brief interglacials and interstadials (the latter being the even shorter warm periods during Ice Ages). The earliest firm evidence of man dates from the Hoxnian interglacial some 250,000 years ago. (The 'chipped flints' from the earlier bone accumulation at Westbury-sub-Mendip are no longer considered to be man-made: that assemblage represents a natural accumulation of animal remains.)

Three sites of Hoxnian age which have yielded remains, both cultural and animal, are Hoxne, Clacton and Swanscombe. At Swanscombe three fragments of a human skull were found. These sites have 'Clactonian' industries containing pebble and biconical choppers, and Acheulian industries with hand axes. Among the mammals found in these sites are the straight-tusked elephant *Palaeoloxodon antiquus*, wild boar, aurochs, lion, horse, an extinct rhinoceros

Dicerorhinus hemitoechus, macaque monkey, wolf, the extinct cave bear *Ursus spelaeus*, the extinct giant deer or 'Irish elk' *Megaceros giganteus*, fallow, red and roe deer, and an extinct giant beaver *Trogontherium cuvieri* (Stuart, 1982; table 7.2). Herds of large herbivorous mammals clearly abounded in Hoxnian Britain.

Identification of the elephant remains provides some clue to the nature of the environment. The number of enamel plates on the grinding surface of elephant teeth is related to toughness of diet. *Palaeoloxodon antiquus* had relatively few plates and fed on the succulent foliage of trees and bushes. *Mammuthus primigenius*, the woolly mammoth, with many more plates, was able to cope with tough fibrous plants of the tundra and steppe. These two forms apparently evolved from the unspecialized Upper Pliocene species *Archidiskodon meridionalis* soon after the first cold phases of the Pleistocene (fig. 8.3, Zeuner, 1958:386, Stuart, 1982:87). At Swanscombe, the presence of *Palaeoloxodon antiquus* suggests a wooded environment, although its decreasing frequency further up that sequence suggests an increasingly open environment, and perhaps a return to colder, steppic conditions (Evans, 1975).

To the Ipswichian Interglacial are assigned, admit-

	1000 AD		1066	Norman conquest
	500 AD			Jutes and Saxons arrive
			410	Britain separated from Roman empire
	0		43	Roman occupation begins
				Belgae arrive
		Iron Age		
FLANDRIAN 'Postglacial'				
	1000 bc			
		Bronze Age		
	1500			
		Neolithic		
	4000			
		Mesolithic		
	8300			
		Later Upper Palaeolithic		
DEVENSIAN mainly cold				
		Earlier Upper Palaeolithic		
	70,000	Middle Palaeolithic		
IPSWICHIAN interglacial				
	125,000			
WOLSTONIAN mainly cold				
	200,000	Lower Palaeolithic		
HOXNIAN interglacial	(370,000)			
	250,000			
ANGLIAN glacial	(400,000)			

Table 8.1 Chronology of the Upper Pleistocene and Holocene in Britain. (From various sources and courtesy J. Wymer and P. Ashbee).

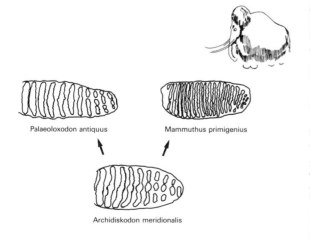

Palaeoloxodon antiquus

Mammuthus primigenius

Archidiskodon meridionalis

8.3 The biting (occlusal) surface of a molar tooth of the Early Pleistocene elephant, *Archidiskodon meridionalis*, and its supposed descendants: the woodland straight-tusked elephant, *Palaeoloxodon antiquus*, and the cold-adapted mammoth, *Mammuthus primigenius*. From Zeuner, 1958. M. Breuil's rendering of an early anonymous artist's sketch of what the mammoth probably looked like is shown above. *From Maska* et al., *1912*

tedly with some doubt, a number of Palaeolithic sites with associated mammal faunas, often showing marked differences. At Ilford and Aveley (Lower Thames valley) there are numerous mammoths and horses but no hippopotami. At Trafalgar Square (London) hippopotamus—often taken to indicate a warm climate—is present but there are no mammoths or horses. Another Thames valley site which is apparently Ipswichian (there are no reindeer) is Crayford. Here a Levalloisian stone-tool industry was found associated with mammoth, woolly rhinoceros (*Coelodonta antiquitatis*), horse and deer. Several other assemblages of mammal bones from southeastern England have been found, but good evidence for the contemporary presence of ancient man is often wanting. During the Ipswichian Interglacial the fallow deer again returned to Britain (fig. 8.4). It was smaller than the Hoxnian fallow, though still larger than the modern English fallow (Lister, 1984).

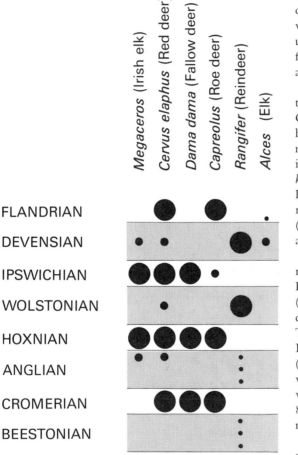

8.4 Deer in Britain. Known occurrences of giant deer ('Irish elk'), red deer, fallow deer, roe deer, reindeer, and elk in the Ice Ages (shaded) and Interglacials (unshaded). Large circles = present through major part of stage; centrally placed medium circles = sporadic occurrence through stage; medium circle at top of zone = known only from late part of stage; small dots = occurrence of uncertain age within stage. *From Lister, 1984*

At Tornewton cave in south Devon, a rich fossiliferous deposit was first excavated in the late nineteenth century, and subsequently re-investigated in the 1950s by Sutcliffe and Zeuner (1962). The mammal faunas of the different strata there suggest a climatic cycle. The bottom levels, which contain glutton and reindeer, represent a cold climate stage. This is followed by an interglacial layer without reindeer or glutton, but containing *Dicerorhinus hemitoechus* (a southern form of the woolly rhino), hippopotamus, and large quantities of hyaena bones and coprolites. The cave may have served as a hyaena den during this period. The interglacial layer is overlain by a 'cold' stratum with reindeer, horse and woolly rhinoceros. The cave had been sporadically used by man in the upper stratum, as evidenced by a few flint artefacts and over 400 fragments of reindeer antler—perhaps evidence for man's antler industry.

The question of which Interglacial is represented in the Tornewton sequence was resolved by Sutcliffe (in Ovey, 1964). He suggested that the presence of hippopotamus and hyaena (both absent in the Hoxnian), the abundance of *Dicerorhinus hemitoechus* (rare in the Hoxnian) and the absence of *Dicerorhinus kirchbergensis* (present in the Hoxnian) all argue for an Ipswichian date. If this is correct, the Tornewton cave may contain deposits from the Wolstonian Glaciation (the last-but-one Ice Age), Ipswichian Interglacial and the Devensian Glaciation.

There is only meagre evidence for the presence of man during the first part of the last Ice Age, the Devensian. But 26,000 years ago Upper Palaeolithic (blade-tool culture) man was sufficiently sophisticated to recolonize Britain; at least southern Britain. There are, however, no human remains known from Britain between Early and Late Upper Palaeolithic (26,000 and 12,500 bc), presumably because the cold was then too severe. The Late Upper Palaeolithic, which commenced in 12,500 bc and lasted until 8000 bc, thus marks the beginning of man's permanent presence in this land.

J.J. Wymer (in Simmons and Tooley, 1981) has summarized a number of findings of large mammals from Upper Palaeolithic sites. For example, lion and woolly rhino were found in a level at Kent's Cavern, south Devonshire, dated to 12,325 bc, and a mammoth carpal was found in a north Wales cave dated to 16,045 bc. He suggests that these large animals may have survived in Britain until they were finally slaughtered to extinction by later Upper Palaeolithic

Culture period				Late Upper Palaeolithic		Early Mesolithic		Late Mesolithic		Neolithic and Bronze Ages	Iron Age
Chronozone	Older Dryas	Allerod	Younger Dryas	Pre-Boreal	Early Boreal	Late Boreal	Atlantic	Sub Boreal	Sub Atlantic
	I	II	III	IV	V	VI	VIIa	VIIb	VIII
Mammoth *Mammuthus primigenius*	?	–	–	–	–	–	–	–	–
Woolly rhinoceros *Coelodonta antiquitatis*	v	–	–	–	–	–	–	–	–
Wild horse *Equus* sp.	v	v	v	v	?	?	?	?	?
Reindeer *Rangifer tarandus*	v	?	v	v	–	–	–	–	–
Irish elk *Megaceros giganteus*	v	?	?	–	–	–	–	–	–
Elk *Alces alces*	–	v	?	v	?	–	–	–	–
Red deer *Cervus elaphus*	?	?	?	v	v	v	v	v	v
Roe deer *Capreolus capreolus*	–	–	–	v	v	v	v	v	v
Aurochs *Bos primigenius*	–	–	–	v	v	v	v	v	–
Bison *Bison priscus*	?	–	–	–	–	–	–	–	–
Wild boar *Sus scrofa*	?	?	?	v	v	v	v	v	v

Table 8.2 Late Glacial and early Holocene wild ungulates of England and Wales (partly from Grigson, 1978 and 1981).

hunters (see also table 8.2 for the possible timing of extinctions).

Elk, horse, reindeer and red deer arrived in Britain during the Late Devensian (Wymer, 1981). At High Furlong, near Blackpool, Lancashire, Barnes *et al.* (1971) found two bone-barbed points associated with the almost complete skeleton of a male elk *Alces alces* dated to between 10,000 and 9600 bc. They noted a number of unhealed lesions on the skeleton, suggesting points where the unfortunate animal had sustained an attack by hunters (fig. 8.5). Some of the lesions, however, must have occurred long before the death of the animal, as they exhibit a reaction: osteoporosis of the bone due to bacterial infection. In addition, a barbed bone projectile point was excavated *in situ* resting in a broad groove in the distal end of the left metatarsal. The groove, it appears, had been eroded in life by pressure of the barbed point causing resorption of bone tissue and infection. This probably occurred 2–3 weeks before the animal's

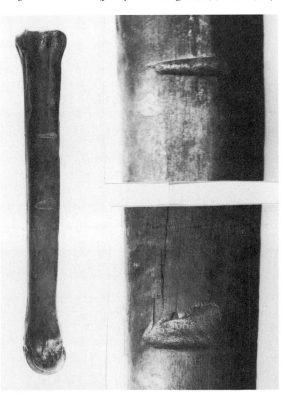

8.5 The late Glacial elk skeleton from High Furlong, near Blackpool. Lateral view of the left metacarpal showing grooves on the lateral surface. Enlarged views of these grooves are shown on the right. *Courtesy John Hallam*

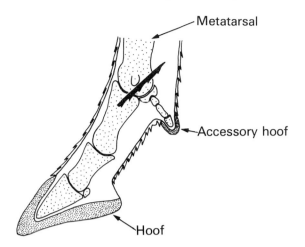

8.6 Left hind foot of the late Glacial elk with an associated barbed point; from High Furlong, near Blackpool, Lancashire, England. *From Hallam et al., 1973*

death (fig. 8.6). At Flixton in Yorkshire another kill site was found (Moore in Clark, 1954). There the incomplete skeletons of three horses associated with flint flakes were found. The Flixton site is dated to just before 8400 bc.

THE MESOLITHIC OF BRITAIN

The climate suddenly and rapidly became warmer approximately 8300 bc—a date which marks the end of the Late Glacial period. As the ice withdrew, open vegetation was replaced by forest. This change of vegetation in northwest Europe meant that man had to give up his Upper Palaeolithic herd-hunting practices and adapt to a forest environment instead. As the ice melted so the sea level rose, and during the seventh millennium bc Britain had again become an island.

The Mesolithic culture period in Britain lasted from about 8000 bc until the elm decline of around 3400–3000 bc, which marks the onset of the Neolithic.

The archaeofaunal evidence suggests that many species of mammals did manage to spread to England before it became an island in 6500 bc. This must have been when Britain gained the bulk of its present-day species. Even so, not every northern European animal made it as far as Britain. Consequently the British mainland terrestrial fauna is a little sparser than that of the continent, lacking beech marten, two species of white-toothed shrew, several vole species, the European mink and the garden dormouse.

Ireland did not receive this post-glacial invasion; this was because of the early presence of a narrowed Irish 'sea'. It was by 'ad hoc means' (Grigson, 1981) that Ireland acquired its mammals such as wild boar, pine marten, badger, wild cat, red squirrel and wood mouse (and perhaps red deer too, see table 8.4). Ireland had, and still has, a rather limited fauna, lacking such species as mole, weasel, common shrew, aurochs, elk and red deer. The same applies to other groups of animals—an impoverished mollusc fauna, for example (Kerney and Cameron, 1979).

The post-glacial climate of Britain was not very different from that in the earlier Interglacials, so why didn't animals like the lion, elephant, rhinoceros and hippopotamus return to Britain? The answer is most probably (Evans, 1975) that competition with man had severely restricted the modern distributions of these animals. We do not know precisely how long many late Glacial species such as mammoth, woolly rhinoceros, bison, cave bear, giant deer, reindeer and hyaena managed to survive into the Holocene, although Juliet Clutton-Brock and Richard Burleigh (1983) have started a long-term radiocarbon project to date late finds of these animals, and also to date the arrival of the first domestic livestock.

Wolf, brown bear, stoat, fox, pygmy shrew, root vole, blue hare, reindeer (Clutton-Brock and Burleigh dated reindeer bone from Kent to 7810 bc) and perhaps the horse (Clutton-Brock and Burleigh dated a horse metapodial from Kent to 7800 bc) may have survived from the late Glacial (see Grigson, 1981). Aurochs, elk, red deer, roe deer, beaver, pine marten, badger, hedgehog, mole, common shrew and water vole were all added to the surviving late Glacial relics. These arrivals are all found at the early Mesolithic site of Thatcham in Berkshire (dated to 8400–7500 bc), and most of them, as well as brown hare, were found at Star Carr in Yorkshire, dated to c7500 bc. These are the earliest and indeed best known Mesolithic sites in England. The earliest evidence for man in Ireland comes from the Mesolithic site Mount Sandel, County Derry, with [14]c dates of c7000–6400 bc.

Early Mesolithic settlements in Britain were probably confined to England. In terms of carcass weight the most important animals which man hunted were the red deer, followed by aurochs, elk, roe deer and wild boar.

Part of Animal	Uses
HIDE	cover for kayak and umiak, line for harpoon, clothing and boots
FLESH	food
BLUBBER	food: eaten with meat, rendered for oil
ORGANS (heart, liver, spleen, kidney)	food
BONES	ribs for root diggers, humerus for club, penis bone for flaker
TEETH	decorative pendants
WHISKERS	decoration of wood hunting hats and visors
SINEW	back sinews for sewing, lashing, cordage
FLIPPERS	soles used for boot soles, contents gelatinised in flipper and eaten
PERICARDIUM	water bottle, general-purpose container
OESOPHAGUS	parka, pants, legging of boots, pouches
STOMACH	storage container (especially for dried salmon)
INTESTINES	parka, pants, pouches

Table 8.3 Some of the many uses to which the northern or Steller Sea Lion (*Eumetopia jubata*) is put by Eskimos (from Grigson, 1981 and Laughlin, 1977).

In later Mesolithic sites the elk is absent. Once Britain became isolated from the continent, during the Mesolithic, the only animal to become extinct rapidly was the elk. It probably disappeared *c*5–6000 bc. Perhaps this was partly due to the late Boreal drying out of its favoured habitat—marshy woodland with abundant undergrowth—and was hastened by hunting by humans.

Grigson lists some of the uses besides meat to which mammal species could have been put by Mesolithic people: antler, bone, wild boar tusks and beaver jaws served as tools; teeth and whiskers were used for decoration, skins for clothing, bedding and possibly for covering huts and boats; leather was used for a variety of purposes; horns were used for carrying and storing liquids; sinews served as thread; fat was used for oil, and so on (see also table 8.3).

Star Carr
The early Mesolithic site of Star Carr, in the vale of Pickering, Yorkshire, is one of the best known Mesolithic sites in Eruope (Clark, 1954). It was excavated between 1949 and 1953 by Grahame Clark (Clarke, 1972). The occupation is dated by two radiocarbon determinations of 7538 and 7607 bc.

The bones from Star Carr were originally studied by Fraser and King. The *Canis* has been re-identified by Magnus Degerbøl (1961). On the basis of its small auditory bullae, small size, and overlapping premolar teeth, he believes it belonged to domestic dog.

(Overlapping of teeth may be the result of poor nourishment when the jaw-bone fails to develop to an extent which is commensurate with the teeth.) This is then the earliest record for a domestic animal in Britain. Since Mesolithic people subsisted by hunting and gathering (as with the Natufians in Israel, Chapter 6), a special relationship between two social beings—one human, the other wolf—may have existed.

Tony Legge and Peter Rowley-Conwy (1986) have restudied the Star Carr fauna. According to their analysis, the Star Carr fauna includes the following animals: red deer (535 bone fragments), elk (243 fragments), aurochs (170 fragments), roe deer (101 fragments), and wild pig (23 fragments). Their study has also revealed that Star Carr was probably occupied in spring and summer (Chapter 4).

One of the novelties retrieved at Star Carr was a series of artificial smoothed stag frontlets with much of the antlers still in place. Clark, drawing upon modern ethnographic parallels such as native Californians (as in the Karok hunter's head dress for decoying deer; Kroeber, 1925:78), interprets them as masks, perhaps used for stalking other deer or for ceremonial activities.

Red-deer antler was used to manufacture barbed points and other tools. First blanks were made by cutting deep longitudinal grooves through the outer hard part and wedging out the splinters between them. Shaping to the desired form followed. As many as 83 out of 102 stag antlers had splinters removed.

Alwyne Wheeler (1978) comments on the remarkable absence of fish remains from the Star Carr assemblage, although the site was, in Mesolithic times, situated close by a large freshwater lake. During the last glaciation all primary freshwater fishes (i.e. those unable to tolerate exposure to salt water) became extinct in Britain. With the early postglacial improvement of the climate, but before the North Sea land bridge was severed, many species of freshwater fish could gradually recolonize English rivers through the system of communicating rivers. This explains the present-day richness of the eastern English fish fauna compared with that of western English rivers, and the poverty of both in comparison with the Rhine and Elbe faunas (Wheeler, 1978). However, this process of recolonization took time, and Wheeler thinks that Star Carr's occupation may well predate the time of arrival of freshwater fish in that region.

THE LATER MESOLITHIC

In the Boreal period, when Britain became an island, man spread into western and northern parts of the British Isles. Several important Mesolithic sites are known from Scotland. For example, the site of Morton Tayport B in Fife (Coles *et al.*, 1971) has dates which range from 4432–4165 bc. This site is situated by the sea, and not surprisingly has yielded abundant remains of marine molluscs (cockles, for example), crabs and various fish (mainly cod, but also haddock, turbot, salmonid and sturgeon). The abundance of cod suggests deep-water fishing from boats. For other possible evidence for Mesolithic deep-water fishing and marine exploration, see Chapter 5. Besides the marine animals, a full range of ungulate species, except elk, was found at Morton Tayport B; on the basis of carcass weight, it seems that ungulates provided some two-thirds of the meat eaten. (Geoff Bailey (1978) has calculated that one red deer carcass is equivalent to 156,800 cockles.)

Several late Mesolithic (Obanian) sites on the west coast and islands of Scotland have been excavated, some in the nineteenth century. They are shell middens, but also contain seal and whale bones, showing that these resources were not ignored.

Oronsay

One Inner Hebridean island which has been subject to careful archaeological investigation is Oronsay (Chapter 4, fig. 4.5). Here Paul Mellars (1978) excavated four shell-midden sites whose dates range from 3700–3200 bc. According to Grigson the island is too small to support a herd of red deer. She found that there were two size groups of red deer, and suggests that the small deer may have been imported from the adjacent island of Colonsay and the larger deer from a larger island such as Islay or Jura, or from the mainland. The ancient inhabitants of Oronsay turned to the sea for sustenance. Apart from huge quantities of molluscs such as limpets, there were seals, birds, and fish as an important part of the diet—especially the saithe or coalfish (*Pollachius virens*), which accounts for at least 95% of the total fish-bones found. The seasonality findings of Mike Wilkinson based upon otolith size variation of this fish are of great interest. His study has been discussed in Chapter 4.

IRELAND IN THE LATE GLACIAL AND POSTGLACIAL (table 8.4)

Mammals are known from a number of caves in southern Ireland which date to the last glaciation (Wijngaarden-Bakker, 1974). Unfortunately the stratigraphy of all these caves is confused. Both lynx and hyaena are known from the warmer interstadials of that glaciation but became extinct during the succeeding stadials (colder stages). Pleistocene remains of other mammals such as mammoth, arctic fox, giant deer, reindeer and lemming have also been found, but never in association with man or his cultural remains. They are presumed to have become extinct once the climate got warmer and forests expanded at the end of the last glacial period. Some mammals, however, such as wolf, fox, brown bear, stoat and mountain hare either did survive through the glacial period or were early immigrants before the land barriers with England and the continent were covered (a matter of much controversy). It is uncertain whether the red deer is a Pleistocene survivor or a Mesolithic introduction. It appears that there were never elk, aurochs or roe deer in Ireland.

The economy of the Mesolithic inhabitants of Ireland was based on collecting molluscs and crus-

1) DELIBERATE INTRODUCTIONS

a) Domestic animals

Cattle	c.2700 bc (3500 BC)
Sheep	c.2700 bc (3500 BC)
Goat	c.2700 bc (3500 BC)
Horse	c.2000 bc
Cat	First centuries AD
Donkey	Eighteenth century AD

b) Other mammal species

Fallow deer	? Norman times
Rabbit	Thirteenth century AD
Brown hare	1850 onwards
Sika deer	1884
Edible dormouse	1885 (unsuccessful)
Grey squirrel	1890, 1911
Musk rat	1927 (extinct in 1934)
Mink	1950 onwards

2) ACCIDENTAL INTRODUCTIONS

House mouse	Roman times or earlier ?Vikings
Black rat	before 1187 AD
Brown rat	1722 onwards
Bank vole	1964 onwards

Already in Ireland in the Mesolithic: wild boar, hare, and red deer, which were probably survivors from the late Glacial south of Ireland (see Woodman in Mellars, 1978).

Table 8.4   List of mammals introduced by man to Ireland (mainly from Van Wijngaarden-Bakker, 1973).

taceans, on fishing and on hunting aquatic animals (seals and whales), birds, red deer, wild boar and brown bear. The Neolithic culture in Ireland may also have begun after *c*3400 bc (perhaps a little later than the advent of the Neolithic in England), when the Mesolithic economy was replaced by one based upon cultivation and animal husbandry.

THE NEOLITHIC

Neolithic culture, technology and economy came to Britain in the middle of the fourth millennium BC. Neolithic people probably began extensive forest clearance and built the first causewayed camps. The Neolithic period ended about 2100 bc.

As far as is known, little change occurred in the wild fauna of Britain: compared with the Ice Ages climatic changes were minor. Most Mesolithic wild animals survived through to the succeeding Bronze Age, except for the elk, though this had probably already become extinct before the Neolithic. Caroline Grigson (1981, 1984) has provided useful summaries of the British Neolithic faunas. These are composed predominantly of domestic animal bones. Wild animals were now, it seems, unimportant in the economy.

The most important archaeofaunal change during the Neolithic was the introduction of domestic livestock: sheep and goat for certain, both species new to Britain, and perhaps cattle and pig. Whether the latter two were introduced is difficult to prove since their wild relatives, the aurochs and wild boar, were already here and could have been locally domesticated. Grigson notes the absence of any cow or pig bones of intermediate size, which argues, though tenuously, for their sudden introduction by boat as domestic animals. Cattle must have been taken by boat to Ireland, since there were no aurochs there. Until quite recently cattle were taken around the west coast of Ireland in small, canvas-covered wickerwork boats known as curraghs (earlier boats were perhaps hide-covered; Grigson, 1984). The earliest English sites reported so far with cattle, sheep or goat are the earthen barrows of Lambourn, Berkshire (*c*3415 bc) and Fussell's Lodge, Wiltshire (*c*3230 bc). However, it is likely that domestic animals were first brought across before that time. The earliest record of small (i.e. domestic) pigs comes from the pre-enclosure occupation at the Cause-wayed camp, Windmill Hill (*c*2960 bc).

The domestic cattle of the Neolithic of Britain were smaller than aurochs but larger than cattle from the succeeding Bronze Age (Jewell, 1962). Withers (shoulder) height may be estimated by multiplying metapodial length by a known constant. Postglacial aurochs had an average height at the withers of 1.47m (cows) and 1.57m (bulls); Neolithic domestic cattle had an average height at the withers of 1.25m; and Middle Bronze Age–Iron Age cattle were just under 1.1m at the withers (fig. 8.7; Grigson, 1982). It has now been shown that most of the Neolithic cattle bones from English sites came from adult cows (Legge, 1981). Could they have been milked? There is no evidence for castration. Presumably most of the bullocks were killed while still very young, so their bones were not preserved. In her reconstruction of English Neolithic cattle, Grigson notes that they had long horns which were fairly slender in cows and stout in bulls. Neolithic bulls did not have the short conical horns of most later prehistoric and many

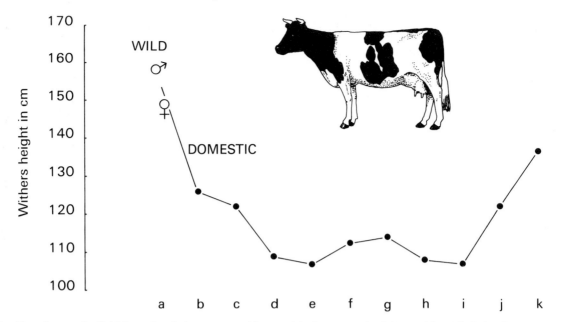

8.7 Size changes in British cattle: their average withers heights in centimetres. (a) Mesolithic, Neolithic and Early Bronze Age male and female aurochs. (b) Earlier Neolithic domestic cattle, 2600 bc. (c) Late Neolithic, Beaker, and Early Bronze, *c*1900 bc. (d) Middle Bronze Age, 1000 bc. (e) Iron Age, 300 BC. (f) Romano-British, first–fourth centuries AD. (g) Anglo-Saxon and Scandinavian, seventh–tenth centuries AD. (h) Saxo-Norman and high medieval, eleventh–thirteenth centuries AD. (i) Later medieval, fourteenth–fifteenth centuries AD. (j) Tudor, late fifteenth–sixteenth centuries AD. (k) Modern, late eighteenth century AD. *From Grigson, 1982; and Armitage, 1982*

modern breeds. In most respects they closely resembled small versions of the aurochs.

An interesting ceremonial use of cattle, with parallels on the continent of Europe, is the so-called 'head and hooves' burial. Several Neolithic barrows such as Tilshead Lodge and Fussell's Lodge have been excavated showing a clear association between the dead person and the feet of a cow. It has been suggested that a cow's hide, complete with feet and tail, and sometimes also the head was draped over the mortuary house before being covered with rubble (Grigson, 1984). Was this to provide protection and food in the next world? An ancient association with the cow seems to have been widespread in many Old World religions (e.g. the golden calf, Veddic India). A good example of a 'head and hooves' burial was uncovered from under a Beaker barrow on Hemp Knoll, near Avebury, Wiltshire (Robertson-

Mackay, 1980). Grigson identified the four feet and almost complete skull of a domestic ox (perhaps an old cow) associated with the human skeleton—a male aged between 35 and 45 lying on his side.

From the middle-Neolithic causewayed enclosure of Etton, near Peterborough in the Fenlands of Suffolk, comes some tantalizing evidence for the possibility that cattle were being used to pull ploughs. Miranda Armour-Chelu (in press) is studying the bones (most from cattle) at this site. She found that several of the cattle acetabula and scapulae show varying degrees of remodelling with the formation of bony outgrowths. According to veterinary opinion (Baker and Brothwell, 1980) this condition is brought about when an animal (typically a working animal) is subjected to excessive strain. It is known as osteoarthritis, a degenerative joint disease.

Indirect evidence for traction (perhaps, though not necessarily, animal-drawn) comes from ploughmarks covered by a long barrow near Avebury in Wiltshire (Fowler and Evans, 1967). They were found over an area of *c*15 metres square: material within and underneath the ploughmarks was dated to 2800–2500 bc (3500–3200 BC). These dates for the earliest use of the plough in Britain are remarkably consistent with others, also between 2800 and 2500 bc, from Denmark, Poland, Hungary, East Germany and Czechoslovakia (see Sherratt, 1981).

From the evidence of both numbers of bones and carcass weight, the early Neolithic economy seems to

orpi ſ745 eſt quint̃ ⁊ ꞇcarius eſt hiere cinctus.

8.8 British domestic pigs being fed on acorns in the month of November, illustrated in Queen Mary's Psalter (early fourteenth century AD). *Courtesy British Library; MS Royal 2BVII f. 81v*

have been based primarily upon cattle, with only moderate numbers of sheep/goat and pig. However, in the light of Payne's sieving experiments (Chapter 1) and since many excavators did not sieve, these data should be viewed with extreme caution. Moreover, Legge (1981) has pointed out that so many of the British Neolithic and Bronze Age sites excavated were of a ceremonial nature where gatherings might have been for some ritual or social purpose, and do not therefore reflect the everyday or domestic economy of Britons at that time. Pigs became very abundant for a short period during the Late Neolithic and their absence from Scottish island sites probably reflects the lack of woodland: 'no pannage, no pig' (Dent, 1977). Pigs were probably very like smaller versions of the wild boar, with long legs and long snout (fig. 8.8). J. Wilfred Jackson (1935) described a dog skeleton from Winterslow in Wiltshire as being 'a small dog of the fox-terrier type'. This of course does not mean that the modern fox-terrier breed has its origin in the Neolithic. Neolithic sheep were usually small and a little more robust than the Soay sheep of today (Legge and Armitage, pers. comm.).

THE BRONZE AGE

This was the time when two waves of migrants from the continent moved into Britain. The first were the so-called Beaker-folk (named after their characteristic drinking cups), who hailed from the Rhineland and the Low Countries. They were probably a martial people and may have been equestrians too (Ashbee, 1978). Their settlement in Britain overlaps with the late Neolithic, and their arrival may mark the beginning of a warrior-dominated 'heroic society' (Ashbee, 1978). They were followed by Celts who came across in the first half of the second millennium BC, bringing with them copper technology.

One major faunal change occurring in Bronze Age Britain was the extinction of the aurochs. It has not been found after the early part of this period. The latest dated remains of aurochs come from Charterhouse Warren Farm, Blagdon in Somerset (1295 bc or 1629 BC; Clutton-Brock and Burleigh, 1983). Grigson suggests that overhunting by man was largely responsible for its demise. Moreover, there is now good evidence that by the early Bronze Age of Britain (most probably during the late Neolithic) peoples' relationship with their livestock had become more complex—they were now exploiting livestock for their secondary products such as milk, wool and energy (Sherratt, 1981).

There was probably a gradual decrease in the amount of hunting in the course of the Bronze Age, which may be linked with forest clearance, the increasing numbers of sheep, and perhaps increased farming efficiency.

Wijngaarden-Bakker (1974) reports horses from the Beaker sites (*c*2000 bc) in Ireland. The absence of wild horse from earlier post-glacial periods there means that the horse must have been introduced by people—and therefore indicates that it was domesticated. She also suggests that the domestic horse was introduced into western Europe by the Beaker people.

Evidence in Bronze Age Britain for the exploitation of animal secondary products comes in the form of spinning and weaving equipment such as spindle whorls and weaving combs (probably for animal fibres) found at Eldon's seat, Dorset (Cunliffe, 1968) and at Bronze Age Deverel-Rimbury sites (Grigson, 1981). The so-called Deverel-Rimbury people were late Bronze Age immigrants from the continent who settled in Wessex and southeast England. No doubt the horse, now fairly frequent in Britain, was exploited for riding and traction.

Indirect evidence for secondary products comes from Anthony Legge's (1981) study of the Middle Bronze Age bones from Grimes Graves in Norfolk (dated to around 850 bc). They consist mostly of cattle (52 per cent, or 64 out of 122 individuals), with some sheep/goat (32 per cent), red deer, pig and horse. In his analysis of the age and sex composition of the animals culled, Legge found that the majority of the adult cattle were female. The cattle mandibles revealed, however, that about half were slaughtered before they reached the age of six months. This kind of age and sex distribution, he argues, indicates a dairy economy, in which a high rate of calving is required to produce lactating cows. Man is competing with the calves for the cows' milk. Calves produced in excess of those needed to maintain herd numbers (especially males) are slaughtered. While these would surely have been eaten, Legge suggests that the emphasis at Grimes Graves was on milk production.

One could argue that the high juvenile cull simply reflects a meat- (or rather, veal-) producing economy, with the adults, most of whom were females, being kept for reproduction. If beef had been the desired food, then the juvenile-culling peak should have been towards the end of the growing period (say 18–24 months). It is more economical in terms of the meat-yield versus fodder-input weight equation to kill at that age, than at below six months as at Grimes Graves.

Legge compares his findings with data spanning the Neolithic and Bronze Ages in Switzerland (Higham, 1968). There, an age shift occurred from a predominantly juvenile cull (less than six months) suggesting dairying, to culling of older calves suggesting beef-production. This coincided with forest clearance and the creation of greater pasture areas in Switzerland. A milk economy is more productive in terms of yield per unit of land. It can be practised on small-holdings. The availability of more pasture as forests were cleared during the Swiss Bronze Age permitted the more extravagant economics of beef production.

THE IRON AGE

The first appearance of iron technology was in the seventh century bc and this period lasted until the Roman invasion of ad 43. It was the time when the great hillforts were constructed. These were perhaps meeting places, or pastoral enclosures, or settlements. At least three invasions from Europe occurred. The last was of the Belgae, who hailed from what is today Belgium and established large-scale settlements in southeastern England. They supposedly introduced the wheel as well as coinage. Contact with Rome is likely: the Belgic chiefs began inscribing their names in Latin characters. Contact with peoples of the Mediterranean (probably the Phoenicians) has also been suggested.

Pioneering studies of British Iron Age animal remains were undertaken during the earlier part of the twentieth century by William Boyd Dawkins and John Wilfrid Jackson. Two notable works of theirs are the report on 'several hundredweights of bones' from the Glastonbury lake village in Somerset (Boyd Dawkins and Wilfrid Jackson, 1917) and the report of animal remains from All Cannings Cross in Wiltshire (Wilfrid Jackson, 1923). At Glastonbury, sheep was the most abundant animal. At All Cannings Cross the frontal (skull) bone of a hornless ox was found, which marks the earliest appearance of polled cattle in Britain.

There are few detailed modern reports of Iron Age animal bones from Britain. The two most notable are

Annie Grant's study of over 100,000 bones from the hillfort at Danebury, occupied during the sixth to first centuries BC in Hampshire, and Ralph Harcourt's study of over 15,000 bones from Gussage All Saints in Dorset. Grant has also summarized the evidence from other Iron Age sites in southern Britain (Grant, 1984). On most of these sites sheep are the most frequently represented animal (70 per cent at Danebury), all the more so on sites that lie on higher ground such as chalk downland. There is a traditional association between sheep farming and chalk downland in Britain. Downland, with its limited water availability and relatively poor grass is not suitable for cattle. Sites in lowland areas with heavy soils and lush grass generally have higher percentages of cattle bones.

The Danebury sheep were small, relatively slender animals (Harcourt gives a figure of 53–64cm at the shoulder for the Gussage All Saints sheep) and generally horned in both sexes, very similar to the modern Soay sheep—a rare breed found on two of the Scottish islands of St Kilda. These primitive sheep breeds had a predominantly hairy coat and shed their 'fleece' annually. The 'wool' therefore had to be plucked. The so-called 'bone-weaving combs' present on many Iron Age sites may have been used for this purpose. Ryder (1983) suggests that the change to sheep with a woolly, continuously growing and therefore shearable coat may have occurred in the Iron Age. This change could have resulted from local selection of mutant forms which retained their fleece. Some have suggested that the Belgae imported a finer-fleeced sheep.

The virtual absence of large samples of sheep remains from sites preceding the Iron Age makes it difficult to interpret the age-culling pattern at Danebury. It seems that approximately one third of the sheep culled at many of the sites were one year old or less, whereas one third were mature animals, beyond the optimum age for meat production. These may represent ewes kept for breeding, and ewes and wethers kept for wool. Grant therefore suggests that the sheep economy was a mixed one: both meat and secondary products were important. Further evidence for wool exploitation comes from finds of loom weights, spindle whorls and the weaving combs already mentioned.

The large number of mandibles from very young calves (and similarly, from lambs) suggests that calving and lambing may have been done within or near the hillfort. The arguments of Legge for the Bronze Age cattle at Grimes Graves would seem to apply here too, so no doubt some milking was undertaken at Danebury. Moreover, the small number of cattle mandibles belonging to juveniles at the optimum age of culling for meat suggests, according to Grant, that the emphasis was not on beef production. Indeed, the majority were from mature or even old individuals. Perhaps some were from oxen used for traction, besides those from milk cows. The cattle were a short-horned variety. Iron Age cattle were small and lightly built with a range of shoulder heights from 100–113cm (Harcourt, 1979).

Most of the pigs culled were young. This is not surprising since the pig is only a source of meat, fat and skin (slaughter products).

Most of the horse bones from Danebury and several other British Iron Age sites belonged to animals 2 or more years old, and a majority of these were males. The horse was, by modern standards, small (fig. 8.9)—the size of a small pony. Boyd Dawkins and Wilfrid Jackson likened British Iron Age ponies to the Exmoor pony. Those from Gussage All Saints were estimated to have been 100–113cm high at the shoulders (Harcourt, 1979). In place of local breeding, horses may have been allowed to run wild and mature horses periodically rounded up for breaking in and riding (Harcourt, 1979). Horses are not generally ready for training until 2–3 years old. They were probably also used as pack animals, and of course to provide their owner with status. Harcourt found evidence for osteoarthrosis at the proximal ends of five horse metatarsals

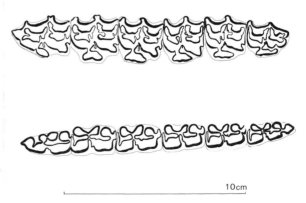

8.9 Occlusal view showing the enamel folds of upper (above) and lower (below) teeth of an Iron Age (third–first centuries BC) pony from Hook, near Warsash, Hampshire, southern England. *From Davis, forthcoming*

from Gussage All Saints, suggesting that Iron Age horses were possibly used for draught purposes. There are also several finds of complete unbutchered horse skeletons from this period. Heavy traction needed to pull ploughs would have been provided by oxen, since the horse harness of antiquity consisted of a soft collar tied round the throat. Owing to its closeness to the windpipe, this collar would interfere with respiration during heavy traction. According to documentary evidence the modern rigid 'breast harness', which rests on the shoulder blade, did not appear in France and England until the tenth and twelfth centuries AD respectively. Traction was then 'through the shoulders' rather than the neck, and allowed horses to be used for pulling ploughs (Lefebvre des Noettes, 1931:122; see also, Trow-Smith, 1957:56 and 92).

Harcourt (1979) has studied the faunal remains from G.J. Wainwright's recent excavations at Gussage All Saints. This was an Iron Age settlement in Dorset occupied throughout the second half of the first millenium BC. Harcourt's findings have revealed some interesting cultural information, new data on the early presence in Britain of cats and mice, and some dramatic evidence concerning cattle mismanagement.

For example, many of the horse bones at Gussage All Saints were complete and unbutchered. Harcourt draws the interesting inference that perhaps even in Iron Age times English people refrained from consuming horse flesh. (In many parts of Europe today there is still a strong prejudice against horsemeat. Even in France, where horsemeat is quite popular, few butchers specializing in this meat existed before 1865. The promotion of 'hippophagie' in France was due in part to the pronouncements in the 1850s of the zoologist Isidore Geoffroy Saint Hilaire and later to the severe food shortage during the siege of Paris in 1870–71; Larousse, 1873:9, 292–3.)

The most remarkable find at Gussage All Saints was the almost complete skeleton of a cow which had died as a result of difficult calving. The fore-limb bones of the calf were found protruding beyond the maternal pelvis, the remaining parts of the calf's skeleton—skull and hind limbs—were on the other side of the pelvis. Clearly the calf was in the process of birth, fore-feet first. Even today this position in calving is very difficult to correct. A caesarean section or even dismembering of the calf may be necessary, and in extreme cases the cow is slaughtered.

Apart from large mammals, remains of several cats (most juvenile) were found. Bones of domestic cats are difficult to distinguish from their wild relatives', but the presence in one locality of five new-born kittens' skeletons makes it most likely that domesticated cats are represented. If this interpretation is correct, then this would be the earliest record so far for domestic cat in Britain—its introduction was hitherto attributed to the Romans. Remains of the house mouse were found in two sealed levels, and represent the earliest secure record of this rodent in Britain.

The presence of small numbers of roe and red deer bones on British Iron Age sites indicates some hunting. But perhaps the most intriguing animal found on late Iron Age (and Roman) British sites is the red jungle fowl or chicken. This had an east or southeast Asian origin and must have been imported into Britain. The chicken is known from Hallstatt-La Tène culture periods in central Europe, and eighth-century BC Phoenician sites in Spain. It was common in the Mediterranean by the sixth century BC, or perhaps even one or two centuries earlier (Crawford, 1984). Julius Caesar, who invaded Britain twice in 55 and 54 BC, and wrote about the inhabitants of these isles (*Gallic War*, V, 12), mentions that *leporem et gallinam et anserem gustare fas non putant; haec tamen alunt animi voluptatisque causa* ('they consider it wrong to eat hare, chicken, and goose, but keep them for pastime and amusement'). There are local traditions in both Cornwall and Scotland that the Phoenicians introduced the chicken. According to Jennie Coy and Mark Maltby the chicken is present consistently in all major Romano-British sites in the Wessex area (see also fig. 8.10).

8.10 The chicken in Britain. Foot print in a Roman tile from Silchester. *Photograph, Silchester collection 12361, courtesy Leslie Cram, Reading Museum and Art Gallery*

ROMAN BRITAIN

The arrival of the Romans in Britain marks the end of British prehistory. Anthony King (1978) has synthesized a large number of reports of Roman-British archaeofaunal assemblages. Most of these comprise sheep, cattle and pigs. He observes several interesting trends. The most distinct one is the progressive decrease of sheep relative to pig and cattle. This trend is not only temporal but also cultural. Native sites, continuing the Iron Age pattern, have more sheep, as do early Roman military sites. The latter finding probably indicates that Roman soldiers relied upon locally available food. The more Romanized sites, like villas, roadside settlements, towns and forts, tend on the other hand to have fewer sheep. At Caerleon fortress baths, O'Connor (1983) reports over 90 per cent cattle in the main rubbish dumps.

One possible explanation for the temporal decrease of sheep would be the location of later Roman sites. Many more of the latter were on land more conducive to pig and cattle husbandry. There may have been a population increase in the fourth century AD which required the exploitation of marginal areas such as woodland: deer bones too are more common on the later Roman sites.

Another factor which King suggests should be taken into account is the economic decline of the Roman empire, which led to the inclusion of livestock in the *capitatio* or poll tax. This could have encouraged the raising of stock with relatively more meat per head, cattle and pig being obvious choices. Woodland animals (like the pig) would also have been easier to conceal from the tax inspector. Moreover, the Romans, like many Mediterranean people of that time, regarded pork as a delicacy. Pliny (*Natural History*, VIII) mentioned a way of improving pig's liver—stuffing a sow with dried figs and, after a drink of mead, killing it. He also noted the very large number of pork dishes compared with other meats. Pork was probably the most commonly eaten meat in Italy, where cattle were kept mainly for traction and sometimes for milk. At the time of Diocletian, beef and mutton commanded a maximum of 8 denarii per pound while pork could command 12 denarii. In Roman Britain sheep were kept mainly for wool and only secondarily for milk and meat (Grant, 1975). Grant also discovered, from her analysis of the cattle bones from Portchester castle in Hampshire, that most were female and were probably exploited for their milk.

Remains of Romano-British cattle exhibit a wide range of sizes; according to Peter Jewell (1963) the larger ones reflect superior Roman organization of agriculture, rather than imports from the continent. And on the subject of size and imports, Armitage (1983) cites evidence for Romano-British polled (hornless) sheep of a size much greater than those from the preceding Iron Age. He suggests that these larger sheep could have been an imported improved strain, and may represent the founding stock of English longwool sheep.

Manfred Teichert (1984) has studied archaeofaunal remains from Roman and free Germany (*Germania Romana* and *Germania libera*). He found that in Roman times an increase in cattle size occurred in Roman provinces on the Rhine and Danube; withers height increased to 1.27m, but this did not occur in *Germania libera*. With the subsequent decline of the Roman empire, the larger cattle disappeared. Back in England, however, the Saxons of the southeast managed to maintain the stocks of large cattle (Armitage, 1982; and see fig. 8.7).

ANGLO-SAXON BRITAIN

By the fourth century AD the Roman empire had split in two and direct control over Britain waned. The years between the fourth and seventh centuries in Europe are known as the migration period because of the dramatic movements of peoples. In the fifth and sixth centuries, Angles, Saxons and Jutes migrated from northwest Europe into southern and eastern England.

England now consisted of a heptarchy, among which the most powerful kingdoms were Wessex, Mercia and Northumbria. This too was the time of the creation of the first Anglo-Saxon towns and the development of a market economy and international trade. By the time of William I's domesday survey (AD 1086) at least 10 per cent of the English population were town-dwellers.

The Anglo-Saxon period is the earliest phase of British history in which man's relationship with animals can be studied from documentary evidence, not just from archaeological bones. Examples of these documents are the *Anglo-Saxon Chronicle*, charters and wills, and the codes of laws. The best known laws are those of King Ine who ruled Wessex from AD 688–726.

According to Juliet Clutton-Brock (1976), Anglo-Saxon peasants lived much as farmers on smallholdings have continued to live until recent times. They kept cattle (the laws of Ine mention ox-drawn ploughs), sheep, goats and poultry, and cats and dogs, ploughed the land, made bacon and rode horses. Pigs were allowed to graze free-range in woodland, and survived the winters by feeding on acorns and beech mast. (This right was known as pannage.) The unimproved livestock probably bore little resemblance to present-day breeds. Much of the forest of Britain was inhabited by boar, deer, wolf and bear, which commoners were allowed to hunt. It was not until William I's game laws that deer preserves were set apart, and the hunting of deer, boars and even hares was prohibited for the common people (see the *Anglo-Saxon Chronicle*). These laws, and the royal forests, did however ensure that the boar and deer survived for many more centuries than they would otherwise have done.

The animal remains from only a few Anglo-Saxon sites have been analysed in any detail (Clutton-Brock, 1976; and Bourdillon and Coy, 1980). All assemblages produced mostly sheep/goat (most common), cattle, pig, and some horse bones (fig. 8.11). Clutton-Brock suggests that pigs were in fact far more common than their bone remains suggest, since boned pork and bacon were probably very popular: their bones must have been dumped somewhere, but where? Free-ranging pigs may have outnumbered all other domestic animals. The fine for felling a 'tree under which 30 swine could stand' was 60 shillings (laws of Ine). However, forest clearance did occur throughout the Anglo-Saxon period and led to a decline in pig numbers. By the time of the domesday, cattle and sheep were the most important sources of food.

The osteological evidence shows (fig. 8.7) that in

8.11 A well-preserved late Anglo-Saxon (tenth century AD) horse skeleton from Ironmonger Lane, City of London. See Armitage, 1981. *Photograph Jon Bailey, courtesy Museum of London*

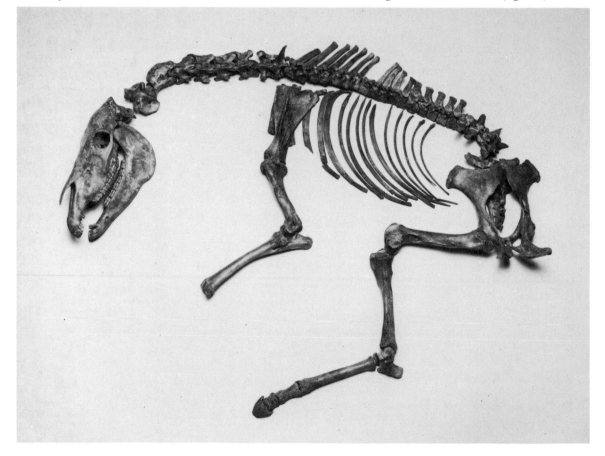

8.12 Medieval British cattle were small. *From Queen Mary's Psalter, courtesy British Library; MS Royal 2.B.VII.f.75*

the seventh to tenth centuries cattle were still quite large. Armitage (1982) suggests that the incentive for keeping such large cattle came from the Saxons' introduction of the heavy plough, or caruca, which enabled them to cultivate heavy clay soils. However, cattle from outlying districts beyond the Anglo-Saxon domain, such as Cornwall and Pictish Orkney, were of the small Iron Age size. English cattle from the eleventh-thirteenth centuries were small: no larger than those from the Iron Age. They were similar in size to present-day Chillingham park cattle—an unimproved feral breed. According to O'Connor (1982) the cattle from medieval Lincoln were also small with a withers height of 1–1.3m (see also fig. 8.12).

It seems that cattle in Britain had now deteriorated. There was widespread neglect of livestock rearing in the twelfth and thirteenth centuries, and much conversion of pasture into arable land to provide grain for the increasing human population. Smaller cattle with less food requirements would have had a better chance of surviving on what grazing land remained, and perhaps they were even preferred for this reason (Armitage, 1982).

Armitage has found in fourteenth- and fifteenth-century London sites a number of long-horned cattle. The longer horns signify larger body size. He discounts the possibility that they originated from the continent, and believes they mark the beginning of a size increase of British cattle, at least in southeast England.

Consider this chain of events: plague in the fourteenth century had killed about one third of the British population. This and inflation had caused widespread abandonment of the English countryside. Tenant farming replaced the manorial system. Much arable land was converted to pasture—a reversal of what happened in the twelfth and thirteenth centuries. These changes probably stimulated livestock husbandry. First, enclosed pasture provided the opportunity for controlled breeding. Second, large estates meant larger herds leading to greater overall variability and therefore more choice for selecting breeding stock. Third, the introduction of crop rotation which included fodder plants, as well as improved techniques for hay-making and storage, would have overcome the problem of long lean winters. This is the chain of events by which Armitage (1980) explains the origin of larger cattle in southeast England in the fourteenth and fifteenth centuries.

Anglo-Saxon sheep were slightly larger than Iron Age and Roman sheep and their size range narrower. But Saxon–early medieval sheep were still much smaller than modern semi-improved breeds like the Romney (O'Connor, pers. comm.; see below). Noddle's measurements taken of the sheep at one site (North Elmham) suggest that the majority were wethers (castrated rams). Wethers produce a heavier fleece than rams or ewes. Large flocks of wethers were kept in the Middle Ages for wool production. At North Elmham most of the sheep, judging by the state of their dentition, were at least six years old at the time of their slaughter. This is further evidence that they were kept for their wool. Correspondence between Offa of Mercia and Charlemagne indicates that woollen garments were being exported from Britain in the eighth century. Indeed the importance of wool production in this country dates back at least to Anglo-Saxon times. The complicated system of customs in Britain can be traced back ultimately to the custom on wool (Hoskins, 1955). Witness too the large numbers of place names beginning with *Shap*, *Shep*, *Skip* and *Ship*—all variants of 'sheep'.

URBAN ZOO-ARCHAEOLOGY —MEDIEVAL AND POST-MEDIEVAL BRITAIN

Marketing

As towns grew from Norman times onwards the economic organization of Britain began to change. The increasing urban population had to be sustained with crops and livestock from the surrounding countryside. Unlike a village, a town, with its middle class, cannot sustain itself. Before such technological innovations as refrigerated motor transport, the only way to supply a town with meat was by bringing in the livestock 'on the hoof', i.e. in droves. From 185,000 in 1557, London's population had grown to over half a million by the second half of the seventeenth century. London's meat supply was coming in droves from as far away as Scotland, Wales and southwest England—all part of a national network. This had developed into an annual cycle. Cattle born and raised in these outlying districts were shod and driven on the hoof along drove roads to graziers in the south Midlands, East Anglia, and Home Counties. Here they were fattened up on grass

or turnips and sent as fattened 'beeves' to London for slaughter (Armitage, 1982). Such long journeys posed immense problems. Perhaps only certain breeds and age groups were capable of withstanding the long trek.

One example suggested by Armitage (1982) is polled (hornless) cattle. The polled condition in cattle arises as a spontaneous mutation perhaps once per 50,000 births (Hammond, 1950). And although this mutant allele (form of the gene) is dominant over the horned one, polled cattle were probably not much favoured by people using cattle for draught purposes, since horns are often used to yoke them to plough or cart. However, polled cattle are much easier and safer to handle in large numbers. They were undoubtedly favoured by drovers.

As towns grew, a complex relationship developed between them and their catchment area, the surrounding countryside. Urban demand presumably eventually became so great as to warrant livestock husbandry systems specially geared to the urban market. This development should reveal itself in the archaeofaunal record.

Zoo-archaeological data from urban sites may indeed provide 'mirror-images' of data from rural contexts as those animals eaten at home were those not sent to market. To date, however, few if any medieval farmsteads surrounding a market town have been excavated to test the economic relationship between town and country.

The animal bones from excavations of various English medieval urban sites—London, Exeter, King's Lynn, Flaxengate (Lincoln) and York—have been extensively reported. The Exeter bone material came from Roman (AD 55–fifth century), medieval (eleventh–fifteenth century), and post-medieval (sixteenth–late eighteenth century) periods. At Flaxengate, the greater part came from the late Anglo-Saxon and early medieval period (c870–c1180) with a smaller amount coming from the period 1200–1500, and at King's Lynn most came from c1050–1500 with some post-medieval remains also. The three species—sheep, cattle and pig—again formed the major part of the faunal remains at these sites.

At both Lincoln and Exeter, O'Connor and Maltby found that: (a) the numbers of sheep bones increased relative to those of cattle and pig—from 35–50 to 50–60 per cent after the thirteenth century at Exeter, and after the early ninth century at Flaxengate with a more marked increase at the end of the thirteenth century; (b) the age of slaughter of the sheep at King's Lynn had risen by the thirteenth century, and at Exeter by post-medieval times. For example, most of the Roman and medieval sheep sold into Exeter were younger than 25 months old, by which age they would have provided at most one fleece of wool. In post-medieval Exeter an age increase occurred, most dramatic in the sixteenth century. This suggests a shift in emphasis from meat to secondary products. Both medieval and post-medieval sheep from King's Lynn were predominantly mature, and Noddle (1977) suggests that the emphasis here may have been on the production of wool as early as AD 1050–1250.

Considering the evidence from all three sites, it seems reasonable to postulate that Lincolnshire and Norfolk became important wool-producing regions before Devon did. O'Connor (1982), in his study of sheep measurements, found that medieval sheep from Exeter and Taunton were appreciably smaller than their contemporaries from elsewhere in England, and has suggested to me that there may be a connection.

These zoo-archaeological findings are borne out by the documentary evidence. Though in Anglo-Saxon times wool already played an important role in the English economy, by the medieval period wool production was an enormous business, and English wool was being exported to Europe on a vast scale. At a more local level thirteenth–fourteenth-century Lincoln and post-medieval Devon experienced a boom in the wool industry. By the fifteenth and

8.13 Medieval pictorial evidence of oxen used for traction. *From the Luttrell Psalter (English c1340 AD), courtesy British Library; MS 42130 f. 170*

sixteenth centuries Devon was exporting the popular cloths known as 'kerseys' (Maltby, 1979). The account books of some great wool merchants in the fifteenth century record single transactions of wool with values of up to £1078 (over £600,000 in today's money!). By the sixteenth century, cloth made up four-fifths of England's exports (Hoskins, 1955).

Pork

At Exeter (Maltby, 1979) the pigs were intensively exploited for their meat, judging by the high proportion of juveniles culled. Sucking pig, a favourite in Roman Italy, was common in Roman Exeter too, but did not regain such popularity again there until the sixteenth century, when the more efficient system of sty husbandry may have replaced the practice of allowing pigs to find pannage in the woods. Pigs in styes were easily fattened up for early slaughter. Moreover, intensively reared sty pigs could be fed surplus whey from the dairy industry, which had become quite important in Tudor Devonshire.

Occasional finds of intact medieval pig skulls show that the pigs then had an elongated facial profile, little different from that of the wild boar. Modern pig skulls, however, exhibit a concave facial profile—a characteristic which may be derived from the short-legged, fleshy Chinese stock that was imported into Europe for interbreeding towards the end of the eighteenth century.

Beef and veal

Most of the cattle remains from Roman and medieval Exeter and early medieval Lincoln belonged to mature animals. The cow, a 'versatile and

multipurpose beast', was probably exploited for both milk and traction (fig. 8.13). This contrasts with the sixteenth–eighteenth centuries, when a much higher proportion of the cattle sold into Exeter and Lincoln was very young. No doubt veal was popular, in the towns at least, and it probably represents a by-product of the now important dairy industry.

Poultry

Archaeofaunal remains from post-Roman sites are beginning to provide a picture of poultry consumption in Britain. Geese and chicken are by far the most common birds represented. The domestic goose may have spread in classical times from its original centre of domestication in southeastern Europe (Zeuner, 1963). In Roman Britain geese appear only sparingly; Bramwell (1980) suggests that the Saxons were responsible for increasing geese rearing. At North Elmham Park, the Saxon site in East Anglia, there were twice as many chickens as geese, but since the goose is more than twice the weight of the chicken, the goose provided the bulk of the bird meat (Bramwell, 1980). Geese increased in importance at the beginning of the medieval period at Exeter (Maltby, 1979), and at Lincoln geese were scarce in the late ninth century but became more common through the tenth century (O'Connor, 1982). The goose trade is traditionally associated with East Anglia, and on the basis of the bird remains from King's Lynn (Bramwell, 1977) was already well established there by the eleventh century AD, and became increasingly important until c1500. At Baynard's Castle, City of London, a large number of bird bones were found in three rubbish dumps. Two, one mid-fourteenth century and one of 1500, are thought to represent refuse of city people. The other dump, dated to 1520, contains refuse from the castle itself. Gillian Carey (1982) has identified these bird bones. Chicken was most common (76 per cent) followed by goose (20 per cent) and duck (4 per cent). A comparison of 'city' with 'castle' geese bones revealed that the inhabitants of the castle seem to have had a more sophisticated diet – consuming a higher proportion of goslings (40 per cent) than city people (20 and 25 per cent). After 1500 geese apparently declined in importance, and chicken took over.

Fishing

From excavations of eleventh- and twelfth-century deposits at Great Yarmouth (where sieving was undertaken) Wheeler and Jones (1976) recovered numerous fish bones. Altogether 19 species, mainly marine fish, were identified. Fishing was probably the basis of the economy. The most abundant species were herring, whiting, cod and mackerel, but plaice, haddock (some of which must have been almost a metre long), and conger eel were also fairly common. Herring as well as horse-mackerel, which was also found, are both pelagic (surface-living) fish, and must therefore have been caught in surface nets.

The East Anglian herring fishery is supposed to have begun cAD 495, and Wheeler and Jones suggest that the drift-net—the traditional herring net of the area—may have been used in medieval Yarmouth. Fish hooks were also recovered from the Great Yarmouth excavations, and these probably served to catch some of the larger fish such as spurdog, conger eel, ling, cod, haddock, turbot and halibut.

At the medieval site at King's Lynn (Norfolk; thirteenth and fourteenth centuries), Wheeler (1977) identified only eight species of sea fish, all rather large. Wet sieving could not be undertaken, owing to the organic nature of the soil. Besides bones of cod, the most abundant species, bones of ling were also found. The ling is rare in the southern and central North Sea, but is more common further north. Wheeler suggests that ling and perhaps some of the other fish may have been imported from distant fishing grounds, salted from fishing ports in Yorkshire or Scotland. However, he does not discount the possibility that King's Lynn boats were fishing in distant northern seas.

The agricultural revolution

From the seventeenth century on, the urban population increased, and so did the average size of cattle, sheep, pig and domestic fowl. Malthus in 1798 commented on the increased size of cattle needed to feed England's multitudes. Meat was now more sought-after than wool, or the power for pulling the plough. Fat for tallow was much in demand for lighting. Moreover oxen tended to be replaced by horses for traction (Clutton-Brock, 1982). Pioneers like Robert Bakewell (1725–95) and his pupils the Colling brothers made great contributions to animal husbandry. Bakewell was the first to practise inbreeding and selection, and he established new breeds of sheep and cattle. However, Noddle (1977) suggests that cattle and sheep may have increased in stature somewhat earlier, in the late seventeenth and early eighteenth centuries, before the 'agricultural revolution and the widely publicized endeavours of Bakewell and others were under way'. O'Connor (1982) suggests that by the sixteenth century there was a general increase of sheep size, although the sheep were still of 'leggy' conformation. A real improvement in modern size and stocky carcass form does not show in bone records until the mid-eighteenth century, and it appears to have occurred quite suddenly.

The social structure

The social status of the inhabitants of a site may also be ascertained by the kinds of animal species represented. Annie Grant (1981) found that while deer bones on medieval sites are usually rare (less than 10 per cent), at the late medieval Portchester castle they constituted 14 per cent of the animal bones. At Lyveden in Northamptonshire over 20 per cent of the bones found in thirteenth- and fourteenth-century contexts were deer bones. Similarly, in the medieval layers excavated in the town of Bedford, deer bones were rare, but in the debris associated with the castle there, they were the most common. We know from documentary evidence that deer-hunting was predominantly the sport of the aristocracy: hence the high numbers of deer bones at these castle sites. Michael Ryder (1961), comparing different kinds of medieval sites in Yorkshire, noted that monastic sites had more deer and wildfowl.

Analysis of body-parts and butchery has also revealed some interesting information. In sixteenth-century Exeter, good meat bones increase at the expense of skull and jaw fragments. At Flaxengate from the mid-eleventh century onwards, and at Exeter in the post-medieval assemblages, large numbers of dorso-ventrally chopped vertebrae indicate that sheep and cattle carcasses were cut lengthwise into sides of meat, as they are today. O'Connor suggests that this may reflect an improvement in the construction of buildings. To cleave a whole cow carcass into two sides requires hanging it by the hind hocks from a supporting beam and then chopping down the mid-line from tail to head. The supporting structure needs to be able to withstand a total downward force of some 400lb (180kg) of carcass plus cleaver blows. In Lincoln, at any rate, we know that the mid-eleventh century saw the requisite improvement in construction techniques.

The bones from Viking Age floor deposits at Coppergate, York, analysed by Terry O'Connor, came from cuts of meat belonging to the poorer parts of cattle and pigs, in particular the heads and feet. These animals were not tender and young but mature, probably (in the case of the cattle) retired traction animals. A few hens and geese were also eaten, but game birds were limited to a few locally available species. The overall impression is of a neighbourhood subsisting on cheap sources of meat, lacking in quality. This O'Connor contrasts with the contents of a series of sixteenth-century pits at Aldwark, also in York. Here most of the bones came from choice cuts of mutton such as shoulders and hind-quarters. Feet and hocks had been removed, and the vertebrae were 'chopped'. Much of the cattle bone was from suckling calves, suggesting veal, and pig was not common. Moreover, besides hens and geese, there was a variety of delicacies such as fallow deer, rabbit, various species of game birds and turkey. Even the fish bones suggest affluence, with salmon and halibut being represented! Were these the remains of a wealthy household, or do they signify the general opulence of sixteenth-century York?

Another urban archaeofaunal collection coming from a 'poor neighbourhood' was excavated in a series of late-seventeenth- to mid-eighteenth-century buildings in Aldgate, to the east of the City of London walls. Here Armitage (in Thompson *et al.*, 1984) analysed the joints of meat represented. Most of the sheep bones derived from skulls, jawbones, and metapodials—parts of the body which support little flesh and represent low-quality cuts of meat traditionally purchased by the poor. In contrast, the joints represented in those found in a late-seventeenth-century refuse pit associated with a wealthy household—the Fulham Pottery site, also in London—came mostly from the shoulder and legs (fig. 8.14). Armitage also identified the Aldgate sheep bones as those of unimproved Leicestershire and Lincolnshire longwool sheep. Throughout the seventeenth and early eighteenth centuries, longwool sheep were kept for their fleeces, used in the manufacture of worsteds. When 3–4 years old, at the end of their economic lives as wool producers, they would be fattened for the London meat market. Their tough, coarse-grained and therefore cheap meat was the main source of mutton for the urban working classes. London's affluent classes preferred the more succulent meat of the smaller short- and middle-woolled breeds such as Welsh sheep, and the Dorset

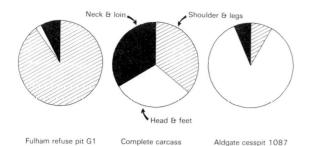

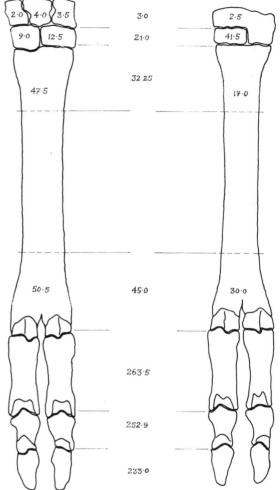

8.14 Carcass cuts and wealth. Proportions of different parts of the sheep skeleton from cesspit (1087) excavated at Aldgate, compared with those from a refuse pit (GI) at Fulham. The people who dined at Fulham were probably better-off than those at Aldgate. *From Armitage in Thompson et al., 1984*

and Wiltshire-horn. At the Fulham Pottery site, Armitage was able to identify sheep metatarsals belonging to small and medium-sized sheep, but none from longwool breeds. (Improvements by farmers like Robert Bakewell, in the late eighteenth century, to the longwool breeds, and selection for a meat-producer resulted in a smaller, shorter-legged animal with a barrel-shaped body; Armitage, 1983.)

Analysis of the animal carcass can sometimes tell us about the activities carried out in a particular locality. O'Connor (1984) found that in a series of late seventeenth- and early eighteenth-century rectangular pits at Walmgate in York, over 99 per cent of the bones in the backfill derived from the lower legs and feet of sheep. Sheep's foot bones comprised 10,203 out of the total of 10,314 bones (fig. 8.15). These are unlikely to be food debris since there is very little meat on sheep metapodia and phalanges. These pits were probably leather-tanning vats used for soaking sheepskins. The skins were probably brought in with the foot bones still attached to provide a convenient handle during stretching. (In medieval Germany it was customary to sell hides with the feet on.) After treatment these bones would then have been discarded.

Another industrial process—horn working—was evidenced at another site in York, the eleventh–twelfth-century pit-deposits at Skeldergate. Here O'Connor found large numbers of cattle and goat horn cores. These presumably represent the waste from a horner's workshop. Beneath the warehouses of the East India Company in Cutler Street, London, over 200 cattle horn cores, dated to the late seventeenth–early eighteenth century, were dis-

8.15 Leather industry refuse. Relative abundance values for different bones of fore- (left) and hind- (right) feet of sheep from late seventeenth/early eighteenth century AD Walmgate, York. Sample WB, context 1097. Note the great abundance of phalanges. *From O'Connor, 1984; The York Archaeological Trust*

covered. These were also, no doubt, the waste from horn working (fig. 8.16; Armitage, 1978). Horn was the first 'plastic', an important commodity for making containers, combs, knife-handles and even windows of lanterns (Ryder, 1984).

From a pit deposit of domestic refuse dated to *c*1770 in Crosswall, City of London, Armitage (1981) has identified a skeleton of an angora rabbit. It showed no evidence of either butchery or skinning. The skull has a feature which distinguishes it from other breeds of rabbit: a narrow width between

8.16 Horner's waste. A late seventeenth-/early eighteenth-century AD deposit in Cutler Street, City of London, containing over 200 cattle horn cores. *Photograph Trevor Hurst, courtesy Museum of London*

supraorbital fissures. It not only represents the earliest report of this rabbit in Britain, but is a rare example of an animal's breed being recognized from archaeological material. Breeds are usually distinguished by means of coat colour and various aspects of soft-part anatomy—not preserved in the skeleton. According to written records the angora was considered suitable as a 'lady's pet'. Armitage thinks that the Crosswall skeleton derives from a pet, an interpretation supported by the finding in the same deposit of a glass bird-feeder and a linnet bone. In the late eighteenth century song-birds like the favoured linnet were caught live on the outskirts of London and sold not for food but as cage-birds. Historical records indicate that England never developed a cottage fur-industry based on the angora rabbit as in France and Switzerland. Only restricted numbers of this breed were ever kept in Britain. The inhabitants of Crosswall, according to Armitage, were reasonably well-off, an interpretation supported by the finds of fine-quality Chinese porcelain and glassware.

The environment

In the last few years archaeologists digging urban sites have increasingly turned their attention to remains of other groups of animals in urban deposits such as insects (Kenward, 1982) and small mammals (parasite eggs were discussed in Chapter 3). James Rackham (1982) emphasizes the important role rodents must have played in damaging stored foods, especially grain, and in transmitting diseases.

In medieval deposits in the convent garden of the Greyfriars, London, and the collegiate grounds at Beverley, Yorkshire, Armitage (1985) found an extremely rich and diverse rodent fauna. At Beverley it included the bank vole *Clethrionomys glareolus*, a timid creature normally associated with entirely rural environments. Both localities then must have been small rural enclaves within the cities.

Dogs

Harcourt (1974) has analysed remains all over Britain of dogs from Mesolithic–Anglo Saxon periods. Although it is not possible to identify breeds, the distribution of sizes reveals something about the kinds of dog which may have been kept in different times. For example, British Iron Age dogs ranged in size from 29–58cm high at the shoulder, but the distribution of sizes suggests a single 'type' of dog. Romano–British dogs, however, exhibit an entirely new feature: great variability in height (from 23–72cm at the shoulder), build and skull shape. There may have been two or even three 'types' of dog. These include, for the first time in Britain, small lap dogs which must have been too small to serve any useful purpose or survive without human shelter. They were no doubt kept as household pets— reflecting settled and affluent times. The larger dogs of Roman and Anglo-Saxon times may have served as guard, hunting or fighting animals. And at several sites Harcourt noticed cut marks on the bones suggesting the interesting possibility that dogs were eaten in Britain.

SOME OTHER ANIMALS INTRODUCED INTO BRITAIN

Besides the chicken, introduced towards the end of the Iron Age, several other exotic species have been introduced, either inadvertently or purposely, into Britain. Some of them have had a major impact on the history and social well-being of the inhabitants of these isles. I shall mention here the fallow deer, mule, black rat, horse, rabbit, turkey, monkey and turtle.

Apart from larger breeds of cattle, the Romans are often thought to have introduced (or re-introduced, since it was common in Hoxnian and Ipswichian inter-glacials) the fallow deer into Britain. Annie Grant (1975) reports several fallow deer bones from a level dated to between AD 290 and 345 at Portchester castle. Fallow deer bones have now been identified from several Romano–British sites—though several of these are multi-period sites, so it is possible that fallow deer bones were from later periods (Grant, pers. comm.).

Another animal which has recently come to light on a Roman site is the mule (Armitage and Chapman, 1979). Philip Armitage, who studied the bones from Roman Billingsgate in London, identified a mule mandible from a rubbish deposit dated between AD 125 and 160. Erosion of bone on the lower part of its external surface (fig. 8.17) suggests that it was probably handled roughly by a rope halter or muzzle, resulting in chafing of the underside of the jaw where there is little flesh to cushion the surface of the underlying bone. The mule is the offspring resulting from crossing two closely related species—female

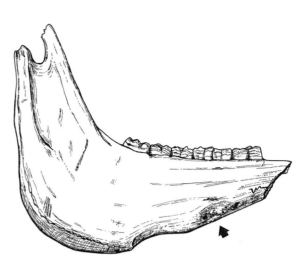

8.17 A Roman mule from Billingsgate buildings, City of London, dated to *c*AD 125–160. External view of the mandible (see also **8.18**). Note the region showing erosion of bone due to pressure, perhaps the result of chafing by a rope halter or a muzzle. Scale 1:2. *Drawing by Katharine Armitage, courtesy K. and Philip Armitage*

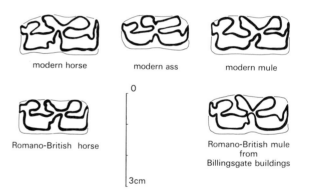

modern horse   modern ass   modern mule

Romano-British horse

Romano-British mule from Billingsgate buildings

0

3cm

8.18 The Roman mule from Billingsgate buildings, City of London. Enamel folds on the occlusal surface of the right lower first molar tooth compared with other equids. *From Armitage and Chapman, 1979*

horse with male donkey—and it is usually infertile. Armitage's find (fig. 8.18) suggests that the Romans either imported mules into Britain or brought in donkeys so that mules could be bred here. The mule played an important role in the Roman economy as both a draught animal and a beast of burden.

Several investigators have discovered remains of the Black rat *Rattus rattus* (fig. 8.19), from Roman Britain (Armitage *et al.* 1984). Rackham (1979) found it in a late Roman (probably fourth-century AD) well at Skeldergate, York. Armitage found it in

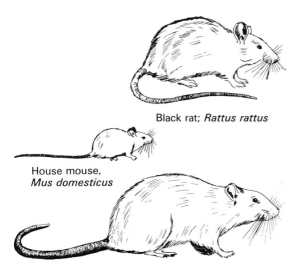

Black rat; *Rattus rattus*

House mouse,
Mus domesticus

Brown rat, *Rattus norvegicus*

8.19 Three rodents which have played and continue to play an important role in our own wellbeing. *Drawings by Evelyn Davis, after Van den Brink:* Field guide to the mammals of Britain and Europe, *1967*

third- and fourth-century AD deposits in the City of London, and O'Connor reports it from second-century AD Wroxeter, and second–third-century York.

The venerable Bede, the eighth-century English historian, wrote about a terrible pestilence which ravaged England in the seventh century and Ireland several times and 'destroyed a great multitude of men'. The pestilence of AD 664 was the most noted (Plummer, 1896) and it is also reported in the Anglo-Saxon Chronicle. Bede even described how St Cuthbert had a 'tumour which arose in his thigh' (*tumor in femore*), referring no doubt to an inguinal bubo of plague (MacArthur, 1949). The plague is even said to have contributed to the decline of London's population in AD 150–250. These epidemics seem to resemble bubonic plague. This disease is carried by the Black rat, which serves as a reservoir. The plague is transmitted from rat to man by the rat flea *Xenopsylla cheopis*. Until recently the Black rat was thought not to have been present in Britain until the Crusaders brought it back from the Near East in the eleventh or twelfth centuries AD. But now the identity of Bede's pestilence may be solved.

The Black rat is closely associated with man, occupying buildings and warehouses, and has accidentally attained a worldwide distribution as a result

of transport on ships between coastal ports—hence its other name, 'Ship rat'. It is thought to have come from the Near East, but it may originally have come from India. It is known from Hyksos times in Egypt (1750–1550 BC; Boessneck, 1976), and the 'ofalim' or 'emerods' (now translated as tumours) in 1 Samuel 5 and 6 that afflicted the Philistines in Ashdod could have been plague. It is also mentioned in this same Biblical text that the Philistines were troubled by rodents (?rats, see MacArthur, 1949). The Black rat must have arrived in Italy before AD 79: it is known from Pompeii, soon after in Switzerland, and from the Roman period in southern Germany. From the Rhineland it could have come to Britain. Alternatively, it may have been imported directly from Mediterranean ports—perhaps in grain or other merchant ships (Armitage *et al.*, 1984).

The Anglo-Saxon invaders brought their own horses with them. Some remains of horses from this period are much larger than the earlier Celtic ponies from the Iron Age (i.e. a withers height of 1.4m or 14 hands compared with 1.2m or 12 hands). Thus the Anglo-Saxon Chronicle mentions the shipment of 'horses and all' from France to Kent in AD 892. It was during the Anglo-Saxon period that an oriental invention, the stirrup, reached Britain (Clutton-Brock, 1976). The Romans did not have stirrups. A cavalry without stirrups has little power in armed combat. On horseback the spear could only be wielded at the end of the arm and a blow could be delivered with the strength of arm and shoulder only. Wars in the ancient world were generally waged with horses harnessed to chariots rather than ridden.

The stirrup provides firm attachment to horseback. The horseman could now use the principle of mounted shock combat. Pikes and swords could be thrust at the enemy at full speed without the cavalier being hurled from the horse. The fighter's hand no longer delivered the blow: it merely guided it. The strength of the whole body could be put into the spear or lance. The stirrup thus replaced human energy with animal power (White, 1962). Armour now became increasingly costly and heavy in order to withstand shock combat, and horses had to be larger, requiring more fodder. Only the rich could afford to be cavaliers; peasants were now heavily taxed, and the feudal system with a mounted warrior class developed.

While the Anglo-Saxons were acquainted with the stirrup, they did not modify their methods of warfare

8.20 Women netting a rabbit in early fourteenth-century England. A ferret is being set in a rabbit burrow. *From Queen Mary's Psalter, courtesy British Library; MS Royal 2.B.VII f.155v*

sufficiently to make the best use of it. They hardly developed an elite of mounted warriors. King Harold was 'sat firmly in his stirrups', on reaching Hastings in order to meet William in 1066, dismounted and fought the old way on foot. The Normans of course, with their mounted cavalry and bowmen, were the victors.

Martin Hinton identified several rabbit bones in the midden at Rayleigh castle, Essex (Hinton, 1912–13). This castle was built soon after the conquest and was no longer in use after 1220. Rabbit bones were also found in twelfth-century levels at Exeter (Maltby, 1979). These finds confirm early documentary evidence of the presence of rabbits in England (fig. 8.20). For example the king in 1235 presented as a gift *decem cuninos vivos* ('ten live rabbits') from his park at Guildford (Veale, 1957). The rabbit was probably introduced from Spain or southern France. Peter des Roches, bishop of Winchester from 1205 to 1238, accustomed to eating rabbits in his native Poitou, is thought to have encouraged their establishment in England (Veale, 1957). Rabbits were expensive in the thirteenth and fourteenth centuries, when they cost four or five times as much as chickens— supporting evidence that they were recent arrivals.

By post-medieval times, judging by the numbers of bones, the rabbit had replaced the hare as an important minor element in the English diet.

Turkey bones are frequently reported from archaeological levels which postdate the mid-sixteenth century. The turkey was introduced into Britain from North America, probably in the 1520s. Maltby (1979), for example, found a turkey bone at Exeter in a context dated to the middle of the sixteenth century.

Armitage (1983) identified a mandible of a South American Weeper Capuchin monkey (*Cebus nigrivittatus*) from a secure post-medieval deposit at Brooks wharf in the City of London. Associated clay pipes indicate a date of *c*1640–80. The capuchin monkey is found in northeastern South America, and Armitage links this unusual find with the unsuccessful seventeenth-century attempts to colonize South America by the English. London, apart from being the supply base, was the administrative centre for Guianan colonization, and in 1619 Captain Roger North had set up the registered company entitled 'The Governor and Company of Noblemen and Gentlemen of the City of London Adventurers in and about the River of the Amazons'. Armitage asked whether this particular specimen derived from a live animal, or one which had been brought back dead and preserved. It is known that monkeys in captivity are prone to suffer bone disease resulting from a calcium-deficient fruit and vegetable diet. Armitage X-rayed mandibles of captive and wild capuchin monkeys from several London collections. The wild specimens showed the expected good cortical development, whereas the captives' bones were more porous and diffuse. The Brooks wharf mandible resembled the bones from captive animals, suggesting that it had been brought back and kept alive for some time. The easily tamed and entertaining capuchin monkey, or 'organ-grinder's monkey', was common in most nineteenth-century European towns.

Armitage (1980) has also identified turtle bones from a well in Leadenhall buildings in the City of London. They date to the period between 1750 and 1815, and provide archaeological evidence of the well documented trade in Green turtles. These were imported live from the West Indies. There is a tradition, going back to 1761, of serving turtle soup at the Lord Mayor's banquet. But turtle soup was for the wealthy only, and the less fortunate had to make do with the 'mock' variety prepared from a calf's head.

Growing interest in the faunal remains from later British archaeological sites will no doubt serve to bring to light an ever-increasing list of exotic animals brought back from the four corners of the world by explorers and international merchants.

WHAT OF THE FUTURE?

With growing interest in many of the new palaeontological discoveries over the last two decades, what are the main research problems which confront zoo-archaeology today?

For a start we need better comparative collections. Few museums are prepared to house series of sexed and aged disarticulated skeletons of such 'boring' animals as domestic livestock. Archaeofaunal reports will have to be more detailed, but few journals are prepared to publish data, such as measurements, in full. Details like measurements are so vital for comparing sites and species through time and across wide geographical areas. We are still ignorant about the way the skeleton and dentition of many of our domestic livestock develop—when teeth erupt and bones cease growth. We barely understand how environmental variables like plane of nutrition, type of food, and temperature affect the skeleton and teeth. Experiments to investigate these are usually expensive but need to be done.

Generally speaking zoo-archaeology can be practised with a minimum of sophisticated equipment and little money. It is (in Sebastian Payne's phrase) a 'low-tech science', often needing little more than a tube of glue and a pair of callipers. Nonetheless there is plenty of scope for electron microscopes and sophisticated equipment. Electron microscopes (especially scanning ones) are now much easier to use and no doubt will be providing us with new kinds of information, as Pat Shipman and others are finding in their analysis of bones associated with early African hominids.

REFERENCES

AGENBROAD, L.D. 1984 New World mammoth distribution. In: Martin, P.S. and Klein, R.G. pp. 90–108

AMBROSETTI, P. 1968 The Pleistocene dwarf elephants of Spinagallo (Siracusa) south-eastern Sicily. *Geologica Romana* 7, 277–397

ANDREWS, M.V., GILBERTSON, D.D., KENT, M., and MELLARS, P.A. 1985 Biometric studies of morphological variation in the intertidal gastropod *Nucella lapillus* (L): environmental and palaeoeconomic significance. *Journal of Biogeography* 12, 71–87

ARMITAGE, P.L. 1978 Hertfordshire cattle and London meat markets in the 17th and 18th centuries. *The London Archaeologist* 3, 217–23

ARMITAGE, P.L. 1980 A preliminary description of British cattle from the late 12th to the early 16th century. *The Ark* 7, 405–12

ARMITAGE, P.L. 1981 Remains of an Angora rabbit from a late 18th century pit at Crosswall. *The London Archaeologist* 4, 87–95

ARMITAGE, P.L. 1981 A late Anglo-Saxon horse skeleton from Ironmonger Lane, City of London, 1980. Unpublished archive report, Museum of London

ARMITAGE, P.L. 1982 Developments in British cattle husbandry from the Romano–British period to early modern times. *The Ark* 9, 50–4

ARMITAGE, P.L. 1982 Studies on the remains of domestic livestock from Roman, medieval, and early modern London: objectives and methods. In: Hall, A.R. and Kenward, H.K. (eds.), *Environmental archaeology in urban context*. pp. 94–106. London, Council for British Archaeology Research Report no. 43

ARMITAGE, P.L. 1983 The early history of English longwool sheep. *The Ark* 10, 90–7

ARMITAGE, P.L. 1983 Jawbone of a South American monkey from Brooks Wharf, City of London. *The London Archaeologist* 4, 262–70

ARMITAGE, P.L. 1985 Small mammal faunas in later mediaeval towns. *The Biologist* 32, 65–71

ARMITAGE, P.L. and CHAPMAN, H. 1979 Roman mules. *The London Archaeologist* 3, 339–46

ARMITAGE, P.L. and McCARTHY, C. 1980 Turtle remains from a late 18th century well at Leadenhall Buildings. *The London Archaeologist* 4, 8–16

ARMITAGE, P.L., WEST, B. and STEADMAN, K. 1984 New evidence of Black rat in Roman London. *The London Archaeologist* 4, 375–83

ARMOUR-CHELU, M. 1985 In: Pryor, F.S.A., French, C. and Taylor, M. An interim report on excavations at Etton, Maxey, Cambridgeshire, 1982–84. *The Antiquaries Journal* 65, 275–311

ASHBEE, P. 1978 *The ancient British a social-archaeological narrative*. Norwich, Geo Abstracts

AVERY, D.M. 1982 Micromammals as palaeoenvironmental indicators and an interpretation of the late Quaternary in the southern Cape province, South Africa. *Annals of the South African Museum* 85, 183–374

AZZAROLI, A. 1981 Cainozoic mammals and the biogeography of the island of Sardinia, western Mediterranean. *Palaeogeography, Palaeoclimatology, Palaeoecology* 36, 107–11

AZZAROLI, A. 1982 Insularity and its effects on terrestrial vertebrates: evolutionary and biogeographic aspects. In: Gallitelli, E.M. (ed.), *Palaeontology, essential of historical geology* pp. 193–213. Modena, Italy, Mucchi

BAILEY, G.N. 1978 Shell middens as indicators of postglacial economies: a territorial perspective. In: Mellars, P. (ed.), *The early postglacial settlement of northern Europe*. London, Duckworth. pp. 37–63

BAILEY, G.N. 1983 Economic change in late Pleistocene Cantabria. In: Bailey, G. (ed.), *Hunter-gatherer economy in prehistory*. Cambridge University Press. pp. 149–65

BAKER, J.R. and BROTHWELL, D.R. 1980 *Animal Diseases in Archaeology*. London, Academic Press

BANKS, W.J. and NEWBREY, J.W. 1983 Antler development as a unique modification of mammalian endochondral ossification. In: Brown, R.D. (ed.), *Antler development in cervidae*. pp. 279–306. Kingsville, Texas, Caesar Kleberg Wildlife Research Institute

BARNES, B., EDWARDS, B.J.N., HALLAM, J.S. and

STUART, A.J. 1971 Skeleton of a late Glacial elk associated with barbed points from Poulton-le-Fylde, Lancashire. *Nature*, 232, 488–9

BATE, D.M.A. 1937 Palaeontology: the fossil fauna of the Wady el-Mughara caves. In: Garrod, D.A.E. and Bate, D.M.A. (eds.), *The Stone Age of Mount Carmel*. Part 2, Oxford, the Clarendon Press. pp. 137–240

BEALE, T.W. 1973 Early trade in highland Iran: a view from a source area. *World Archaeology* 5, 133–48

BEEK, G.W. van 1969 The rise and fall of Arabia Felix. *Scientific American* 221, 36–46

BELLWOOD, P. 1978 *Man's conquest of the Pacific*. London, Collins

BERRY, R.J. 1977 *Inheritance and natural history*. London, Collins

BLOOM, W. and FAWCETT, D.W. 1975 *A textbook of histology*. 10th Edition. Philadelphia, Saunders

BLUMENBERG, B. 1979 The origins of hominid megafaunal carnivory. *Carnivore* 2, 71–2

BOEKSCHOTEN, G.J. and SONDAAR, P.Y. 1972 On the fossil mammalia of Cyprus. *Koninklijke Nederlandse Akademie van Wetenschappen. Proceedings, Series B* 75, 306–38

BOESSNECK, J. 1964 Uber die osteologischen arbeiten und probleme des tieranatomischen instituts der Universitat Munchen. *Zeitschrift fur Agrargeschichte und Agrarsoziologie* 12, 216–30

BOESSNECK, J. 1969 Osteological differences between sheep (*Ovis aries* Linne) and goat (*Capra hircus* Linne). In Brothwell, D. and Higgs, E.S. (eds.), *Science in archaeology* 2nd ed. pp. 331–58. London, Thames and Hudson

BOESSNECK, J. 1976 Tell el-Dab'a III. Die Tierknochenfunde 1966–1969. *Osterreichischen Akademie der Wissenschaften Denkschriften der Gesamtakademie* 5, 7–42

BOESSNECK, J. and DRIESCH, A. von den 1976 Pferde im 4/3 jahrtausend v. Chr. in Ostanatolien. *Saugetierkundliche Mitteilungen* 24, 81–7

BOESSNECK, J. and DRIESCH, A. von den 1978 The significance of measuring animal bones from archaeological sites. In: Meadow, R.H. and Zeder, M.A. (eds.), *Approaches to faunal analysis in the Middle East*, pp. 25–39. Peabody Museum Bulletin 2, Harvard University, Cambridge, Mass.

BOESSNECK, J., MULLER, H.-H. and TEICHERT, M. 1964 Osteologische unterscheidungsmerkmale zwischen schaf (*Ovis aries* LINNE) und ziege (*Capra hircus* LINNE). *Kuhn–Archiv* 78, 1–129

BÖKÖNYI, S. 1969 Archaeological problems and methods of recognizing animal domestication. In: Ucko, P. and Dimbleby, G. (eds.), *The domestication and exploitation of plants and animals*, pp. 219–29 London, Duckworth

BÖKÖNYI, S. 1978 The earliest waves of domestic horses in East Europe. *Journal of Indo-European Studies* 6, 17–76

BORDES, F. and PRAT, F. 1965 Observations sur les faunes du Riss et du Wurm I en Dordogne. *L'Anthropologie* 69, 31–46

BOSMA, A.A., HAAN, N.A. and MACDONALD, A.A. 1984 Karyotype variability in the wild boar (*Sus scrofa*). In: Spitz, F. and Pepin, D. (eds.), *Symposium international sur le sanglier*. Toulouse, Institut National de la Recherche Agronomique. pp. 53–6

BOURDILLON, J. and COY, J. 1980 The animal bones, in: Holdsworth, P. (ed.), *Excavations at Melbourne Street, Southampton 1971–76*. Council for British Archaeology Research Report 33, 79–120

BOWDLER, S. 1984 *Hunter Hill, Hunter Island archaeological investigations of a prehistoric Tasmanian site*. Terra Australis 8, Canberra, Australian National University, department of Prehistory

BOYD DAWKINS, W. and WILFRID JACKSON, J. 1917 The wild animals of the lake village, and the domestic animals of the lake village. In: Bulleid, A. and St. George Gray, H. *The Glastonbury lake village* Vol. II. pp. 641–72. The Glastonbury Antiquarian Society

BRAIN, C.K. 1967 Hottentot food remains and their bearing on the interpretation of fossil bone assemblages. *Scientific papers of the Namib Desert Research Institute* 32, 1–11

BRAIN, C.K. 1981 *The hunters or the hunted? An introduction to African cave taphonomy*. Chicago University Press

BRAMWELL, D. 1977 Bird bone. In: Clarke, H. and Carter, A. Excavations in King's Lynn 1963–70. *Society for Medieval Archaeology Monograph Series* 7, 399–402

BRAMWELL, D. 1980 Identification and interpretation of bird bones. In: Wade Martins, P. (ed.), Excavations in North Elmham Park. *East Anglian Archaeological Report* 9, 409–12

BRASH, J.C. 1934 Some problems in the growth and developmental mechanics of bone. *Edinburgh Medical Journal* 41, 305–19; 363–87

BULL, G. and PAYNE, S. 1982 Tooth eruption and epiphyseal fusion in pigs and wild boar. In: Wilson, B., Grigson, C. and Payne, S. (eds.), *Ageing and sexing animal bones from archaeological sites*, pp. 55–71. Oxford, BAR British series 109

BULLIET, R.W. 1975 *The camel and the wheel*. Cambridge, Mass., Harvard University Press

BUNCH, T.D., FOOTE, W.C. and SPILLETT, J.J. 1976 Translocations of acrocentric chromosomes and their implications in the evolution of sheep (*Ovis*). *Cytogenetics and Cell Genetics* 17, 122–36

BUNN, H.T. 1981 Archaeological evidence for meat-eating by Plio-Pleistocene hominids from Koobi Fora and Olduvai Gorge. *Nature* 291, 574–7

BUTZER, K.W. 1971 *Environment and archaeology an ecological approach to prehistory*. 2 edn. London, Methuen

CAESAR, Julius C. *The Gallic War*. Translated by H.J. Edwards. The Loeb Classical Library. London, Heinemann

CAMPBELL, J.B. 1977 *The Upper Palaeolithic of Britain*. Oxford University Press

CAREY, G. 1982 Ageing and sexing domestic bird bones

from some late medieval deposits at Baynard's castle, city of London. pp. 263–8. Oxford, BAR British series, 109

CASSELS, R. 1984 The role of prehistoric man in the faunal extinctions of New Zealand and other Pacific islands. In: Martin, P.S. and Klein, R.G. (eds.). pp. 741–67

CASTEEL, R.W. 1972 Some archaeological uses of fish remains. *American Antiquity* 37, 404–19

CHALINE, J. 1976 Les rongeurs. In: Lumley, H. de (ed.) *La Préhistoire Française* I pp. 420–4. Editions du Centre National de la Recherche Scientifique

CHAPLIN, R.E. 1971 *The Study of Animal Bones from Archaeological Sites.* London, Seminar Press

CHERRY, J.F. 1981 Pattern and process in the earliest colonization of the Mediterranean, *Proceedings of the Prehistoric Society* 47, 41–68

CHILDE, V.G. 1928 *The most ancient East: the oriental prelude to European prehistory.* London, Kegan Paul, Trench, Trubner

CHOW B.-S., 1984 Animal domestication in Neolithic China. In: Clutton-Brock, J. and Grigson, C. (eds.), *Animals and Archaeology: 3. Early herders and their flocks.* pp. 363–9. Oxford, BAR International Series 202

CLARK, G.A. and STRAUS, L.G. 1983 Late Pleistocene hunter-gatherer adaptations in Cantabrian Spain. In: Bailey, G. (ed.), *Hunter-gatherer economy in prehistory.* pp. 131–48. Cambridge University Press

CLARK, J.G.D. 1954 *Excavations at Star Carr, an early Mesolithic site at Seamer, near Scarborough, Yorkshire.* Cambridge University Press

CLARK, J.G.D. 1972 Star Carr—a case study in bioarchaeology. *McCaleb module in Anthropology* 10, 1–42

CLEVEDON BROWN, J. and YALDEN, D.W. 1973 The description of mammals—2 limbs and locomotion of terrestrial mammals. *Mammal Review* 3, 107–34

CLUTTON-BROCK, J. 1971 The primary food animals of the Jericho Tell from the proto-Neolithic to the Byzantine period. *Levant* 3, 41–55

CLUTTON-BROCK, J. 1974 The Buhen horse. *Journal of Archaeological Science* 1, 89–100

CLUTTON-BROCK, J. 1976 The animal resources. In: Wilson, D.M. (ed.), *The archaeology of Anglo-Saxon England,* pp. 373–92. London, Methuen

CLUTTON-BROCK, J. 1978 Bones for the zoologist. In: Meadow, R.H. and Zeder, M.A. (eds.), *Approaches to faunal analysis in the Middle East. pp. 49–51.* Harvard University, Peabody Museum Bulletin 2

CLUTTON-BROCK, J. 1982 British cattle in the eighteenth century. *The Ark* 9, 55–9

CLUTTON-BROCK, J. and BURLEIGH, R. 1983 Some archaeological applications of the dating of animal bone by radiocarbon with particular reference to post-Pleistocene extinctions. In: Mook, W.G. and Waterbolk, H.T. (eds.), *Proceedings of the first International symposium 14C and archaeology.* pp. 409–19. Strasbourg, Council of Europe PACT 8.

COHEN, M.N. 1977 *The food crisis in prehistory.* New Haven, Yale University Press

COLES, J.M. 1971 The early settlement of Scotland: excavations at Morton Fife. *Proceedings of the Prehistoric Society* 37, 284–366

COMPAGNONI, B. and TOSI, M. 1978 The camel: its distribution and state of domestication in the Middle East during the third millennium BC in light of finds from Shahr-i Sokhta. In: Meadow, R.H. and Zeder, M.A. (eds.), *Approaches to faunal analysis in the Middle East.* pp. 91–103. Harvard University, Peabody Museum Bulletin 2

COON, C.S. 1951 *Cave explorations in Iran, 1949.* Museum monographs, Philadelphia: the university museum

COOPE, G.R. 1977 Fossil coleopteran assemblages as sensitive indicators of climatic changes during the Devensian (Last) cold stage. *Philosophical Transactions of the Royal Society London* 280, 313–40

CORNWALL, I.W. 1964 *Bones for the archaeologist.* Third impression, London, Phoenix house

COUTTS, P. and HIGHAM, C. 1971 The seasonal factor in prehistoric New Zealand. *World Archaeology* 2, 266–77

CRAM, L. 1984 Footprints in the sands of time. In: Grigson, C. and Clutton-Brock, J. (eds.), *Animals and archaeology, 4. Husbandry in Europe.* pp. 229–35. Oxford, BAR International series 227

CRAWFORD, H.E.W. 1973 Mesopotamia's invisible exports in the third millennium BC. *World Archaeology* 5, 232–41

CRAWFORD, R.D. 1984 Domestic fowl. In: Mason, I.L. (ed.), *Evolution of domesticated animals.* pp. 298–311. London, Longman

CRAWFORD, R.D. 1984 Turkey. In: Mason, I.L. (ed.), *Evolution of domesticated animals.* pp. 325–34. London, Longman

CROTHERS, J.H. 1978 The dog-whelk, *Nucella lapillus* (L.), as an indicator of exposure and pollution on rocky sea shores. *Haliotis* 9, 33–41

CUNLIFFE, B. 1968 Excavations at Eldon's seat, Encombe, Dorset. *Proceedings of the Prehistoric Society* 34, 191–226

DANIEL, G. 1975 *A hundred and fifty years of archaeology.* London, Duckworth

DANSGAARD, W., JOHNSON, S.J., MØLLER, J. and LANGWAY, C.C. 1969 One thousand centuries of climatic record from Camp Century on the Greenland ice sheet. *Science* 166, 377–81

DARWIN, C. 1839 *Journal and remarks 1832–1836* in: Fitzroy, R. (ed.), *Narrative of the surveying voyages of His Majesty's ships Adventure and Beagle between the years 1826 and 1836 describing their examination of the southern shores of South America and the Beagle's circumnavigation of the globe.* Vol III. London, Henry Colburn

DAVIS, S.J.M. 1976 Mammal bones from the Early Bronze Age city of Arad, northern Negev, Israel: some implications concerning human exploitation. *Journal of Archaeological Science* 3, 153–64

DAVIS, S.J.M. 1980 Late Pleistocene and Holocene equid remains from Israel. *Zoological Journal of the Linnean Society* 70, 289–312

DAVIS, S.J.M. 1980 A note on the dental and skeletal ontogeny of *Gazella. Israel Journal of Zoology* 29, 129–34

DAVIS, S.J.M. 1981 The effects of temperature change and domestication on the body size of late Pleistocene to Holocene mammals of Israel. *Paleobiology* 7, 101–14

DAVIS, S.J.M. 1982 Climatic change and the advent of domestication: the succession of ruminant artiodactyls in the late Pleistocene-Holocene in the Israel region. *Paléorient* 8, 5–15

DAVIS, S.J.M. 1983 The age profiles of gazelles predated by ancient man in Israel: possible evidence for a shift from seasonality to sedentism in the Natufian. *Paléorient* 9, 55–62

DAVIS, S.J.M. 1984 The advent of milk and wool production in western Iran: some speculations. In: Clutton-Brock, J. and Grigson, C. (eds.), *Animals and archaeology: 3. Early herders and their flocks.* pp. 265–78. Oxford, BAR International series 202

DAVIS, S.J.M. 1985 A preliminary report of the fauna from Hatoula: a Natufian-Khiamian (PPNA) site near Latroun, Israel. pp. 71–98. In: Lechevallier, M. and Ronen, A. *Le site Natoufien-Khiamien de Hatoula, prés de Latroun, Israel.* Centre de Recherche Français de Jérusalem. Service de documentation 1

DAVIS, S.J.M. and VALLA, F.R. 1978 Evidence for domestication of the dog 12,000 years ago in the Natufian of Israel. *Nature* 276, 608–610

DEGERBØL, M. 1961 On a find of a Preboreal domestic dog (*Canis familiaris* L.) from Star Carr, Yorkshire, with remarks on other Mesolithic dogs. *Proceedings of the Prehistoric Society* 3, 35–55

DEITH, M.R. 1983 Molluscan calendars: the use of growth-line analysis to establish seasonality of shellfish collection at the Mesolithic site of Morton, Fife. *Journal of Archaeological Science* 10, 423–40

DELPECH, F. 1983 *Les faunes du Paléolithique supérieur dans le sud-ouest de la France.* Bordeaux, éditions du Centre National de la Recherche Scientifique: Cahiers du Quaternaire 6

DELPECH, F. and HEINTZ, E. 1976 Les artiodactyls: bovidés. In: Lumley, H. de (ed.), *La préhistoire Française* I. pp. 386–394. Editions du Centre National de la Recherche Scientifique

DENIZ, E. and PAYNE, S. 1982 Eruption and wear in the mandibular dentition as a guide to ageing Turkish Angora goats. In: Wilson, B., Grigson, C. and Payne, S. (eds.), *Ageing and sexing animal bones from archaeological sites.* pp. 155–205. Oxford, BAR British series 109

DENT, A. 1977 Orkney pigs. *The Ark* 4, 304

DERMITZAKIS, M.D. and SONDAAR, P.Y. 1978 The importance of fossil mammals in reconstructing paleogeography with special reference to the Pleistocene

Aegean archipelago. *Annales Géologiques des Pays Helléniques* 29, 808–40

DEWAR, R.E. 1984 Extinctions in Madagascar. The loss of the subfossil fauna. In: Martin, P.S. and Klein, R.G. (eds.), pp. 574–93

DIXON, J.E. and RENFREW, C. 1973 The source of the Franchthi obsidians. *Hesperia* 42, 82–83

DONNER, J.J. and KURTEN, B. 1958 The floral and faunal succession of Cueva del Toll, Spain. *Eiszeitalter u. Gegenwart* 9, 72–82

DRIESCH, A. von den, 1976 *Das vermessen von tierknochen aus vor und fruhgeschichtlichen siedlungen.* Munich, Institut fur Palaoanatomie, Universitat Munchen. (Translated into English as: *A guide to the measurement of animal bones from archaeological sites.* Peabody Museum Bulletin 1, Cambridge Mass., Harvard University

DRIESCH, A. von den, and BOESSNECK, J. 1975 Schnittspuren an Neolithischen tierknochen. *Germania* 53, 1–23

DROWER, M.S. 1969 The domestication of the horse. in: Ucko, P.J. and Dimbleby, G.W. (eds.), *The domestication and exploitation of plants and animals.* pp. 471–8. London, Duckworth

DUERST, J.U. 1908 Animal remains from the excavations at Anau. In: Pumpelly, R. *Explorations in Turkestan. Expedition of 1904* pp. 341–99. Washington, Carnegie Institute

DUERST, J.U. 1928 Vergleichende untersuchungsmethoden am skelett bei saugern. In: Abderhalden, E. (ed.), *Handbuch der biologischen arbeitsmethoden* 7. pp. 125–530

EFREMOV, J.A. 1940 Taphonomy: new branch of paleontology. *Pan-American Geologist* 74, 81–93

ELDER, W.H. 1965 Primaeval deer hunting pressures revealed by remains from American Indian middens. *Journal of Wildlife Management* 29, 366–70

ENLOW, D.H. 1963 *Principles of bone remodeling.* Springfield, Illinois; Charles Thomas

EPSTEIN, H. 1972 The Chandella horse of Khajuraho, with comments on the origin of early Indian horses. *Zeitschrift fur Tierzuchtung und Zuchtungsbiologie* 89, 170–77

EVANS, A. 1935 *The palace of Minos at Knossos* 4. London, Macmillan

EVANS, J.D. 1977 Island archaeology in the Mediterranean: problems and opportunities. *World Archaeology* 9, 12–26

EVANS, J.G. 1975 *The environment of early man in the British Isles.* London, Paul Elek

FLANNERY, K.V. 1969 The animal bones. In: Hole, F., Flannery, K.V. and Neely, J.A. *Prehistory and human ecology of the Deh Luran plain an early village sequence from Khuzistan, Iran.* Memoirs of the Museum of Anthropology, University of Michigan 1. pp. 262–330

FLEISCH, H. and NEUMAN, W.F. 1961 Mechanisms of calcification: role of collagen, poly-phosphates and phosphatase. *American Journal of Physiology* 200, 1296–300

FLOOD, J. 1983 *Archaeology of the dreamtime.* Sydney, Collins

FOCK, J. 1966 *Metrische untersuchungen an metapodien einiger Europaischer rinderrassen.* Dissertation, University of Munich

FOWLER, P. and EVANS, J. 1967 Plough-marks, lynchets and early fields. *Antiquity* 41, 289–94

FRERE, J. 1800 Account of flint weapons discovered at Hoxne in Suffolk. *Archaeologia* 13, 204–5

FRISON, G.C. 1971 The buffalo pound in northwestern plains prehistory: site 48CA302, Wyoming. *American Antiquity* 36, 77–91

FRISON, G.C. (ed.) 1974 *The Casper site. A Hell Gap bison kill on the high plains.* New York, Academic Press

FRISON, G.C. and STANFORD, D.J. 1982 *The Agate Basin site. A record of Paleoindian occupation of the northwestern high plains.* New York, Academic Press

GARCIA-GONZALEZ, R. 1981 Estudio de la osificacion postnatal en ovinos de raza rasa aragonesa. *Munibe* 33, 259–79

GARRARD, A.N. 1982 The environmental implications of a re-analysis of the large mammal fauna from the wadi el-Mughara caves, Palestine. In: Bintliff, J.N. and Van Zeist, W. (eds.), *Palaeoclimates, palaeoenvironments and human communities in the eastern Mediterranean region in later prehistory.* pp. 165–87. Oxford, BAR International series 133

GAUTHIER-PILTERS, H. and DAGG, A.I. 1981 *The camel.* Chicago, Chicago University Press

GELDER-OTTWAY, S. 1979 Faunal remains from Dokkum. *Palaeohistoria* 21, 110–26

GILBERT, B.M. and BASS, W.M. 1967 Seasonal dating of burials from the presence of fly pupae. *American Antiquity* 32, 534–5

GILLESPIE, R., HORTON, D.R. LADD, P., MACUMBER, P.G., RICH, T.H., THORNE, R. and WRIGHT, R.V.S. 1978 Lancefield swamp and the extinction of the Australian megafauna. *Science* 200, 1044–8

GLIOZZI, E. and MALATESTA, A. 1980 The Quaternary goat of Capo Figari (northeastern Sardinia). *Geologica Romana* 19, 295–347

GLIOZZI, E. and MALATESTA, A. 1982 A megacerine in the Pleistocene of Sicily. *Geologica Romana* 21, 311–95

GOLDBERG, P. and BAR YOSEF, O. 1982 Environmental and archaeological evidence for climatic change in the southern Levant. In: Bintliff, J.N. and Van Zeist, W. (eds.), *Palaeoclimates, palaeoenvironments and human communities in the eastern Mediterranean region in later prehistory.* pp. 399–418. Oxford, BAR International series 133 (ii)

GOODE, A.W. and RAMBAUT, P.C. 1985 The skeleton in space. *Nature* 317, 204–5

GORDON, C.C. and BUIKSTRA, J.E. 1979 Soil pH, bone preservation, and sampling bias at mortuary sites. Paper presented at the 44th annual meeting of the Society for American Archaeology, Vancouver, British Columbia

GOWLETT, J.A.J., HARRIS, J.W.K., WALTON, D. and WOOD, B.A. 1981 Early archaeological sites, hominid remains and traces of fire from Chesowanja, Kenya. *Nature* 294, 125–9

GRANT, A. 1975 The animal bones. In: Cunliffe, B. (ed.), *Excavations at Portchester castle* I Roman. pp. 378–408. Reports of the research committee, society of antiquaries of London 32

GRANT, A. 1981 The significance of deer remains at occupation sites of the Iron Age to the Anglo-Saxon period. In: Jones, M. and Dimbleby, G. (eds.), *The environment of man: the Iron Age to the Anglo-Saxon period.* pp. 205–13. Oxford, BAR British series 87

GRANT, A. 1984 Animal husbandry in Wessex and the Thames valley. In: Cunliffe, B. and Miles, D. (eds.), *Aspects of the Iron Age in central southern Britain.* pp. 102–19. University of Oxford: committee for archaeology

GRIGSON, C. 1981 In: Simmons, I.G. and Tooley, M.J. (eds.), *The environment in British prehistory.* London, Duckworth

GRIGSON, C. 1982 Cattle in prehistoric Britain. *The Ark* 9, 47–9

GRIGSON, C. 1982 Sex and age determination of some bones and teeth of domestic cattle: a review of the literature. In: Wilson, B., Grigson, C. and Payne, S. (eds.), *Ageing and sexing animal bones from archaeological sites.* pp. 7–23. Oxford, BAR British series 109

GRIGSON, C. 1983 In: Evans, J.G. et al. Excavations at Cherhill, north Wiltshire, 1967. *Proceedings of the Prehistoric Society* 49, 43–117

GRIGSON, C. 1984 The domestic animals of the earlier Neolithic in Britain. In: Nobis, G. (ed.), *Der beginn der haustierhaltung in der "alten welt".* pp. 205–20. Koln, Bohlau

GRUE, H. and JENSEN, B. 1979 Review of the formation of incremental lines in tooth cementum of terrestrial mammals. *Danish Review of Game Biology* 11, 1–48

GUILDAY, J.E. 1970 Animal remains from archaeological excavations at Fort Ligonier. *Annals of the Carnegie Museum* 42, 177–86

GUILLIEN, Y. and HENRI-MARTIN, G. 1968 Dentures de rennes et saisons de chasse: l'abri Aurignacien de la Quina. *L'Anthropologie* 72, 337–48

GUTHRIE, R.D. 1984 Mosaics, allelochemics and nutrients. An ecological theory of late Pleistocene megafaunal extinctions. In: Martin, P.S. and Klein, R.G. (eds.). pp. 259–98

HAHN, E. 1896 *Die haustiere und ihre beziehungen zur wirtschaft des menschen. Eine geographische studie.* Liepzig, Duncker and Humblot

HALL, H.R. and WOOLLEY, C.L. (eds.), 1927 *Ur excavations I: al'Ubaid*. London

HALLAM, J.S., EDWARDS, B.J.N., BARNES, B. and STUART, A.J. 1973 The remains of a late Glacial elk with associated barbed points from High Furlong, near Blackpool, Lancashire. *Proceedings of the Prehistoric Society* 39, 100–28

HALSTEAD, L.B. 1974 *Vertebrate hard tissues*. London, Wykeham

HAMMOND, J. 1950 Polled cattle. *Endeavour* 9, 85–90

HANSEN, R.M. 1978 Shasta ground sloth food habits, Rampart cave, Arizona. *Paleobiology* 4, 302–19

HARCOURT, R.A. 1974 The dog in prehistoric and early historic Britain. *Journal of Archaeological Science* 1, 151–75

HARCOURT, R.A. 1979 The animal bones. In: Wainwright, G.J. *Gussage All Saints: an Iron Age settlement in Dorset*. pp. 150–160. London, Department of the Environment Archaeological reports 10, Her Majesty's Stationery Office

HARRIS, S. 1978 Age determination in the Red fox (*Vulpes vulpes*)—an evaluation of technique efficiency as applied to a sample of suburban foxes. *Journal of Zoology, London* 184, 91–117

HARRISON, D.L. 1968 *The mammals of Arabia Vol 2. Carnivora, Artiodactyla, Hyracoidea*. London, Ernest Benn

HATTING, T. 1983 Osteological investigations on *Ovis aries* L. *Dansk naturhistorisk Forening* 144, 115–35

HAURY, E.W., ANTEVS, E. and LANCE, J.F. 1953 Artifacts with mammoth remains, Naco, Arizona: I, II, III. *American Antiquity* 19, 1–24

HAURY, E.W., SAYLES, E.B. and WASLEY, W.W. 1959 The Lehner mammoth site, southeastern Arizona. *American Antiquity* 25, 2–30

HAYNES, C.V. 1980 The Clovis culture. *Canadian Journal of Anthropology* 1, 115–21

HAYNES, C.V. 1984 Stratigraphy and late Pleistocene extinction in the United States. In: Martin, P.S. and Klein, R.G. (eds.), pp. 345–53

HEANEY, L.R. 1978 Island area and body size of insular mammals: evidence from the tri-colored squirrel (*Callosciurus prevosti*) of southeast Asia. *Evolution* 32, 29–44

HEHN, V. 1888 *The wanderings of plants and animals from their first home*. London, Swan Sonnenschein

HELMER, D. 1984 Le parcage des moutons et des chèvres au Néolithique ancien et moyen dans le sud de la France. In: Clutton-Brock, J. and Grigson, C. (eds.), *Animals and Archaeology: 3. Early herders and their flocks*. pp. 39–45. Oxford, BAR International series 202

HERREID, C.F. and KESSEL, B. 1967 Thermal conductance in birds and mammals. *Comparative Biochemistry and Physiology* 21, 405–14

HESSE, B.C. 1978 *Evidence for husbandry from the early Neolithic site of Ganj Dareh in western Iran*. Columbia University, PhD. thesis. University Microfilms International: Ann Arbor, Michigan.

HESSE B. and WAPNISH, P. 1985 *Animal bone archaeology*. Washington, D.C. Taraxacum

HIGGS, E.S. 1967 Environment and chronology: the evidence from mammalian fauna. In: McBurney, C.B.M. (ed.), *The Haua Fteah (Cyrenaica) and the Stone Age of the south-east Mediterranean* pp. 16–44. Cambridge University Press

HIGHAM, C.F.W. 1968 Size trends in prehistoric European domestic fauna, and the problem of local domestication. *Acta Zoologica Fennica* 120, 3–21

HIGHAM, C.F.W. 1968 Patterns of prehistoric economic exploitation on the Alpine foreland: a statistical analysis of faunal remains in the zoological museum of Zurich University. *Vierteljahrsschrift der Naturforschenden Gesellschaft in Zurich* 113, 41–92

HIND, H.Y. 1860 *Narrative of the Canadian Red River exploring expedition of 1857 and of the Assinniboine and Saskatchewan exploring expedition of 1858*. 2 vols. London, Longman

HINTON, M.A.C. 1912–13 On the remains of vertebrate animals found in the middens of Rayleigh castle. *Essex Naturalist* 17, 16–21

HODGES, H.W.M. 1976 *Artefacts: an introduction to early materials and technology*. 2nd edition. London, Baker

HOLMES, W. 1981 Cattle. *The Biologist* 28, 273–9

HOROWITZ, A. 1979 *The Quaternary of Israel*. New York, Academic Press

HORTON, D. 1984 Red kangaroos: last of the Australian megafauna. In: Martin, P.S. and Klein, R.G. (eds.), pp. 639–80

HOSKINS, W.G. 1955 *Sheep farming in Saxon and medieval England*. London, department of education of the International Wool Secretariat

HOUTEKAMER, J.L. and SONDAAR, P.Y. 1979 Osteology of the fore limb of the Pleistocene dwarf hippopotamus from Cyprus with special reference to phylogeny and function. *Koninklijke Nederlandse Akademie van Wetenschappen. Proceedings series B* 82, 411–48

HOWELL, F.C. 1959 Upper Pleistocene stratigraphy and early man in the Levant. *Proceedings of the American Philosophical Society* 103, 1–65

HSU, K.J. 1978 Mediterranean sea. In: *McGraw Hill yearbook science and technology*

HSU, T.C. and BENIRSCHKE, K. 1967–1977 *An atlas of mammalian chromosomes* 1–10. Berlin and New York, Springer

HUE, E. 1907 *Musée osteologique—étude de la faune Quaternaire. Osteometrie des mammifères*. I–II. Paris, Schleicher frères

ISAAC, E. 1962 On the domestication of cattle. *Science* 137, 195–204

ISAAC, E. 1970 *Geography of Domestication*. Englewood Cliffs, New Jersey, Prentice-Hall

ISAAC, G.L. 1977 *Olorgesailie: archaeological studies of a Middle Pleistocene lake basin in Kenya*. Chicago, University of Chicago Press

ISAAC, G.L. 1983 Bones of contention: competing explanations for the juxtaposition of early Pleistocene artifacts and faunal remains. In: Clutton-Brock, J. and Grigson, C. (eds.), *Animals and Archaeology 1. Hunters and their prey.* pp. 3–19. Oxford, BAR International series 163

JACKSON, J.W. 1935 Report on the skeleton of the dog from Ash Pit C. In: Stone, J.F.S., Excavations at Easton Down, Winterslow. *Wiltshire Archaeology and Natural History Magazine* 47, 76–8

JACOBSEN, T.W. 1976 17,000 years of Greek prehistory. *Scientific American* 234, (6) 76–87

JARMAN, M.R. and WILKINSON, P.F. 1972 Criteria of animal domestication. In: Higgs, E.S. (ed.), *Papers in economic prehistory.* pp. 83–96. Cambridge University Press

JEWELL, P. 1962 Changes in the size and type of cattle from prehistoric to medieval times in Britain. *Zeitschrift fur Tierzuchtung und Zuchtungsbiologie* 77, 159–67

JEWELL, P. 1963 Cattle from British archaeological sites. In: Mourant, A. and Zeuner, F. (eds.), *Man and cattle.* pp. 80–91. London

JOHN, B. 1976 *Population cytogenetics.* The Institute of Biology's studies in Biology no. 70. London, Edward Arnold

JOHNSON, D.L. 1978 The origin of island mammoths and the Quaternary land bridge history of the northern Channel Islands, California. *Quaternary Research* 10, 204–25

JONES, A.K.G. 1982 Recent finds of intestinal parasite ova at York, England. *Proceedings of the Palaeopathology Association. Fourth European meeting. Middleburg/Antwerpen,* 229–233

JONES, A.K.G. 1982 Human parasite remains: prospects for a quantitative approach. In: Hall, A.R. and Kenward, H.K. *Environmental archaeology in the urban context.* pp. 66–70. London, Council for British Archaeology research report 43

JONES, A.K.G. 1983 A coprolite from 6–8 Pavement. In: Hall, A.R., Kenward, H.K., Williams, D. and Greig, J.R.A. *Environment and living conditions at two Anglo-Scandinavian sites.* The archaeology of York. The past environment of York 14/4, 225–30

JONES, W.E. and BOGART, R. 1971 *Genetics of the horse.* Fort Collins, Colorado, Caballus

KAPLAN, J. 1969 'Ein el Jarba, Chalcolithic remains in the plain of Esdraelon. Bulletin of the American Schools of Oriental Research 194, 2–39

KEELEY, L. and TOTH, N. 1981 Microwear polishes on early stone tools from Koobi Fora, Kenya. *Nature* 293, 464–5

KEHOE, T.F. 1973 *The Gull Lake site: a prehistoric bison drive site in southwestern Saskatchewan.* Milwaukee Public Museum publications in Anthropology and History 1

KENWARD, H. 1982 Insect communities and death assemblages, past and present. In: Hall, A.R. and Kenward, H.K. (eds.), *Environmental archaeology in the urban context.* pp. 71–8. London, Council for British archaeology, research report 43

KERNEY, M.P. and CAMERON, R.A.D. 1979 *A field guide to the land snails of Britain and north-west Europe.* London, Collins

KERSHAW, A.P. 1984. Late Cenozoic plant extinctions in Australia. In: Martin, P.S. and Klein, R.G. (eds.), pp. 691–707

KING, A. 1978 A comparative survey of bone assemblages from Roman sites in Britain. *Bulletin of the Institute of Archaeology* (London) 15, 207–32

KING, J.E. and SAUNDERS, J.J. 1984 Environmental insularity and the extinction of the American mastodont. In: Martin, P.S. and Klein, R.G. (eds.), pp. 315–39

KLEIN, R.G. 1973 *Ice-Age hunters of the Ukraine.* Chicago University Press

KLEIN, R.G. 1975 Palaeoanthropological implications of the nonarchaeological bone assemblage from Swartklip 1, south-western Cape Province, South Africa. *Quaternary Research* 5, 275–88

KLEIN, R.G. 1975 Ecology of Stone Age man at the southern tip of Africa. *Archaeology* 28, 238–47

KLEIN, R.G. 1979 Stone Age exploitation of animals in southern Africa. *American Scientist* 67, 151–60

KLEIN, R.G. 1983 Palaeoenvironmental implications of Quaternary large mammals in the Fynbos region. In: *Fynbos palaeoecology: a preliminary synthesis* Deacon, H.J., Hendey, Q.B. and Lambrechts, J.J.N. (eds.), pp. 116–38. South African National Scientific Programmes report 75

KLEIN, R.G. and CRUZ-URIBE, K. 1984 *The analysis of animal bones from archaeological sites.* Chicago, Chicago University Press

KOIKE, H. 1975 The use of daily and annual growth lines of the clam *Meretrix lusoria* in estimating seasons of Jomon period shell gathering. In: Suggate, R.P. and Cresswell, M.M. (eds.), *Quaternary Studies,* pp. 189–92. Wellington, New Zealand, The Royal Society

KOIKE, H. 1979 Seasonal dating and the valve-pairing technique in shell-midden analysis. *Journal of Archaeological Science* 6, 63–74

KROEBER, A.L. 1925 *Handbook of the Indians of California.* Washington DC. Smithsonian Institution Bureau of American Ethnology, Bulletin 78

KRUUK, H. 1972 *The spotted hyaena: a study of predation and social behaviour.* Chicago, Chicago University Press

KUBIAK, H. 1977 Hutten aus mammutknochen. *Umschau* 77, 116–17

KURTÉN, B. 1960 Chronology and faunal evolution of the earlier European glaciations. *Commentationes Biologicae* 21, 3–62

KURTÉN, B. 1965 Carnivora of the Palestine caves. *Acta Zoologica Fennica* 107, 1–74

KURTÉN, B. 1973 Geographic variation in size in the puma (*Felis concolor*). *Commentationes Biologicae* 63, 3–8

KURTÉN, B. and ANDERSON, E. 1972 The sediments

and fauna of Jaguar cave: II—the fauna. *Tebiwa* 15, 21–45

KURTÉN, B. and ANDERSON, E. 1980 *Pleistocene mammals of North America*. New York, Columbia University Press

LAMB, H.H. 1977 *Climate: present, past and future. 2. Climatic history and the future*. London, Methuen

LAROUSSE, P. 1873 *Grand dictionnaire universel du XIXe siècle 9*, 292–3. Paris, Administration du grand dictionnaire universel

LAVOCAT, R. (ed.), 1966 *Faunes et flores préhistoriques de l'Europe occidentale*. Paris, Boubée

LECHEVALLIER, M., MEADOW, R.H. and QUIVRON, G. 1982 Dépôts d'animaux dans les sépultures néolithiques de Mehrgarh, Pakistan. *Paléorient 8*, 99–106

LEE, R.B. 1968 What hunters do for a living or how to make out on scarce resources. In: Lee, R.B. and DeVore, I. (eds.), *Man the hunter*, pp. 30–48. Chicago, Aldine

LEE, R.B. 1972 Population growth and the beginnings of sedentary life among the !Kung Bushmen. In: Spooner, B. (ed.), *Population growth: Anthropological implications*, pp. 329–42. Cambridge, Mass., MIT Press

LEE, R.B. and DeVORE, I 1968 Problems in the study of hunters and gatherers. In: Lee, R.B. and DeVore, I. (eds.), *Man the hunter*. pp. 3–12. Chicago, Aldine

LEEMANS, W.F. 1977 The importance of trade. *Iraq 39*, 1–10

LEFEBVRE des NOETTES, R.J.E.C. 1931 *L'Attelage. Le cheval de selle à travers les âges Contribution à l'histoire de l'esclavage*. Paris, Picard

LEGGE, A.J. 1981 The agricultural economy. In: Mercer, R. (ed.), *Excavation at Grimes Graves 1971–2*. pp. 79–118. London, HMSO

LEGGE, A.J. 1981 Aspects of cattle husbandry. In: Mercer, R. (ed.), *Farming practice in British prehistory*. pp. 169–181. Edinburgh, University Press

LEGGE, A.J. and ROWLEY-CONWY, P.A. 1986 Some preliminary results of a re-examination of the Star Carr fauna. In: Bonsall, C. (ed.), *The Mesolithic in Europe: Proceedings of the IIIrd International Symposium Edinburgh 1985*. Edinburgh, Department of Archaeology, University of Edinburgh

LEINDERS, J.J.M. and SONDAAR, P.Y. 1974 On functional fusions in footbones of ungulates. *Zeitschrift fur Saugetierkunde 39*, 109–15

LISTER, A.M. 1984 Evolutionary and ecological origins of British deer. *Proceedings of the Royal Society of Edinburgh 82B*, 205–29

LIU, T-S, and LI, X-G. 1984 Mammoths in China. In: Martin, P.S. and Klein, R.G. (eds.), pp. 517–27

MacARTHUR, R.H. 1972 *Geographical ecology, patterns in the distribution of species*. New York, Harper and Row

MacARTHUR, W.P. 1949 The identification of some pestilences recorded in the Irish annals. *Irish Historical Studies 6*, 169–88

MacGREGOR, A. 1985 *Bone, antler, ivory and horn. The technology of skeletal materials since the Roman period*. London, Croom Helm

MACINTOSH, N.W.G. 1975 The origin of the dingo: an enigma. In: Fox, M.W. (ed.), *The wild canids: their systematics, behavioural ecology and evolution*, pp. 87–106. New York, London, Van Nostrand Reinhold

MALTBY, M. 1979 *The animal bones from Exeter 1971–1975*. Exeter Archaeological reports (2). Sheffield University, Department of Prehistory and Archaeology

MALTHUS, T.R. 1798 *An essay on the principle of population, as it affects the future improvement of society; with remarks on the speculations of W. Godwin, M. Condorcet and other writers*. London. (1970; Harmondsworth, Penguin)

MANWELL, C. and BAKER, C.M.A. 1984 Domestication of the dog: hunter, food, bed-warmer, or emotional object? *Zeitschrift fur Tierzuchtung und Zuchtungsbiologie 101*, 241–56

MARTIN, P. 1973 The discovery of America. *Science 179*, 969–74

MARTIN, P.S. 1984 Prehistoric overkill: the global model. In: Martin, P.S. and Klein, R.G. (eds.), pp. 354–403

MARTIN, P.S. and KLEIN, R.G. 1984 (eds.), *Quaternary extinctions: a prehistoric revolution*. Arizona University Press

MARTIN, P.S. and WRIGHT, H.E. 1967 *Pleistocene extinctions, the search for a cause*. New Haven, Yale University Press

MASKA, Ch., OBERMAIER, H. and BREUIL, H. 1912. La statuette de mammouth de Predmost. *L'Anthropologie 23*, 273–85

MATEESCU, C.N. 1975 Remarks on cattle breeding and agriculture in the Middle and Late Neolithic on the Lower Danube. *Dacia 19*, 13–18

MAYR, E. 1956 Geographical character gradients and climatic adaptation. *Evolution 10*, 105–8

MAZZAOUI, M.F. 1981 *The Italian cotton industry in the later Middle Ages 1100–1600*. Cambridge University Press

McCRACKEN, R.D. 1971. Lactase deficiency: an example of dietary evolution. *Current Anthropology 12*, 479–518

McDONALD, J.N. 1984 The reordered North American selection regime and late Quaternary megafaunal extinctions. In: Martin, P.S. and Klein, R.G. (eds.), pp. 404–39

McMILLAN, R.B. 1970 Early canid burial from the western Ozark highland. *Science 167*, 1246–7

MEADOW, R.H. 1980 Animal bones: problems for the archaeologist together with some possible solutions. *Paléorient 6*, 65–77

MEADOW, R.H. 1984 Animal domestication in the Middle East: a view from the eastern margin. In: Clutton-Brock, J. and Grigson, C. (eds.), *Animals and Archaeology: 3. Early herders and their flocks*. pp. 309–37. Oxford, BAR International Series 202

MEADOW, R.H. 1984 A camel skeleton from Mohenjodaro. In: Lal, B.B. and Gupta, S.P. (eds.), *Frontiers of the*

Indus civilization. pp. 133–9. New Delhi, Indian Archaeological Society

MELLARS, P. 1978 Excavation and economic analysis of Mesolithic shell middens on the island of Oronsay (Inner Hebrides). In: Mellars, P. (ed.), *The early postglacial settlement of northern Europe*, pp. 371–96. London, Duckworth

MELLARS, P.A. and WILKINSON, M.R. 1980 Fish otoliths as evidence of seasonality in prehistoric shell middens: the evidence from Oronsay. *Proceedings of the Prehistoric Society* 46, 19–44

MELTZER, D.J. and MEAD, J.I. 1983 The timing of late Pleistocene mammalian extinctions in North America. *Quaternary Research* 19, 130–5

MIDANT-REYNES, B. and BRAUNSTEIN-SILVESTRE, F. 1977 Le chameau en Egypte. *Orientalia n.s.* 46, 337–62

MODELL, W. 1969 Horns and antlers. *Scientific American* 220, 114–22

MOOREY, P.R.S. and GURNEY, O.R. 1978 Ancient Near Eastern cylinder seals acquired by the Ashmolean Museum, Oxford 1963–1973. *Iraq* 40, 41ff, 23

MOSIMANN, J.E. and MARTIN, P.S. 1975 Stimulating overkill by Paleoindians. *American Scientist* 63, 304–13

MUNSON, P.J. 1984 Teeth of juvenile woodchucks as seasonal indicators on archaeological sites. *Journal of Archaeological Science* 11, 395–403

MURDOCK, G.P. 1968 The current status of the world's hunting and gathering peoples. In: Lee, R.B. and DeVore, I. (eds.), *Man the hunter*, pp. 13–20. Chicago, Aldine

MURRAY, P. 1984 Extinctions downunder: a bestiary of extinct Australian late Pleistocene monotremes and marsupials. In: Martin, P.S. and Klein, R.G. (eds.), pp. 600–28

NADLER, C.F., KOROBITSINA, K.V., HOFFMANN, R.S. and VORONTSOV, N.N. 1973 Cytogenetic differentiation, geographic distribution, and domestication in Palearctic sheep (*Ovis*). *Zeitschrift fur Saugetierkunde* 38, 109–25

NEEV, D. and HALL, J.K. 1977 Climatic fluctuations during the Holocene as reflected by the Dead Sea levels. Paper presented at the International Conference on Terminal Lakes. Weber State College, Ogden, Utah 84408

NIKOLSKY, G.V. 1963 *The ecology of fishes*. New York, Academic Press

NODDLE, B.A. 1974 Ages of epiphyseal closure in feral and domestic goats and ages of dental eruption. *Journal of Archaeological Science* 1, 195–204

NODDLE, B.A. 1977 Mammal bone. In: Clarke, H. and Carter, A. (eds.), *Excavations in King's Lynn 1963–70*. pp. 378–99. Society for Medieval Archaeology, Monographs 7

NOVOA, C. and WHEELER, J.C. 1984 Lama and alpaca. In: Mason, I.L. (ed.), *Evolution of domesticated animals*. pp. 116–28. London, Longman

O'CONNOR, T.P. 1982 *The archaeozoological interpretation of morphometric variability in British sheep limb bones*. PhD thesis, University of London

O'CONNOR, T. 1982 *Animal bones from Flaxengate, Lincoln c870–1500*. The Archaeology of Lincoln 18 (1), Council for British Archaeology

O'CONNOR, T. 1983 Aspects of site environment and economy at Caerleon fortress baths, Gwent. In: Proudfoot, B. (ed.), *Site, Environment and Economy* pp. 105–13. Oxford, BAR International series 173

O'CONNOR, T. 1984 *Selected groups of bones from Skeldergate and Walmgate*. The Archaeology of York 15 (1): The animal bones, Council for British Archaeology

OVEY, C.D. 1964 (ed.), The Swanscombe skull. A survey of research on a Pleistocene site. *Royal Anthropological Institute of Great Britain and Ireland, Occasional Paper* 20

OWEN, R. 1877 *Researches on the fossil remains of the extinct mammals of Australia*. 2 vols. London, Erxleben

PAYNE, S. 1973 Kill-off patterns in sheep and goats: the mandibles from Aşvan Kale. *Anatolian Studies* 23, 281–303

PAYNE, S. 1975 Faunal change at Franchthi cave from 20,000 BC to 3,000 BC. In: Clason, A.T. (ed.), *Archaeozoological studies*. pp. 120–31. Amsterdam, New York, North Holland

PAYNE, S. 1975 Partial recovery and sample bias. In Clason, A.T. (ed.), *Archaeozoological studies*. pp. 7–17. Amsterdam, New York, North Holland

PAYNE, S. 1983 The animal bones from the 1974 excavations at Douara cave. *University Museum, University of Tokyo, Bulletin* 21, 1–108

PAYNE, S. 1985 Zoo-archaeology in Greece: a reader's guide. In: Wilkie, N.C. and Coulson, W.D.E. (eds.), *Contributions to Aegean archaeology*. University of Minnesota, Center for Ancient studies.

PAYNE, S. 1985 Morphological distinctions between the mandibular teeth of young sheep, *Ovis*, and goats, *Capra*. *Journal of Archaeological Science* 12, 139–47

PAYNE, S. 1985 Animal bones from Asıklı Hüyük. *Anatolian Studies* 35, 109–122

PAYNE, S. and MUNSON, P.J. 1986 Ruby and how many squirrels? the destruction of bones by dogs. Oxford, BAR

PERKINS, D. 1964 Prehistoric fauna from Shanidar, Iraq. *Science* 144, 1565–6

PETRONIO, C. 1970 I roditori pleistocenici della grotta di Spinagallo. *Geologica Romana* 9, 149–94

PHILLIPS, A.M. 1984 Shasta ground sloth extinction: fossil packrat midden evidence from the western grand canyon. In: Martin, P.S. and Klein, R.G. (eds.), pp. 148–58

PIDOPLICHKO, I.G. 1969 *Upper Palaeolithic mammoth bone dwellings in the Ukraine*. Kiev, Mukova dumka

PIDOPLICHKO, I.G. 1976 *Mezhirichskie zhilischa iz kosti mamonta*. Kiev

PIGGOT, S. 1952 *Prehistoric India*. London, Penguin

PITTS, M. 1979 Hides and antlers: a new look at the hunter-gatherer site at Star Carr, North Yorkshire, England. *World Archaeology* 11, 32–42

PLINY, C. *Natural History*. Translated by H. Rackham, 1940. The Loeb classical library. London, Heinemann

PLUMMER, C. 1896 *Venerabilis Baedae historiam ecclesiasticam gentis anglorum historiam abbatum epistolam ad ecgberctum*. 2 vols. Oxford, Clarendon Press

POPESCU, C.P., QUERE, J.P. and FRANCESCHI, P. 1980 Observations chromosomiques chez le sanglier français (*Sus scrofa scrofa*). *Annales de Génétique et de Sélection animale* 12, 395–400

POPLIN, F. 1979 Origine du mouflon de Corse dans une nouvelle perspective paléontologique: par marronage. *Annales de Génétique et de Sélection animale* 11, 133–43

POTTS, R. and SHIPMAN, P. 1981 Cutmarks made by stone tools on bones from Olduvai Gorge, Tanzania. *Nature* 291, 577–80

PRESTWICH, J. 1861 On the occurrence of flint implements, associated with the remains of animals of extinct species in beds of a late geological period, in France at Amiens and Abbeville, and in England at Hoxne. *Philosophical Transactions of the Royal Society* 150, 277–317

RACKHAM, D.J. 1979 *Rattus rattus:* the introduction of the black rat into Britain. *Antiquity* 53, 112–20

RACKHAM, D.J. 1982 The smaller mammals in the urban environment: their recovery and interpretation from archaeological deposits. In: Hall, A.R. and Kenward, H.K. (eds.), *Environmental archaeology in the urban context* pp. 86–93. London, Council for British Archaeology research report 43

READER, J. 1981 *Missing links. The hunt for earliest man*. London, Collins

REED, C.A. 1961 Osteological evidences for prehistoric domestication in southwestern Asia. *Zeitschrift fur Tierzuchtung und Zuchtungsbiologie* 76, 31–38

RICHARDSON, C.A., CRISP, D.J. and RUNHAM, N.W. 1979 Tidally deposited growth bands in the shell of the common cockle, *Cerastoderma edule* (L). *Malacologia* 18, 277–90

RICHTER, J. 1982 Adult and juvenile Aurochs, *Bos primigenius* Boj. from the Maglemosian site of Ulkestrup Lyng Øst, Denmark. *Journal of Archaeological Science* 9, 247–59

ROBERTSON-MACKAY, M.E. 1980 A "Head and Hooves" burial beneath a round barrow, with other Neolithic and Bronze Age sites, on Hemp Knoll, near Avebury, Wiltshire. *Proceedings of the Prehistoric Society* 46, 123–76

ROWLEY-CONWY, P. 1983 Sedentary hunters: the Ertebølle example. In: Bailey, G. (ed.), *Hunter-Gatherer economy in prehistory*. pp. 111–26. Cambridge University Press

ROWLEY-CONWY, P. 1984 The laziness of the short-distance hunter: the origins of agriculture in western Denmark. *Journal of Anthropological Archaeology* 3, 300–24

RUST, A. 1937 *Das Altsteinzeitliche Rentierjagerlager Meiendorf*. Archaeologisches Institut des Deutschen Reiches. Neumunster in Holstein, Karl Wachholtz

RYDER, M.L. 1961 Livestock remains from four medieval sites in Yorkshire. *The Agricultural History Review* 9, 105–11

RYDER, M.L. 1968 *Animal Bones in Archaeology*. Oxford, Blackwell

RYDER, M.L. 1969 Changes in the fleece of sheep following domestication (with a note on the coat of cattle). In: Ucko, P.J. and Dimbleby, G.W. (eds.), *The domestication and exploitation of plants and animals*. pp. 495–521. London, Duckworth

RYDER, M.L. 1983 A re-assessment of Bronze Age wool. *Journal of Archaeological Science* 10, 327–31

RYDER, M.L. 1984 Mediaeval animal products. *The Biologist* 31, 281–7

RYDER, M.L. 1984 Skin, hair and cloth remains from the ancient Kerma civilization of northern Sudan. *Journal of Archaeological Science* 11, 477–82

RYDER, M.L. and GABRA-SANDERS, T. (in press) The application of microscopy to textile history. *Textile History*

RYDER, O.A., EPEL, N.C. and BENIRSCHKE, K. 1978 Chromosome banding studies of the Equidae. *Cytogenetics and Cell Genetics* 20, 323–50

SAKELLARIDIS, M. 1979 *The Mesolithic and Neolithic of the Swiss area*. Oxford, BAR International series 67

SAUNDERS, J.J. 1980 A model for man-mammoth relationships in late Pleistocene North America. *Canadian Journal of Anthropology* 1, 87–98

SCHMID, E. 1972 *Atlas of animal bones for prehistorians, archaeologists and Quaternary geologists*. Amsterdam, London, New York, Elsevier

SEAL, U.S. 1975 Molecular approaches to taxonomic problems in the Canidae. In: Fox, M.W. (ed.), *The wild canids, their systematics, behavioural ecology and evolution*. pp. 27–39. New York, Van Nostrand Reinhold

SHACKLETON, N. 1973 Oxygen isotope analysis as a means of determining season of occupation of prehistoric midden sites. *Archaeometry* 15, 133–41

SHERRATT, A. 1981 Plough and pastoralism: aspects of the secondary products revolution. In: Hodder, I., Isaac, G. and Hammond, N. (eds.), *Pattern of the past: studies in honour of David Clarke*. pp. 261–305. Cambridge University Press

SHERRATT, A. 1983 The secondary exploitation of animals in the Old World. *World Archaeology* 15, 90–104

SHIPMAN, P. 1983 Early hominid lifestyle: hunting and gathering or foraging and scavenging? In: Clutton-Brock, J. and Grigson, C. (eds.), *Animals and archaeology: 1. Hunters and their prey*. pp. 31–49. BAR International series 163

SHIPMAN, P., BOSLER, W. and DAVIS, K.L. 1981

Butchering of giant geladas at an Acheulian site. *Current Anthropology* 22, 257–68

SIMKISS, K. 1975 *Bone and biomineralization.* The Institute of Biology's studies in biology 53. London, Edward Arnold

SIMONSEN, V. 1976 Electrophoretic studies on the blood proteins of domestic dogs and other Canidae. *Hereditas* 82, 7–18

SIMOONS, F.J. 1971 The antiquity of dairying in Asia and Africa. *The Geographical Review* 61, 431–9

SIMOONS, F.J. 1979 Dairying, milk use, and lactose malabsorption in Eurasia: a problem in culture history. *Anthropos* 74, 61–80

SIMOONS, F.J. 1980 The determinants of dairying and milk use in the Old World: ecological, physiological and cultural. In: Robson, J.R.K. (ed.), *Food, ecology and culture.* pp. 83–91. New York, Gordon and Breach

SIMPSON, G.G., ROE, A. and LEWONTIN, R.C. 1960 *Quantitative zoology.* New York, Harcourt, Brace

SINCLAIR, A.R.E. 1977 *The African buffalo.* Chicago University Press

SMITH, R.N. and ALLCOCK, J. 1960 Epiphyseal fusion in the greyhound. *The Veterinary Record* 72, 75–9

SOKAL, R.R. and ROHLF, F.J. 1969 *Biometry, the principles and practise of statistics in biological research.* San Francisco, Freeman.

SONDAAR, P.Y. 1971 Paleozoogeography of the Pleistocene mammals from the Aegean. *Opera Botanica* 30, 65–70

SONDAAR, P.Y. 1977 Insularity and its effect on mammal evolution. In: Hecht, M.K., Goody, P.C. and Hecht, B.M. (eds.), *Major patterns in vertebrate evolution.* pp. 671–707. New York, Plenum.

SONDAAR, P.Y. 1987 Pleistocene man and extinctions of island endemics. *Bulletin de la Société Géologique Française*

SONDAAR, P.Y., SANGES, M., KOTSAKIS, T. and de BOER, P.L. 1986 The Pleistocene deer hunter of Sardinia. *Geobios* 19, 17–25

SOWLS, L.K. 1984 *The peccaries.* Tucson, Arizona, University of Arizona Press

SPAULDING, W.G. 1983 The overkill hypothesis as a plausible explanation for the extinctions of late Wisconsin megafauna. *Quaternary Research* 20, 110–12

SPETH, J. 1983 *Bison kills and bone counts. Decision making by ancient hunters.* Chicago, Chicago University Press

SPIESS, A.E. 1979 *Reindeer and caribou hunters. An archaeological study.* New York, Academic Press

SPINAGE, C.A. 1972 Age estimation of zebra. *East African Wildlife Journal* 10, 273–77

SPINAGE, C.A. 1973 A review of the age determination of mammals by means of teeth, with special reference to Africa. *East African Wildlife Journal* 11, 165–87

STEIN, G. and WATTENMAKER, P. 1984 An archaeological study of pastoral production in the Karababa basin of the Turkish lower Euphrates valley. Paper presented at the ASOR annual meetings, Chicago, Illinois

STRAUS, L.G. 1982 Carnivores and cave sites in Cantabrian Spain. *Journal of Anthropological Research* 38, 75–96

STUART, A.J. 1982 *Pleistocene vertebrates in the British Isles.* London, Longman

SUSSMAN, R.M. 1972 Child transport, family size and increase in human population during the Neolithic. *Current Anthropology* 13, 258–59

SUTCLIFFE, A.J. and ZEUNER, F.E. 1958 Excavations in the Torbryan caves, Devonshire I. Tornewton cave. *Proceedings of the Devon Archaeological and Exploration Society* 5, 127–45

SYMEONIDES, N. and SONDAAR, P.Y. 1975 A new otter from the Pleistocene of Crete. *Annales géologiques des pays Hélleniques, Athènes* 27, 11–24

TEICHERT, M. 1984 Size variation in cattle from Germania Romana and Germania libera. In: Grigson, C. and Clutton-Brock, J. (eds.), *Animals and archaeology: 4. Husbandry in Europe.* pp. 93–103. Oxford, BAR International series 227

TELEKI, G. 1975 Primate subsistence patterns: collector-predators and gatherer-hunters. *Journal of Human Evolution* 4, 125–84

THOMPSON, A., GREW, F. and SCHOFIELD, J. 1984 Excavations at Aldgate, 1974. *Post Medieval Archaeology* 18, 1–148

TROTTER, M.M. and McCULLOCH, B. 1984 Moas, men and middens. In Martin, P.S. and Klein R.G. (eds.), pp. 708–27

TROW-SMITH, R. 1957 *A history of British livestock husbandry to 1700.* London, Routledge and Kegan Paul

TURNBULL, P. and REED, C. 1974 The fauna from the terminal Pleistocene of Palegawra cave, a Zarzian occupation site in northeast Iraq. *Fieldiana Anthropology* 63, 81–146

UERPMANN, H.-P. 1978 Metrical analysis of faunal remains from the Middle East. In: Meadow, R.H. and Zeder, M.A. (eds.), *Approaches to faunal analysis in the Middle East.* pp. 41–5. Peabody Museum Bulletin 2, Harvard University.

UERPMANN, H.-P. 1979 *Probleme der Neolithisierung des Mittelmeerraums.* Tubinger Atlas des Vorderen Orients, B. 28. Wiesbaden, Ludwig Reichert.

UERPMANN, H.-P. 1982 Faunal remains from Shams ed-din Tannira, a Halafian site in northern Syria. *Berytus* 30, 3–52

UREY, H.C. 1947 The thermodynamic properties of isotopic substances. *Journal of the Chemical Society,* 562–81

VANCOUVER, G. 1798 *A voyage of discovery to the north Pacific Ocean, and round the world; in which the coast of north-west America has been carefully examined and accurately surveyed.* 3 vols. London, Robinson and Edwards

VEALE, E.M. 1957 The rabbit in England. *The Agricultural History Review* 5, 85–90

VIGNE, J.-D. 1983 Le remplacement des faunes de petits mammifères en Corse, lors de l'arrivée de l'homme. *Comptes Rendues de la Societé de Biogéographie* 59, 41–51

VIGNE, J.-D. 1984 Premières données sur le début de l'élevage du mouton, de la chèvre et du porc dans le sud de la Corse (France). In: Clutton-Brock, J. and Grigson, C. (eds.), *Animals and Archaeology: 3. Early Herders and their Flocks.* pp. 47–65. BAR International Series 202.

VIGNE, J.-D., MARINVAL-VIGNE, M.-Ch., LANFRANCHI, F. de and WEISS, M.-C. 1981 Consommation du "Lapin-rat" (*Prolagus sardus* WAGNER) au Néolithique ancien mediterranéen. Abri d'Araguina-Sennola (Bonifacio, Corse). *Bulletin de la Societé préhistorique Française* 78, 222–4

VOORHIES, M.R, 1969 *Taphonomy and population dynamics of an early Pliocene vertebrate fauna, Knox county, Nebraska.* University of Wyoming, Contributions to Geology, Special paper 1. Laramie, Wyoming

VRBA, E.S. 1975 Some evidence of chronology and palaeoecology of Sterkfontein, Swartkrans and Kromdraai from the fossil bovidae. *Nature* 254, 301–4

WALDREN, W.H. 1982 *Balearic prehistoric ecology and culture. The excavation and study of certain caves, rock shelters and settlements.* Oxford, BAR International series 149

WALKER, A. 1981 Dietary hypotheses and human evolution. *Philosophical Transactions of the Royal Society, London* B 292, 57–64

WALKER, A., ZIMMERMAN, M.R. and LEAKEY, R.E.F. 1982 A possible case of hypervitaminosis A in *Homo erectus. Nature* 296, 248–50

WALKER, R. 1985 *A guide to post-cranial bones of East African animals.* Norwich, England, Hylochoerus press

WAPNISH, P. 1981 Camel caravans and camel pastoralists at Tell Jemmeh. *Journal of the Ancient Near Eastern Society of Columbia University* 13, 101–121

WASHBURN, S. and LANCASTER, 1968 The evolution of hunting. In: Lee, R.B. and DeVore, I. (eds.), *Man the hunter*, pp. 293–303. Chicago, Aldine

WATSON, J.P.N. 1979 The estimation of the relative frequencies of mammalian species: Khirokitia 1972. *Journal of Archaeological Science* 6, 127–37

WEBB, D.S. 1984 Ten million years of mammal extinctions in North America. In: Martin, P.S. and Klein, R.G. (eds.), pp. 189–210

WHEAT, J.B. 1972 The Olsen-Chubbuck site. A Paleo-Indian bison kill. *American Antiquity* 27, 1–180

WHEELER, A. 1977 Fish bone. In: Clarke, H. and Carter, A. Excavations in King's Lynn 1963–1970. *Society for Medieval Archaeology monograph series* 7, 403–8

WHEELER, A. 1978 Why were there no fish remains at Star Carr? *Journal of Archaeological Science* 5, 85–89

WHEELER, A. and JONES, A. 1976 Report on the fish bones. In: Rogerson, A. Excavations on Fuller's Hill, Great Yarmouth, 1974. *East Anglian Archaeology* 2, 208–26

WHEELER, J.C. 1984 On the origin and early development of camelid pastoralism in the Andes. In: Clutton-Brock, J. and Grigson, C. (eds.), *Animals and archaeology: 3. Early herders and their flocks.* pp. 395–410. Oxford, BAR International series 202

WHITE, L.T. 1962. *Medieval technology and social change.* Oxford, Clarendon Press

WIDDOWSON, E.M. and McCANCE, R.A. 1975 A review: new thoughts on growth. *Pediatric Research* 9, 154–56

WIJNGAARDEN-BAKKER, L.H. 1974 The animal remains from the Beaker settlement at Newgrange, Co. Meath: first report. *Proceedings of the Royal Irish Academy* 74C, 313–83

WILFRID JACKSON, J. 1923 Notes on animal remains found at All Cannings Cross, Wilts. In: Cunnington, M.E. *The Early Iron Age inhabited site at All Cannings Cross Farm, Wiltshire.* pp. 43–50. Devizes, George Simpson.

WILLOUGHBY, D.P. 1974 *The empire of Equus.* New York, Barnes

WILSON, B., GRIGSON, C. and PAYNE, S. 1982 (eds.), *Ageing and sexing animal bones from archaeological sites.* Oxford, BAR British series 109

WING, E. 1978 Animal domestication in the Andes. In: Browman, D.L. (ed.), *Advances in Andean archaeology.* pp. 167–88. The Hague, Mouton

YALDEN, D.W. 1977 *The identification of remains in owl pellets.* An occasional publication of the Mammal Society of Britain and Ireland

YALDEN, D.W. 1982 When did the mammal fauna of the British Isles arrive? *Mammal Review* 12, 1–57

ZAKY, A. and ISKANDER, Z. 1942 Ancient Egyptian cheese. *Annales du Service des Antiquités de l'Egypte* 41, 195–313

ZAMMIT MAEMPEL, G. and DE BRUIJN, H. 1982 The Plio/Pleistocene Gliridae from the Mediterranean islands reconsidered. *Proceedings of the Koninklijke Nederlandse Akademie van Wetenschappen, Series B* 85, 113–28

ZEUNER, F.E. 1958 *Dating the past.* London, Methuen

ZEUNER, F.E. 1963 *A history of domesticated animals.* London, Hutchinson

Orkney

St. Kilda—

Oronsay

Jura

Islay

Mount Sandel

Morton Tayport

York
Star Carr
Flixton
Cresswell Crags
Lincoln
King's Lynn
North Elmham
Great Yarmouth
Hoxne
Grimes Graves
Clacton
Rayleigh castle
Crayford
Swanscombe
Hastings

High Furlong
Wroxeter

Etton·
Lyveden·

Caerleon

Uley

Lambourne
Aveley
London

Charterhouse Warren Farm

Taunton

Exeter

Tornewton cave

Guildford
Thatcham
Winchester
Portchester Castle
Danebury
Winterslow
Fussell's Lodge

Kent's Cavern
Glastonbury
All Cannings Cross
Hambledon Hill
Eldon's seat
Windmill Hill
Tilshead Lodge

Buhen ●

Melka Kunture ●

Koobi Fora ●

Chesowanja ●

Olorgesailie ●

Olduvai gorge ●

Makapansgat ●

Swartkrans ●
Sterkfontein

Elands Bay
Paternoster
Sea Harvest
Hoedjies Punt

Boomplaas

Klasies River Mouth
Nelson Bay

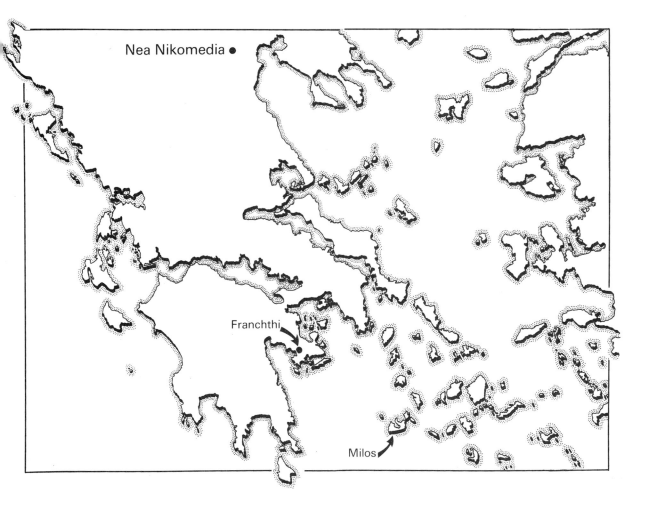

Nea Nikomedia ●

Franchthi

Milos

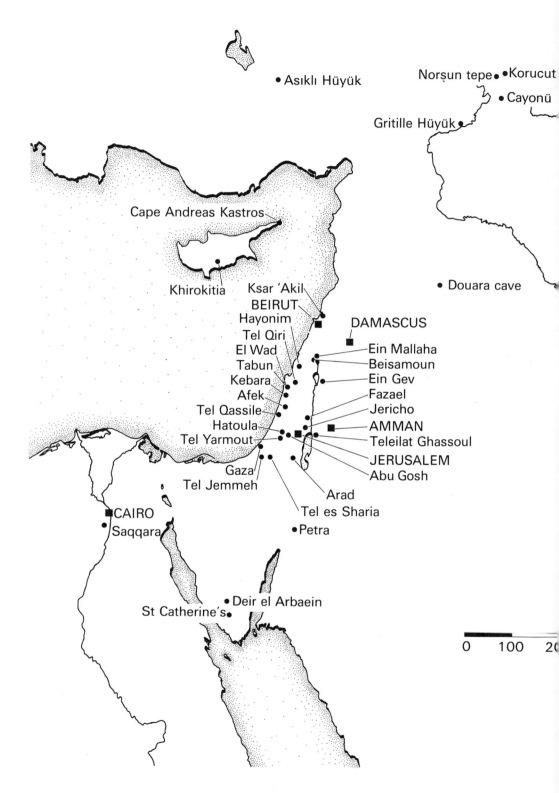

ANKARA■

● Asıklı Hüyük

Norşun tepe ●●Korucut
● Cayonü

Gritille Hüyük ●

Cape Andreas Kastros

● Douara cave

Khirokitia

Ksar 'Akil
BEIRUT
Hayonim
Tel Qiri
El Wad
Tabun
Kebara
Afek
Tel Qassile
Hatoula
Tel Yarmout

DAMASCUS ■

Ein Mallaha
Beisamoun
Ein Gev
Fazael
Jericho
AMMAN ■
Teleilat Ghassoul
JERUSALEM
Abu Gosh

Gaza
Tel Jemmeh

Arad

Tel es Sharia

● Petra

■CAIRO
Saqqara

● Deir el Arbaein
St Catherine's ●

0   100   20

Zawi Chemi Shanidar

Belt cave

Palegawra cave

TEHRAN

Choga Maran

KERMANSHAH

Ganj Dareh

Jammeh Shuran

Siahbid

Sarab

BAGHDAD

Deh Luran

Uruk

al 'Ubaid

Ur

Index